The Lost Books Of The Bible

Published by Timothy Green Beckley
Ed

THE LOST BOOKS OF THE BIBLE

BEING ALL THE GOSPELS, EPISTLES, AND OTHER PIECES NOW EXTANT ATTRIBUTED IN THE FIRST FOUR CENTURIES TO JESUS CHRIST, HIS APOSTLES AND THEIR COMPANIONS, NOT INCLUDED, BY ITS COMPILERS, IN THE AUTHORIZED NEW TESTAMENT; AND, THE RECENTLY DISCOVERED SYRIAC MSS. OF PILATE'S LETTERS TO TIBERIUS, ETC.

TRANSLATED FROM THE ORIGINAL TONGUES

Published by Timothy Green Beckley
Edited by William Kern
This edition Copyright 2014
by Global Communications/Conspiracy Journal

Revised Edition

Published in the United States of America By
Global Communications/Conspiracy Journal
Box 753 · New Brunswick, NJ 08903

Staff Members
Timothy G. Beckley, Publisher
Carol Ann Rodriguez, Assistant to the Publisher
Sean Casteel, General Associate Editor
Tim R. Swartz, Graphics and Editorial Consultant
William Kern, Editorial and Art Consultant

Sign Up On The Web For Our Free Weekly Newsletter
and Mail Order Version of Conspiracy Journal
and Bizarre Bazaar
www.Conspiracy Journal.com
PayPal: MrUFO8@hotmail.com
Order Hot Line: 1-732-602-3407

"Christ was the joyous boy of the fields. We are not permitted to think that the shadows of Calvary darkened His pathway as a youth, and the Apocryphal Books of the New Testament show a great deal of the early life of Christ not to be found in the four Evangelists."

—DR. TALMAGE

THE ORDER OF ALL THE BOOKS OF THE LOST BOOKS OF THE BIBLE
WITH THEIR PROPER NAMES

INTRODUCTION TO THE LOST BOOKS OF THE BIBLE

By DR. FRANK CRANE

THE great things in this world are growths. This applies to books as well as to institutions.

The Bible is a growth. Many people do not understand that it is not a book written by a single person, but it is a library of several books which were composed by various people in various countries. It is interesting to know how this library grew and upon what principle some books were accepted and some rejected.

Of course we may take people's word for the reasons why certain books were chosen, but it is always satisfactory to come to our own conclusions by examining our own evidence.

This is what this Lost Books of the Bible enables us to do. We can examine the books of the Scriptures which we have in the authorized version, and then in this book we can read those scriptures which have been eliminated by various councils in order to make up our standard Bible.

It is safe to say that a comparison of the accepted books with those rejected may be relied upon, for those books which were accepted are far superior in value to the others.

These others which are included in the Lost Books of the Bible comprise all kinds of stories, tales and myths.

No great figure appears in history without myths growing up about him. Every great personage becomes a nucleus or center about which folk tales cluster.

There are apocryphal tales about Napoleon, about Charlemagne, about Julius Caesar and other outstanding characters.

It is impossible that a man representing so great a force as Jesus of Nazareth should appear in the world without finding many echoes of His personality in contemporary literature—many stories which grew up about Him as time elapsed.

What these tales and stories are, just how He appears to the fictional minds of His day and afterwards, it is interesting to note.

Very often the fiction writer depicts life and the great truth of life better than the historian. He does not pretend to write down what is exactly true, but he tinges all things with his imagination. His feelings, however, may be just and reliable.

The reading of this Lost Books of the Bible is interesting as a matter of course. All who in any way are attracted by the personage of Jesus are interested to know any stories that may have grown up about Him.

They are also valuable because they enable us to get many a point of view which otherwise would have been lost.

History may be true, but in a sense tradition is even truer. It has been said that history records what has been, but tradition tells what ought to have been.

It must be remembered also that such a thing as historical accuracy is a comparatively novel product. The older writers never dreamed of it. They wrote in order to be interesting, not to tell the truth. And it is a remarkable fact that the events recorded in the Holy Scriptures, as far as we can find out, were most of them veritable, and the chroniclers were truthful.

In this volume all these apocryphal volumes are presented without argument or commentation. The reader's own judgment and common sense are appealed to. It makes no difference whether he is Catholic or Protestant or Hebrew. The facts are plainly laid before him. These facts for a long time have been the peculiar esoteric property of the learned. They were available only in the original Greek and Latin and so forth. Now they have been translated and brought in plain English before the eye of every reader.

The ordinary man has therefore the privilege of seeing upon what grounds the commonly accepted Scriptures rest. He can examine the pile of evidence and do his own sifting.

Thousands of people to-day look to the New Testament narrative as their leader and guide. It is important to know upon what authority this rests, and many a man will be delighted to find the evidence thus clearly presented before him.

The Lost Books of the Bible present all sorts of matter before the curious eye. There are stories about Mary and instances of her personal life. There are other stories about the boyhood of Jesus and instances about His crucifixion. All of these become important because of the central figure about whom they revolve.

No man has ever appealed to the imagination of the world and so played upon its feelings as has Jesus of Nazareth.

It is interesting to know what forms of stories and speculations about Him took place in the early period of the Christian era.

In other words, the ordinary man is invited to take his place in that council chamber which accepts and rejects the various writings of Scripture. It is safe to say that the conclusions desired can safely be left to his common sense. It can no longer be said that our Scriptures were accepted by learned men; you do not know that, but you must accept their conclusions. Now it is shown you upon what grounds these conclusions rest.

As a believer in the authenticity of our accepted Scriptures I have no hesitancy in saying that I am perfectly satisfied to let the common sense of the world decide upon the superiority of the accepted text.

The publication of this book will do good because it takes away the veil of secrecy that has hidden for many years the act of the church in accepting certain Scriptures and rejecting others. All of the grounds are rendered perfectly intelligible to the common man.

PREFACE

YOU will find between these covers all the ecclesiastical writings of early Christian authorities that are known to exist, and yet were omitted from the authorized New Testament.

They are published here as a matter of record. Whether they are canonical or not, at least these writings are of very great antiquity.

Origins are noted in paragraphs at the front of each book. This will enable the reader to form his own conclusions as to the genuineness of the writings. These writings are a vivid picture of the minds of men in the post-Apostolic period of the Church. Discount the statements from the historical viewpoint as you will—there remains in these gospels and epistles an earnestness of purpose, and zeal to express a message, similar to that of our authorized Bible.

An interesting question naturally arises as to why these writings were cast out in the selection of the material that has come down to us in the authorized version.

The compilation of the Bible was not an act of any definite occurrence. It was a matter complicated and abstruse. It was an evolution at the hands of Churchmen of various beliefs and purposes. In the formulation of early church doctrines there was dissension, personal jealousy, intolerance, persecution, bigotry. That out of this welter should have arisen the Bible, with its fine inspiration, would seem to present a plausible basis for belief in its Divine origin.

But who can deny that under such vicious and human circumstances much writing of as pure purpose and as profound sincerity as other that is included in the authorized Bible, must have been omitted? The story of the first council of Nice, when Arius was commanded by the Bishop of Alexandria to quit his beliefs or be declared a heretic, and his writings were ordered destroyed, is eloquent of many things that happened. Good men were engaged on both sides of the ecclesiastical controversies.

About two thirds of this volume is occupied with epistles. Beginning on page 91 you will discover otherwise generally unknown letters of Paul; and the illuminating letters of Clement and others, concluding with correspondence and reports of Herod, Pontius Pilate, and Tiberius Caesar.

Concerning these epistles Archbishop of Canterbury Wake, who translated them from the originals, says that here is a full and perfect collection of "all the genuine writings that remain to us of the Apostolic Fathers, and carry on the antiquity of the Church from the time of the Holy Scriptures of the New Testament to about a hundred and fifty years after Christ; that except the Holy Scriptures, there is nothing remaining of the truly genuine Christian antiquity more early; that they contain all that can with any certainty be depended upon of the most Primitive Fathers, who had not only the advantage of living in the apostolical times, of hearing the Holy Apostles, and conversing with them, but were most of them persons of a very eminent character in the church, too: that we cannot with any reason doubt of what they deliver to us as the Gospel of Christ, but ought to receive it, if not with equal veneration, yet but a little less respect than we do the Sacred Writings of those who were their masters and instructors;" and, "if," says the Archbishop, "it shall be asked how I came to choose the drudgery of a translator, rather than the more ingenious part of publishing somewhat of my own composing, it was, in short, this; because I hoped that such writings as these would find a more general and unprejudiced acceptance with all sorts of men than anything that could be written by anyone now living."

This collection of The Lost Books of the Bible is published without prejudice or motive save that the reader may find whatever pleases and instructs him, and may be free to enjoy his own speculation and hold his own opinion of these ancient and beautiful writings.

R.H.P., Jr.

New York, January 1, 1926.

Lamentations Over The Body Of Jesus

The Holy Family With Young Saint John

EDITOR'S PRELUDE

Religions have always stood in opposition to science. Copernicus – Mendel – Darwin – blasphemy! The first human quest for knowledge was severely punished by marching Adam and his sinful common-law wife out of heaven. The whole idea of religion is based on unconditional belief and not on tangible proof. Thus the very probing of science to break through the "cloud of unknowing" was a threatening and therefore sinful act. Why? Why would it be a disaster to get a little closer to the knowledge of how it all works? Curiously enough, most religions operate under a similar belief system of sequestering God from human eyes and the desire to know and understand. In both Islamic and Judaic traditions, it is unthinkable to paint or to have any kind of representation of divinity; so much so that in the Hebrew language, one cannot even say the word "God". In this case, the very act of uttering the word is criminal.

Catholics are simply appalled by the limits of human disbelief. The position of the church is: "Why do you need proof?" Well, fortunately or not, the human being is designed with a yearning need for knowledge. Any of us who have been exposed to children know how many times they repeat the question "Why?" and how many times we are unable to give an answer. For instance, even the 'simplest' one of all, "Why are we here?"

If we look at the biblical tale of Adam and Eve, it follows that the human being was designed to want to know. And even if he/she was too ignorant to ask, then he/she was insistently given hints – "Have all you want but don't go near that tree!" Well, we did taste the apple, and so now we are faced with such moral questions as "Is it ethical to make a human clone?" Personally, I don't take any sides, but simply think that it is unavoidable – just as it was unavoidable for Adam or Eve to taste from the *forbidden fruit.* (Just in case they didn't get the point, God let his former employee remind Adam and Eve again and again about it, even if only by naming him a "fallen angel.")

Recently I was watching a documentary which definitely had some moral undertones toward the side of "do not". It was pretty much a traditional argument. However, at the very end, they interviewed a priest who declared with trepidation and fear in his eyes that scientists are discussing the use of a drop of blood found on the Shroud of Turin (you might guess whose DNA we are talking about) for their evil experiments with cloning. *An unthinkable, shocking proposition – to clone Christ!*

An unrelated fact is that the insistence of the return of the prophet suddenly becomes dangerous. We together as a society at large are expecting: Christ, Messiah, Mohammed, and a number of other prophets. Most religions believe that this would signify the end of the world; the small detail they don't agree on is who will be saved. Jews believe they will be the ones, Christians would feel quite the opposite – so, nobody wants to share the pie.

Here is the main point. Assuming that it is Christ's blood on the Shroud of Turin, the cloning, then, *is* the Second Coming. This would explain the subconscious fear carried out by religious dogma against science. The choice is clear – you either believe and you'll live or you know and you'll die.

But, perhaps the **greater** fear in the church is that science might clone Jesus and still nothing untoward would happen. What, then, becomes of the words of disaster in their mouths?

I am sure one can study the signs mentioned in the holy texts that are supposed to warn us about the second coming and apply them to contemporary life. Things like "Watch out for a red beast." What is interesting is that we have been told to behave, and if we don't, we should expect the return of the savior [the final and fatal visit]. We were warned once, at which time Christ took the suffering upon himself. However, according to the scripture, we should not be forgiven twice. When one thinks of the second coming, one imagines the story repeating itself with miraculous things like "the Annunciation" and all the rest of the attributes. But we don't expect that it is we ourselves who would make it happen (not through an Immaculate Conception but by the scientific method and laboratory experiment).

By the way, this gives a new perspective to the creation of Eve (cloned from Adam's rib) and to the Divine Birth itself. Mystic ideas such as "how do you remain a virgin after conceiving a child" can then be solved.

True, we do suspect that even if the clone were genetically identical to its original, the character of the person would still be different, since it would be conditioned by the environment. Therefore, we do not know if Christ will be as we know him or as an Other-Christ. By any chance, if the drop of blood does not belong to God's son but to the cunning, ingenious artist, then the meaning of eternalization by a work of art will definitely be seen in a new light. And how well deserved would be the rebirth of that artist!

Intelligent readers can scarcely fail to find a striking discrepancy between the two accounts of the creation of man recorded in the first and second chapters of Genesis (to say nothing of the **Lost and Forgotten Books** that follow). In the first chapter of Genesis, we read how, on the fifth day of creation, God created the fishes and the birds, all the creatures that live in the water or in the air; and how on the sixth day he created all terrestrial animals, and last of all man, whom he fashioned in his own image, both male and female. From this narrative we infer that man was the last to be created of all living beings on earth, and incidentally we gather that the distinction of the sexes, which is characteristic of humanity, is shared also by the divinity; though how the distinction can be reconciled with the unity of the Godhead is a point on which the authors of Genesis offer no information.

Passing by this theological problem, as perhaps too deep for human comprehension, we turn to the simpler question of chronology and take note of the statements that God created the lower animals first and human beings afterwards, and that the human beings consisted of a man and a woman, produced, from all indications, simultaneously, and each of them reflecting in equal measure the glory of their divine parent. So it is in the first chapter. But when we proceed to examine the second chapter, it is somewhat disconcerting to discover a totally different and extraordinarily contradictory account of the same momentous event. For here we learn with surprise that God created man first, the lower animals next, and woman last of all, fashioning her as a mere afterthought out of a rib which was excised from the man while he slept. The order of merit in the two narratives is clearly reversed. In the first narrative the deity begins with fishes and works steadily up through birds and beasts to man and woman. In the second narrative he begins with man and works downwards through the lower animals to woman, who apparently marks the lowest point of the divine workmanship. And in this second version nothing at all is said about man and woman being made in the image of God. We are simply told that "the Lord God formed man of the dust of the ground, and breathed into his nostrils the breath of life; and man became a living soul." Afterwards, to relieve the loneliness of the man, who wandered vagrantly about without a living companion in the beautiful garden which had been created for him, God fashioned all the birds and beasts and brought them to man, apparently to amuse him and keep him company. Man looked at them and gave to them all their names; but still he was not content with these playthings, so at last, as if in despair, God created woman out of an insignificant portion of the masculine frame, introduced her to man and claimed that she was to be his wife.

The flagrant contradiction between the two accounts is explained very simply by the circumstance that they are derived from two different and originally independent documents which were afterwards combined into a single book by an editor, who pieced the two narratives together without taking pains to soften or harmonize their discrepancies. The account of the creation in the first chapter is derived from what is called the Priestly Document, which was composed by priestly writers during or after the Babylonian captivity. The account of the creation of man and the animals in the second chapter is derived from what is called the Jehovistic Document, which was written several hundred years before the other, probably in the ninth or eighth century before our era.

The difference between the religious standpoints of the two writers is clear. The later or priestly writer conceives God in an abstract form as withdrawn from human sight, and creating all things by a simple fiat. The earlier or Jehovistic writer conceives God in a very concrete form as acting and speaking like a man, modeling a human being out of clay, planting a garden, walking in it at the cool of the day, calling to the man and woman to come out from among the trees behind which they had hidden themselves, and making coats of skin to replace the scanty fig-leaves with which our embarrassed first parents sought to conceal their nakedness.

The charming naiveté, almost the gaiety, of the earlier narrative contrasts with the dark seriousness of the later; though we cannot but be struck by a theme of sadness and pessimism running under the brightly colored picture of life in the age of innocence, which the great Jehovistic artist has painted for us. Above all, he hardly attempts to hide his deep disdain for woman. The lateness of her creation, and the irregular and undignified manner of it—made out of a piece of her lord and master, after all the lower animals had been created in a regular and perfectly decent manner—sufficiently mark the low opinion he held of her nature; and in the sequel his hatred of and contempt for women, as we may safely describe it, takes a still darker tone, when he ascribes all the misfortunes and sorrows of humanity to the credulous folly and unbridled innocence of its first mother.

Of the two narratives, the earlier Jehovistic is not only the more picturesque but also the richer in folklore, retaining many features suggestive of primitive simplicity which have been carefully abridged by the later writer. Accordingly, it offers more points of comparison with the childlike ghost stories by which men in many ages and countries have sought to explain the great mystery of the beginning of life on earth.

The Jehovistic writer seems to have imagined that God moulded the first man out of clay, just as a potter might, or as a child moulds a doll of mud; and that having parallels, kneaded and patted the clay into the proper shape, the deity animated it by breathing into the mouth and nostrils of the figure, exactly as the prophet Elisha is said to have restored to life the dead child of the Shunammite by lying on him, and putting his eyes to the child's eyes and his mouth to the child's mouth, no doubt to impart his breath to the corpse; after which the child sneezed seven times and opened its eyes. To the Hebrews this derivation of our species from the dust of the ground suggested itself all the more naturally because, in their language, the word for "ground" (adamah) is in feminine form the word for "man" (adam).

From various allusions in Babylonian literature it would seem that the they also conceived man to have been moulded from clay. According to Berosus, the Babylonian priest, whose account of creation has been preserved in a Greek version, the god Bel cut off his own head, and the other gods caught the flowing blood, mixed it with earth, and fashioned men from the bloody paste; and that, they said, is why men are so wise—because their mortal clay is tempered with divine DNA.

In Egyptian mythology Khnoumou, the Father of the Gods, is said to have moulded men out of clay on his potter's wheel. So in Greek legend the sage Prometheus is said to have moulded the first men out of clay at Panopeus in Phocis. When he had done his work, some of the clay was left over, and might be seen on the spot long afterwards in the shape of two large boulders lying at the edge of a ravine. A Greek traveler, who visited the place in the second century of our era, thought that the boulders had the color of clay, and that they smelt strongly of human flesh. I, too, visited the spot some seventeen hundred and fifty years later. It is a forlorn little glen, on the southern side of the hill of Panopeus, below the long line of ruined but still stately walls and towers which crowns the gray rocks of the summit. It was a hot day in late autumn—the first of November—and after the long arid summer of Greece the little glen was quite dry; no water trickled down its bushy sides, but in the bottom I found a reddish crumbling earth, perhaps a relic of the clay out of which Prometheus modeled our first parents. The place was solitary and deserted: not a human being, not a sign of human habitation was to be seen; only the line of moldering towers and battlements on the hill above spoke of the busy life that had long passed away.

The entire scene, like so many others in Greece, was fitted to impress the mind with a sense of the impermanence of man's little bustling existence on earth compared with the lasting quality and, at least, the outward peace and tranquility of nature. The impression was deepened when I rested, in the heat of the day, on the summit of the hill under the shade of some fine holly-oaks, and surveyed the distant prospect, rich in memories of the past, while the sweet perfume of the wild thyme scented all the air. To the south the finely cut peak of Helicon peered over the low intervening ridges. In the west loomed the mighty mass of Parnassus, its middle slopes darkened by pine woods like shadows of clouds brooding on the mountain side; while at its skirts nestled the ivy-mantled walls of Daulis overhanging the deep glen, whose romantic beauty accords so well with the loves and sorrows of Procne and Philomela, which Greek legend associated with the spot.

Northwards, across the broad plain to which the steep bare hill of Panopeus descends, the eye rested on the gap in the hills through which the Cephissus winds his tortuous way to flow under grey willows, at the foot of barren stony hills, till his turbid waters lose themselves, no longer in the vast reedy swamps of the now vanished Copaic Lake, but in a dark cavern of the limestone rock. Eastward, clinging to the slopes of the bleak range of which the hill of Panopeus forms part, were the ruins of Chaeronea, the birthplace of Plutarch; and out there in the plain raged the fatal engagement which laid Greece at the feet of Macedonia.

There, too, in a later age, East and West met in deadly conflict, when the Roman armies under Sulla defeated the Asiatic hosts of Mithridates. Such was the landscape spread out before me on one of those farewell autumn days of almost pathetic splendor, when the departing summer seems to linger fondly, as if loath to resign to winter the enchanted mountains of Greece. Next day the scene had changed: summer was gone. A grey November mist hung low on the hills which only yesterday had shone splendidly in the sun, and under its melancholy curtain the dead flat of the Chaeronea plain, a wide, treeless expanse shut in by desolate slopes, wore an aspect of chilly sadness befitting the battlefield where a nation's freedom was lost.

We cannot doubt that such rude conceptions of the origin of mankind, common to Greeks, Hebrews, Babylonians, and Egyptians, were handed down to the civilized peoples of antiquity by their savage or barbarous forebears. Certainly stories of the same sort have been recorded among savages and barbarians for untold centuries.

Thus the Australian blacks near Melbourne said that Pund-jel, the Creator, cut three large sheets of bark with his big knife. On one of these he placed some clay and worked it up with his knife into a proper consistence. He then laid a portion of the clay on one of the other pieces of bark and shaped it into a human form; first he made the feet, then the legs, then the trunk, the arms, and the head. Thus he made a clay man on each of the two pieces of bark; and being well pleased with his handiwork, he danced round them for joy. Next he took stringy bark from the eucalyptus tree, made hair of it, and stuck it on the heads of his clay men. Then he looked at them again, was pleased with his work, and again danced round them for joy. He then lay down on them, blew his breath hard into their mouths, their noses, and their navels; and presently they stirred, spoke, and rose up fully grown men.

The Maoris of New Zealand say that a certain god, variously named Tu, Tiki, and Tane, took red riverside clay, kneaded it with his own blood into a likeness or image of himself, with eyes, legs, arms, and all complete, in fact, an exact copy of the deity; and having perfected the model, animated it by breathing into its mouth and nostrils, whereupon the clay effigy came to life and sneezed. "Of all these things," said a Maori, in relating the story of man's creation, "the most important is the fact that the clay sneezed, forasmuch as that sign of the power of the gods remains with us even to this day in order that we may be reminded of the great work Tu accomplished on the altar of the Kauhanga-nui, and hence it is that when men sneeze the words of Tu are repeated by those who are present;" for they say, "Sneeze, O spirit of life." So like himself was the man whom the Maori Creator Tiki fashioned that he called him Tiki-ahua; that is, Tiki's likeness.

It must be admitted that language is a weak and inadequate vehicle even for the expression of our usual understanding of things, to say nothing of those moments when the understanding unexpectedly expands and becomes deeper, and we see revealed an entire panoply of facts and relations for the description of which we have neither words nor expressions. But quite aside from this, in ordinary conditions of thinking and feeling, we are frequently at a loss for words, and we use one word at different times to describe different events or objects. The thoughts and words might all be considered correct for any given occasion or, on the other hand, when examined in the light of new understanding, might be, not only misleading, but completely wrong.

And so it was for the authors of **The Forgotten Books Of Eden** and **The Lost Books Of The Bible.**

William Kern; Editor

xvii

THE LOST BOOKS OF THE BIBLE

THE LOST BOOKS OF THE BIBLE

THE GOSPEL OF THE BIRTH OF MARY.

[In the primitive ages there was a Gospel extant bearing this name, attributed to St. Matthew, and received as genuine and authentic by several of the ancient Christian sects. It is to be found in the works of Jerome, a Father of the Church, who flourished in the fourth century, from whence the present translation is made. His contemporaries, Epiphanius, Bishop of Salamis, and Austin, also mention a Gospel under this title. The ancient copies differed from Jerome's, for from one of them the learned Faustus, a native of Britain, who became Bishop of Riez, in Provence, endeavoured to prove that Christ was not the Son of God till after his baptism; and that he was not of the house of David and tribe of Judah, because, according to the Gospel he cited, the Virgin herself was not of this tribe, but of the tribe of Levi; her father being a priest of the name of Joachim. It was likewise from this Gospel that the sect of the Collyridians, established the worship and offering of manchet bread and cracknels, or fine wafers, as sacrifices to Mary, whom they imagined to have been born of a Virgin, as Christ is related in the Canonical Gospel to have been born of her. Epiphanius likewise cites a passage concerning the death of Zacharias, which is not in Jerome's copy, viz. "That it was the occasion of the death of Zacharias in the temple, that when he had seen a vision, he, through surprise, was willing to disclose it, and his mouth was stopped. That which he saw was at the time of his offering incense, and it was a man standing in the form of an ass. When he was gone out, and had a mind to speak thus to the people, Woe unto you, whom do ye worship? he who had appeared to him in the temple took away the use of his speech. Afterwards when he recovered it, and was able to speak, he declared this to the Jews, and they slew him. They add (viz. the Gnostics in this book), that on this very account the high-priest was appointed by their lawgiver (by God to Moses), to carry little bells, that whensoever he went into the temple to sacrifice, he, whom they worshipped, hearing the noise of the bells, might have time enough to hide himself; and not be caught in that ugly shape and figure."—The principal part of this Gospel is contained in the Protevangelion of James, which follows next in order.]

THE LOST BOOKS OF THE BIBLE

CHAPTER I.

The parentage of Mary. Joachim her father, and Anna her mother, go to Jerusalem to the feast of the dedication. Issachar the high priest reproaches Joachim for being childless.

THE blessed and ever glorious Virgin Mary, sprung from the royal race and family of David, was born in the city of Nazareth, and educated at Jerusalem, in the temple of the Lord.

Her father's name was Joachim, and her mother's Anna. The family of her father was of Galilee and the city of Nazareth. The family of her mother was of Bethlehem.

Their lives were plain and right in the sight of the Lord, pious and faultless before men. For they divided all their substance into three parts:

One of which they devoted to the temple and officers of the temple; another they distributed among strangers, and persons in poor circumstances; and the third they reserved for themselves and the uses of their own family.

In this manner they lived for about twenty years chastely, in the favour of God, and the esteem of men, without any children.

But they vowed, if God should favour them with any issue, they would devote it to the service of the Lord; on which account they went at every feast in the year to the temple of the Lord.

And it came to pass, that when the feast of the dedication drew near, Joachim, with some others of his tribe, went up to Jerusalem, and at that time, Issachar was high-priest;

Who, when he saw Joachim along with the rest of his neighbours, bringing his offering, despised both him and his offerings, and asked him,

Why he, who had no children, would presume to appear among those who had? Adding, that his offerings could never be acceptable to God, who was judged by him unworthy to have children; the Scripture having said, Cursed is every one who shall not beget a male in Israel.

He further said, that he ought first to be free from that curse by begetting some issue, and then come with his offerings into the presence of God.

But Joachim being much confounded with the shame of such reproach, retired to the shepherds, who were with the cattle in their pastures;

For he was not inclined to return home, lest his neighbours, who were present and heard all this from the high-priest, should publicly reproach him in the same manner.

CHAPTER II.

An angel appears to Joachim, and informs him that Anna shall conceive and bring forth a daughter, who shall be called Mary, be brought up in the temple, and while yet a virgin, in a way unparalleled, bring forth the Son of God: gives him a sign, and departs.

BUT when he had been there for some time, on a certain day when he was alone, the angel of the Lord stood by him with a prodigious light.

To whom, being troubled at the appearance, the angel who had appeared to him, endeavouring to compose him said:

Be not afraid, Joachim, nor troubled at the sight of me, for I am an angel of the Lord sent by him to you, that I might inform you, that your prayers are heard, and your alms ascended in the sight of God.

For he hath surely seen your shame, and heard you unjustly reproached for not having children: for God is the avenger of sin, and not of nature;

And so when he shuts the womb of any person, he does it for this reason, that he may in a more wonderful manner again open it, and that which is born appear to be not the product of lust, but the gift of God.

For the first mother of your nation Sarah, was she not barren even till her eightieth year: And yet even in the end of her old age brought forth Isaac, in whom the promise was made a blessing to all nations.

Rachel also, so much in favour with God, and beloved so much by holy Jacob, continued barren for a long time, yet afterwards was the mot her of Joseph, who was not only governor of Egypt, but delivered many nations from perishing with hunger.

Who among the judges was more valiant than Samson, or more holy than Samuel? And yet both their mothers were barren.

But if reason will not convince you of the truth of my words, that there are frequent conceptions in advanced years, and that those who were barren have brought forth to their great surprise; therefore Anna your wife shall bring you a daughter, and you shall call her name Mary;

She shall, according to your vow, be devoted to the Lord from her infancy, and be filled with the Holy Ghost from her mother's womb;

She shall neither eat nor drink anything which is unclean, nor shall her conversation be without among the common people, but in the temple of the Lord; that so she may not fall under any slander or suspicion of what is bad.

So in the process of her years, as she shall be in a miraculous manner born of one that was barren, so she shall, while yet a virgin, in a way unparalleled, bring forth the Son of the most High God, who shall, be called Jesus, and, according to the signification of his name, be the Saviour of all nations.

And this shall be a sign to you of the things which I declare, namely, when you come to the golden gate of Jerusalem, you shall there meet your wife Anna, who being very much troubled that you returned no sooner, shall then rejoice to see you.

When the angel had said this he departed from him.

CHAPTER III.

The angel appears to Anna; tells her a daughter shall be born unto her, devoted to the service of the Lord in the temple, who, being a virgin and not knowing man, shall bring forth the Lord, and gives her a sign therefore. Joachim and Anna meet and rejoice, and praise the Lord. Anna conceives, and brings forth a daughter called Mary.

AFTERWARDS the angel appeared to Anna his wife saying: Fear not, neither think that which you see is a spirit.

For I am that angel who hath offered up your prayers and alms before God, and am now sent to you, that I may inform you, that a daughter will be born unto you, who shall be called Mary, and shall be blessed above all women.

She shall be, immediately upon her birth, full of the grace of the Lord, and shall continue during the three years of her weaning in her father's house, and afterwards, being devoted to the service of the Lord, shall not depart from the temple, till she arrives to years of discretion.

In a word, she shall there serve the Lord night and day in fasting and prayer, shall abstain from every unclean thing, and never know any man;

But, being an unparalleled instance without any pollution or defilement, and a virgin not knowing any man, shall bring forth a son, and a maid shall bring forth the Lord, who both by his grace and name and works, shall be the Saviour of the world.

Arise therefore, and go up to Jerusalem, and when you shall come to that which is called the golden gate (because it is gilt with gold), as a sign of what I have told you, you shall meet your husband, for whose safety you have been so much concerned.

When therefore you find these things thus accomplished, believe that all the rest which I have told you, shall also undoubtedly be accomplished.

According therefore to the command of the angel, both of them left the places where they were, and when they came to the place specified in the angel's prediction, they met each other.

Then, rejoicing at each other's vision, and being fully satisfied in the promise of a child, they gave due thanks to the Lord, who exalts the humble.

After having praised the Lord, they returned home, and lived in a cheerful and assured expectation of the promise of God.

So Anna conceived, and brought forth a daughter, and, according to the angel's command, the parents did call her name Mary.

CHAPTER IV.

Mary brought to the temple at three years old. Ascends the stairs of the temple by miracle. Her parents sacrificed and returned home.

AND when three years were expired, and the time of her weaning complete, they brought the Virgin to the temple of the Lord with offerings.

And there were about the temple, according to the fifteen Psalms of degrees, fifteen stairs to ascend.

For the temple being built in a mountain, the altar of burnt-offering, which was without, could not be come near but by stairs;

The parents of the blessed Virgin and infant Mary put her upon one of these stairs;

But while they were putting off their clothes, in which they had travelled, and according to custom putting on some that were more neat and clean,

In the mean time the Virgin of the Lord in such a manner went up all the stairs one after another, without the help of any to lead or lift her, that any one would have judged from hence that she was of perfect age.

Thus the Lord did, in the infancy of his Virgin, work this extraordinary work, and evidence by this miracle how great she was like to be hereafter.

But the parents having offered up their sacrifice, according to the custom of the law, and perfected their vow, left the Virgin with other virgins in the apartments of the temple, who were to be brought up there, and they returned home.

CHAPTER V.

Mary ministered unto by angels. The high-priest orders all virgins of fourteen years old to quit the temple and endeavour to be married. Mary refuses, having vowed her virginity to the Lord. The high-priest commands a meeting of the chief persons of Jerusalem, who seek the Lord for counsel in the matter. A voice from the mercy-seat. The high priest obeys it by ordering all the unmarried men of the house of David to bring their rods to the altar, that his rod which should flower, and on which the Spirit of God should sit, should betroth the Virgin.

BUT the Virgin of the Lord, as she advanced in fears, increased also in perfections, and according to the saying of the Psalmist, her father and mother forsook her, but the Lord took care of her.

For she every day had the conversation of angels, and every day received visitors from God, which preserved her from all sorts of evil, and caused her to abound with

THE LOST BOOKS OF THE BIBLE

all good things;

So that when at length she arrived to her fourteenth year, as the wicked could not lay anything to her charge worthy of reproof, so all good persons, who were acquainted with her, admired her life and conversation.

At that time the high-priest made a public order. That all the virgins who had public settlements in the temple, and were come to this age, should return home, and, as they were now of a proper maturity, should, according to the custom of their country, endeavour to be married.

To which command, though all the other virgins readily yielded obedience, Mary the Virgin of the Lord alone answered, that she could not comply with it.

Assigning these reasons, that both she and her parents had devoted her to the service of the Lord; and besides, that she had vowed virginity to the Lord, which vow she was resolved never to break through by lying with a man.

The high priest being hereby brought into a difficulty,

Seeing he durst neither on the one hand dissolve the vow, and disobey the Scripture, which says, Vow and pay,

Nor on the other hand introduce a custom, to which the people were strangers, commanded,

That at the approaching feast all the principal persons both of Jerusalem and the neighbouring places should meet together, that he might have their advice, how he had best proceed in so difficult a case.

When they were accordingly met, they unanimously agreed to seek the Lord, and ask counsel from him on this matter.

And when they were all engaged in prayer, the high-priest, according to the usual way, went to consult God.

And immediately there was a voice from the ark, and the mercy seat, which all present heard, that it must be inquired or sought out by a prophecy of Isaiah to whom the Virgin should be given and be betrothed;

For Isaiah saith, there shall come forth a rod out of the stem of Jesse, and a flower shall spring out of its root,

And the Spirit of the Lord shall rest upon him, the Spirit of Wisdom and Understanding, the Spirit of Counsel and Might, the Spirit of Knowledge and Piety, and the Spirit of the fear of the Lord shall fill him.

Then, according to this prophecy, he appointed, that all the men of the house and family of David, who were marriageable, and not married, should bring their several rods to the altar,

And out of whatsoever person's rod after it was brought, a flower should bud forth,

6

and on the top of it the Spirit of the Lord should sit in the appearance of a dove, he should be the man to whom the Virgin should be given and be betrothed.

CHAPTER VI.

Joseph draws back his rod. The dove pitches on it. He betroths Mary and returns to Bethlehem. Mary returns to her parents' house at Galilee.

AMONG the rest there was a man named Joseph, of the house and family of David, and a person very far advanced in years, who drew back his rod, when every one besides presented his.

So that when nothing appeared agreeable to the heavenly voice, the high-priest judged it proper to consult God again,

Who answered that he to whom the Virgin was to be betrothed was the only person of those who were brought together, who had not brought his rod.

Joseph therefore was betrayed.

For, when he did bring his rod, and a dove coming from Heaven pitched upon the top of it, every one plainly saw, that the Virgin was to be betrothed to him:

Accordingly, the usual ceremonies of betrothing being over, he returned to his own city of Bethlehem, to set his house in order, and make the needful for the marriage.

But the Virgin of the Lord, Mary, with seven other virgins of the same age, who had been weaned at the same time, and who had been appointed to attend her by the priest, returned to her parents' house in Galilee.

CHAPTER VII.

The salutation of the Virgin by Gabriel, who explains to her that she shall conceive, without lying with a man, while a Virgin, by the Holy Ghost coming upon her without the heats of lust. She submits.

NOW at this time of her first coming into Galilee, the angel Gabriel was sent to her from God, to declare to her the conception of our Saviour, and the manner and way of her conceiving him.

Accordingly going into her, he filled the chamber where she was with a prodigious light, and in a most courteous manner saluting her, he said,

Hail, Mary! Virgin of the Lord most acceptable! O Virgin full of Grace! The Lord is with you, you are blessed above all women, you are blessed above all men, that. have been hitherto born.

But the Virgin, who had before been well acquainted with the countenances of angels, and to whom such light from heaven was no uncommon thing,

Was neither terrified with the vision of the angel, nor astonished at the greatness of the light, but only troubled about the angel's words:

And began to consider what so extraordinary a salutation should mean, what it did portend, or what sort of end it would have.

To this thought the angel, divinely inspired, replies;

Fear not, Mary, as though I intended anything inconsistent with your chastity in this salutation:

For you have found favour with the Lord, because you made virginity your choice.

Therefore while you are a Virgin, you shall conceive without sin, and bring forth a son.

He shall be great, because he shall reign from sea to sea, and from the rivers to the ends of the earth.

And he shall be called the Son of the Highest; for he who is born in a mean state on earth reigns in an exalted one in heaven.

And the Lord shall give him the throne of his father David, and he shall reign over the house of Jacob for ever, and of his kingdom there shall be no end.

For he is the King of Kings, and Lord of Lords, and his throne is for ever and ever.

To this discourse of the angel the Virgin replied not, as though she were unbelieving, but willing to know the manner of it.

She said, How can that be? For seeing, according to my vow, I have never known any man, how can I bear a child without the addition of a man's seed?

To this the angel replied and said, Think not, Mary, that you shall conceive in the ordinary way.

For, without lying with a man, while a Virgin, you shall conceive; while a Virgin, you shall bring forth; and while a Virgin shall give suck.

For the Holy Ghost shall come upon you, and the power of the Most High shall overshadow you, without any of the heats of lust.

So that which shall be born of you shall be only holy, be. cause it only is conceived without sin, and being born, shall be called the Son of God.

Then Mary stretching forth her hands, and lifting her eyes to heaven, said, Behold the handmaid of the Lord! Let it be unto me according to thy word.

CHAPTER VIII.

Joseph returns to Galilee to marry the Virgin he had betrothed. perceives she is with child, is uneasy, purposes to put her away privily, is told by the angel of the Lord it is not the work of man but the Holy Ghost, Marries her, but keeps chaste, removes with her to Bethlehem, where she brings forth Christ.

JOSEPH therefore went from Judaea to Galilee, with intention to marry the Virgin who was betrothed to him:

For it was now near three months since she was betrothed to him.

At length it plainly appeared she was with child, and it could not be hid from Joseph:

For going to the Virgin in a free manner, as one espoused, and talking familiarly with her, he perceived her to be with child.

And thereupon began to be uneasy and doubtful, not knowing what course it would be best to take;

For being a just man, he was not willing to expose her, nor defame her by the suspicion of being a whore, since he was a pious man.

He purposed therefore privately to put an end to their agreement, and as privately to put her away.

But while he was meditating these things, behold the angel of the Lord appeared to him in his sleep, and said Joseph, son of David, fear not;

Be not willing to entertain any suspicion of the Virgin's being guilty of fornication, or to think any thing amiss of her, neither be afraid to take her to wife;

For that which is begotten In her and now distresses your mind, is not the work of man, but the Holy Ghost.

For she of all women is that only Virgin who shall bring forth the Son of God, and you shall call his name Jesus, that is, Saviour: for he will save his people from their sins.

Joseph thereupon, according to the command of the angel, married the Virgin, and did not know her, but kept her in chastity.

And now the ninth month from her conception drew near, when Joseph took his wife and what other things were necessary to Bethlehem, the city from whence he came.

And it came to pass, while they were there, the days were fulfilled for her bringing forth.

And she brought forth her first-born son, as the holy Evangelists have taught, even our Lord Jesus Christ, who with the Father, Son, and Holy Ghost, lives and reigns to everlasting ages.

THE PROTEVANGELION; OR, AN HISTORICAL ACCOUNT OF THE BIRTH OF CHRIST, AND THE PERPETUAL VIRGIN MARY, HIS MOTHER, BY JAMES THE LESSER, COUSIN AND BROTHER OF THE LORD JESUS, CHIEF APOSTLE AND FIRST BISHOP OF THE CHRISTIANS IN JERUSALEM.

[This Gospel is ascribed to James. The allusions to it in the ancient Fathers are frequent, and their expressions indicate that it had obtained a very general credit in the Christian world. The controversies founded upon it chiefly relate to the age of Joseph at the birth of Christ, and to his being a widower with children, before his marriage with

THE LOST BOOKS OF THE BIBLE

the Virgin. It seems material to remark, that the legends of the latter ages affirm the virginity of Joseph, notwithstanding Epiphanius, Hilary, Chrysostom, Cyril, Euthymius, Thephylact, Occumenius, and indeed all the Latin Fathers till Ambrose, and the Greek Fathers afterwards, maintain the opinions of Joseph's age and family, founded upon their belief in the authenticity of this book. It is supposed to have been originally composed in Hebrew. Postellus brought the MS. of this Gospel from the Levant, translated it into Latin, and sent it to Oporimus, a printer at Basil, where Bibliander, a Protestant Divine, and the Professor of Divinity at Zurich, caused it to be printed in 1552. Postellus asserts that it was publicly read as canonical in the eastern churches, they making no doubt that James was the author of it. It is, nevertheless, considered apocryphal by some of the most learned divines in the Protestant and Catholic churches.]

CHAPTER I.

Joachim, a rich man,offers to the Lord,is opposed by Reuben the high-priest, because he has not begotten issue in Israel, retires into the wilderness and fasts forty days and forty nights.

IN the history of the twelve tribes of Israel we read there was a certain person called Joachim, who being very rich, made double offerings to the Lord God, having made this resolution: my substance shall be for the benefit of the whole people, and that I may find mercy from the Lord God for the forgiveness of my sins.

But at a certain great feast of the Lord, when the children of Israel offered their gifts, and Joachim also offered his, Reuben the high-priest opposed him, saying it is not lawful for thee to offer thy gifts, seeing thou hast not begot any issue in Israel.

At this Joachim being concerned very much, went away to consult the registries of the twelve tribes, to see whether he was the only person who had begot no issue.

But upon inquiry he found that all the righteous had raised up seed in Israel:

Then he called to mind the patriarch Abraham, How that God in the end of his life had given him his son Isaac; upon which he was exceedingly distressed, and would not be seen by his wife:

But retired into the wilderness, and fixed his tent there, and fasted forty days and forty nights, saying to himself,

I will not go down either to eat or drink, till the Lord my God shall look down upon me, but prayer shall be my meat and drink.

CHAPTER II.

Anna, the wife of Joachim, mourns her barrenness, is reproached with it by Judith her maid, sits under a laurel tree and prays to the Lord.

IN the meantime his wife Anna was distressed and perplexed on a double account, and said I will mourn both for my widowhood and my barrenness.

Then drew near a great feast of the Lord, and Judith her maid said, How long will you thus afflict your soul? The feast of the Lord is now come, when it is unlawful for any one to mourn.

Take therefore this hood which was given by one who makes such things, for it is not fit that I, who am a servant, should wear it, but it well suits a person of your greater character.

But Anna replied, Depart from me, I am not used to such things; besides, the Lord hath greatly humbled me.

I fear some ill-designing person hath given thee this, and thou art come to pollute me with my sin.

Then Judith her maid answered, What evil shall I wish you when you will not hearken to me?

I cannot wish you a greater curse than you are under, in that God hath shut up your womb, that you should not be a mother in Israel.

At this Anna was exceedingly troubled, and having on her wedding garment, went about three o'clock in the afternoon to walk in her garden.

And she saw a laurel-tree, and sat under it, and prayed unto the Lord, saying,

O God of my fathers, bless me and regard my prayer as thou didst bless the womb of Sarah, and gavest her a son Isaac.

CHAPTER III.

Anna perceiving a sparrow's nest in the laurels bemoans her barrenness.

AND as she was looking towards heaven she perceived a sparrow's nest in the laurel,

And mourning within herself, she said, Wo is me, who begat me? and what womb did bear me, that I should be thus accursed before the children of Israel, and that they should reproach and deride me in the temple of my God: Wo is me, to what can I be compared?

I am not comparable to the very beasts of the earth, for even the beasts of the earth are fruitful before thee, O Lord! Wo is me, to what can I be compared?

I am not comparable to the brute animals, for even the brute animals are fruitful before thee, O Lord! Wo is me, to what am I comparable?

I cannot be compared to these waters, for even the waters are fruitful before thee, O Lord! Wo is me, to what can I be compared?

I am not comparable to the waves of the sea; for these, whether they are calm, or in motion, with the fishes which are in them, praise thee, O Lord! Wo is me, to what can I be compared?

I am not comparable to the very earth, for the earth produces its fruits, and praises thee, O Lord!

CHAPTER IV.

An Angel appears to Anna and tells her she shall conceive; two angels appear to her on the same errand. Joachim sacrifices. Anna goes to meet him, rejoicing that she shall conceive.

THEN an angel of the Lord stood by her and said, Anna, Anna, the Lord hath heard thy prayer; thou shalt conceive and bring forth, and thy progeny shall be spoken of in all the world.

And Anna answered, As the Lord my God liveth, whatever I bring forth, whether it be male or female, I will devote it to the Lord my God, and it shall minister to him in holy things, during its whole life.

And behold there appeared two angels, saying unto her, Behold Joachim thy husband is coming with his shepherds.

For an angel of the Lord hath also come down to him, and said, The Lord God hath heard thy prayer, make haste and go hence, for behold Anna thy wife shall conceive.

And Joachim went down and called his shepherds, saying Bring me hither ten she-lambs without spot or blemish, and they shall be for the Lord my God.

And bring me twelve calves without blemish, and the twelve calves shall be for the priests and the elders.

Bring me also a hundred goats, and the hundred goats shall be for the whole people.

And Joachim went down with the shepherds, and Anna stood by the gate and saw Joachim coming with the shepherds.

And she ran, and hanging about his neck, said, Now I know that the Lord hath greatly blessed me:

For behold, I who was a widow am no longer a widow, and I who was barren shall conceive.

CHAPTER V.

Joachim abides the first day in his house, but sacrifices on the morrow. consults the plate on the priest's forehead. And is without sin. Anna brings forth a daughter, whom she calls Mary.

AND Joachim abode the first day in his house, but on the morrow he brought his offerings and said,

If the Lord be propitious to me let the plate which is on the priest's forehead make it manifest.

And he consulted the plate which the priest wore, and saw it, and behold sin was not found in him.

And Joachim said, Now I know that the Lord is propitious to me, and hath taken away all my sins.

And he went down from the temple of the Lord justified, and he went to his own house.

And when nine months were fulfilled to Anna, she brought forth, and said to the midwife, What have I brought forth?

And she told her, a girl.

Then Anna said, the Lord hath this day magnified my soul; and she laid her in bed.

And when the days of her purification were accomplished, she gave suck to the child, and called her name Mary.

CHAPTER VI.

Mary at nine months old, walks nine steps, Anna keeps her holy. When she is a year old, Joachim makes a great feast. Anna gives her the breast, and sings a song to the Lord.

AND the child increased in strength every day, so that when she was nine months old, her mother put her upon the ground to try if she could stand; and when she had walked nine steps, she came again to her mother's lap.

Then her mother caught her up, and said, As the Lord my God liveth, thou shalt not walk again on this earth till I bring thee into the temple of the Lord.

Accordingly she made her chamber a holy place, and suffered nothing uncommon or unclean to come near her, but invited certain undefiled daughters of Israel, and they drew her aside.

But when the child was a year old, Joachim made a great feast, and invited the priests, scribes, elders, and all the people of Israel;

And Joachim then made an offering of the girl to the chief priests, and they blessed her, saying, The God of our fathers bless this girl, and give her a name famous and lasting through all generations. And all the people replied, So be it, Amen.

Then Joachim a second time offered her to the priests, and they blessed her, saying, O most high God, regard this girl, and bless her with an everlasting blessing.

Upon this her mother took her up, and gave her the breast, and sung the following song to the Lord.

I will sing a new song unto the Lord my God, for he hath visited me, and taken away from me the reproach of mine enemies, and hath given me the fruit of his righteousness, that it may now be told the sons of Reuben, that Anna gives suck.

Then she put the child to rest in the room which she had consecrated, and she went out and ministered unto them.

And when the feast was ended, they went away rejoicing and praising the God of Israel.

CHAPTER VII.

Mary being three years old, Joachim causes certain virgins to light each a lamp, and goes with her to the temple. The high-priest places her on the third step of the altar, and she dances with her feet.

BUT the girl grew, and when she was two years old, Joachim said to Anna, Let us lead her to the temple of the Lord, that we may perform our vow, which we have vowed unto the Lord God, lest he should be angry with us, and our offering be unacceptable.

But Anna said, Let us wait the third year, lest she should be at a loss to know her father. And Joachim said, Let us then wait.

And when the child was three years old, Joachim said, Let us invite the daughters of the Hebrews, who are undefiled, and let them take each a lamp, and let them be lighted, that the child may not turn back again, and her mind be set against the temple of the Lord.

And they did thus till they ascended into the temple of the Lord. And the high-priest received her, and blessed her, and said, Mary, the Lord God hath magnified thy name to all generations, and to the very end of time by thee will the Lord shew his redemption to the children of Israel,

And he placed her upon the third step of the altar, and the Lord gave unto her grace, and she danced with her feet, and all the house of Israel loved her.

CHAPTER VIII.

Mary fed in the temple by angels, when twelve years old the priests consult what to do with her. The angel of the Lord warns Zacharias to call together all the widowers, each bringing a rod. The people meet by sound of trumpet. Joseph throws away his hatchet, and goes to the meeting, a dove comes forth from his rod, and alights on his head. He is chosen to betroth the Virgin. refuses because he is an old man, is compelled, takes her home, and goes to mind his trade of building.

AND her parents went away filled with wonder, and praising God, because the girl did not return back to them.

But Mary continued in the temple as a dove educated there, and received her food from the hand of an angel.

And when she was twelve years of age, the priests met in a council, and said, Behold, Mary is twelve years of age; what shall we do with her, for fear lest the holy place of the Lord our God should be defiled?

Then replied the priests to Zacharias the high-priest, Do you stand at the altar of the Lord, and enter into the holy place, and make petitions concerning her, and whatsoever the Lord shall manifest unto you, that do.

Then the high-priest entered into the Holy of Holies, and taking away with him the breastplate of judgment made prayers concerning her;

And behold the angel of the Lord came to him, and said, Zacharias, Zacharias, Go forth and call together all the widowers among the people, and let every one of them bring his rod, and he by whom the Lord shall shew a sign shall be the husband of Mary.

And the criers went out through all Judaea, and the trumpet of the Lord sounded, and all the people ran and met together.

Joseph also, throwing away the hatchet, went out to meet them; and when they were met, they went to the high-priest, taking every man his rod.

After the high-priest had received their rods, he went into the temple to pray;

And when he had finished his prayer, he took the rods, And went forth and distributed them, and there was no miracle attended them.

The last rod was taken by Joseph, and behold a dove proceeded out of the rod, and flew upon the head of Joseph.

And the high-priest said, Joseph, Thou art the person chosen to take the Virgin of the Lord, to keep her for him:

But Joseph refused, saying, I am an old man, and have children, but she is young, and I fear lest I should appear ridiculous in Israel.

Then the high-priest replied, Joseph, fear the Lord thy God, and remember how God dealt with Dathan, Korah, and Abiram, how the earth opened and swallowed them up, because of their contradiction.

Now therefore, Joseph, fear God, lest the like things should happen in your family.

Joseph then being afraid, took her unto his house, and Joseph said unto Mary, Behold, I have taken thee from the temple of the Lord, and now I will leave thee in my house; I must go to mind my trade of building. he Lord be with thee.

CHAPTER IX.

The priests desire a new veil for the temple, seven virgins cast lots for making different parts of it, the lot to spin the true purple falls to Mary. Zacharias, the high priest, becomes dumb. Mary takes a pot to draw water, and hears a voice, trembles and begins to work,an angel appears, and salutes her, and tells her she shall conceive by the Holy Ghost, she submits, visits her cousin Elizabeth, whose child in her womb leaps.

AND it came to pass, in a council of the priests, it was said, Let us make a new veil for the temple.

And the high-priest said, Call together to me seven undefiled virgins of the tribe of David.

And the servants went and brought them into the temple of the Lord, and the high-priest said unto them Cast lots before me now, who of you shall spin the golden thread, who the blue, who the scarlet, who the fine linen, and who the true purple.

Then the high-priest knew Mary, that she was of the tribe of David; and he called her, and the true purple fell to her lot to spin, and she went away to her own house.

But from that time Zacharias the high-priest became dumb, and Samuel was placed in his room till Zacharias spoke again.

But Mary took the true purple, and did spin it.

And she took a pot, and went out to draw water, and heard a voice saying unto her, Hail thou who art full of grace, the Lord is with thee; thou art blessed among women.

And she looked round to the right and to the left (to see) whence that voice came, and then trembling went into her house, and laying down the water-pot she took the purple, and sat down in her seat to work it.

And behold the angel of the Lord stood by her, and said, Fear not, Mary, for thou hast found favour in the sight of God;

Which when she heard, she reasoned with herself what that sort of salutation meant.

And the angel said unto her, The Lord is with thee, and thou shalt conceive:

To which she replied, What! shall I conceive by the living God, and bring forth as all other women do?

But the angel returned answer, Not so, O Mary, but the Holy Ghost shall come upon thee, and the power of the Most High shall overshadow thee;

Wherefore that which shall be born of thee shall be holy, and shall be called the Son of the Living God, and thou shalt call his name Jesus; for he shall save his people from their sins.

And behold thy cousin Elizabeth, she also hath conceived a son in her old age.

And this now is the sixth month with her, who was called barren; for nothing is impossible with God.

And Mary said, Behold the handmaid of the Lord; let it be unto me according to thy word.

And when she had wrought her purple, she carried it to the high-priest, and the high-priest blessed her, saying, Mary, the Lord God hath magnified thy name, and thou shalt be blessed in all the ages of the world.

Then Mary, filled with joy, went away to her cousin Elizabeth, and knocked at the door.

Which when Elizabeth heard, she ran and opened to her, and blessed her, and said, Whence is this to me, that the mother of my Lord should come unto me?

For lo! as soon as the voice of thy salutation reached my ears, that which is in me leaped and blessed thee.

But Mary, being ignorant of all those mysterious things which the archangel Gabriel had spoken to her, lifted up her eyes to heaven, and said, Lord! What am I, that all the generations of the earth should call me blessed?

But perceiving herself daily to grow big, and being afraid, she went home, and hid herself from the children of Israel; and was fourteen years old when all these things happened.

CHAPTER X.

Joseph returns from building houses, finds the Virgin grown big, being six months' gone with child, is jealous and troubled, reproaches her, she affirms her innocence, he leaves her, determines to dismiss her privately, is warned in a dream that Mary is with child by the Holy Ghost, and glorifies God who hath shewn him such favour.

AND when her sixth month was come, Joseph returned from his building houses abroad, which was his trade, and entering into the house, found the Virgin grown big:

Then smiting upon his face, he said, With what face can I look up to the Lord my God? or, what shall I say concerning this young woman?

For I received her a Virgin out of the temple of the Lord my God, and have not preserved her such!

Who has thus deceived me? Who has committed this evil in my house, and seducing the Virgin from me, hath defiled her?

Is not the history of Adam exactly accomplished in me?

For in the very instant of his glory, the serpent came and found Eve alone, and seduced her.

Just after the same manner it has happened to me.

Then Joseph arising from the ground, called her, and said, O thou who hast been so much favoured by God, why hast thou done this?

Why hast thou thus debased thy soul, who wast educated in the Holy of Holies, and received thy food from the hand of angels?

But she, with a flood of tears, replied, I am innocent, and have known no man.

Then said Joseph, How comes it to pass you are with child?

Mary answered, As the Lord my God liveth, I know not by what means.

Then Joseph was exceedingly afraid, and went away from her, considering what he should do with her; and he thus reasoned with himself:

If I conceal her crime, I shall be found guilty by the law of the Lord;

And if I discover her to the children of Israel, I fear, lest she being with child by an angel, I shall be found to betray the life of an innocent person:

What therefore shall I do? I will privately dismiss her.

Then the night was come upon him, when behold an angel of the Lord appeared to him in a dream, and said,

Be not afraid to take that young woman, for that which is within her is of the Holy Ghost; .

And she shall bring forth a son, and thou shalt call his name Jesus, for he shall save his people from their sins.

Then Joseph arose from his sleep, and glorified the God of Israel, who had shown him such favour, and preserved the Virgin.

CHAPTER XI.

Annas visits Joseph, perceives the Virgin big with child, informs the high priest that Joseph had privately married her. Joseph and Mary brought to trial on the charge. Joseph drinks the water of the Lord as an ordeal, and receiving no harm, returns home.

THEN came Annas the scribe, and said to Joseph, Wherefore have we not seen you since your return?

And Joseph replied, Because I was weary after my journey, and rested the first day.

But Annas turning about perceived the Virgin big with child.

And went away to the priest, and told him, Joseph in whom you placed so much confidence, is guilty of a notorious crime, in that he hath defiled the Virgin whom he received out of the temple of the Lord, and hath privately married her, not discovering it to the children of Israel.

Then said the priest, Hath Joseph done this?

Annas replied, If you send any of your servants, you will find that she is with child.

And the servants went, and found it as he said.

Upon this both she and Joseph were brought to their trial, and the priest said unto her, Mary, what hast thou done?

Why hast thou debased thy soul, and forgot thy God, seeing thou wast brought up in the Holy of Holies, and didst receive thy food from the hands of angels, and heardest their songs?

Why hast thou done this?

To which with a flood of tears she answered, As the Lord my God liveth, I am innocent in his sight, seeing I know no man.

Then the priest said to Joseph, Why hast thou done this?

And Joseph answered, As the Lord my God liveth, I have not been concerned with her.

But the priest said, Lie not, but declare the truth; thou hast privately married her, and not discovered it to the children of Israel, and humbled thyself under the mighty hand (of God), that thy seed might be blessed.

And Joseph was silent.

Then said the priest (to Joseph), You must restore to the temple of the Lord the Virgin which you took thence.

But he wept bitterly, and the priest added, I will cause you both to drink the water of the Lord, which is for trial, and so your iniquity shall be laid open before you.

Then the priest took the water, and made Joseph drink, and sent him to a mountainous place.

And he returned perfectly well, and all the people wondered that his guilt was not discovered.

So the priest said, Since the Lord hath not made your sins evident, neither do I condemn you.

So he sent them away.

Then Joseph took Mary, and went to his house, rejoicing and praising the God of Israel.

CHAPTER XII.

A decree from Augustus for taxing the Jews. Joseph puts Mary on an ass, to return to Bethlehem, she looks sorrowful, she laughs, Joseph inquires the cause of each, she tells him she sees two persons, one mourning and the other rejoicing, the delivery being near, he takes her from the ass, and places her in a cave.

AND it came to pass, that there went forth a decree from the Emperor Augustus, that all the Jews should be taxed, who were of Bethlehem in Judaea:

And Joseph said, I will take care that my children be taxed: but what shall I do with this young woman?

To have her taxed as my wife I am ashamed; and if I tax her as my daughter, all Israel knows she is not my daughter.

When the time of the Lord's appointment shall come, let him do as seems good to him.

And he saddled the ass, and put her upon it, and Joseph and Simon followed after her, and arrived at Bethlehem within three miles.

Then Joseph turning about saw Mary sorrowful, and said within himself, Perhaps she is in pain through that which is within her.

But when he turned about again he saw her laughing, and said to her,

Mary, how happens it, that I sometimes see sorrow, and sometimes laughter and joy in thy countenance?

And Mary replied to him, I see two people with mine eyes, the one weeping and mourning, the other laughing and rejoicing.

And he went again across the way, and Mary said to Joseph, Take me down from the ass, for that which is in me presses to come forth.

But Joseph replied, Whither shall I take thee? for the place is desert.

Then said Mary again to Joseph, take me down, for that which is within me mightily presses me.

And Joseph took her down.

And he found there a cave, and let her into it.

CHAPTER XIII.

Joseph seeks a Hebrew midwife, perceives the fowls stopping in their flight, the working people at their food not moving, the sheep standing still, the shepherd fixed and immoveable, and kids with their mouths touching the water but not drinking.

AND leaving her and his sons in the cave, Joseph went forth to seek a Hebrew midwife in the village of Bethlehem.

But as I was going (said Joseph) I looked up into the air, and I saw the clouds astonished, and the fowls of the air stopping in the midst of their flight.

And I looked down towards the earth, and saw a table spread, and working people sitting around it, but their hands were upon the table, and they did not move to eat.

They who had meat in their mouths did not eat.

They who lifted their hands up to their heads did not draw them back:

And they who lifted them up to their mouths did not put anything in;

But all their faces were fixed upwards.

And I beheld the sheep dispersed, and yet the sheep stood still.

And the shepherd lifted up his hand to smite them, and his hand continued up.

And I looked unto a river, and saw the kids with their mouths close to the water, and touching it, but they did not drink.

CHAPTER XIV.

Joseph finds a midwife. A bright cloud overshadows the cave. A great light in the cave, gradually increases until the infant is born. The midwife goes out, and tells Salome that she has seen a virgin bring forth. Salome doubts it. her hand withers, she supplicates the Lord, is cured, but warned not to declare what she had seen.

THEN I beheld a woman coming down from the mountains, and she said to me, Where art thou going, O man?

And I said to her, I go to inquire for a Hebrew midwife.

She replied to me, Where is the woman that is to be delivered?

And I answered, In the cave, and she is betrothed to me.

Then said the midwife, Is she not thy wife?

Joseph answered, It is Mary, who was educated in the Holy of Holies, in the house of the Lord, and she fell to my lot, and is not my wife, but has conceived by the Holy Ghost.

The midwife said, Is this true?

He answered, Come and see.

And the midwife went along with him, and stood in the cave.

Then a bright cloud overshadowed the cave, and the midwife said, This day my soul is magnified, for mine eyes have seen surprising things, and salvation is brought forth to Israel.

But on a sudden the cloud became a great light in the cave, so that their eyes could not bear it.

But the light gradually decreased, until the infant appeared, and sucked the breast of his mother Mary.

Then the midwife cried out, and said, How glorious a day is this, wherein mine eyes have seen this extraordinary sight!

And the midwife went out from the cave, and Salome met her.

And the midwife said to her, Salome, Salome, I will tell you a most surprising thing which I saw,

A virgin hath brought forth, which is a thing contrary to nature.

To which Salome replied, As the Lord my God liveth, unless I receive particular proof of this matter, I will not believe that a virgin hath brought forth.

Then Salome went in, and the midwife said, Mary, shew thyself, for a great controversy is risen concerning thee.

And Salome received satisfaction.

But her hand was withered, and she groaned bitterly.

And said, Woe to me, because of mine iniquity; for I have tempted the living God, and my hand is ready to drop off.

Then Salome made her supplication to the Lord, and said, O God of my fathers, remember me, for I am of the seed of Abraham, and Isaac, and Jacob.

Make me not a reproach among the children of Israel, but restore me sound to my parents.

For thou well knowest, O Lord, that I have performed many offices of charity in thy name, and have received my reward from thee.

Upon this an angel of the Lord stood by Salome, and said, The Lord God hath heard thy prayer, reach forth thy hand to the child, and carry him, and by that means thou shalt be restored.

Salome, filled with exceeding joy, went to the child, and said, I will touch him:

And she purposed to worship him, for she said, This is a great king which is born in Israel.

And straightway Salome was cured.

Then the midwife went out of the cave, being approved by God.

And lo! a voice came to Salome, Declare not the strange things which thou hast seen, till the child shall come to Jerusalem.

So Salome also departed, approved by God.

CHAPTER XV.

Wise men come from the east. Herod alarmed; desires them if they find the child, to bring him word. They visit the cave, and offer the child their treasure, and being warned in a dream, do not return to Herod, but go home another way.

THEN Joseph was preparing to go away, because there arose a great disorder in Bethlehem by the coming of some wise men from the east,

Who said, Where is the king of the Jews born? For we have seen his star in the east, and are come to worship him.

When Herod heard this, he was exceedingly troubled, and sent messengers to the wise men, and to the priests, and inquired of them in the town-hall,

And said unto them, Where have you it written concerning Christ the king, or where should he be born?

Then they say unto him, In Bethlehem of Judaea; for thus it is written: And thou Bethlehem in the land of Judah, art not the least among the princes of Judah, for out of thee shall come a ruler, who shall rule my people Israel.

And having sent away the chief priests, he inquired of the men in the town-hall, and said unto them, What sign was it ye saw concerning the king that is born?

They answered him, We saw an extraordinary large star shining among the stars of heaven, and so out-shined all the other stars, as that they became not visible, and we knew thereby that a great king was born in Israel, and therefore we are come to worship him.

Then said Herod to them, Go and make diligent inquiry; and if ye find the child, bring me word again, that I may come and worship him also.

So the wise men went forth, and behold, the star which they saw in the east went before them, till it came and stood over the cave where the young child was with Mary his mother

Then they brought forth oat of their treasures, and offered unto him gold and frankincense, and myrrh.

And being warned in a dream by an angel, that they should not return to Herod through Judaea, they departed into their own country by another way.

CHAPTER XVI.

Herod enraged, orders the infants in Bethlehem to be slain. Mary puts her infant in an ox manger. Elizabeth flees with her son John to the mountains. A mountain miraculously divides and receives them. Herod incensed at the escape of John, causes Zacharias to be murdered at the altar, the roofs of the temple rent, the body miraculously conveyed, and the blood petrified. Israel mourns for him. Simeon chosen his successor by lot.

THEN Herod perceiving that e he was mocked by the wise men, and being very angry, commanded certain men to go and to kill all the children that were in Bethlehem, from two years old and under.

But Mary hearing that the children were to be killed, being under much fear, took the child, and wrapped him up in swaddling clothes, and laid him in an ox-manger, because there was no room for them in the inn.

Elizabeth also, hearing that her son John was about to be searched for, took him and went up unto the mountains, and looked around for a place to hide him;

And there was no secret place to be found.

Then she groaned within herself, and said, O mountain of the Lord, receive the mother with the child.

For Elizabeth could not climb up.

And instantly the mountain was divided and received them.

And there appeared to them an angel of the Lord, to preserve them.

But Herod made search after John, and sent servants to Zacharias, when he was (ministering) at the altar, and said unto him, Where hast thou hid thy son?

He replied to them, I am a minister of God, and a servant at the altar; how should

THE LOST BOOKS OF THE BIBLE

I know where my son is?

So the servants went back, and told Herod the whole; at which he was incensed, and said, Is not this son of his like to be king in Israel?

He sent therefore again his servants to Zacharias, saying, Tell us the truth, where is thy son, for you know that your life is in my hand.

So the servants went and told him all this:

But Zacharias replied to them, I am a martyr for God, and if he shed my blood, the Lord will receive my soul.

Besides know that ye shed innocent blood.

However Zacharias was murdered in the entrance of the temple and altar, and about the partition;

But the children of Israel knew not when he was killed.

Then at the hour of salutation the priests went into the temple, but Zacharias did not according to custom meet them and bless them;

Yet they still continued waiting for him to salute them;

And when they found he did not in a long time come, one of them ventured into the holy place where the altar was, and he saw blood lying upon the ground congealed;

When, behold, a voice from heaven said, Zacharias is murdered, and his blood shall not be wiped away, until the revenger of his blood come.

But when he heard this, he was afraid, and went forth and told the priests what he had seen and heard; and they all went in, and saw the fact.

Then the roofs of the temple howled, and were rent from the top to the bottom:

And they could not find the body, but only blood made hard like stone.

And they went awry, and told the people, that Zacharias was murdered, and all the tribes of Israel heard thereof, and mourned for him, and lamented three days.

Then the priests took counsel together concerning a person to succeed him.

And Simeon and the other priests cast lots, and the lot fell upon Simeon.

For he had been assured by the Holy Spirit, that he should not die, till he had seen Christ come in the flesh.

I James wrote this History in Jerusalem: and when the disturbance was I retired into a desert place, until the death of Herod. And the disturbance ceased at Jerusalem. That which remains is, that I glorify God that he hall; given me such wisdom to write unto you who are spiritual, and who love God: to whom (be ascribed) glory and dominion for ever and ever, Amen.

THE FIRST GOSPEL OF THE INFANCY OF JESUS CHRIST.

THE LOST BOOKS OF THE BIBLE

[Mr. Henry Sike, Professor of Oriental Languages at Cambridge, first translated and published this Gospel in 1697. It was received by the Gnostics, a sect of Christians in the second century, and several of its relations were credited in the following ages by other Christians, viz., Eusebius, Athanasius, Epiphanius, Chrysostom, &c. Sozomen says, he was told by many, and he credits the relations, of the idols in Egypt falling down on Joseph, and Mary's flight thither with Christ; and of Christ making a well to wash his clothes in a sycamore tree, from whence balsam afterwards proceeded. These stories are from this Gospel. Chemnitlus out of Stipulensis, who had it from Peter Martyr, Bishop of Alexandria, in the third century, says, that the place in Egypt where Christ was banished is now called Matarea, about ten miles beyond Cairo; that the inhabitants constantly burn a lamp in remembrance of it; and that there is a garden of trees yielding a balsam, which were planted by Christ when a boy. M. La Crosse cites a synod at Angamala, in the mountains of Malabar, A.D. 1599, which condemns this Gospel as commonly read by the Nestorians in that country. Ahmed Ibn Idris, a Mahometan divine, says, it was used by some Christians in common with the other four Gospels; and Ocobius de Castro mentions a Gospel of Thomas, which he says, he saw and had translated to him by an Armenian Archbishop at Amsterdam, that was read in very many churches of Asia and Africa, as the only rule of their faith. Fabricius takes it to be this Gospel. It has been supposed, that Mahomet and his coadjutors used it in compiling the Koran. There are several stories believed of Christ proceeding from this Gospel; as that which Mr. Sike relates out of La Brosse's Persic Lexicon, that Christ practised the trade of a dyer, and his working a miracle with the colours; from whence the Persian dyers honour him as their patron, and call a dye-house the shop of Christ. Sir John Chardin mentions Persian legends concerning Christ's dispute with his schoolmaster about his A B C; and his lengthening the cedar-board which Joseph sawed too short.]

CHAPTER I.

Caiaphas relates, that Jesus when in his cradle, informed his mother, that he was the Son. of God. Joseph and Mary going to Bethlehem to be taxed, Mary's time of bringing forth arrives, and she goes into a cave. Joseph fetches in a Hebrew woman, the cave with great lights. The infant born, cures the woman, arrival of the shepherds.

THE following accounts we found in the book of Joseph the high-priest, called by some Caiaphas

He relates, that Jesus spake even when he was in the cradle, and said to his mother:

Mary, I am Jesus the Son of God, that word which thou didst bring forth according to the declaration of the angel Gabriel to thee, and my father hath sent me for the salvation of the world.

In the three hundred and ninth year of the aera of Alexander, Augustus published a decree that all persons should go to be taxed in their own country.

Joseph therefore arose, and with Mary his spouse he went to Jerusalem, and then came to Bethlehem, that he and his family might be taxed in the city of his fathers.

And when they came by the cave, Mary confessed to Joseph that her time of bringing forth was come, and she could not go on to the city, and said, Let us go into this cave.

At that time the sun was very near going down.

But Joseph hastened away, that he might fetch her a midwife; and when he saw an old Hebrew woman who was of Jerusalem, he said to her, Pray come hither, good woman, and go into that cave, and you will there see a woman just ready to bring forth.

It was after sunset, when the old woman and Joseph with her reached the cave, and they both went into it.

And behold, it was all filled with lights, greater than the light of lamps and candles, and greater than the light of the sun itself.

The infant was then wrapped up in swaddling clothes, and sucking the breasts of his mother St. Mary.

When they both saw this light, they were surprised; the old woman asked St. Mary, Art thou the mother of this child?

St. Mary replied, She was.

On which the old woman said, Thou art very different from all other women.

St. Mary answered, As there is not any child like to my son, so neither is there any woman like to his mother.

The old woman answered, and said, O my Lady, I am come hither that I may obtain an everlasting reward.

Then our Lady, St. Mary, said to her, Lay thine hands upon the infant; which, when she had done, she became whole.

And as she was going forth, she said, From henceforth, all the days of my life, I will attend upon and be a servant of this infant.

After this, when the shepherds came, and had made a fire, and they were exceedingly rejoicing, the heavenly host appeared to them, praising and adoring the supreme God.

And as the shepherds were engaged in the same employment, the cave at that time seemed like a glorious temple, because both the tongues of angels and men united to adore and magnify God, on account of the birth of the Lord Christ.

But when the old Hebrew woman saw all these evident miracles, she gave praises to God, and said, I thank thee, O God, thou God of Israel, for that mine eyes have seen the birth of the Saviour of the world.

CHAPTER II.

The child circumcised in the cave, and the old woman preserving his foreskin or navel-string in a box of spikenard, Mary afterwards anoints Christ with it. Christ brought to the temple, shines, angels stand around him adoring. Simeon praises Christ.

AND when the time of his circumcision was come, namely, the eighth day, on which the law commanded the child to be circumcised, they circumcised him in the cave.

And the old Hebrew woman took the foreskin (others say she took the navel-string), and preserved it in an alabaster-box of old oil of spikenard.

And she had a son who was a druggist, to whom she said, Take heed thou sell not this alabaster box of spikenard-ointment, although thou shouldst be offered three hundred pence for it.

Now this is that alabaster-box which Mary the sinner procured, and poured forth the ointment out of it upon the head and the feet of our Lord Jesus Christ, and wiped it off with the I hairs of her head.

Then after ten days they brought him to Jerusalem, and on the fortieth day from his birth they presented him in the temple before the Lord, making the proper offerings for him, according to the requirement of the law of Moses: namely, that every male which opens the womb shall be called holy unto God.

At that time old Simeon saw him shining as a pillar of light, when St. Mary the Virgin, his mother, carried him in her arms, and was filled with the greatest pleasure at the sight.

And the angels stood around him, adoring him, as a king's guards stand around him.

Then Simeon going near to St. Mary, and stretching forth his hands towards her, said to the Lord Christ, Now, O my Lord, thy servant shall depart in peace, according to thy word;

For mine eyes have seen thy mercy, which thou hast prepared for the salvation of all nations; a light to all people, and the glory of thy people Israel.

Hannah the prophetess was also present, and drawing near, she gave praises to God, and celebrated the happiness of Mary.

CHAPTER III.

The wise men visit Christ. Mary gives them one of his swaddling clothes. An angel appears to them in the form of a star. They return and make a fire, and worship the swaddling cloth, and put it in the fire, where it remains unconsumed.

AND it came to pass, when the Lord Jesus was born at Bethlehem, a city of Judaea, in the time of Herod the King; the wise men came from the East to Jerusalem, according to the prophecy of Zoradascht, and brought with them offerings: namely, gold, frankincense, and myrrh, and worshipped him, and offered to him their gifts.

Then the Lady Mary took one of his swaddling clothes in which the infant was wrapped, and gave it to them instead of a blessing, which they received from her as a most noble present.

And at the same time there appeared to them an angel in the form of that star which had before been their guide in their journey; the light of which they followed till they returned into their own country.

On their return their kings and princes came to them inquiring, What they had seen and done? What sort of journey and return they had? What company they had on the road?

But they produced the swaddling cloth which St. Mary had given to them, on account whereof they kept a feast.

And having, according to the custom of their country, made a fire, they worshipped it.

And casting the swaddling cloth into it, the fire took it, and kept it.

And when the fire was put out, they took forth the swaddling cloth unhurt, as much as if the fire had not touched it.

Then they began to kiss it, and put it upon their heads and their eyes, saying, This is certainly an undoubted truth, and it is really surprising that the fire could not burn it, and consume it.

Then they took it, and with the greatest respect laid it up among their treasures.

CHAPTER IV.

Herod intends to put Christ to death. An angel warns Joseph to take the child and its mother into Egypt. Consternation on their arrival. The idols fall down. Mary washes Christ's swaddling clothes, and hangs them to dry on a post. A son of the chief priest puts one on his head, and being possessed of devils, they leave him.

NOW Herod, perceiving that the wise men did delay, and not return to him, called together the priests and wise men and said, Tell me in what place the Christ should be born?

And when they replied, in Bethlehem, a city of Judaea, he began to contrive in his own mind the death of the Lord Jesus Christ.

But an angel of the Lord appeared to Joseph in his sleep, and said, Arise, take the child and his mother, and go into Egypt as soon as the cock crows. So he arose, and went.

And as he was considering with himself about his journey, the morning came upon him.

In the length of the journey the girts of the saddle broke.

And now he drew near to a great city, in which there was an idol, to which the other idols and gods of Egypt brought their offerings and vows.

And there was by this idol a priest ministering to it, who, as often as Satan spoke out of that idol, related the things he said to the inhabitants of Egypt, and those countries.

This priest had a son three years old, who was possessed with a great multitude of devils, who uttered many strange things, and when the devils seized him, walked about naked with his clothes torn, throwing stones at those whom he saw.

Near to that idol was the inn of the city, into which when Joseph and St. Mary were come, and had turned into that inn, all the inhabitants of the city were astonished.

And all the magistrates and priests of the idols assembled before that idol, and made inquiry there, saying, What means all this consternation, and dread, which has fallen upon all our country?

The idol answered them, The unknown God is come hither, who is truly God; nor is there any one besides him, who is worthy of divine worship; for he is truly the Son of God.

At the fame of him this country trembled, and at his coming it is under the present commotion and consternation; and we ourselves are affrighted by the greatness of his power.

And at the same instant this idol fell down, and at his fall all the inhabitants of Egypt, besides others, ran together.

But the son of the priest, when his usual disorder came upon him, going into the inn, found there Joseph and St. Mary, whom all the rest had left behind and forsook.

And when the Lady St. Mary had washed the swaddling clothes of the Lord Christ, and hanged them out to dry upon a post, the boy possessed with the devil took down one of them, and put it upon his head.

And presently the devils began to come out of his mouth, and fly away in the shape of crows and serpents.

From that time the boy was healed by the power of the Lord Christ, and he began to sing praises, and give thanks to the Lord who had healed him.

When his father saw him restored to his former state of health, he said, My son, what has happened to thee, and by what means wert thou cured?

The son answered, When the devils seized me, I went into the inn, and there found a very handsome woman with a boy, whose swaddling clothes she had just before washed, and hanged out upon a post.

One of these I took, and put it upon my head, and immediately the devils left me, and fled away.

At this the father exceedingly rejoiced, and said, My son, perhaps this boy is the son of the living God, who made the heavens and the earth.

For as soon as he came amongst us, the idol was broken, and all the gods fell down, and were destroyed by a greater power.

Then was fulfilled the prophecy which saith, Out of Egypt I have called my son.

CHAPTER V.

Joseph and Mary leave Egypt. Go to the haunts of robbers, Who, hearing a mighty noise as of a great army, flee away.

NOW Joseph and Mary, when they heard that the idol was fallen down and destroyed, were seized with fear and trembling, and said, When we were in the land of Israel, Herod, intending to kill Jesus, slew for that purpose all the infants at Bethlehem, and that neighbourhood.

And there is no doubt but the Egyptians if they come to hear that this idol is broken and fallen down, will burn us with fire.

They went therefore hence to the secret places of robbers, who robbed travellers as they pass by, of their carriages and their clothes, and carried them away bound.

These thieves upon their coming heard a great noise, such as the noise of a king with a great army and many horses, and the trumpets sounding at his Overture from his own city, at which they were so affrighted as to leave all their booty behind them, and fly away in haste.

Upon this the prisoners arose, and loosed each other's bonds, and taking each man his bags, they went away, and saw Joseph and Mary coming to wards them, and inquired, Where is that king, the noise of whose approach the robbers heard, and left us, so that we are now come off safe?

Joseph answered, He will come after us.

CHAPTER VI.

Mary looks on a woman in whom Satan had taken up his abode, and she becomes dispossessed. Christ kissed by a bride made dumb by sorcerers, cures her, miraculously cures a gentlewoman in whom Satan had taken up his abode. A leprous girl cured by the water in which he was washed, and becomes the servant of Mary and Joseph. The leprous son of a prince's wife cured in like manner. His mother offers large gifts to Mary, and dismisses her.

THEN they went into another where there was a woman possessed with a devil, and in whom Satan, that cursed rebel, had taken up his abode.

One night, when she went to fetch water, she could neither endure her clothes on, nor to be in any house; but as often as they tied her with chains or cords, she brake them, and went out into desert places, and sometimes standing where roads crossed, and in churchyards, would throw stones at men.

When St. Mary saw this woman, she pitied her; whereupon Satan presently left her, and fled away in the form of a young man, saying, Wo to me, because of thee, Mary, and thy son.

So the woman was delivered from her torment; but considering herself naked, she blushed, and avoided seeing any man, and having put on her clothes, went home, and gave au account of her case to her father and relations, who, as they were the best of the city, entertained St. Mary and Joseph with the greatest respect.

The next morning having received a sufficient supply of provisions for the road, they went from them, and about the evening of the day arrived at another town, where a marriage was then about to be solemnized; but by the arts of Satan and the practices of some sorcerers, the bride was become so dumb, that she could not so much as open her mouth.

But when this dumb bride saw the Lady St. Mary entering into the town, and carrying the Lord Christ in her arms, she stretched out her hands to the Lord Christ, and took him in her arms, and closely hugging him, very often kissed him, continually moving him and pressing him to her body.

Straightway the string of her tongue was loosed, and her ears were opened, and she began to sing praises unto God, who had restored her.

So there was great joy among the inhabitants of the town that night, who thought that God and his angels were come down among them.

In this place they abode three days, meeting with the greatest respect and most splendid entertainment.

And being then furnished by the people with provisions for the road, they departed and went to another city, in which they were inclined to lodge, because it was a famous place.

There was in this city a gentlewoman, who, as she went down one day to the river to bathe, behold cursed Satan leaped upon her in the form of a serpent,

And folded himself about her belly, and every night lay upon her.

This woman seeing the Lady St. Mary, and the Lord Christ the infant in her bosom, asked the Lady St. Mary, that she would give her the child to kiss, and carry in her arms.

When she had consented, and as soon as the woman had moved the child, Satan left her, and fled away, nor did the woman ever afterwards see him.

Hereupon all the neighbours praised the Supreme God, and the woman rewarded them with ample beneficence.

On the morrow the same woman brought perfumed water to wash the Lord Jesus; and when she had washed him, she preserved the water.

And there was a girl there, whose body was white with a leprosy, who being sprinkled with this water, and washed, was instantly cleansed from her leprosy.

The people therefore said Without doubt Joseph and Mary, and that boy are Gods, for they do not look like mortals.

And when they were making ready to go away, the girl, who had been troubled with the leprosy, came and desired they would permit her to go along with them; so they consented, and the girl went with them till. they came to a city, in which was the palace of a great king, and whose house was not far from the inn.

Here they staid, and when the girl went one day to the prince's wife, and found her in a sorrowful and mournful condition, she asked her the reason of her tears.

She replied, Wonder not at my groans, for I am under a great misfortune, of which I dare not tell any one.

But, says the girl, if you will entrust me with your private grievance, perhaps I may find you a remedy for it.

Thou, therefore, says the prince's wife, shalt keep the secret, and not discover it to any one alive!

I have been married to this prince, who rules as king over large dominions, and lived long with him, before he had any child by me.

At length I conceived by him, but alas! I brought forth a leprous son; which, when he saw, he would not own to be his, but said to me,

Either do thou kill him, or send him to some nurse in such a place, that he may be never heard of; and now take care of yourself; I will never see you more.

So here I pine, lamenting my wretched and miserable circumstances. Alas, my son! alas, my husband! Have I disclosed it to you?

The girl replied, I have found a remedy for your disease, which I promise you, for I also was leprous, but God hath cleansed me, even he who is called Jesus, the son of the Lady Mary.

The woman inquiring where that God was, whom she spake of, the girl answered He lodges with you here in the same house.

But how can this be? says she; where is he? Behold, replied the girl, Joseph and Mary; and the infant who is with them is called Jesus: and it is he who delivered me from my disease and torment.

But by what means, says she, were you cleansed from your leprosy? Will you not tell me that?

Why not? says the girl; I took the water with which his body had been washed, and poured it upon me, and my leprosy vanished.

The prince's wife then arose and entertained them, providing a great feast for Joseph among a large company of men.

And the next day took perfumed water to wash the Lord Jesus, and afterwards poured the same water upon her son, whom she had brought with her, and her son was instantly cleansed from his leprosy.

Then she sang thanks and praises unto God, and said, Blessed is the mother that bare thee, O Jesus!

Dost thou thus cure men of the same nature with thyself, with the water with which thy body is washed?

She then offered very large gifts to the Lady Mary, and sent her away with all imaginable respect.

CHAPTER VII.

A man who could not enjoy his wife, freed from his disorder. A young man who had been bewitched, and turned into a mule, miraculously cured by Christ being put on his back, and is married to the girl who had been cured of leprosy.

THEY came afterwards to another city, and had a mind to lodge there.

Accordingly they went to a man's house, who was newly married, but by the influence of sorcerers could not enjoy his wife:

But they lodging at his house that night, the man was freed of his disorder:

And when they were pre paring early in the morning to go forward on their journey, the new married person hindered them, and provided a noble entertainment for them?

But going forward on the morrow, they came to another city, and saw three women going from a certain grave with great weeping.

When St. Mary saw them, she spake to the girl who was their companion, saying, Go and inquire of them, what is the matter with them, and what misfortune has befallen them?

When the girl asked them, they made her no answer, but asked her again, Who are ye, and where are ye going? For the day is far spent, and the night is at hand.

We are travellers, saith the girl, and are seeking for an inn to lodge at.

They replied, Go along with us, and lodge with us.

They then followed them, and were introduced into a new house, well furnished with all sorts of furniture.

It was now winter-time, and the girl went into the parlour where these women were, and found them weeping and lamenting, as before.

By them stood a mule, covered over with silk, and an ebony collar hanging down from his neck, whom they kissed, and were feeding.

But when the girl said, How handsome, ladies, that mule is! they replied with tears, and said, This mule, which you see, was our brother, born of this same mother as we:

For when our father died, and left us a very large estate, and we had only this brother, and we endeavoured to procure him a suitable match, and thought he should be married as other men, some giddy and jealous woman bewitched him without our knowledge.

And we, one night, a little before day, while the doors of the house were all fast shut, saw this our brother was changed into a mule, such as you now see him to be:

And we, in the melancholy condition in which you see us, having no father to comfort us, have applied to all the wise men, magicians, and diviners in the world, but they have been of no service to us.

As often therefore as we find ourselves oppressed with grief, we rise and go with this our mother to our father's tomb, where, when we have cried sufficiently we return home.

When the girl had heard this, she said, Take courage, and cease your fears, for you have a remedy for your afflictions near at hand, even among you and in the midst of your house,

For I was also leprous; but when I saw this woman, and this little infant with her, whose name is Jesus, I sprinkled my body with the water with which his mother had washed him, and I was presently made well.

And I am certain that he is also capable of relieving you under your distress. Wherefore, arise, go to my mistress, Mary, and when you have brought her into your own parlour, disclose to her the secret, at the same time, earnestly beseeching her to compassionate your case.

As soon as the women had heard the girl's discourse, they hastened away to the Lady St. Mary, introduced themselves to her, and sitting down before her, they wept.

And said, O our Lady St. Mary, pity your handmaids, for we have no head of our family, no one older than us; no father, or brother to go in and out before us.

But this mule, which you see, was our brother, which some woman by witchcraft have brought into this condition which you see: we therefore entreat you to compassionate us.

Hereupon St. Mary was grieved at their case, and taking the Lord Jesus, put him upon the back of the mule.

And said to her son, O Jesus Christ, restore (or heal) according to thy extraordinary power this mule, and grant him to have again the shape of a man and a rational creature, as he had formerly.

This was scarce said by the Lady St. Mary, but the mule immediately passed into a human form, and became a young man without any deformity.

Then he and his mother and the sisters worshipped the Lady St. Mary, and lifting the child upon their heads, they kissed him, and said, Blessed is thy mother, O Jesus, O Saviour of the world! Blessed are the eyes which are so happy as to see thee.

Then both the sisters told their mother, saying, Of a truth our brother is restored to his former shape by the help of the Lord Jesus Christ, and the kindness of that girl, who told us of Mary and her son.

And inasmuch as our brother is unmarried, it is fit that we marry him to this girl their servant.

When they had consulted Mary in this matter, and she had given her consent, they made a splendid wedding for this girl.

And so their sorrow being turned into gladness, and their mourning into mirth, they began to rejoice. and to make merry, and sing, being dressed in their richest attire, with bracelets.

Afterwards they glorified and praised God, saying, O Jesus son of David who changest sorrow into gladness, and mourning into mirth!

After this Joseph and Mary tarried there ten days, then went away, having received great respect from those people;

Who, when they took their leave of them, and returned home, cried,

But especially the girl.

CHAPTER VIII.

 Joseph and Mary pass through a country infested by robbers, Titus, a humane thief, offers Dumachus, his comrade, forty groats to let Joseph and Mary pass unmolested. Jesus prophesies that the thieves, Dumachus and Titus, shall be crucified with him, and that Titus shall go before him into Paradise. Christ causes a well to spring from a sycamore tree, and Mary washes his coat in it. A balsam grows there from his sweat: They go to Memphis, where Christ works more miracles. Return to Judaea. being warned, depart for Nazareth.

IN their journey from hence they came into a desert country, and were told it was infested with robbers; so Joseph and St. Mary prepared to pass through it in the night.

And as they were going along, behold they saw two robbers asleep in the road, and with them a great number of robbers, who were their confederates, also asleep.

The names of these two were Titus and Dumachus; and Titus said to Dumachus, I beseech thee let those persons go along quietly, that our company may not perceive anything of them:

But Dumachus refusing, Titus again said, I will give thee forty groats, and as a pledge take my girdle, which he gave him he had done speaking, that he might not open his mouth, or make a noise.

When the Lady St. Mary saw the kindness which this robber did shew them, she said to him, The Lord God will receive thee to his right hand, and grant thee pardon of thy sins.

Then the Lord Jesus answered, and said to his mother, When thirty years are expired, O mother, the Jews will crucify me at Jerusalem;

And these two thieves shall be with me at the same time upon the cross, Titus on my right hand, and Dumachus on my left, and from that time Titus shall go before me into paradise:

THE LOST BOOKS OF THE BIBLE

And when she had said, God forbid this should be thy lot, O my son, they went on to a city in which were several idols; which, as soon as they came near to it, was turned into hills of sand.

Hence they went to that sycamore tree, which is now called Matarea;

And in Matarea the Lord Jesus caused a well to spring forth, in which St. Mary washed his coat;

And a balsam is produced, or grows, in that country from the sweat which ran down there from the Lord Jesus.

Thence they proceeded to Memphis, and saw Pharaoh, and abode three years in Egypt.

And the Lord Jesus did very many miracles in Egypt, which are neither to be found in the Gospel of the Infancy nor in the Gospel of Perfection.

At the end of three years he returned out of Egypt, and when he came near to Judas, Joseph was afraid to enter;

For hearing that Herod was dead, and that Archelaus his son reigned in his stead, he was afraid;

And when he went to Judaea, an angel of God appeared to him, and said, O Joseph, go into the city Nazareth, and abide there.

It is strange indeed that he, who is the Lord of all countries, should be thus carried backward and forward through so many countries.

CHAPTER IX.

Two sick children cured by water wherein Christ was washed.

WHEN they came afterwards into the city Bethlehem, they found there several very desperate distempers, which became so troublesome to children by seeing them, that most of them died.

There was there a woman who had a sick son, whom she brought, when he was at the point of death, to the Lady St. Mary, who saw her when she was washing Jesus Christ.

Then said the woman, O my Lady Mary, look down upon this my son, who is afflicted with most dreadful pains.

St. Mary hearing her, said, Take a little of that water with which I have washed my son, and sprinkle it upon him.

Then she took a little of that water, as St. Mary had commanded, and sprinkled it upon her son, who being wearied with his violent pains, had fallen asleep; and after he had slept a little, awaked perfectly well and recovered.

The mother being abundantly glad of this success, went again to St. Mary, and St. Mary said to her, Give praise to God, who hath cured this thy son.

There was in the same place another woman, a neighbour of her, whose son was now cured.

This woman's son was afflicted with the same disease, and his eyes were now almost quite shut, and she was lamenting for him day and night.

The mother of the child which was cured, said to her, Why do you not bring your son to St. Mary, as I brought my son to her, when he was in the agonies of death; and he was cured by that water, with which the body of her son Jesus was washed?

When the woman heard her say this, she also went, and having procured the same water, washed her son with it, whereupon his body and his eyes were instantly restored to their former state.

And when she brought her son to St. Mary, and opened his case to her, she commanded her to give thanks to God for the recovery of her son's health, and tell no one what had happened.

CHAPTER X.

Two wives of one man, each have a son sick. One of them, named Mary, and whose son's name was Caleb, presents the Virgin with a handsome carpet, and Caleb is cured; but the son of the other wife dies, which occasions a difference between the women. The other wife puts Caleb into a hot oven, and he is miraculously preserved; she afterwards throws him into a well, and he is again preserved; his mother appeals to the Virgin against the other wife, whose downfall the Virgin prophesies, and who accordingly falls into the well, therein fulfilling a saying of old.

THERE were in the same city two wives of one man, who had each a son sick. One of them was called Mary and her son's name was Caleb.

She arose, and taking her son, went to the Lady St. Mary, the mother of Jesus, and offered her a very handsome carpet, saying, O my Lady Mary accept this carpet of me, and instead of it give me a small swaddling cloth.

To this Mary agreed, and when the mother of Caleb was gone, she made a coat for her son of the swaddling cloth, put it on him, and his disease was cured; but the son of the other wife died.

Hereupon there arose between them, a difference in doing the business of the family by turns, each her week.

And when the turn of Mary the mother of Caleb came, and she was heating the oven to bake bread, and went away to fetch the meal, she left her son Caleb by the oven;

Whom, the other wife, her rival, seeing to be by himself, took and cast him into the oven, which was very hot, and then went away.

Mary on her return saw her son Caleb lying in the middle of the oven laughing, and the oven quite as cold as though it had not been before heated, and knew that her rival the other wife had thrown him into the fire.

THE LOST BOOKS OF THE BIBLE

When she took him out, she brought him to the Lady St. Mary, and told her the story, to whom she replied, Be quiet, I am concerned lest thou shouldest make this matter known.

After this her rival, the other wife, as she was drawing water at the well, and saw Caleb playing by the well, and that no one was near, took him, and threw him into the well.

And when some men came to fetch water from the well, they saw the boy sitting on the superficies of the water, and drew him out with ropes, and were exceedingly surprised at the child, and praised God.

Then came the mother and took him and carried him to the Lady St. Mary, lamenting and saying, O my Lady, see what my rival hath done to my son, and how she hath cast him into the well, and I do not question but one time or other she will be the occasion of his death.

St. Mary replied to her, God will vindicate your injured cause.

Accordingly a few days after, when the other wife came to the well to draw water, her foot was entangled in the rope, so that she fell headlong into the well, and they who ran to her assistance, found her skull broken, and bones bruised.

So she came to a bad end, and in her was fulfilled that saying of the author, They digged a well, and made it deep, but fell themselves into the pit which they prepared.

CHAPTER XI.

Bartholomew, when a child and sick, miraculously restored by being laid on Christ's bed.

ANOTHER woman in that city had likewise two sons sick.

And when one was dead, the other, who lay at the point of death, she took in her arms to the Lady St. Mary, and in a flood of tears addressed herself to her, saying,

O my Lady, help and relieve me; for I had two sons, the one I have just now buried, the other I see is just at the point of death, behold how I (earnestly) seek favour from God, and pray to him.

Then she said, O Lord, thou art gracious, and merciful, and kind; thou hast given me two sons; one of them thou hast taken to thyself, O spare me this other.

St. Mary then perceiving the greatness of her sorrow, pitied her and said, Do thou place thy son in my son's bed, and cover him with his clothes.

And when she had placed him in the bed wherein Christ lay, at the moment when his eyes were just closed by death; as soon as ever the smell of the garments of the Lord Jesus Christ reached the boy, his eyes were opened, and calling with a loud voice to his mother, he asked for bread, and when he had received it, he sucked it.

Then his mother said, O Lady Mary, now I am assured that the powers of God do

38

dwell in you, so that thy son can cure children who are of the same sort as himself, as soon as they touch his garments.

This boy who was thus cured, is the same who in the Gospel is called Bartholomew.

CHAPTER XII.

A leprous woman healed by Christ's washing water. A princess healed by it and restored to her husband.

AGAIN there was a leprous woman who went to the Lady St. Mary, the mother of Jesus, and said, O my Lady, help me.

St. Mary replied, what help dost thou desire? Is it gold or silver, or that thy body be cured of its leprosy?

Who, says the woman, can grant me this?

St. Mary replied to her, Wait a little till I have washed my son Jesus, and put him to bed.

The woman waited, as she was commanded; and Mary when she had put Jesus in bed, giving her the water with which she had washed his body, said, Take some of the water, and pour it upon thy body;

Which when she had done, she instantly became clean, and praised God, and gave thanks to him.

Then she went away, after she had abode with her three days:

And going into the city, she saw a certain prince, who had married another prince's daughter;

But when he came to see her, he perceived between her eyes the signs of leprosy like a star, and thereupon declared the marriage dissolved and void.

When the woman saw these persons in this condition, exceedingly sorrowful, and shedding abundance of tears, she inquired of them the reason of their crying.

They replied, Inquire not into our circumstances; for we are not able to declare our misfortunes to any person whatsoever.

But still she pressed and desired them to communicate their case to her, intimating, that perhaps she might be able to direct them to a remedy.

So when they shewed the young woman to her, and the signs of the leprosy, which appeared between her eyes,

She said, I also, whom ye see in this place, was afflicted with the same distemper, and going on some business to Bethlehem, I went into a certain cave, and saw a woman named Mary, who had a son called Jesus.

She seeing me to be leprous, was concerned for me, and gave me some water with which she had washed her son's body; with that I sprinkled my body, and became clean.

Then said these women, Will you, Mistress, go along with us, and shew the Lady St. Mary to us?

To which she consenting, they arose and went to the Lady St. Mary, taking with them very noble presents.

And when they came in and offered their presents to her, they showed the leprous young woman what they brought with them to her.

Then said St. Mary, The mercy of the Lord Jesus Christ rest upon you;

And giving them a little of that water with which she had washed the body of Jesus Christ, she bade them wash the diseased person with it; which when they had done, she was presently cured;

So they, and all who were present, praised God; and being filled with joy, they went back to their own city, and gave praise to God on that account.

Then the prince hearing that his wife was cured, took her home and made a second marriage, giving thanks unto God for the recovery of his wife's health.

CHAPTER XIII.

A girl, whose blood Satan sucked, receives one of Christ's swaddling clothes from the Virgin. Satan comes like a dragon, and she shews it to him; flames and burning coals proceed from it and fall upon him; he is miraculously discomfited, and leaves the girl.

THERE was also a girl, who was afflicted by Satan;

For that cursed spirit did frequently appear to her in the shape of a dragon, and was inclined to swallow her up, and had so sucked out all her blood, that she looked like a dead carcase.

As often as she came to herself, with her hands wringed about her head she would cry out, and say, Wo, Wo is me, that there is no one to be found who can deliver me from that impious dragon!

Her father and mother, and all who were about her and saw her, mourned and wept over her;

And all who were present would especially be under sorrow and in tears, when they heard her bewailing, and saying, My brethren and friends, is there no one who can deliver me from this murderer?

Then the prince's daughter, who had been cured of her leprosy, hearing the complaint of that girl, went upon the top of her castle, and saw her with her hands twisted about her head, pouring out a flood of tears, and all the people that were about her in sorrow.

Then she asked the husband of the possessed person, Whether his wife's mother was alive? He told her, That her father and mother were both alive.

THE LOST BOOKS OF THE BIBLE

Then she ordered her mother to be sent to her: to whom, when she saw her coming, she said, Is this possessed girl thy daughter? She moaning and bewailing said, Yes, madam, I bore her.

The prince's daughter answered, Disclose the secret of her case to me, for I confess to you that I was leprous, but the Lady Mary, the mother of Jesus Christ, healed me.

And if you desire your daughter to be restored to her former state, take her to Bethlehem, and inquire for Mary the mother of Jesus, and doubt not but your daughter will be cured; for I do not question but you will come home with great joy at your daughter's recovery.

As soon as ever she had done speaking, she arose and went with her daughter to the place appointed, and to Mary, and told her the case of her daughter.

When St. Mary had heard her story, she gave her a little of the water with which she had washed the body of her son Jesus, and bade her pour it upon the body of her daughter.

Likewise she gave her one of the swaddling cloths of the Lord Jesus, and said, Take this swaddling cloth and shew it to thine enemy as often as thou seest him; and she sent them away in peace.

After they had left that city and returned home, and the time was come in which Satan was wont to seize her, in the same moment this cursed spirit appeared to her in the shape of a huge dragon, and the girl seeing him was afraid.

The mother said to her, Be not afraid daughter; let him alone till he come nearer to thee! then shew him the swaddling cloth, which the Lady Mary gave us, and we shall see the event.

Satan then coming like a dreadful dragon, the body of the girl trembled for fear.

But as soon as she had put the swaddling cloth upon her head, and about her eyes, and shewed it to him, presently there issued forth from the swaddling cloth flames and burning coals, and fell upon the dragon.

Oh! how great a miracle was this, which was done: as soon as the dragon saw the swaddling cloth of the Lord Jesus, fire went forth and was scattered upon his head and eyes; so that he cried out with a loud voice, What have I to do with thee, Jesus, thou son of Mary, Whither shall I flee from thee?

So he drew back much affrighted, and left the girl.

And she was delivered from this trouble, and sang praises and thanks to God, and with her all who were present at the working of the miracle.

CHAPTER XIV.

Judas when a boy possessed by Satan, and brought by his parents to Jesus to be cured, whom he tries to bite, but failing, strikes Jesus and makes him cry out. Whereupon Satan goes from Jesus in the shape of a dog.

41

THE LOST BOOKS OF THE BIBLE

ANOTHER woman likewise lived there, whose son was possessed by Satan.

This boy, named Judas, as often as Satan seized him, was inclined to bite all that were present; and if he found no one else near him, he would bite his own hands and other parts.

But the mother of this miserable boy, hearing of St. Mary and her son Jesus, arose presently, and taking her son in her arms, brought him to the Lady Mary.

In the meantime, James and Joses had taken away the infant, the Lord Jesus, to play at a proper season with other children; and when they went forth, they sat down and the Lord Jesus with them.

Then Judas, who was possessed, came and sat down at the right hand of Jesus.

When Satan was acting upon him as usual, he went about to bite the Lord Jesus.

And because he could not do it, he struck Jesus on the right side, so that he cried out.

And in the same moment Satan went out of the boy, and ran away like a mad dog.

This same boy who struck Jesus, and out of whom Satan went in the form of a dog, was Judas Iscariot, who betrayed him to the Jews.

And that same side, on which Judas struck him, the Jews pierced with a spear.

CHAPTER XV.

Jesus and other boys play together, and make day figures of animals. Jesus causes them to walk, also makes clay birds, which he causes to fly, and eat and drink. The children's parents alarmed, and take Jesus for a sorcerer. He goes to a dyer's shop, and throws all the cloths into the furnace, and works a miracle therewith. Whereupon the Jews praise God.

AND when the Lord Jesus was seven years of age, he was on a certain day with other boys his companions about the same age.

Who when they were at play, made clay into several shapes, namely, asses, oxen, birds, and other figures,

Each boasting of his work, and endeavouring to exceed the rest.

Then the Lord Jesus said to the boys, I will command these figures which I have made to walk.

And immediately they moved, and when he commanded them to return, they returned.

He had also made the figures of birds and sparrows, which, when he commanded to fly, did fly, and when he commanded to stand still, did stand still; and if he gave them meat and drink, they did eat and drink.

When at length the boys went away, and related these things to their parents, their fathers said to them, Take heed, children, for the future, of his company, for he is a sorcerer; shun and avoid him, and from henceforth never play with him.

On a certain day also, when the Lord Jesus was playing with the boys, and running about, he passed by a dyer's shop, whose name was Salem.

And there were in his shop many pieces of cloth belonging to the people of that city, which they designed to dye of several colours.

Then the Lord Jesus going into the dyer's shop, took all the cloths, and threw them into the furnace.

When Salem came home, and saw the cloths spoiled, he began to make a great noise, and to chide the Lord Jesus, saying,

What hast thou done to me, O thou Son of Mary? Thou hast injured both me and my neighbours; they all desired their cloths of a proper colour; but .thou hast come, and spoiled them all.

The Lord Jesus replied, I will change the colour of every cloth to what colour thou desirest;

And then he presently began to take the cloths out of the furnace, and they were all dyed of those same colours which the dyer desired.

And when the Jews saw this surprising miracle, they praised God

CHAPTER XVI.

Christ miraculously widens or contracts the gates, milk-pails, sieves, or bones, not properly made by Joseph, he not being skilful at his carpenter's trade. The King of Jerusalem gives Joseph an order for a throne. Joseph works on it for two years in the king's palace, and makes it two spans too short. The king being angry with. him, Jesus comforts him, commands him to pull one side of the throne, while he pulls the other, and brings it to its proper dimensions. Whereupon the bystanders praise God.

AND Joseph, wheresoever he went in the city, took the Lord Jesus with him, where he was sent for to work to make gates, or milk-pails, or sieves, or boxes; the Lord Jesus was with him wheresoever he went.

And as often as Joseph had anything in his work, to make longer or shorter, or wider, or narrower, the Lord Jesus would stretch his hand towards it.

And presently it became as Joseph would have it.

So that he had no need to finish anything with his own hands, for he was not very skilful at his carpenter's trade.

On a certain time the King of Jerusalem sent for him, and said, I would have thee make me a throne of the same dimensions with that place in which I commonly sit.

Joseph obeyed, and forthwith began the work, and continued two years in the king's palace before he finished it.

And when he came to fix it in its place, he found it wanted two spans on each side of the appointed measure.

Which, when the king saw, he was very angry with Joseph;

And Joseph afraid of the king's anger, went to bed without his supper, taking not any thing to eat.

Then the Lord Jesus asked him, What he was afraid of?

Joseph replied, Because I have lost my labour in the work which I have been about these two years.

Jesus said to him, Fear not, neither be cast down;

Do thou lay hold on one side of the throne, and I will the other, and we will bring it to its just dimensions.

And when Joseph had done as the Lord Jesus said, and each of them had with strength drawn his side, the throne obeyed, and was brought to the proper dimensions of the place:

Which miracle when they who stood by saw, they were astonished, and praised God.

The throne was made of the same wood, which was in being in Solomon's time, namely, wood adorned with various shapes and figures.

CHAPTER XVII.

Jesus plays with boys at hide and seek. Some women put his playfellows in a furnace, where they are transformed by Jesus into kids. Jesus calls them to go and play, and they are restored to their former shape.

ON another day the Lord Jesus going out into the street, and seeing some boys who were met to play, joined himself to their company:

But when they saw him, they hid themselves, and left him to seek for them:

The Lord Jesus came to the gate of a certain house, and asked some women who were standing there, Where the boys were gone?

And when they answered, That there was no one there; the Lord Jesus said, Who are those whom ye see in the furnace?

They answered, They were kids of three years old.

Then Jesus cried out aloud, and said, Come out hither, O ye kids, to your shepherd;

And presently the boys came forth like kids, and leaped about him; which when the women saw, they were exceedingly amazed, and trembled.

Then they immediately worshipped the Lord Jesus, and beseeched him, saying,

O our Lord Jesus, son of Mary, thou art truly that good shepherd of Israel! have mercy on thy handmaids, who stand before thee, who do not doubt, but that thou, O Lord, art come to save, and not to destroy.

After that, when the Lord Jesus said, the children of Israel are like Ethiopians among the people; the women said, Thou, Lord, knowest all things, nor is any thing concealed from thee; but now we entreat thee, and beseech of thy mercy that thou wouldst restore those boys to their former state.

Then Jesus said, Come hither O boys, that we may go and play; and immediately, in the presence of these women, the kids were changed and returned into the shape of boys.

CHAPTER XVIII.

Jesus becomes the king of his playfellows, and they crown him with flowers, miraculously causes a serpent who had bitten Simon the Cananite, then a boy, to suck our all the poison again; the serpent bursts, and Christ restores the boy to health.

IN the month Adar Jesus gathered together the boys, and ranked them as though he had been a king.

For they spread their garments on the ground for him to sit on; and having made a crown of flowers, put it upon his head, and stood on his right and left as the guards of a king.

And if any one happened to pass by, they took him by force, and said, Come hither, and worship the king, that you may have a prosperous journey.

In the mean time, while these things were doing, there came certain men, carrying a boy upon a couch;

For this boy having gone with his companions to the mountain to gather wood, and having found there a partridge's nest, and put his hand in to take out the eggs, was stung by a poisonous serpent, which leaped out of the nest; so that he was forced to cry out for the help of his companions: who, when they came, found him lying upon the earth like a dead person.

After which his neighbours came and carried him back into the city.

But when they came to the place where the Lord Jesus was sitting like a king, and the other boys stood around him like his ministers, the boys made haste to meet him, who was bitten by the serpent, and said to his neighbours, Come and pay your respects to the king;

But when, by reason of their sorrow, they refused to come, the boys drew them, and forced them against their wills to come.

And when they came to the Lord Jesus, he inquired, On what account they carried that boy?

And when they answered, that a serpent had bitten him, the Lord Jesus said to the boys, Let us go and kill that serpent.

But when the parents of the boy desired to be excused, because their son lay at the point of death; the boys made answer, and said, Did not ye hear what the king said? Let us go and kill the serpent; and will not ye obey him?

So they brought the couch back again, whether they would or not.

And when they were come to the nest, the Lord Jesus said to the boys, Is this the serpent's lurking place? They said, It was.

Then the Lord Jesus calling the serpent, it presently came forth and submitted to him; to whom he said, Go and suck out all the poison which thou hast infused into that boy;

So the serpent crept to the boy, and took away all its poison again.

Then the Lord Jesus cursed the serpent so that it immediately burst asunder, and died.

And he touched the boy with his hand to restore him to his former health;

And when he began to cry, the Lord Jesus said, Cease crying, for hereafter thou shalt be my disciple;

And this is that Simon the Canaanite, who is mentioned in the Gospel.

CHAPTER XIX.

James being bitten by a viper, Jesus blows on the wound and cures him. Jesus charged with throwing a boy from the roof of a house, miraculously causes the dead boy to acquit him, fetches water for his mother, breaks the pitcher and miraculously gathers the water in his mantle and brings it home, makes fish-pools on the Sabbath, causes a boy to die who broke them down, another boy run against him, whom he also causes to die.

ON another day Joseph sent his son James to gather wood and the Lord Jesus went with him;

And when they came to the place where the wood was, and James began to gather it, behold, a venomous viper bit him, so that he began to cry, and make a noise.

The Lord Jesus seeing him in this condition, came to him, and blowed upon the place where the viper had bit him, and it was instantly well.

On a certain day the Lord Jesus was with some boys, who were playing on the housetop, and one of the boys fell down, and presently died.

Upon which the other boys all running away, the Lord Jesus was left alone on the house-top.

And the boy's relations came to him and said to the Lord Jesus, Thou didst throw our son down from the housetop.

But he denying it, they cried out, Our son is dead, and this is he who killed him.

The Lord Jesus replied to them, Do not charge me with a crime, of which you are not able to convict me, but let us go ask the boy himself, who will bring the truth to light.

Then the Lord Jesus going down stood over the head of the dead boy, and said with a loud voice, Zeinunus, Zeinunus, who threw thee down from the housetop?

Then the dead boy answered, thou didst not throw me down, but such a one did.

And when the Lord Jesus bade those who stood by to take notice of his words, all who were present praised God on account of that miracle.

On a certain time the Lady St. Mary had commanded the Lord Jesus to fetch her some water out of the well;

And when he had gone to fetch the water, the pitcher, when it was brought up full, brake.

But Jesus spreading his mantle gathered up the water again, and brought it in that to his mother.

Who, being astonished at this wonderful thing, laid up this, and all the other things which she had seen, in her memory.

Again on another day the Lord Jesus was with some boys by a river and they drew water out of the river by little channels, and made little fish-pools.

But the Lord Jesus had made twelve sparrows, and placed them about his pool on each side, three on a side.

But it was the Sabbath day, and the son of Hanani a Jew came by, and saw them making these things, and said, Do ye thus make figures of clay on the Sabbath? And he ran to them, and broke down their fish-pools.

But when the Lord Jesus clapped his hands over the sparrows which he had made, they fled away chirping.

At length the son of Hanani coming to the fish-pool of Jesus to destroy it, the water vanished away, and the Lord Jesus said to him,

In like manner as this water has vanished, so shall thy life vanish; and presently the boy died.

Another time, when the Lord Jesus was coming home in the evening with Joseph, he met a boy, who ran so hard against him, that he threw him down;

To whom the Lord Jesus said, As thou hast thrown me down, so shalt thou fall, nor ever rise.

And that moment the boy fell down and died.

CHAPTER XX.

Sent to school to Zaccheus to learn his letters, and teaches Zaccheus. Sent to another schoolmaster. refuses to tell his letters, and the schoolmaster going to whip him his hand withers and he dies.

THERE was also at Jerusalem one named Zaccheus, who was a schoolmaster.

And he said to Joseph, Joseph, why dost thou not send Jesus to me, that he may learn his letters?

Joseph agreed, and told St. Mary;

So they brought him to that master; who, as soon as he saw him, wrote out an alphabet for him.

And he bade him say Aleph; and when he had said Aleph, the master bade him pronounce Beth.

Then the Lord Jesus said to him, Tell me first the meaning of the letter Aleph, and then I will pronounce Beth.

And when the master threatened to whip him, the Lord Jesus explained to him the meaning of the letters Aleph and Beth;

Also which were the straight figures of the letters, which the oblique, and what letters had double figures; which had points, and which had none; why one letter went before another; and many other things he began to tell him, and explain, of which the master himself had never heard, nor read in any book.

The Lord Jesus farther said to the master, Take notice how I say to thee; then he began clearly and distinctly to say Aleph, Beth, Gimel, Daleth, and so on to the end of the alphabet.

At this the master was so surprised, that he said, I believe this boy was born before Noah;

And turning to Joseph, he said, Thou hast brought a boy to me to be taught, who is more learned than any master.

He said also unto St. Mary, This your son has no need of any learning.

They brought him then to a more learned master, who, when he saw him, said, say Aleph.

And when he had said Aleph, the master bade him pronounce Beth; to which the Lord Jesus replied, Tell me first the meaning of the letter Aleph, and then I will pronounce Beth.

But this master, when he lift up his hand to whip him, had his hand presently withered, and he died.

Then said Joseph to St. Mary, henceforth we will not allow him to go out of the house; for every one who displeases him is killed.

THE LOST BOOKS OF THE BIBLE

CHAPTER XXI.

Disputes miraculously with the doctors in the temple, on law, on astronomy, on physics and metaphysics, is worshipped by a philosopher, and fetched home by his mother.

AND when he was twelve years old, they brought him to Jerusalem to the feast; and when the feast was over, they returned.

But the Lord Jesus continued behind in the temple among the doctors and elders, and learned men of Israel; to whom he proposed several questions of learning, and also gave them answers:

For he said to them, Whose son is the Messiah? They answered, the son of David:

Why then, said he, does he in the spirit call him Lord? when he saith, The Lord said to my Lord, sit thou at my right hand, till I have made thine enemies thy footstool.

Then a certain principal Rabbi asked him, Hast thou read books?

Jesus answered, he had read both books, and the things which were contained in books.

And he explained to them the books of the law, and precepts, and statutes: and the mysteries which are contained in the books of the prophets; things which the mind of no creature could reach.

Then said that Rabbi, I never yet have seen or heard of such knowledge! What do you think that boy will be!

When a certain astronomer, who was present, asked the Lord Jesus, Whether he had studied astronomy?

The Lord Jesus replied, and told him the number of the spheres and heavenly bodies, as also their triangular, square, and sextile aspect; their progressive and retrograde motion; their size and several prognostications; and other things which the reason of man had never discovered.

There was also among them a philosopher well skilled in physic and natural philosophy, who asked the Lord Jesus, Whether he had studied physic?

He replied, and explained to him physics and metaphysics.

Also those things which were above and below the power of nature;

The powers also of the body, its humours, and their effects.

Also the number of its members, and bones, veins, arteries, and nerves;

The several constitutions of body, hot and dry, cold and moist, and the tendencies of them;

How the soul operated upon the body;

What its various sensations and faculties were;

The faculty of speaking, anger, desire;

And lastly the manner of its composition and dissolution; and other things, which the understanding of no creature had ever reached.

Then that philosopher arose, and worshipped the Lord Jesus, and said, O Lord Jesus, from henceforth I will be thy disciple and servant.

While they were discoursing on these and such like things, the Lady St. Mary came in, having been three days walking about with Joseph, seeking for him.

And when she saw him sitting among the doctors, and in his turn proposing questions to them, and giving answers, she said to him, My son, why hast thou done thus by us? Behold I and thy father have been at much pains in seeking thee.

He replied, Why did ye seek me? Did ye not know that I ought to be employed in my father's house?

But they understood not the words which he said to them.

Then the doctors asked Mary, Whether this was her son? And when she said, He was, they said, O happy Mary, who hast borne such a son.

Then he returned with them to Nazareth, and obeyed them in all things.

And his mother kept all these things in her mind;

And the Lord Jesus grew in stature and wisdom, and favour with God and man.

CHAPTER XXII.

Conceals his miracles, studies the law and is baptised.

NOW from this time Jesus began to conceal his miracles and secret works,

And he gave himself to the study of the law, till he arrived to the end of his thirtieth year;

At which time the Father publicly owned him at Jordan, sending down this voice from heaven, This is my beloved son, in whom I am well pleased;

The Holy Ghost being also present in the form of a dove.

This is he whom we worship with all reverence, because he gave us our life and being, and brought us from our mother's womb.

Who, for our sakes, took a human body, and hath redeemed us, so that he might so embrace us with everlasting mercy, and shew his free, large, bountiful grace and goodness to us.

To him be glory and praise, and power, and dominion, from henceforth and for evermore, Amen.

THE LOST BOOKS OF THE BIBLE

The end of the whole Gospel of the Infancy, by the assistance of the Supreme God, according to what we found in the original.

THOMAS'S GOSPEL OF THE INFANCY OF JESUS CHRIST.

[The original in Greek, from which this translation is made, will be found printed by Cotelerius, in his notes on the constitutions of the Apostles, from a MS. in the French King's Library, No. 2279—It is attributed to Thomas, and conjectured to have been originally connected with the Gospel of Mary.]

An Account of the ACTIONS and MIRACLES of our Lord and Saviour JESUS CHRIST in his INFANCY.

CHAPTER I.

Jesus miraculously dears the water after rain. plays with clay sparrows, which he animates on the sabbath day.

I THOMAS, an Israelite, judged it necessary to make known to our brethren among the Gentiles, the actions and miracles of Christ in his childhood, which our Lord and God Jesus Christ wrought after his birth in Bethlehem in our country, at which I myself was astonished; the beginning of which was as followeth.

When the child Jesus was five years of age and there had been a shower of rain, which was now over, Jesus was playing with other Hebrew boys by a running stream; and the water running over the banks, stood in little lakes;

But the water instantly became clear and useful again; he having smote them only by his word, they readily obeyed him.

Then he took from the bank of the stream some soft clay, and formed out of it twelve sparrows; and there were other boys playing with him.

But a certain Jew seeing the things which he was doing, namely, his forming clay into the figures of sparrows on the sabbath day, went presently away, and told his father Joseph, and said,

Behold, thy boy is playing by the river side, and has taken clay, and formed it into twelve sparrows, and profaneth the sabbath.

Then Joseph came to the place where he was, and when he saw him, called to him, and said, Why doest thou that which it is not lawful to do on the sabbath day?

Then Jesus clapping together the palms of his hands, called to the sparrows, and said to them: Go, fly away; and while ye live remember me.

So the sparrows fled away, making a noise.

The Jews seeing this, were astonished, and went away, and told their chief persons what a strange miracle they had seen wrought by Jesus.

CHAPTER II.

51

Causes a boy to wither who broke down his fish pools, partly restores him, kills another boy, causes blindness to fall on his accusers, for which Joseph pulls him by the ear.

BESIDES this, the son of Anna the scribe was standing there with Joseph, and took a bough of a willow tree, and scattered the waters which Jesus had gathered into lakes.

But the boy Jesus seeing what he had done, became angry, and said to him, Thou fool, what harm did the lake do thee, that thou shouldest scatter the water?

Behold, now thou shalt wither as a tree, and shalt not bring forth either leaves, or branches, or fruit.

And immediately he became withered all over.

Then Jesus went away home. But the parents of the boy who was withered, lamenting the misfortune of his youth, took and carried him to Joseph, accusing him, and said, Why dost thou keep a son who is guilty of such actions?

Then Jesus at the request of all who were present did heal him, leaving only some small member to continue withered, that they might take warning.

Another time Jesus went forth into the street, and a boy running by, rushed upon his shoulder;

At which Jesus being angry, said to him, thou shalt go no farther.

And he instantly fell down dead:

Which when some persons saw, they said, Where was this boy born, that everything which he says presently cometh to pass?

Then the parents of the dead buy going to Joseph complained, saying, You are not fit to live with us, in our city, having such a boy as that:

Either teach him that he bless and not curse, or else depart hence with him, for he kills our children.

Then Joseph calling the boy Jesus by himself, instructed him saying, Why doest thou such things to injure the people so, that they hate us and prosecute us?

But Jesus replied, I know that what thou sayest is not of thyself, but for thy sake I will say nothing;

But they who have said these things to thee, shall suffer everlasting punishment.

And immediately they who had accused him became blind.

And all they who saw it were exceedingly afraid and confounded, and said concerning him, Whatsoever he saith, whether good or bad, immediately cometh to pass: and they were amazed.

And when they saw this action of Christ, Joseph arose, and plucked him by the ear, at which the boy was angry, and said to him, Be easy;

THE LOST BOOKS OF THE BIBLE

For if they seek for us, they shall not find us: thou hast done very imprudently.

Dost thou not know that I am thine? Trouble me no more.

CHAPTER III.

Astonishes his schoolmaster by his learning.

A CERTAIN schoolmaster named Zacchaeus, standing in a certain place, heard Jesus speaking these things to his father.

And he was much surprised, that being a child, he should speak such things; and after a few days he came to Joseph, and said,

Thou hast a wise and sensible child, send him to me, that he may learn to read.

When he sat down to teach the letters to Jesus, he began with the first letter Aleph;

But Jesus pronounced the second letter Mpeth (Beth) Cghimel (Gimel), and said over all the letters to him to the end.

Then opening a book, he taught his master the prophets: but be was ashamed, and was at a loss to conceive how he came to know the letters.

And he arose and went home, wonderfully surprised at so strange a thing.

CHAPTER IV.

Fragment of an adventure at a dyer's.

AS Jesus was passing by a certain shop, he saw a young man dipping (or dyeing) some cloths and stockings in a furnace, of a sad colour, doing them according to every person's particular order;

The boy Jesus going to the young man who was doing this, took also some of the cloths.

* * * * * *

Here endeth the Fragment of Thomas's Gospel of the Infancy of Jesus Christ.

THE EPISTLES OF JESUS CHRIST AND ABGARUS KING OF EDESSA.

[The first writer who makes any mention of the Epistles that passed between Jesus Christ and Abgarus, is Eusebius, Bishop of Caesarea, in Palestine, who flourished in the early part of the fourth century. For their genuineness, he appeals to the public registers and records of the City of Edessa in Mesopotamia, where Abgarus reigned, affirms that he found them written, in the Syriac language. He published a Greek translation of them, in his Ecclesiastical History. The learned world have been much divided on this subject; but, notwithstanding that the erudite Grabe, with Archbishop Cave, Dr. Parker, and other divines, has strenuously contended for their admission into the canon of Scripture, they are deemed apocryphal. The Rev. Jeremiah Jones observes, that the common people in England have this Epistle in their houses, in many places, fixed in a frame, with the picture of Christ before it; and that they generally, with much honesty and devotion, regard it as the word of God, and the genuine Epistle of Christ.]

CHAPTER I.

A copy of a letter written by King Abgarus to Jesus, and sent to him by Ananias, his footman, to Jerusalem, 5 inviting him to Edessa.

ABGARUS, king of Edessa, to Jesus the good Saviour, who appears at Jerusalem, greeting.

I have been informed concerning you and your cures, which are performed without the use of medicines and herbs.

For it is reported, that you cause the blind to see, the lame to walk, do both cleanse lepers, and cast out unclean spirits and devils, and restore them to health who have been long diseased, and raisest up the dead;

All which when I heard, I was persuaded of one of these two, viz: either that you are God himself descended from heaven, who do these things, or the son of God.

On this account therefore I have wrote to you, earnestly to desire you would take the trouble of a journey hither, and cure a disease which I am under.

For I hear the Jews ridicule you, and intend you mischief.

My city is indeed small, but neat, and large enough for us both.

CHAPTER II.

The answer of Jesus by Ananias the footman to Abgarus the king, declining to visit Edessa.

ABGARUS, you are happy, forasmuch as you have believed on me, whom ye have not seen.

For it is written concerning me, that those who have seen me should not believe on me, that they who have not seen might believe and live.

As to that part of your letter, which relates to my giving you a visit, I must inform you, that I must fulfil all the ends of my mission in this country, and after that be received up again to him who sent me.

But after my ascension I will send one of my disciples, who will cure your disease, and give life to you, and all that are with you.

THE GOSPEL OF NICODEMUS,
FORMERLY CALLED THE ACTS OF PONTIUS PILATE.

[Although this Gospel is, by some among the learned, supposed to have been really written by Nicodemus, who became a disciple of Jesus Christ, and conversed with him; others conjecture that it was a forgery towards the close of the third century by some zealous believer, who observing that there had been appeals made by the Christians of the former age, to the Acts of Pilate, but that such Acts could not be produced, imagined it would be of service to Christianity to fabricate and publish this Gospel; as it would both confirm the Christians under persecution, and convince the Heathens of the truth of the Christian religion. The Rev. Jeremiah Jones says, that such pious frauds were very common among Christians even in the first three centuries; and that a forgery of this nature, with the view above mentioned, seems natural and probable. The same author, in noticing that Eusebius, in his Ecclesiastical history, charges the Pagans with having forged and published a book, called "The Acts of Pilate," takes occasion to observe, that the internal evidence of this Gospel shows it was not the work of any Heathen; but that if in the latter end of the third century we find it in use among Christians (as it was then certainly in some churches) and about the same time find a forgery of the Heathens under the same title, it seems exceedingly probable that some Christians, at that time, should publish such a piece as this, in order partly to confront the spurious one of the Pagans, and partly to support those appeals which had been made by former Christians to the Acts of Pilate; and Mr. Jones says, he thinks so more particularly as we have innumerable instances of forgeries by the faithful in the primitive ages, grounded on less plausible reasons. Whether it be canonical or not, it is of very great antiquity, and is appealed to by several of the ancient Christians. The present translation is made from the Gospel published by Grynaeus in the Orthodoxographa, vol. i. tom. ii. p. 643.]

The Gospel of NICODEMUS the disciple, concerning the Sufferings and Resurrection of our Master and Saviour JESUS CHRIST.

CHAPTER I.

Christ accused to Pilate by the Jews of healing on the sabbath, summoned before Pilate by a messenger who does him honour, worshipped by the standards bowing down to him.

ANNAS and Caiaphas, and Summas, and Datam, Gamaliel, Judas, Levi, Nepthalim, Alexander, Cyrus, and other Jews, went to Pilate about Jesus, accusing him with many bad crimes.

And said, We are assured that Jesus is the son of Joseph the carpenter, land born of Mary, and that he declares himself the Son of God, and a king; and not only so, but attempts the dissolution of the sabbath, and the laws of our fathers.

Pilate replied; What is it which he declares? and what is it which he attempts dissolving?

The Jews told him, We have a law which forbids doing cures on the sabbath day; but he cures both the lame and the deaf, those afflicted with the palsy, the blind, and lepers, and demoniacs, on that day by wicked methods.

Pilate replied, How can he do this by wicked methods? They answered, He is a conjurer, and casts out devils by the prince of the devils; and so all things become subject to him.

Then said Pilate, Casting out devils seems not to be the work of an unclean spirit, but to proceed from the power of God.

THE LOST BOOKS OF THE BIBLE

The Jews replied to Pilate, We entreat your highness to summon him to appear before your tribunal, and hear him yourself.

Then Pilate called a messenger and said to him, By what means will Christ be brought hither?

Then went the messenger forth, and knowing Christ, worshipped him; and having spread the cloak which he had in his hand upon the ground, he said, Lord, walk upon this, and go in, for the governor calls thee.

When the Jews perceived what the messenger had done they exclaimed (against him) to Pilate, and said, Why did you not give him his summons by a beadle, and not by a messenger?—For the messenger, when he saw him, worshipped him, and spread the cloak which he had in his hand upon the ground before him, and said to him, Lord, the governor calls thee.

Then Pilate called the messenger, and said, Why hast thou done thus?

The messenger replied, When thou sentest me from Jerusalem to Alexander, I saw Jesus sitting in a mean figure upon a she-ass, and the children of the Hebrews cried out, Hosannah, holding boughs of trees in their hands.

Others spread their garments in the way, and said, Save us, thou who art in heaven; blessed is he who cometh in the name of the Lord.

Then the Jews cried out, against the messenger, and said, The children of the Hebrews made their acclamations in the Hebrew language; and how couldst thou, who art a Greek, understand the Hebrew?

The messenger answered them and said, I asked one of the Jews and said, What is this which the children do cry out in the Hebrew language?

And he explained it to me, saying, they cry out Hosannah, which being interpreted, is, O, Lord, save me; or, O Lord, save.

Pilate then said to them, Why do you yourselves testify to the words spoken by the children, namely, by your silence? In what has the messenger done amiss? And they were silent.

Then the governor said unto the messenger, Go forth and endeavour by any means to bring him in.

But the messenger went forth, and did as before; and said, Lord, come in, for the governor calleth thee.

And as Jesus was going in by the ensigns, who carried the standards, the tops of them bowed down and worshipped Jesus.

Whereupon the Jews exclaimed more vehemently against the ensigns.

But Pilate said to the Jews, I know it is not pleasing to you that the tops of the standards did of themselves bow and worship Jesus; but why do ye exclaim against the ensigns, as if they had bowed and worshipped?

They replied to Pilate, We saw the ensigns themselves bowing and worshipping Jesus.

Then the governor called the ensigns and said unto them, Why did you do thus?

The ensigns said to Pilate, We are all Pagans and worship the gods in temples; and how should we think anything about worshipping him? We only held the standards in our hands and they bowed themselves and worshipped him.

Then said Pilate to the rulers of the synagogue, Do ye yourselves choose some strong men, and let them hold the standards, and we shall see whether they will then bend of themselves.

So the elders of the Jews sought out twelve of the most strong and able old men, and made them hold the standards and they stood in the presence of the governor.

Then Pilate said to the messenger, Take Jesus out, and by some means bring him in again. And Jesus and the messenger went out of the hall.

And Pilate called the ensigns who before had borne the standards, and swore to them, that if they had not borne the standards in that manner when Jesus before entered in, he would cut off their heads.

Then the governor commanded Jesus to come in again.

And the messenger did as he had done before, and very much entreated Jesus that he would go upon his cloak, and walk on it, and he did walk upon it, and went in.

And when Jesus went in, the standards bowed themselves as before, and worshipped him.

CHAPTER II.

Is compassionated by Pilate's wife, charged with being born in fornication. Testimony to the betrothing of his parents. Hatred of the Jews to him.

NOW when Pilate saw this, he was afraid, and was about to rise from his seat.

But while he thought to rise, his own wife who stood at a distance, sent to him, saying Have thou nothing to do with that just man; for I have suffered much concerning him in a vision this night.

When the Jews heard this they said to Pilate, Did we not say unto thee, He is a conjuror? Behold, he hath caused thy wife to dream.

Pilate then calling Jesus, said, thou hast heard what they testify against thee, and makest no answer?

Jesus replied, If they had not a power of speaking, they could not have spoke; but because every one has the command of his own tongue, to speak both good and bad, let him look to it.

But the elders of the Jews answered, and said to Jesus, What shall we look to?

In the first place, we know this concerning thee, that thou wast born through fornication; secondly, that upon the account of thy birth the infants were slain in Bethlehem; thirdly, that thy father and mother Mary fled into Egypt, because they could not trust their own people.

Some of the Jews who stood by spake more favourably, We cannot say that he was born through fornication; but we know that his mother Mary was betrothed to Joseph, and so he was not born through fornication.

Then said Pilate to the Jews who affirmed him to be born through fornication, This your account is not true, seeing there was a betrothment, as they testify who are of your own nation.

Annas and Caiaphas spake to Pilate, All this multitude of people is to be regarded, who cry out, that he was born through fornication, and is a conjuror; but they who deny him to be born through fornication, are his proselytes and disciples.

Pilate answered Annas and Caiaphas, Who are the proselytes? They answered, They are those who are the children of Pagans, and are not become Jews, but followers of him.

Then replied Eleazer, and Asterius, and Antonius, and James, Caras and Samuel, Isaac and Phinees, Crispus and Agrippa, Annas and Judas, We are not proselytes, but children of Jews, and speak the truth, and were present when Mary was betrothed.

Then Pilate addressing himself to the twelve men who spake this, said to them, I conjure you by the life of Caesar, that ye faithfully declare whether he was born through fornication, and those things be true which ye have related.

They answered Pilate, We have a law, whereby we are forbid to swear, it being a sin: Let them swear by the life of Caesar that it is not as we have said, and we will be contented to be put to death.

Then said Annas and Caiaphas to Pilate, Those twelve men will not believe that we know him to be basely born, and to be a conjuror, although he pretends that he is the son of God, and a king: which we are so far from believing, that we tremble to hear.

Then Pilate commanded every one to go out except the twelve men who said he was not born through fornication, and Jesus to withdraw to a distance, and said to them, Why have the Jews a mind to kill Jesus?

They answered him, They are angry because he wrought cures on the Sabbath day. Pilate said, Will they kill him for good work? They say unto him, Yes, Sir.

CHAPTER III.

Is exonerated by Pilate. Disputes with Pilate concerning Truth.

THEN Pilate, filled with anger, went out of the hall, and said to the Jews, I call the whole world to witness that I find no fault in that man.

The Jews replied to Pilate, If he had not been a wicked person, we had not brought him before thee.

Pilate said to them, Do ye take him and try him by your law.

Then the Jews said, It is not lawful for us to put any one to death.

Pilate said to the Jews, The command, therefore thou shalt not kill, belongs to you, but not to me.

And he went again into the hall, and called Jesus by himself, and said to him, Art thou the king of the Jews?

And Jesus answering, said to Pilate, Dost thou speak this of thyself, or did the Jews tell it thee concerning me?

Pilate answering, said to Jesus, Am I a Jew? The whole nation and rulers of the Jews have delivered thee up to me. What hast thou done?

Jesus answering, said, My kingdom is not of this world: if my kingdom were of this world, then would my servants fight, and I should not have been delivered to the Jews; but now my kingdom is not from hence.

Pilate said, Art thou a king then? Jesus answered, Thou sayest that I am a king: to this end was I born, and for this end came I into the world; and for this purpose I came, that I should bear witness to the truth; and every one who is of the truth, heareth my voice.

Pilate saith to him, What is truth?

Jesus said, Truth is from heaven.

Pilate said, Therefore truth is not on earth.

Jesus said to Pilate, Believe that truth is on earth among those, who when they have the power of judgment, are governed by truth, and form right judgment.

CHAPTER IV.

Pilate finds no fault in Jesus. The Jews demand his crucifixion.

THEN Pilate left Jesus in the hall, and went out to the Jews, and said, I find not any one fault in Jesus.

The Jews say unto him, But he said, I can destroy the temple of God, and in three days build it up again.

Pilate saith unto them, What sort of temple is that of which he speaketh?

The Jews say unto him, That which Solomon was forty-six years in building, he said he would destroy, and in three days build up.

Pilate said to them again, I am innocent from the blood of that man; do ye look to it.

The Jews say to him, His blood be upon us and our children. Then Pilate calling together the elders and scribes, priests and Levites, saith to them privately, Do not act thus; I have found nothing in your charge (against him) concerning his curing sick persons, and breaking the sabbath, worthy of death.

The Priests and Levites replied to Pilate, By the life of Caesar, if any one be a blasphemer, he is worthy of death; but this man hath blasphemed against the Lord.

Then the governor again commanded the Jews to depart out of the hall; and calling Jesus, said to him, What shall I do with thee?

Jesus answered him, Do according as it is written.

Pilate said to him, How is it written?

Jesus saith to him, Moses and the prophets have prophesied concerning my suffering and resurrection.

The Jews hearing this, were provoked, and said to Pilate, Why wilt thou any longer hear the blasphemy of that man?

Pilate saith to them, If these words seem to you blasphemy, do ye take him, bring him to your court, and try him according to your law.

The Jews reply to Pilate, Our law saith, he shall be obliged to receive nine and thirty stripes, but if after this manner he shall blaspheme against the Lord, he shall be stoned.

Pilate saith unto them, If that speech of his was blasphemy, do ye try him according to your law.

The Jews say to Pilate, Our law commands us not to put any one to death: we desire that he may be crucified, because he deserves the death of the cross.

Pilate saith to them, It is not fit he should be crucified: let him be only whipped and sent away.

But when the governor looked upon the people that were present and the Jews, he saw many of the Jews in tears, and said to the chief priests of the Jews, All the people do not desire his death.

The elders of the Jews answered to Pilate, We and all the people came hither for this very purpose, that he should die.

Pilate saith to them, Why should he die?

They said to him, Because he declares himself to be the Son of God, and a King.

CHAPTER V.

Nicodemus speaks in defence of Christ, and relates his miracles. Another Jew, with Veronica, Centurio, and others, testify of other miracles.

BUT Nicodemus, a certain Jew, stood before the governor, and said, I entreat thee, O righteous judge, that thou wouldst favour me with the liberty of speaking a few words.

Pilate said to him, Speak on.

Nicodemus said, I spake to the elders of the Jews, and the scribes, and priests and Levites, and all the multitude of the Jews, in their assembly; What is it ye would do with this man?

He is a man who hath wrought many useful and glorious miracles, such as no man on earth ever wrought before, nor will ever work. Let him go, and do him no harm; if he cometh from God, his miracles, (his miraculous cures) will continue; but if from men, they will come to nought.

Thus Moses, when he was sent by God into Egypt, wrought the miracles which God commanded him, before Pharaoh king of Egypt; and though the magicians of that country, Jannes and Jambres, wrought by their magic the same miracles which Moses did, yet they could not work all which he did;

And the miracles which the magicians wrought, were not of God, as ye know, O Scribes and Pharisees; but they who wrought them perished, and all who believed them.

And now let this man go; because the very miracles for which ye accuse him, are from God; and he is not worthy of death.

The Jews then said to Nicodemus, Art thou become his disciple, and making speeches in his favour?

Nicodemus said to them, Is the governor become his disciple also, and does he make speeches for him? Did not Caesar place him in that high post?

When the Jews heard this they trembled, and gnashed their teeth at Nicodemus, and said to him, Mayest thou receive his doctrine for truth, and have thy lot with Christ!

Nicodemus replied, Amen; I will receive his doctrine, and my lot with him, as ye have said.

Then another certain Jew rose up, and desired leave of the governor to hear him a few words.

And the governor said, Speak what thou hast a mind.

And he said, I lay for thirty-eight years by the sheep-pool at Jerusalem, labouring under a great infirmity, and waiting for a cure which should be wrought by the coming of an angel, who at a certain time troubled the water; and whosoever first after the troubling of the water stepped in, was made whole of whatsoever disease he had.

And when Jesus saw me languishing there, he said to me, Wilt thou be made whole? And I answered, Sir, I have no man, when the water is troubled, to put me into the pool.

And he said unto me, Rise, take up thy bed and walk. And I was immediately made whole, and took up my bed and walked.

The Jews then said to Pilate, Our Lord Governor, pray ask him what day it was on which he was cured of his infirmity.

The infirm person replied, It was on the sabbath.

The Jews said to Pilate, Did we not say that he wrought his cures on the sabbath, and cast out devils by the prince of devils?

Then another certain Jew came forth, and said, I was blind, could hear sounds, but could not see any one; and as Jesus was going along, I heard the multitude passing by, and I asked what was there?

They told me that Jesus was passing by: then I cried out, saying, Jesus, Son of David, have mercy on me. And he stood still, and commanded that I should be brought to him, and said to me, What wilt thou?

I said, Lord, that I may receive my sight.

He said to me, Receive thy sight: and presently I saw, and followed him, rejoicing and giving thanks.

Another Jew also came forth, and said, I was a leper, and he cured me by his word only, saying, I will, be thou clean; and presently I was cleansed from my leprosy.

And another Jew came forth, and said, I was crooked, and he made me straight by his word.

And a certain woman named Veronica, said, I was afflicted with an issue of blood twelve years, and I touched the hem of his garments, and presently the issue of my blood stopped.

The Jews then said, We have a law, that a woman shall not be allowed as an evidence.

And, after other things, another Jew said, I saw Jesus invited to a wedding with his disciples, and there was a want of wine in Cana of Galilee;

And when the wine was all drank, he commanded the servants that they should fill six pots which were there with water, and they filled them up to the brim, and he blessed them, and turned the water into wine, and all the people drank, being surprised at this miracle.

And another Jew stood forth, and said, I saw Jesus teaching in the synagogue at Capernaum; and there was in the synagogue a certain man who had a devil; and he cried out, saying, let me alone; what have we to do with thee, Jesus of Nazareth? Art thou come to destroy us? I know that thou art the Holy One of God.

And Jesus rebuked him, saying, Hold thy peace, unclean spirit, and come out of the man; and presently he came out of him, and did not at all hurt him.

The following things were also said by a Pharisee; I saw that a great company came to Jesus from Galilee and Judaea, and the sea-coast, and many countries about Jordan, and many infirm persons came to him, and he healed them all.

And I heard the unclean spirits crying out, and saying, Thou art the Son of God.

And Jesus strictly charged them, that they should not make him known.

After this another person, whose name was Centurio, said, I saw Jesus in Capernaum, and I entreated him, saying, Lord, my servant lieth at home sick of the palsy.

And Jesus said to me, I will come and cure him.

But I said, Lord, I am not worthy that thou shouldst come under my roof; but only speak the word, and my servant shall be healed.

And Jesus said unto me, Go thy way; and as thou hast believed, so be it done unto thee. And my servant was healed from that same hour.

Then a certain nobleman said, I had a son in Capernaum, who lay at the point of death; and when I heard that Jesus was come into Galilee, I went and besought him that he would come down to my house, and heal my son, for he was at the point of death.

He said to me, Go thy way, thy son liveth.

And my son was cured from that hour.

Besides these, also many others of the Jews, both men and women, cried out and said, He is truly the Son of God, who cures all diseases only by his word, and to whom the devils are altogether subject.

Some of them farther said,, This power can proceed fro none but God.

Pilate said to the Jews Why are not the devils subject your doctors?

Some of them said, The power of subjecting devils can not proceed but from God.

But others said to Pilate That he had raised Lazarus from the dead, after he had been four days in his grave.

The governor hearing this, trembling said to the multitude of the Jews, What will it profit you to shed innocent blood?

CHAPTER VI.

Pilate dismayed by the turbulence of the Jews, who demand Barabbas to be released, and Christ to be crucified, Pilate warmly expostulates with them, washes his hands of Christ's blood, and sentences him to be whipped and crucified.

THEN Pilate having called together Nicodemus, and the fifteen men who said that Jesus was not born through fornication, said to them, What shall I do, seeing there is like to be a tumult among the people.

They said unto him, We know not; let them look to it who raise the tumult.

Pilate then called the multitude again, and said to them, Ye know that ye have a custom, that I should release to you one prisoner at the feast of the passover;

I have a noted prisoner, a murderer, who is called Barabbas, and Jesus who is called Christ, in whom I find nothing that deserves death; which of them therefore have you a mind that I should release to you?

They all cry out, and say, Release to us Barabbas.

Pilate saith to them, What then shall I do with Jesus who, is called Christ?

They all answer, Let him be crucified.

Again they cry out and say to Pilate, You are not the friend of Caesar, if you release this man? for he hath declared that he is the Son of God, and a king. But are you inclined that he should be king, and not Caesar?

Then Pilate filled with anger said to them, Your nation hath always been seditious, and you are always against those who have been serviceable to you?

The Jews replied, Who are those who have been serviceable to us?

Pilate answered them, Your God who delivered you from the hard bondage of the Egyptians, and brought you over the Red Sea as though it had been dry land, and fed you in the wilderness with manna and the flesh of quails, and brought water out of the rock, and gave you a law from heaven:

Ye provoked him all ways, and desired for yourselves a molten calf, and worshipped it, and sacrificed to it, and said, These are Thy Gods, O Israel, which brought thee out of the land of Egypt

On account of which your God was inclined to destroy you; but Moses interceded for you, and your God heard him, and forgave your iniquity.

Afterwards ye were enraged against, and would have killed your prophets, Moses and Aaron, when they fled to the tabernacle, and ye were always murmuring against God and his prophets.

And arising from his judgment seat, he would have gone out; but the Jews all cried out, We acknowledge Caesar to be king, and not Jesus.

Whereas this person, as soon as he was born, the wise men came and offered gifts unto him; which when Herod heard, he was exceedingly troubled, and would have killed him.

When his father knew this, he fled with him and his mother Mary into Egypt. Herod, when he heard he was born, would have slain him; and accordingly sent and slew all the children which were in Bethlehem, and in all the coasts thereof, from two years old and under.

When Pilate heard this account, he was afraid; and commanding silence among the people, who made a noise, he said to Jesus, Art thou therefore a king?

All the Jews replied to Pilate, he is the very person whom Herod sought to have slain.

Then Pilate taking water, washed his hands before the people and said, I am innocent of the blood of this just person; look ye to it.

The Jews answered and said, His blood be upon us and our children.

Then Pilate commanded Jesus to be brought before him, and spake to him in the following words:

Thy own nation hath charged thee as making thyself a king; wherefore I, Pilate, sentence thee to be whipped according to the laws of former governors; and that thou be first bound, then hanged upon a cross in that place where thou art now a prisoner; and also two criminals with thee, whose names are Dimas and Gestas.

CHAPTER VII.

Manner of Christ's crucifixion with the two thieves.

THEN Jesus went out of the hall, and the two thieves with him.

And when they came to the place which is called Golgotha, they stript him of his raiment, and girt him about with a linen cloth, and put a crown of thorns upon his head, and put a reed in his hand.

And in like manner did they to the two thieves who were crucified with him, Dimas on his right hand and Gestas on his left.

But Jesus said, My Father, forgive them; For they know not what they do.

And they divided his garments, and upon his vesture they cast lots.

The people in the mean time stood by, and the chief priests and elders of the Jews mocked him, saying, he saved others, let him now save himself if he can; if he be the son of God, let him now come down from the cross.

The soldiers also mocked him, and taking vinegar and gall offered it to him to drink, and said to him, If thou art king of the Jews deliver thyself.

Then Longinus, a certain soldier, taking a spear, pierced his side, and presently there came forth blood and water.

And Pilate wrote the title upon the cross in Hebrew, Latin, and Greek letters, viz. This is the king of the Jews.

But one of the two thieves who were crucified with Jesus, whose name was Gestas, said to Jesus, If thou art the Christ, deliver thyself and us.

But the thief who was crucified on his right hand, whose name was Dimas, answering, rebuked him, and said, Dost not thou fear God, who art condemned to this punishment? We indeed receive rightly and justly the demerit of our actions; but this Jesus, what evil hath he done?

After this groaning, he said to Jesus, Lord, remember me when thou comest into thy kingdom.

Jesus answering, said to him, Verily I say unto thee, that this day thou shalt be with me in Paradise.

CHAPTER VIII.

Miraculous appearance at his death. The Jews say the eclipse was natural. Joseph of Arimathaea embalms Christ's body and buries it.

AND it was about the sixth hour, and darkness was upon the face of the whole earth until the ninth hour.

And while the sun was eclipsed, behold the vail of the temple was rent from the top to the bottom; and the rocks also were rent, and the graves opened, and many bodies of saints, which slept, arose.

And about the ninth hour Jesus cried out with a loud voice, saying, Hely, Hely, lama zabacthani? which being interpreted, is, My God, My God, why hast thou forsaken me?

And after these things, Jesus said, Father, into thy hands I commend my spirit; and having said this, he gave up the ghost.

But when the centurion saw that Jesus thus crying out gave up the ghost, he glorified God, and said, Of a truth this was a just man.

And all the people who stood by, were exceedingly troubled at the sight; and reflecting upon what had passed, smote upon their breasts, and then returned to the city of Jerusalem.

The centurion went to the governor, and related to him all that had passed;

And when he had heard all these things, he was exceeding sorrowful;

And calling the Jews together, said to them, Have ye seen the miracle of the sun's eclipse, and the other things which came to pass, while Jesus was dying?

Which when the Jews heard, they answered to the governor, The eclipse of the sun happened according to its usual custom.

But all those who were the acquaintance of Christ, stood at a distance, as did the women who had followed Jesus from Galilee, observing all these things.

And behold a certain man of Arimathaea, named Joseph, who also was a disciple of Jesus, but not openly so, for fear of the Jews, came to the governor, and entreated the governor that he would give him leave to take away the body of Jesus from the cross.

And the governor gave him leave.

And Nicodemus came, bringing with him a mixture of myrrh and aloes about a hundred pound weight; and they took down Jesus from the cross with tears, and bound him with linen cloths with spices, according to the custom of burying among the Jews,

And placed him in a new tomb, which Joseph had built, and caused to be cut out of a rock, which never any man had been put; and they rolled a great stone to the door of the sepulchre.

CHAPTER IX.

The Jews angry with Nicodemus; and with Joseph of Arimathaea, whom they imprison.

WHEN the unjust Jews heard that Joseph had begged and buried the body of Jesus, they sought after Nicodemus; and those fifteen men who had testified before the Governor, that Jesus was not born through fornication, and other good persons who had shewn any good actions towards him.

But when they all concealed themselves through fear of the Jews Nicodemus alone shewed himself to them, and said, How can such persons as these enter into the synagogue?

The Jews answered him, But how durst thou enter into the synagogue who wast a confederate with Christ? Let thy lot be along with him in the other world.

Nicodemus answered, Amen; so may it be, that I may have my lot with him in his kingdom.

In like manner Joseph, when he came to the Jews, said to them Why are ye angry with me for desiring the body of Jesus of Pilate? Behold, I have put him in my tomb, and wrapped him up in clean linen, and put a stone at the door of the sepulchre:

I have acted rightly towards him; but ye have acted unjustly against that just person, in crucifying him, giving him vinegar to drink, crowning him with thorns, tearing his body with whips, and prayed down the guilt of his blood upon you.

The Jews at the hearing of this were disquieted, and troubled; and they seized Joseph, and commanded him to be put in custody before the sabbath, and kept there till the sabbath was over.

And they said to him, Make confession; for at this time it is not lawful to do thee any harm, till the first day of the week come. But we know that thou wilt not be thought worthy of a burial; but we will give thy flesh to the birds of the air, and the beasts of the earth.

Joseph answered, That speech is like the speech of proud Goliath, who reproached the living God in speaking against David. But ye scribes and doctors know that God saith by the prophet, Vengeance is mine, and I will repay to you evil equal to that which ye have threatened to me.

The God whom you have hanged upon the cross, is able to deliver me out of your hands. All your wickedness will return upon you.

For the governor, when he washed his hands, said, I am clear from the blood of this just person. But ye answered and cried out, His blood be upon us and our children. According as ye have said, may ye perish for ever.

The elders of the Jews hearing these words, were exceedingly enraged; and seizing Joseph, they put him into a chamber where there was no window; they fastened the door, and put a seal upon the lock;

And Annas and Caiaphas placed a guard upon it, and took counsel with the priests and Levites, that they should all meet after the sabbath, and they contrived to what death they should put Joseph.

When they had done this, the rulers, Annas and Caiaphas, ordered Joseph to be brought forth.

In this place there is a portion of the Gospel lost or omitted, which cannot be supplied.

CHAPTER X.

Joseph's escape. The soldiers relate Christ's resurrection. Christ is seen preaching in Galilee. The Jews repent of their cruelty to him.

WHEN all the assembly heard this, they admired and were astonished, because they found the same seal upon the lock of the chamber, and could not find Joseph.

Then Annas and Caiaphas went forth, and while they were all admiring at Joseph's being gone, behold one of the soldiers, who kept the sepulchre of Jesus, spake in the assembly.

That while they were guarding the sepulchre of Jesus, there was an earthquake; and we saw an angel of God roll away the stone of the sepulchre and sit upon it;

And his countenance was like lightning and his garment like snow; and we became through fear like persons dead.

And we heard an angel saying to the women at the sepulchre of Jesus, Do not fear; I know that you seek Jesus who was crucified; he is risen as he foretold.

Come and see the place where he was laid; and go presently, and tell his disciples that he is risen from the dead, and he will go before you into Galilee; there ye shall see him as he told you.

Then the Jews called together all the soldiers who kept the sepulchre of Jesus, and said to them, Who are those women, to whom the angel spoke? Why did ye not seize them?

The soldiers answered and said, We know not whom the women were; besides we became as dead persons through fear, and how could we seize those women?

The Jews said to them, As the Lord liveth we do not believe you.

The soldiers answering said to the Jews, when ye saw and heard Jesus working so many miracles, and did not believe him, how should ye believe us? Ye well said, As the Lord liveth, for the Lord truly does live.

We have heard that ye shut up Joseph, who buried the body of Jesus, in a chamber, under a lock which was sealed; and when ye opened it, found him not there.

Do ye then produce Joseph whom ye put under guard in the chamber, and we will produce Jesus whom we guarded in the sepulchre.

The Jews answered and said, We will produce Joseph, do ye produce Jesus. But Joseph is in his own city of Arimathaea.

The soldiers replied, If Joseph be in Arimathaea, and Jesus in Galilee, we heard the angel inform the women.

The Jews hearing this, were afraid, and said among themselves, If by any means these things should become public, then every body will believe in Jesus.

Then they gathered a large sum of money, and gave it to the soldiers, saying, Do ye tell the people that the disciples of Jesus came in the night when ye were asleep and stole away the body of Jesus; and if Pilate the governor should hear of this, we will satisfy him and secure you.

The soldiers accordingly took the money, and said as they were instructed by the Jews; and their report was spread abroad among the people.

But a certain priest Phinees, and a schoolmaster, and a Levite, named Ageus, they three came from Galilee to Jerusalem, and told the chief priests and all who were in the synagogues, saying,

We have seen Jesus, whom ye crucified, talking with his eleven disciples, and sitting in the midst of them in Mount Olivet, and saying to them,

Go forth into the whole world, preach the Gospel to all nations, baptizing them in the name of the Father, and the Son, and the Holy Ghost; and whosoever shall believe and be baptized, shall be saved.

And when he had said these things to his disciples, we saw him ascending up to heaven.

When the chief priests, and elders, and Levites heard these things, they said to these three men, Give glory to the God of Israel, and make confession to him, whether those things are true, which ye say ye have seen and heard.

They answering said, As the Lord of our fathers liveth, the God of Abraham, and the God of Isaac, and the God of Jacob, according as we heard Jesus talking with his disciples, and according as we saw him ascending up to heaven, so we have related the truth to you.

And the three men farther answered, and said, adding these words, If we should not own the words which we heard Jesus speak, and that we saw him ascending into heaven, we should be guilty of sin.

Then the chief priests immediately rose up, and holding the book of the law in their hands, conjured these men, saying, Ye shall no more hereafter declare those things which ye have spoke concerning Jesus.

And they gave them a large sum of money, and sent other persons along with them, who should conduct them to their own country, that they might not by any means make any stay at Jerusalem.

Then the Jews did assemble all together, and having expressed the most lamentable concern, said, What is this extraordinary thing which is come to pass in Jerusalem?

But Annas and Caiaphas comforted them, saying, Why should we believe the soldiers who guarded the sepulchre of Jesus, in telling us, that an angel rolled away the stone from the door of the sepulchre?

Perhaps his own disciples told them this, and gave them money that they should say so, and they themselves took away the body of Jesus.

Besides, consider this, that there is no credit to be given to foreigners, because they also took a large sum of us, and they have declared to us according to the instructions which we gave them. They must either be faithful to us, or to the disciples of Jesus.

CHAPTER XI.

Nicodemus counsels the Jews. Joseph found. Invited by the Jews to return. Relates the manner of his miraculous escape.

THEN Nicodemus arose, and said, Ye say right, O sons of Israel, ye have heard what those three men have sworn by the Law of God, who said, We have seen Jesus speaking with his disciples upon Mount Olivet, and we saw him ascending up to heaven.

And the scripture teacheth us that the blessed prophet Elijah was taken up to heaven; and Elisha being asked by the sons of the prophets, Where is our father Elijah? He said to them, that he is taken up to heaven.

And the sons of the prophets said to him, Perhaps the spirit hath carried him into one of the mountains of Israel, there perhaps we shall find him. And they besought Elisha, and he walked about with them three days, and they could not find him.

And now hear me, O sons of Israel, and let us send men into the mountains of Israel, lest perhaps the spirit hath carried away Jesus, and there perhaps we shall find him, and be satisfied.

And the counsel of Nicodemus pleased all the people; and they sent forth men who sought for Jesus, but could not find him: and they returning, said, We went all about, but could not find Jesus, but we have found Joseph in his city of .

The rulers hearing this, and all the people, were glad, and praised the God of Israel, because Joseph was found, whom they had shut up in a chamber, and could not find.

And when they had formed a large assembly, the chief priests said, By what means shall we bring Joseph to us to speak with him?

And taking a piece of paper, they wrote to him, and said, Peace be with thee, and all thy family. We know that we have offended against God and thee. Be pleased to give a visit to us your fathers, for we were perfectly surprised at your escape from prison.

We know that it was malicious counsel which we took against thee, and that the Lord took care of thee, and the Lord himself delivered thee from our designs. Peace be unto thee, Joseph, who art honourable among all the people.

And they chose seven of Joseph's friends, and said to them, When ye come to Joseph, salute him in peace, and give him this letter.

Accordingly, when the men came to Joseph, they did salute him in peace, and gave him the letter.

And when Joseph had read it, he said, Blessed be the Lord God, who didst deliver me from the Israelites, that they could not shed my blood. Blessed be God, who has protected me under thy wings.

And Joseph kissed them, and took them into his house. And on the morrow, Joseph mounted his ass, and went along with them to Jerusalem.

And when all the Jews heard these things, they went out to meet him, and cried out, saying, Peace attend thy coming hither, father Joseph.

To which he answered, Prosperity from the Lord attend all the people.

And they all kissed him; and Nicodemus took him to his house, having prepared a large entertainment.

But on the morrow, being a preparation-day, Annas, and Caiaphas, and Nicodemus, said to Joseph, Make confession to the God of Israel, and answer to us all those questions which we shall ask thee;

For we have been very much troubled, that thou didst bury the body of Jesus; and that when we had locked thee in a chamber, we could not find thee; and we have been afraid ever since, till this time of thy appearing among us. Tell us therefore before God, all that came to pass.

Then Joseph answering, said, Ye did indeed put me under confinement, on the day of preparation, till the morning.

But while I was standing at prayer in the middle of the night, the house was surrounded with four angels; and I saw Jesus as the brightness of the sun, and fell down upon the earth for fear.

But Jesus laying hold on my hand, lifted me from the ground, and the dew was then sprinkled upon me; but he, wiping my face, kissed me, and said unto me, Fear not, Joseph; look upon me, for it is I.

Then I looked upon him, and said, Rabboni Elias! He answered me, I am not Elias, but Jesus of Nazareth, whose body thou didst bury.

I said to him, Shew me the tomb in which I laid thee.

Then Jesus, taking me by the hand, led me unto the place where I laid him, and shewed me the linen clothes, and napkin which I put round his head. Then I knew that it was Jesus, and worshipped him, and said, Blessed be he who cometh in the name of the Lord.

Jesus again taking me by the hand, led me to Arimathaea to my own house, and said to me, Peace be to thee; but go not out of thy house till the fortieth day; but I must go to my disciples.

CHAPTER XII.

The Jews astonished and confounded. Simeon's two sons, Charinus and Lenthius, rise from the dead at Christ's crucifixion. Joseph proposes to get them to relate the mysteries of their resurrection. They are sought and found, brought to the synagogue, privately sworn to secrecy, and undertake to write what they had seen.

WHEN the chief priests and heard all these things, they were astonished, and fell down with their faces on the ground as dead men, and crying out to one another said, What is this extraordinary sign which is come to pass in Jerusalem? We know the father and mother of Jesus.

And a certain Levite said, I know many of his relations, religious persons, who are wont to offer sacrifices and burnt-offerings to the God of Israel, in the temple, with prayers.

And when the high priest Simeon took him up in his arms. he said to him, Lord, now lettest thou thy servant depart in peace, according to thy word; for mine eyes have seen thy salvation, which thou hast prepared before the face of all people: a light to enlighten the Gentiles, and the glory of thy people Israel.

Simeon in like manner blessed Mary the mother of Jesus, and said to her, I declare to thee concerning that child; He is appointed for the fall and rising again of many, and for a sign which shall be spoken against.

Yea, a sword shall pierce through thine own soul also, and the thoughts of many hearts shall be revealed.

Then said all the Jews, Let us send to those three men, who said they saw him talking with his disciples in Mount Olivet.

After this, they asked them what they had seen; who answered with one accord, In the presence of the God of Israel we affirm, that we plainly saw Jesus talking with his disciples in Mount Olivet, and ascending up to heaven.

Then Annas and Caiaphas took them into separate places, and examined them separately; who unanimously confessed the truth, and said, they had seen Jesus.

Then Annas and Caiaphas said "Our law saith, By the mouth of two or three witnesses every word shall be established."

But what have we said? The blessed Enoch pleased God, and was translated by the word of God; and the burying-place of the blessed Moses is known.

But Jesus was delivered to Pilate, whipped, crowned with thorns, spit upon, pierced with a spear, crucified, died upon the cross, and was buried, and his body the honorable

THE LOST BOOKS OF THE BIBLE

Joseph buried in a new sepulchre, and he testifies that he saw him alive.

And besides these men have declared, that they saw him talking with his disciples in Mount Olivet, and ascending up to heaven.

Then Joseph rising up. said to Annas and Caiaphas, Ye may be justly under a great surprise, that you have been told, that Jesus is alive, and gone up to heaven.

It is indeed a thing really surprising, that he should not only himself arise from the dead, but also raise others from their graves, who have been seen by many in Jerusalem.

And now hear me a little: We all knew the blessed Simeon, the high-priest, who took Jesus when an infant into his arms in the temple.

This same Simeon had two sons of his own, and we were all present at their death and funeral.

Go therefore and see their tombs, for these are open, and they are risen: and behold, they are in the city of Arimathaea, spending their time together in offices of devotion.

Some, indeed, have heard the sound of their voices in prayer, but they will not discourse with any one, but they continue as mute as dead men.

But come, let us go to them, and behave ourselves towards them with all due respect and caution. And if we can bring them to swear, perhaps they will tell us some of the mysteries of their resurrection.

When the Jews heard this, they were exceedingly rejoiced.

Then Annas and Caiaphas, Nicodemus, Joseph, and Gamaliel, went to Arimathaea, but did not find them in their graves; but walking about the city, they bound them on their bended knees at their devotions:

Then saluting them with all respect and deference to God, they brought them to the synagogue at Jerusalem: and having shut the gates, they took the book of the law of the Lord,

And putting it in their hands, swore them by God Adonai, and the God of Israel, who spake to our fathers by the law and the prophets, saying, If ye believe him who raised you from the dead, to be Jesus, tell us what ye have seen, and how ye were raised from the dead.

Charinus and Lenthius, the two sons of Simeon, trembled when they heard these things, and were disturbed, and groaned; and at the same time looking up to heaven, they made the sign of the cross with their fingers on their tongues.

And immediately they spake, and said, Give each of us some paper, and we will write down for you all those things which we have seen. And they each sat down and wrote, saying,

THE LOST BOOKS OF THE BIBLE

CHAPTER XIII.

The narrative of Charinus and Lenthius commences. A great light in hell. Simeon arrives, and announces the coming of Christ.

O LORD Jesus and Father, who art God, also the resurrection and life of the dead, give us leave to declare thy mysteries, which we saw after death, belonging to thy cross; for we are sworn by thy name.

For thou hast forbid thy servants to declare the secret things, which were wrought by thy divine power in hell.

When we were placed with our fathers in the depth of hell, in the blackness of darkness, on a sudden there appeared the colour of the sun like gold, and a substantial purple-coloured light enlightening the place.

Presently upon this, Adam, the father of all mankind, with all the patriarchs and prophets, rejoiced and said, That light is the author of everlasting light, who hath promised to translate us to everlasting light.

Then Isaiah the prophet cried out, and said, This is the light of the Father, and the Son of God, according to my prophecy, when I was alive upon earth.

The land of Zabulon, and the land of Nephthalim beyond Jordan, a people who walked in darkness, saw a great light; and to them who dwelled in the region of the shadow of death, light is arisen. And now he is come, and hath enlightened us who sat in death.

And while we were all rejoicing in the light which shone upon us, our father Simeon came among us, and congratulating all the company, said, Glorify the Lord Jesus Christ the Son of God.

Whom I took up in my arms when an infant in the temple, and being moved by the Holy Ghost, said to him, and acknowledged, That now mine eyes have seen thy salvation, which thou hast prepared before the face of all people, a light to enlighten the Gentiles and the glory of thy people Israel.

All the saints who were in the depth of hell, hearing this, rejoiced the more.

Afterwards there came forth one like a little hermit, and was asked by every one, Who art thou?

To which he replied, I am the voice of one crying in the wilderness, John the Baptist, and the prophet of the Most High, who went before his coming to prepare his way, to give the knowledge of salvation to his people for the forgiveness of sins.

And I John, when I saw Jesus coming to me, being moved by the Holy Ghost, I said, Behold the Lamb of God, behold him who takes away the sins of the world.

And I baptized him in the river Jordan, and saw the Holy Ghost descending upon him in the form of a dove, and heard a voice from heaven, saying, This is my beloved Son, in whom I am well pleased.

And now while I was going before him, I came down hither to acquaint you, that the Son of God will next visit us, and, as the day-spring from on high, will come to us, who are in darkness and the shadow of death.

CHAPTER XIV.

Adam causes Seth to relate what he heard from Michael the archangel, when he sent him to Paradise to entreat God to anoint his head in his sickness.

BUT when the first man our father Adam heard these things, that Jesus was baptized in Jordan, he called out to his son, Seth, and said,

Declare to your sons, the patriarchs and prophets, all those things, which thou didst hear from Michael, the archangel, when I sent thee to the gates of Paradise, to entreat God that he would anoint my head when I was sick.

Then Seth, coming near to the patriarchs and prophets, said, I Seth, when I was praying to God at the gates of Paradise, beheld the angel of the Lord, Michael appear unto me saying, I am sent unto thee from the Lord; I am appointed to preside over human bodies.

I tell thee Seth, do not pray to God in tears, and entreat him for the oil of the tree of mercy wherewith to anoint thy father Adam for his head-ache;

Because thou canst not by any means obtain it till the last day and times, namely, till five thousand and five hundred years be past.

Then will Christ, the most merciful Son of God, come on earth to raise again the human body of Adam, and at the same time to raise the bodies of the dead, and when he cometh he will be baptized in Jordan:

Then with the oil of his mercy he will anoint all those who believe on him; and the oil of his mercy will continue to future generations, for those who shall be born of the water and the Holy Ghost unto eternal life.

And when at that time the most merciful Son of God, Christ Jesus, shall come down on earth, he will introduce our father Adam into Paradise, to the tree of mercy.

When all the patriarchs and prophets heard all these things from Seth, they rejoiced more.

CHAPTER XV.

Quarrel between Satan and the prince of hell concerning the expected arrival of Christ in hell.

WHILE all the saints were vv rejoicing, behold Satan, the prince and captain of death, said to the prince of hell,

Prepare to receive Jesus of Nazareth himself, who boasted that he was the Son of God, and yet was a man afraid of death, and said, My soul is sorrowful even to death.

Besides he did many injuries to me and to many others; for those whom I made blind and lame and those also whom I tormented with several devils, he cured by his word; yea, and those whom I brought dead to thee, he by force takes away from thee.

To this the prince of hell replied to Satan, Who is that so-powerful prince, and yet a man who is afraid of death?

For all the potentates of the earth are subject to my power, whom thou broughtest to subjection by thy power.

But if be be so powerful in his human nature, I affirm to thee for truth, that he is almighty in his divine nature, and no man can resist his power.

When therefore he said be was afraid of death, he designed to ensnare thee, and unhappy it will be to thee for everlasting ages.

Then Satan replying, said to the prince of hell, Why didst thou express a doubt, and wast afraid to receive that Jesus of Nazareth, both thy adversary and mine?

As for me, I tempted him and stirred up my old people the Jews with zeal and anger against him?

I sharpened the spear for his suffering; I mixed the gall and vinegar, and commanded that he should drink it; I prepared the cross to crucify him, and the nails to pierce through Ibis hands and feet; and now his death is near at hand, I will bring him hither, subject both to thee and me.

Then the prince of hell answering, said, Thou saidst to me just now, that he took away the dead from me by force.

They who have been kept here till they should live again upon earth, were taken away hence, not by their own power, but by prayers made to God, and their almighty God took them from me.

Who then is that Jesus of Nazareth that by his word hath taken away the dead from me without prayer to God?

Perhaps it is the same who took away from me Lazarus, after he had been four days dead, and did both stink and was rotten, and of whom I had possession as a dead person, yet he brought him to life again by his power.

Satan answering, replied to the prince of hell, It is the very same person, Jesus of Nazareth.

Which when the prince of hell heard, he said to him, I adjure thee by the powers which belong to thee and me, that thou bring him not to me.

For when I heard of the power of his word, I trembled for fear, and all my impious company were at the same time disturbed;

And we were not able to detain Lazarus, but he gave himself a shake, and with all the signs of malice, he immediately went away from us; and the very earth, in which the dead body of Lazarus was lodged, presently turned him out alive.

And I know now that he is Almighty God who could perform such things, who is mighty in his dominion, and mighty in his human nature, who is the Saviour of mankind.

Bring not therefore this person hither, for he will set at liberty all those whom I hold in prison under unbelief, and bound with the fetters of their sins, and will conduct them to everlasting life.

CHAPTER XVI.

Christ's arrival at hell-gates; the confusion thereupon. He descends into hell.

AND while Satan and the prince of hell were discoursing thus to each other, on a sudden there was a voice as of thunder and the rushing of winds, saying, Lift up your gates, O ye princes; and be ye lift up, O everlasting gates, and the King of Glory shall come in.

When the prince of hell heard this, he said to Satan, Depart from me, and begone out of my habitations; if thou art a powerful warrior, fight with the King of Glory. But what hast thou to do with him?

And he cast him forth from his habitations.

And the prince said to his impious officers, Shut the brass gates of cruelty, and make them fast with iron bars, and fight courageously, lest we be taken captives.

But when all the company of the saints heard this they spake with a loud voice of anger to the prince of hell:

Open thy gates that the King of Glory may come in.

And the divine prophet David, cried out saying, Did not I when on earth truly prophesy and say, O that men would praise the Lord for his goodness, and for his wonderful works to the children of men.

For he hath broken the gates of brass, and cut the bars of iron in sunder. He hath taken them because of their iniquity, and because of their unrighteousness they are afflicted.

After this another prophet, namely, holy Isaiah, spake in like manner to all the saints, did not I rightly prophesy to you when I was alive on earth?

The dead men shall live, and they shall rise again who are in their graves, and they shall rejoice who are in earth; for the dew which is from the Lord shall bring deliverance to them.

And I said in another place, O death, where is thy victory? O death, where is thy sting?

When all the saints heard these things spoken by Isaiah, they said to the prince of hell, Open now thy gates, and take away thine iron bars; for thou wilt now be bound, and have no power.

Then there was a great voice, as of the sound of thunder saying, Lift up your gates,

O princes; and be ye lifted up, ye gates of hell, and the King of Glory will enter in.

The prince of hell perceiving the same voice repeated, cried out as though he had been ignorant, Who is that King of Glory?

David replied to the prince of hell, and said, I understand the words of that voice, because I spake them by his spirit. And now, as I have above said, I say unto thee, the Lord strong and powerful, the Lord mighty in battle: he is the King of Glory, and he is the Lord in heaven and in earth;

He hath looked down to hear the groans of the prisoners, and to set loose those that are appointed to death.

And now, thou filthy and stinking prince of hell, open thy gates, that the King of Glory may enter in; for he is the Lord of heaven and earth.

While David was saying this, the mighty Lord appeared in the form of a man, and enlightened those places which had ever before been in darkness,

And broke asunder the fetters which before could not be broken; and with his invincible power visited those who sat in the deep darkness by iniquity, and the shadow of death by sin.

CHAPTER XVII.

Death and the devils in great horror at Christ's coming. He tramples on death, seizes the prince of hell, and takes Adam with him to heaven.

IMPIOUS Death and her cruel officers hearing these things, were seized with fear in their several kingdoms, when they saw the clearness of the light,

And Christ himself on a sudden appearing in their habitations; they cried out therefore, and said, We are bound by thee; thou seemest to intend our confusion before the Lord.

Who art thou, who hast no sign of corruption, but that bright appearance which is a full proof of thy greatness, of which yet thou seemest to take no notice?

Who art thou, so powerful and so weak, so great and so little, a mean and yet a soldier of the first rank, who can command in the form of a servant as a common soldier?

The King of Glory, dead and alive, though once slain upon the cross?

Who layest dead in the grave, and art come down alive to us, and in thy death all the creatures trembled, and all the stars were moved, and now hast thou thy liberty among the dead, and givest disturbance to our legions?

Who art thou, who dost release the captives that were held in chains by original sin, and bringest them into their former liberty

Who art thou, who dost spread so glorious and divine a light over those who were made blind by the darkness of sin?In like manner all the legions of devils were seized with the like horror, and with the most submissive fear cried out, and said,

Whence comes it, O thou Jesus Christ, that thou art a man so powerful and glorious in majesty, so bright as to have no spot, and so pure as to have no crime? For that lower world of earth, which was ever till now subject to us, and from whence we received tribute, never sent us such a dead man before, never sent such presents as these to the princes of hell.

Who therefore art thou, who with such courage enterest among our abodes, and art not only not afraid to threaten us with the greatest punishments, but also endeavourest to rescue all others from the chains in which we hold them?

Perhaps thou art that Jesus, of whom Satan just now spoke to our prince, that by the death of the cross thou wert about to receive the power of death.

Then the King of Glory trampling upon death, seized the prince of hell, deprived him of all his power, and took our earthly father Adam with him to his glory.

CHAPTER XVIII.

Beelzebub, prince of hell, vehemently upbraids Satan for persecuting Christ and bringing him to hell. Christ gives Beelzebub dominion over Satan for ever, as a recompense for taking away Adam and his sons.

THEN the prince of hell took Satan, and with great indication said to him, O thou prince of destruction, author of

Beelzebub's defeat and banishment, the scorn of God's angels and loathed by all righteous persons! What inclined thee to act thus?

Thou wouldst crucify the King of Glory, and by his destruction, hast made us promises of very large advantages, but as a fool wert ignorant of what thou wast about.

For behold now that Jesus of Nazareth, with the brightness of his glorious divinity, puts to flight all the horrid powers of darkness and death;

He has broke down our prisons from top to bottom, dismissed all the captives, released all who were bound, and all who were wont formerly to groan under the weight of their torments have now insulted us, and we are like to be defeated by their prayers.

Our impious dominions are subdued, and no part of mankind is now left in our subjection, but on the other hand, they all boldly defy us;

Though, before, the dead never durst behave themselves insolently towards us, nor, being prisoners, could ever on any occasion be merry.

O Satan, thou prince of all the wicked, father of the impious and abandoned, why wouldest thou attempt this exploit, seeing our prisoners were hitherto always without the least hopes of salvation and life?

But now there is not one of them does ever groan, nor is there the least appearance of a tear in any of their faces.

O prince Satan, thou great keeper of the infernal regions, all thy advantages which thou didst acquire by the forbidden tree, and the loss of Paradise, thou hast now lost by the wood of the cross;

And thy happiness all then expired, when thou didst crucify Jesus Christ the King of Glory.

Thou hast acted against thine own interest and mine, as thou wilt presently perceive by those large torments and infinite punishments which thou art about to suffer.

O Satan, prince of all evil, author of death, and source of all pride, thou shouldest first have inquired into the evil crimes of Jesus of Nazareth, and then thou wouldest have found that he was guilty of no fault worthy of death.

Why didst thou venture, without either reason or justice, to crucify him, and hast brought down to our regions a person innocent and righteous, and thereby hast lost all the sinners, impious and unrighteous persons in the whole world?

While the prince of hell was thus speaking to Satan, the King of Glory said to Beelzebub, the prince of hell, Satan, the prince shall be subject to thy dominion for ever, in the room of Adam and his righteous sons, who are mine.

CHAPTER XIX.

Christ takes Adam by the hand, the rest of the saints join hands, and they all ascend with him to Paradise.

THEN Jesus stretched forth his hand, and said, Come to me, all ye my saints, who were created in my image, who were condemned by the tree of forbidden fruit, and by the devil and death;

Live now by the wood of my cross; the devil, the prince of this world, is overcome, and death is conquered.

Then presently all the saints were joined together under the hand of the most high God; and the Lord Jesus laid hold on Adam's hand and said to him, Peace be to thee, and all thy righteous posterity, which is mine.

Then Adam, casting himself at the feet of Jesus, addressed himself to him, with tears, in humble language, and a loud voice, saying,

I will extol thee, O Lord, for thou hast lifted me up, and hast not made my foes to rejoice over me. O Lord my God, I cried unto thee, and thou hast healed me.

O Lord thou hast brought up my soul from the grave; thou hast kept me alive, that I should not go down to the pit.

Sing unto the Lord, all ye saints of his, and give thanks at the remembrance of his holiness. For his anger endureth but for a moment; in his favour is life.

In like manner all the saints, prostrate at the feet of Jesus, said with one voice, Thou art come, O Redeemer of the world, and hast actually accomplished all things, which thou didst foretell by the law and thy holy prophets.

Thou hast redeemed the living by thy cross, and art come down to us, that by the death of the cross thou mightest deliver us from hell, and by thy power from death.

O, Lord, as thou hast put the ensigns of thy glory in heaven, and hast set up the sign of thy redemption, even thy cross on earth! so, Lord, set the sign of the victory of thy cross in hell, that death may have do minion no longer.

Then the Lord stretching forth his hand, made the sign of the cross upon Adam, and upon all his saints.

And taking hold of Adam by his right hand, he ascended from hell, and all the saints of God followed him.

Then the royal prophet David boldly cried, and said, O sing unto the Lord a new song, for he hath done marvellous things; his right hand and his holy arm have gotten him the victory.

The Lord hath made known his salvation, his righteousness hath he openly shewn in the sight of the heathen.

And the whole multitude of saints answered, saying, This honour have all his saints, Amen, Praise ye the Lord.

Afterwards, the prophet Habakkuk cried out, and said, Thou wentest forth for the salvation of thy people, even for the salvation of thy people.

And all the saints said, Blessed is he who cometh in the name of the Lord; for the Lord hath enlightened us. This is our God for ever and ever; he shall reign over us to everlasting ages, Amen.

In like manner all the prophets spake the sacred things of his praise, and followed the Lord.

CHAPTER XX.

Christ delivers Adam to Michael the archangel. They meet Enoch and Elijah in heaven, and also the blessed thief, who relates how he cares to Paradise.

THEN the Lord holding Adam by the hand, delivered him to Michael the archangel; and he led them into Paradise, filled with mercy and glory;

And two very ancient men met them, and were asked by the saints, Who are ye, who have not yet been with us in hell, and have had your bodies placed in Paradise?

One of them answering, said, I am Enoch, who was translated by the word of God: and this man who is with me, is Elijah the Tishbite, who was translated in a fiery chariot.

Here we have hitherto been, and have not tasted death, but are now about to return at the coming of Antichrist, being armed with divine signs and miracles, to engage with him in battle, and to be slain by him at Jerusalem, and to be taken up alive again into the clouds, after three days and a half.

And while the holy Enoch and Elias were relating this, behold there came another man in a miserable figure carrying the sign of the cross upon his shoulders.

And when all the saints saw him, they said to him, Who art thou? For thy countenance is like a thief's; and why dost thou carry a cross upon thy shoulders?

To which he answering, said, Ye say right, for I was a thief who committed all sorts of wickedness upon earth.

And the Jews crucified me with Jesus; and I observed the surprising things which happened in the creation at the crucifixion of the Lord Jesus.

And I believed him to be the Creator of all things, and the Almighty King; and I prayed to him, saying, Lord, remember me, when thou comest into thy kingdom.

He presently regarded my supplication, and said to me, Verily I say unto thee, this day thou shalt be with me in Paradise.

And he gave me this sign of the cross saying, Carry this, and go to Paradise; and if the angel who is the guard of Paradise will not admit thee, shew him the sign of the cross, and say unto him: Jesus Christ who is now crucified, hath sent me hither to thee.

When I did this, and told the angel who is the guard of Paradise all these things, and he heard them, he presently opened the gates, introduced me, and placed me on the right-hand in Paradise,

Saying, Stay here a little time, till Adam, the father of all mankind, shall enter in, with all his sons, who are the holy and righteous servants of Jesus Christ, who was crucified.

When they heard all this account from the thief, all the patriarchs said with one voice, Blessed be thou, O Almighty God, the Father of everlasting goodness, and the Father of mercies, who hast shewn such favour to those who were sinners against him, and hast brought them to the mercy of Paradise, and hast placed them amidst thy large and spiritual provisions, in a spiritual and holy life. Amen.

CHAPTER XXI.

Charinus and Lenthius being only allowed three days to remain on earth, deliver in their narratives, which miraculously correspond; they vanish, and Pilate records these transactions.

THESE are the divine and sacred mysteries which we saw and heard. I, Charinus and Lenthius are not allowed to declare the other mysteries of God, as the archangel Michael ordered us,

Saying, ye shall go with my brethren to Jerusalem, and shall continue in prayers, declaring and glorifying the resurrection of Jesus Christ, seeing he hath raised you from the dead at the same time with himself.

And ye shall not talk with any man, but sit as dumb persons till the time come when the Lord will allow you to relate the mysteries of his divinity.

The archangel Michael farther commanded us to go beyond Jordan, to an excellent and fat country, where there are many who rose from the dead along with us for the proof of the resurrection of Christ.

For we have only three days allowed us from the dead, who arose to celebrate the passover of our Lord with our parents, and to bear our testimony for Christ the Lord, and we have been baptized in the holy river of Jordan. And now they are not seen by any one.

This is as much as God allowed us to relate to you; give ye therefore praise and honour to him, and repent, and he will have mercy upon you. Peace be to you from the Lord God Jesus Christ, and the Saviour of us all. Amen, Amen, Amen.

And after they had made an end of writing and had wrote in two distinct pieces of paper, Charinus gave what he wrote into the hands of Annas, and Caiaphas, and Gamaliel.

Lenthius likewise gave what he wrote into the hands of Nicodemus and Joseph; and immediately they were changed into exceeding white forms and were seen no more.

But what they had wrote was found perfectly to agree, the one not containing one letter more or less than the other.

When all the assembly of the Jews heard all these surprising relations of Charinus and Lenthius, they said to each other, Truly all these things were wrought by God, and blessed be the Lord Jesus for ever and ever, Amen.

And they went about with great concern, and fear, and trembling, and smote upon their breasts and went away every one to his home.

But immediately all these things which were related by the Jews in their synagogues concerning Jesus, were presently told by Joseph and Nicodemus to the governor.

And Pilate wrote down all these transactions, and placed all these accounts in the public records of his hall.

CHAPTER XXII.

Pilate goes to the temple; calls together the rulers, and scribes, and doctors. Commands the gates to be shut; orders the book of the Scripture; and causes the Jews to relate what they really knew concerning Christ. They declare that they crucified Christ in ignorance, and that they now know him to be the Son of God, according to the testimony of the Scriptures; which, after they put him to death, they are examined.

AFTER these things Pilate went to the temple of the Jews, and called together all the rulers and scribes, and doctors of the law, and went with them into a chapel of the temple.

And commanding that all the gates should be shut, said to them, I have heard that ye have a certain large book in this temple; I desire you therefore, that it may be brought before me.

And when the great book, carried by four ministers of the temple, and adorned with gold and precious stones, was brought, Pilate said to them all, I adjure you by the God of your Fathers, who made and commanded this temple to be built, that ye conceal not the truth from me.

Ye know all the things which are written in that book; tell me therefore now, if ye in the Scriptures have found any thing of that Jesus whom ye crucified, and at what time of the world he ought to have come: shew it me.

Then having sworn Annas and Caiaphas, they commanded all the rest who were with them to go out of the chapel.

And they shut the gates of the temple and of the chapel, and said to Pilate, Thou hast made us to swear, O judge, by the building of this temple, to declare to thee that which is true and right.

After we had crucified Jesus, not knowing that he was the Son of God, but supposing he wrought his miracles by some magical arts, we summoned a large assembly in this temple.

And when we were deliberating among one another about the miracles which Jesus had wrought, we found many witnesses of our own country, who declared that they had seen him alive after his death, and that they heard him discoursing with his disciples, and saw him ascending unto the height of the heavens, and entering into them;

And we saw two witnesses, whose bodies Jesus raised from the dead, who told us of many strange things which Jesus did among the dead, of which we have a written account in our hands.

And it is our custom annually to open this holy book before an assembly, and to search there for the counsel of God.

And we found in the first of the seventy books, where Michael the archangel is speaking to the third son of Adam the first man, an account that after five thousand five hundred years, Christ the most beloved Son of God was come on earth,

And we further considered, that perhaps he was the very God of Israel who spoke to Moses, Thou shalt make the ark of the testimony; two cubits and a half shall be the length thereof, and a cubit and a half the breadth thereof, and a cubit and a half the height thereof.

By these five cubits and a half for the building of the ark of the Old Testament, we perceived and knew that in five thousand years and a half (one thousand) years, Jesus Christ was to come in the ark or tabernacle of a body;

And so our scriptures testify that he is the son of God, and the Lord and King of Israel.

And because after his suffering, our chief priests were surprised at the signs which were wrought by his means, we opened that book to search all the generations down to the generation of Joseph and Mary the mother of Jesus, supposing him to be of the seed of David;

And we found the account of the creation, and at what time he made the heaven and the earth and the first man Adam, and that from thence to the flood, were two thousand, two hundred and twelve years.

And from the flood to Abraham, nine hundred and twelve. And from Abraham to Moses, four hundred and thirty. And from Moses to David the king, five hundred and ten.

And from David to the Babylonish captivity, five hundred years. And from the Babylonish captivity to the incarnation of Christ, four hundred years.

The sum of all which amounts to five thousand and half (a thousand).

And so it appears, that Jesus whom we crucified, is Jesus Christ the Son of God, and true and Almighty God. Amen.

In the name of the Holy Trinity, thus end the Acts of our Saviour Jesus Christ, which the Emperor Theodosius the Great found at Jerusalem, in the hall of Pontius Pilate among the public records; the things were acted in the nineteenth year of Tiberius Caesar, Emperor of the Romans, and in the seventeenth year of the government of Herod the son of Herod king of Galilee, on the eighth of the calends of April, which is the twenty-third day of the month of March, in the CCIId Olympiad, when Joseph and Caiaphas were Rulers of the Jews; being a History written in Hebrew by Nicodemus, of what happened after our Saviour's crucifixion.

THE APOSTLES' CREED.

[It is affirmed by Ambrose "that the twelve Apostles, as skilful artificers assembled together, and made a key by their common advice, that is, the Creed; by which the darkness of the devil is disclosed, that the light of Christ may appear." Others fable that every Apostle inserted an article, by which the creed is divided into twelve articles; and a sermon, fathered upon St. Austin, and quoted by the Lord Chancellor King, fabricates that each particular article was thus inserted by each particular Apostle

"Peter.—1. I believe in God the Father Almighty;

"John.—2. Maker of heaven and earth;

"James.—3. And in Jesus Christ his only Son, our Lord;

"Andrew.—4. Who was conceived by the Holy Ghost, born of the Virgin Mary;

"Philip.—5. Suffered under Pontius Pilate, was crucified, dead and buried;

"Thomas.—6. He descended into hell, the third day he rose again from the dead;

"Bartholomew.—7. He ascended into heaven, sitteth at the right hand of God the Father Almighty;

"Matthew.—8. From thence he shall come to judge the quick and the dead;

"James, the son of Alpheus.—9. I believe in the Holy Ghost, the holy Catholic

THE LOST BOOKS OF THE BIBLE

Church;

"Simon Zelotes.—10. The communion of saints, the forgiveness of sins;

"Jude the brother of James.—11. The resurrection of the body;

"Matthias.—12. Life everlasting. Amen."

Archbishop WAKE says: "With respect to the Apostles being the authors of this Creed, it is not my intention to enter on any particular examination of this matter, which has been so fully handled, not only by the late critics of the Church of Rome, Natalia Alexander, Du Pin, &c., but yet more especially by Archbishop Usher, Gerard Vossius, Suicer, Spanhemius, Tentzelius, and Sam. Basnage, among the Protestants. It shall suffice to say, that as it is not likely, that had any such thing as this been done by the Apostles, St. Luke would have passed it by, without taking the least notice of it: so the diversity of Creeds in the ancient Church, and that not only in expression, but in some whole Articles too, sufficiently shows, that the Creed which we call by that name, was not composed by the twelve Apostles, much less in the same form in which it now is."

Mr. Justice BAILEY says: "It is not to be understood that this Creed was framed by the Apostles, or indeed that it existed as a Creed in their time;" and after giving the Creed as it existed in the year 600, and which is here copied from his Common Prayer Book, he says, "how long this form had existed before the year 600 is not exactly known. The additions were probably made in opposition to particular heresies and errors."

The most important "addition," since the year of Christ 600, is that which affirms, that Christ descended into hell. This has been proved not only to have been an invention after the Apostles' time, but even after the time of Eusebius. Bishop Pearson says, that the descent into hell was not in the ancient creeds or rules of faith. "It is not to be found in the rules of faith delivered by Irenaeus, by Origen, or by Tertullian. It is not expressed in those creeds which were made by the councils as larger explications of the Apostles' Creed; not in the Nicene, or Constantinopolitan; not in those of Ephesus, or Chalcedon; not in those confessions made at Sardica, Antioch, Selucia, Sirmium, &c. It is not mentioned in several confessions of faith delivered by particular persons; not in that of Eusebius Caesariensis, presented to the council of Nice; not in that of Marcellus, bishop of Ancyra, delivered to Pope Julius; not in that of Arius and Euzoius, presented to Constantine; not in that of Acacius, bishop of Caesarea, delivered into the synod of Selucia; not in that of Eustathius, Theophilus, and Sylvanus, sent to Liberius; there is no mention of it in the creed of St. Basil; in the creed of Epiphanus, Gelasius, Damascus, Macarius, &c. It is not in the creed expounded by St. Cyril, though some have produced that creed to prove it. It is not in the creed expounded by St. Augustine; not in that other, attributed to St. Augustine in another place; not in that expounded by Maximus Taurinensis; nor in that so often interpreted by Petrus Chrysologus; nor in that of the church of Antioch, delivered by Cassianus; neither is it to be seen in the MS. creeds set forth by the learned Archbishop of Armagh. It is affirmed by Ruffinus, that in his time it was neither in the Roman nor the Oriental Creeds."

As it stood An. Dom. 600. Copied from Mr. Justice Bailey's Edition of the book of

Common Prayer.

"Before the year 600, it was no more than this."—MR. JUSTICE BAILEY. p. 9 n.

1 I BELIEVE in God the Father Almighty:

2 And in Jesus Christ his only begotten Son, our Lord;

3 Who was born of the Holy Ghost and Virgin Mary,

4 And was crucified under Pontius Pilate, and was buried;

5 And the third day rose again from the dead.

6 Ascended into heaven, sitteth on the right hand of the Father;

7 Whence he shall come to judge the quick and the dead;

8 And in the Holy Ghost;

9 The Holy Church;

10 The remission of sins;

11 And the resurrection of the flesh, Amen.

As it stands in the book of Common Prayer of the United Church of England and Ireland as by law established.

1 I BELIEVE in God the Father Almighty, maker of heaven and earth:

2 And in Jesus Christ his only Son, our Lord:

3 Who was conceived by the Holy Ghost, born of the Virgin Mary,

4 Suffered under Pontius Pilate, was crucified, dead and buried;

5 He descended into hell;

6 The third day he rose again from the dead;

7 He ascended into heaven, and sitteth on the right hand of God the Father Almighty;

8 From thence he shall come to judge the quick and the dead.

9 I believe in the Holy Ghost;

10 The holy Catholic Church; the communion of saints;

11 The forgiveness of sins;

12 The resurrection of the body and the life everlasting, Amen.

THE EPISTLE OF PAUL THE APOSTLE TO THE LAODICEANS.

[This Epistle has been highly esteemed by several learned men of the church of

Rome and others. The Quakers have printed a translation and plead for it, as the reader may see, by consulting Poole's Annotations on Col. vi. 16. Sixtus Senensis mentions two MSS., the one in the Sorbonne Library at Paris, which is a very ancient copy, and the other in the Library of Joannes a Viridario, at Padua, which he transcribed and published, and which is the authority for the following translation. There is a very old translation of this Epistle in the British Museum, among the Harleian MSS., Cod. 1212.]

He salutes the brethren. exhorts them to persevere in good works, and not to be moved by vain speaking. Rejoices in his bonds, desires them to live in the fear of the Lord.

PAUL an Apostle, not of men, neither by man, but by Jesus Christ, to the brethren which are at Laodicea.

Grace be to you, and Peace, from God the Father and our Lord Jesus Christ.

I thank Christ in every prayer of mine, that ye may continue and persevere in good works looking for that which is promised in the day of judgment.

Let not the vain speeches of any trouble you who pervert the truth, that they may draw you aside from the truth of the Gospel which I have preached.

And now may God grant, that my converts may attain to a perfect knowledge of the truth of the Gospel, be beneficent, and doing good works which accompany salvation.

And now my bonds, which I suffer in Christ, are manifest, in which I rejoice and am glad.

For I know that this shall turn to my salvation for ever, which shall be through your prayer, and the supply of the Holy Spirit.

Whether I live or die; (for) to me to live shall be a life to Christ, to die will be joy.

And our Lord will grant us his mercy, that ye may have the same love, and be like-minded.

Wherefore, my beloved, as ye have heard of the coming of the Lord, so think and act in fear, and it shall be to you life eternal;

For it is God who worketh in you;

And do all things without sin.

And what is best, my beloved, rejoice in the Lord Jesus Christ, and avoid all filthy lucre.

Let all your requests be made known to God, and be steady in the doctrine of Christ.

And whatsoever things are sound and true, and of good report, and chaste, and just, and lovely, these things do.

Those things which ye have heard, and received, think on these things, and peace shall be with you.

All the saints salute you.

The grace of our Lord Jesus Christ be with your spirit. Amen.

Cause this Epistle to be read to the Colossians, and the Epistle of the Colossians to be read among you.

THE EPISTLES OF PAUL THE APOSTLE TO SENECA, WITH SENECA'S TO PAUL.

[Several very learned writers have entertained a favourable opinion of these Epistles. They are undoubtedly of high antiquity. Salmeron cites them to prove that Seneca was one of Car's household, referred to by Paul, Philip. iv. 22, as saluting the brethren at Philippi. In Jerome's enumeration of illustrious men, he places Seneca, on account of these Epistles, amongst the ecclesiastical and holy writers of the Christian Church. Sixtus Senensis has published them in his Bibliotheque, pp. 89, 90; and it is from thence that the present translation is made. Baronius, Bellarmine, Dr. Cave, Spanheim, and others, contend that they are not genuine.]

CHAPTER I.

ANNAEUS SENECA TO PAUL GREETING.

I SUPPOSE, Paul, you have been informed of that conversation, which passed yesterday between me and my Lucilius, concerning hypocrisy and other subjects; for there were some of your disciples in company with us;

For when we were retired into the Sallustian gardens, through which they were also passing, and would have gone another way, by our persuasion they joined company with us.

I desire you to believe, that we much wish for your conversation:

We were much delighted with your book of many Epistles, which you have wrote to some cities and chief towns of provinces, and contain wonderful instructions for moral conduct:

Such sentiments, as I suppose you were not the author of, but only the instrument of conveying, though sometimes both the author and the instrument.

For such is the sublimity of those doctrines, and their grandeur, that I suppose the age of a man is scarce sufficient to be instructed and perfected in the knowledge of them. I wish your welfare, my brother. Farewell.

CHAPTER II.

PAUL TO SENECA GREETING.

I RECEIVED your letter yesterday with pleasure: to which I could immediately have wrote an answer, had the young man been at home, whom I intended to have sent to you:

For you know when, and by whom, at what seasons, and to whom I must deliver every thing which I send.

I desire therefore you would not charge me with negligence, if I wait for a proper person.

I reckon myself very happy in having the judgment of so valuable a person, that you are delighted with my Epistles:

For you would not be esteemed a censor, a philosopher, or be the tutor of so great a prince, and a master of every thing, if you were not sincere. I wish you a lasting prosperity.

CHAPTER III.

ANNAEUS SENECA TO PAUL GREETING.

I HAVE completed some volumes, and divided them into their proper parts.

I am determined to read them to Caesar, and if any favourable opportunity happens, you also shall be present, when they are read;

But if that cannot be, I will appoint and give you notice of a day, when we will together read over the performance.

I had determined, if I could with safety, first to have your opinion of it, before I published it to Caesar, that you might be convinced of my affection to you. Farewell, dearest Paul.

CHAPTER IV.

PAUL TO SENECA GREETING.

AS often as I read your letters, I imagine you present with me; nor indeed do I think any other, than that you are always with us.

As soon therefore as you begin to come, we shall presently see each other. I wish you all prosperity.

CHAPTER V.

ANNAEUS SENECA TO PAUL GREETING.

WE are very much concerned at your too long absence from us.

2 What is it, or what affairs are they, which obstruct your coming?

3 If you fear the anger of Caesar, because you have your former religion, and made proselytes also of others, you have this to plead, that your acting thus proceeded not from inconstancy, but judgment. Farewell.

CHAPTER VI.

PAUL TO SENECA AND LUCILIUS GREETING.

CONCERNING those things about which ye wrote to me it is not proper for me to mention anything in writing with pen and ink: the one of which leaves marks, and the other evidently declares things.

Especially since I know that there are near you, as well as me, those who will understand my meaning.

Deference is to be paid to all men, and so much the more, as they are more likely to take occasions of quarrelling.

And if we show a submissive temper, we shall overcome effectually in all points, if so be they are, who are capable of seeing and acknowledging themselves to have been in the wrong. Farewell.

CHAPTER VII.

ANNAEUS SENECA TO PAUL GREETING.

I PROFESS myself extremely pleased with the reading your letters to the Galatians, Corinthians, and people of Achaia.

For the Holy Ghost has in them by you delivered those sentiments which are very lofty, sublime, deserving of all respect, and beyond your own invention.

I could wish therefore, that when you are writing things so extraordinary, there might not be wanting an elegancy of speech agreeable to their majesty.

And I must own my brother, that I may not at once dishonestly conceal anything from you, and be unfaithful to my own conscience, that the emperor is extremely pleased with the sentiments of your Epistles;

For when he heard the beginning of them read, he declared, That he was surprised to find such notions in a person, who had not had a regular education.

To which I replied, That the Gods sometimes made use of mean (innocent) persons to speak by, and gave him an instance of this in a mean countryman, named Vatienus, who, when he was in the country of Reate, had two men appeared to him, called Castor and Pollux, and received a revelation from the gods. Farewell.

CHAPTER VIII.

PAUL TO SENECA GREETING.

ALTHOUGH I know the emperor is both an admirer and favourer of our (religion), yet give me leave to advise you against your suffering any injury, (by shewing favour to us.)

I think indeed you ventured upon a very dangerous attempt, when you would declare to the emperor) that which is so very contrary to his religion, and way of worship; seeing he is a worshipper of the heathen gods.

THE LOST BOOKS OF THE BIBLE

I know not what you particularly had in view, when you told him of this; but I suppose you did it out of too great respect for me.

But I desire that for the future you would not do so; for you had need be careful, lest by shewing your affection for me, you should offend your master:

His anger indeed will do us no harm, if he continue a heathen; nor will his not being angry be of any service to us:

And if the empress act worthy of her character, she will not be angry; but if she acts as a woman, she will be affronted. Farewell.

CHAPTER IX.

ANNAEUS SENECA TO PAUL GREETING.

I KNOW that my letter, wherein I acquainted you, that I had read to the Emperor your Epistles, does not so much affect of as the nature of the things (contained in them),

Which do so powerfully divert men's minds from their former manners and practices, that I have always been surprised, and have been fully convinced of it by many arguments heretofore.

Let us therefore begin afresh; and if any thing heretofore has been imprudently acted, do you forgive.

I have sent you a book de copia verborum. Farewell, dearest Paul.

CHAPTER X.

PAUL TO SENECA GREETING.

AS often as I write to you, and place my name before yours, I do a thing both disagreeable to myself; and contrary to our religion:

For I ought, as I have often declared, to become all things to all men, and to have that regard to your quality, which the Roman law has honoured all senators with; namely, to put my name last in the (inscription of the) Epistle, that I may not at length with uneasiness and shame be obliged to do that which it was always my inclination to do. Farewell, most respected master. Dated the fifth of the calends of July, in the fourth consulship of Nero, and Messala.

CHAPTER XI.

ANNAEUS SENECA TO PAUL GREETING.

ALL happiness to you, my dearest Paul.

If a person so great, and every way agreeable as you are, become not only a common, but a most intimate friend to me, how happy will be the case of Seneca!

You therefore, who are so eminent, and so far exalted above all, even the greatest, do not think yourself unfit to be first named in the inscription of an Epistle;

Lest I should suspect you intend not so much to try me, as to banter me; for you know yourself to be a Roman citizen.

And I could wish to be in that circumstance or station which you are, and that you were in the same that I am. Farewell, dearest Paul. Dated the xth of the calends of April, in the consulship of Aprianus and Capito.

CHAPTER XII.

ANNAEUS SENECA TO PAUL GREETING.

ALL happiness to you, my dearest Paul. Do you not suppose I am extremely concerned and grieved that your innocence should bring you into sufferings?

And that all the people should suppose you (Christians) so criminal, and imagine all the misfortunes that happen to the city, to be caused by you?

But let us bear the charge with a patient temper, appealing (for our innocence) to the court (above), which is the only one our hard fortune will allow us to address to, till at length our misfortunes shall end in unalterable happiness.

Former ages have produced (tyrants) Alexander the son of Philip, and Dionysius; ours also has produced Caius Caesar; whose inclinations were their only laws.

As to the frequent burnings of the city of Rome, the cause is manifest; and if a person in my mean circumstances might be allowed to speak, and one might declare these dark things without danger, every one should see the whole of the matter.

The Christians and Jews are indeed commonly punished for the crime of burning the city; but that impious miscreant, who delights in murders and butcheries, and disguises his villanies with lies, is appointed to, or reserved till, his proper time.

And as the life of every excellent person is now sacrificed instead of that one person (who is the author of the mischief), so this one shall be sacrificed for many, and he shall be devoted to be burnt with fire instead of all.

One hundred and thirty-two houses, and four whole squares (or islands) were burnt down in six days: the seventh put an end to the burning. I wish you all happiness.

Dated the fifth of the calends of April, in the consulship of Frigius and Bassus.

CHAPTER XIII.

ANNAEUS SENECA TO PAUL GREETING.

ALL happiness to you, my dearest Paul.

You have wrote many volumes in an allegorical and mystical style, and therefore such mighty matters and business being committed to you, require not to be set off with any rhetorical flourishes of speech, but only with some proper elegance.

I remember you often say, that many by affecting such a style do injury to their subjects, and lose the force of the matters they treat of.

But in this I desire you to regard me, namely, to have respect to true Latin, and to choose just words, that so you may the better manage the noble trust which is reposed in you.

Farewell. Dated with of the names of July, Leo and Savinus consuls.

CHAPTER XIV.

PAUL TO SENECA GREETING.

YOUR serious consideration requited with these discoveries, which the Divine Being has granted but to few.

I am thereby assured that I sow the most strong seed in a fertile soil, not anything material, which is subject to corruption, but the durable word of God, which shall increase and bring forth fruit to eternity.

That which by your wisdom you have attained to, shall abide without decay for ever.

Believe that you ought to avoid the superstitions of Jews and Gentiles.

The things which you have in some measure arrived to, prudently make known to the emperor, his family, and to faithful friends;

And though your sentiments will seem disagreeable, and not be comprehended by them, seeing most of them will not regard your discourses, yet the Word of God once infused into them, will at length make them become new men, aspiring towards God.

Farewell Seneca, who art most dear to us. Dated on the Calends of August, in the consulship of Leo and Savinus.

THE ACTS OF PAUL AND THECLA.

[Tertullian says that this piece was forged by a Presbyter of Asia, who being convicted, "confessed that he did it out of respect of Paul," and Pope Gelasius, in his Decree against apocryphal books, inserted it among them. Notwithstanding this, a large part of the history was credited, and looked upon as genuine among the primitive Christians. Cyprian, Eusebius, Epiphanius, Austin, Gregory Nazianzen, Chrysostom, and Severus Sulpitius, who all lived within the fourth century, mention Thecla, or refer to her history. Basil of Seleucia wrote her acts, sufferings, and victories, in verse; and Euagrius Scholasticus, an ecclesiastical historian, about 590, relates that "after the Emperor Zeno had abdicated his empire, and Basilik had taken possession of it, he had a vision of the holy and excellent martyr Thecla, who promised him the restoration of his empire; for which, when it was brought about, he erected and dedicated a most noble and sumptuous temple to this famous martyr Thecla, at Seleucia, a city of Isauria, and bestowed upon it very noble endowments, which (says the author) are preserved even till this day." Hist. Eccl., lib. 3, cap. 8.—Cardinal Baronius, Locrinus, Archbishop Wake, and others; and also the learned Grabe, who edited the Septuagint, and revived the Acts of Paul and Thecla, consider them as having been written in the Apostolic age; as containing nothing superstitious, or disagreeing from the opinions and belief of those times; and, in short, as a genuine and authentic history. Again, it is said, that this is not the original book of the early Christians; but however that may be, it is published from the Greek MS. in the Bodleian Library at Oxford, which Dr. Mills copied and transmitted to Dr. Grabe.]

THE MARTYRDOM OF THE HOLY AND GLORIOUS FIRST MARTYR AND APOSTLE THECLA.

CHAPTER I.

Demas and Hermogenes become Paul's companions. Paul visits Onesiphorus. Invited by Demas and Hermogenes. Preaches to the household of Onesiphorus. His sermon.

WHEN Paul went up to Iconium, after his flight from Antioch, Demas and Hermogenes became his companions, who were then full of hypocrisy.

But Paul looking only at the goodness of God, did them no harm, but loved them greatly.

Accordingly he endeavoured to make agreeable to them, all the oracles and doctrines of Christ, and the design of the Gospel of God's well-beloved Son, instructing them in the knowledge of Christ, as it was revealed to him.

And a certain man named Onesiphorus, hearing that Paul was come to Iconium, went out speedily to meet him, together with his wife Lectra, and his sons Simmia and Zeno, to invite him to their house.

For Titus had given them a description of Paul's personage, they as yet not knowing him in person, but only being acquainted with his character.

They went in the king's highway to Lystra, and stood there waiting for him, comparing all who passed by, with that description which Titus had given them.

At length they saw a man coming (namely Paul), of a low stature, bald (or shaved) on the head, crooked thighs, handsome legs, hollow-eyed; had a crooked nose; full of grace; for sometimes he appeared as a man, sometimes he had the countenance of an angel. And Paul saw Onesiphorus, and was glad.

And Onesiphorus said: Hail, thou servant of the blessed God. Paul replied, The grace of God be with thee and thy family.

But Demos and Hermogenes were moved with envy, and, under a show of great religion, Demas said, And are not we also servants of the blessed God? Why didst thou not salute us?

Onesiphorus replied, Because I have not perceived in, you the fruits of righteousness; nevertheless, if ye are of that sort, ye shall be welcome to my house also.

Then Paul went into the house of Onesiphorus, and there was great joy among the family on that account: and they employed themselves in prayer, breaking of bread, and hearing Paul preach the word of God concerning temperance and the resurrection, in

THE LOST BOOKS OF THE BIBLE

the following manner:

Blessed are the pure in heart; for they shall see God.

Blessed are they who keep their flesh undefiled (or pure); for they shall be the temple of God.

Blessed are the temperate (or chaste); for God will reveal himself to them.

Blessed are they who abandon their secular enjoyments; for they shall be accepted of God.

Blessed are they who have wives, as though they had them not; for they shall be made angels of God.

Blessed are they who tremble at the word of God; for they shall be comforted.

Blessed are they who keep their baptism pure; for they shall find peace with the Father, Son, and Holy Ghost.

Blessed are they who pursue the wisdom (or doctrine) of Jesus Christ; for they shall be called the sons of the Most High.

Blessed are they who observe the instructions of Jesus Christ; for they shall dwell in eternal light.

Blessed are they, who for the love of Christ abandon the glories of the world; for they shall judge angels, and be placed at the right hand of Christ, and shall not suffer the bitterness of the last judgment.

Blessed are the bodies and souls of virgins; for they are acceptable to God, and shall not lose the reward of their virginity; for the word of their (heavenly) Father shall prove effectual to their salvation in the day of his Son, and they shall enjoy rest for evermore.

CHAPTER II.

Thecla listens anxiously to Paul's preaching. Thamyris, her admirer, concerts with Theoclia her mother to dissuade her, in vain. Demos and Hermogenes deliver Paul to Thamyria.

WHILE Paul was preaching this sermon in the church which was in the house of Onesiphorus, a certain virgin, named Thecla (whose mother's name was Theoclia, and who was betrothed to a man named Thamyris) sat at a certain window in her house.

From whence, by the advantage of a window in the house where Paul was, she both night and day heard Paul's sermons concerning God, concerning charity, concerning faith in Christ, and concerning prayer;

Nor would she depart from the window, till with exceeding joy she was subdued to the doctrines of faith.

At length, when she saw many women and virgins going in to Paul, she earnestly desired that she might be thought worthy to appear in his presence, and hear the word of Christ; for she had not yet seen Paul's person, but only heard his sermons, and that alone.

But when she would not be prevailed upon to depart from the window, her mother sent to Thamyris, who came with the greatest pleasure, as hoping now to marry her. Accordingly he said to Theoclia, Where is my Thecla?

Theoclia replied, Thamyris, I have something very strange to tell you; for Thecla, for the space of three days, will not move from the window not so much as to eat or drink, but is so intent in hearing the artful and delusive discourses of a certain foreigner, that I perfectly admire, Thamyris, that a young woman of her known modesty, will suffer herself to be so prevailed upon.

For that man has disturbed the whole city of Iconium, and even your Thecla, among others, All the women and young men flock to him to receive his doctrine; who, besides all the rest, tells them that there is but one God, who alone is to be worshipped, and that we ought to live in chastity.

Notwithstanding this, my daughter Thecla, like a spider's web fastened to the window, is captivated by the discourses of Paul, and attends upon them with prodigious eagerness, and vast delight; and thus, by attending on what he says, the young woman is seduced. Now then do you go, and speak to her, for she is betrothed to you.

Accordingly Thamyris went, and having saluted her, and taking care not to surprise her, he said, Thecla, my spouse, why sittest thou in this melancholy posture? What strange impressions are made upon thee? Turn to Thamyris, and blush.

Her mother also spake to her after the same manner, and said, Child, why dost thou sit so melancholy, and, like one astonished, makest no reply?

Then they wept exceedingly, Thamyria, that he had lost his spouse; Theoclia, that she had lost her daughter; and the maids, that they had lost their mistress; and there was an universal mourning in the family.

But all these things made no impression upon Thecla, so as to incline her so much as to turn to them, and take notice of them; for she still regarded the discourses of Paul.

Then Thamyris ran forth into the street to observe who they were who went into Paul, and came out from him; and he saw two men engaged in a very warm dispute, and said to them;

Sirs, what business have you here? and who is that man within, belonging to you, who deludes the minds of men, both young men and virgins, persuading them, that they ought not to marry, but continue as they are?

I promise to give you a considerable sum, if you will give me a just account of him; for I am the chief person of this city.

Demas and Hermogenes replied, We cannot so exactly tell who he is; but this we know, that he deprives young men of their (intended) wives, and virgins of their (intended) husbands, by teaching, There can be no future resurrection, unless ye continue in chastity, and do not defile your flesh.

CHAPTER III.

They betray Paul. Thamyris arrests him with officers.

THEN said Thamyris, Come along with me to my house, and refresh yourselves. So they went to a very splendid entertainment, where there was wine in abundance, and very rich provision.

They were brought to a table richly spread, and made to drink plentifully by Thamyris, on account of the love he had for Thecla and his desire to marry her.

Then Thamyris said, I desire ye would inform me what the doctrines of this Paul are, that I may understand them; for I am under no small concern about Thecla, seeing she so delights in that stranger's discourses, that I am in danger of losing my intended wife.

Then Demas and Hermogenes answered both together, and said, Let him be brought before the governor Castellius, as one who endeavours to persuade the people into the new religion of the Christians, and he, according to the order of Caesar, will put him to death, by which means you will obtain your wife;

While we at the same time will teach her, that the resurrection which he speaks of is already come, and consists in our having children; and that we then arose again, when we came to the knowledge of God.

Thamyris having this account from them, was filled with hot resentment:

And rising early in the morning he went to the house of Onesiphorus, attended by the magistrates, the jailor, and a great multitude of people with staves, and said to Paul;

Thou hast perverted the city of Iconium, and among the rest, Thecla, who is betrothed to me, so that now she will not marry me. Thou shalt therefore go with us to the governor Castellius.

And all the multitude cried out, Away with this impostor (magician), for he has perverted the minds of our wives, and all the people hearken to him.

CHAPTER IV.

Paul accused before the governor by Thamyris. Defends himself. Is committed to Prison, and visited by Thecla.

THEN Thamyris standing before the governor's judgment-seat, spake with a loud voice in the following manner.

O governor, I know not whence this man cometh; but he is one who teaches that matrimony is unlawful. Command him therefore to declare before you for what reason he publishes such doctrines.

While he was saying thus, Demas and Hermogenes (whispered to Thamyris, and) said; Say that he is a Christian, and he will presently be put to death.

But the governor was more deliberate, and calling to Paul, he said, Who art thou? What dost thou teach? They seem to lay gross crimes to thy charge.

Paul then spake with a loud voice, saying, As I am now called to give an account, O governor, of my doctrines, I desire your audience.

That God, who is a God of vengeance, and who stands in need of nothing but the salvation of his creatures, has sent me to reclaim them from their wickedness and corruptions, from all (sinful) pleasures, and from death; and to persuade them to sin no more.

On this account, God sent his Son Jesus Christ, whom I preach, and in whom I instruct men to place their hopes as that l person who only had such compassion on the deluded world, that it might not, O governor, be condemned, but have faith, the fear of God, the knowledge of religion, and the love of truth.

So that if I only teach those things which I have received by revelation from God, where is my crime?

When the governor heard this, he ordered Paul to be bound, and to be put in prison, till he should be more at leisure to hear him more fully.

But in the night, Thecla taking off her ear-rings, gave them to the turnkey of the prison, who then opened the doors to her, and let her in;

And when she made a present of a silver looking-glass to the jailor, was allowed to go into the room where Paul was; then she sat down at his feet, and heard from him the great things of God.

And as she perceived Paul not to be afraid of suffering, but that by divine assistance he behaved himself with courage, her faith so far increased that she kissed his chains.

CHAPTER V.

Thecla sought and found by her relations. Brought with Paul before the governor. Ordered to be burnt, and Paul to be whipt. Thecla miraculously saved.

AT length Thecla was missed, and sought for by the family and by Thamyris in every street, as though she had been lost, but one of the porter's fellow-servants told them, that she had gone out in the night-time.

Then they examined the porter, and he told them, that she was gone to the prison to the strange man.

They went therefore according to his direction, and there found her; and when they came out, they got a mob together, and went and told the governor all that happened.

Upon which he ordered Paul to be brought before his judgment seat.

Thecla in the mean time lay wallowing on the ground in the prison, in that same place where Paul had sat to teach her; upon which the governor also ordered her to be brought before his judgment-seat; which summons she received with joy, and went.

When Paul was brought thither, the mob with more vehemence cried out, He is a magician, let him die.

Nevertheless the governor attended with pleasure upon Paul's discourses of the holy works of Christ; and, after a council called, he summoned Thecla, and said to her, Why do you not, according to the law of the Iconians, marry Thamyris?

She stood still, with her eyes fixed upon Paul; and finding she made no reply, Theoclia, her mother, cried out, saying, Let the unjust creature be burnt; let her be burnt in the midst of the theatre, for refusing Thamyris, that all women may learn from her to avoid such practices.

Then the governor was exceedingly concerned, and ordered Paul to be whipt out of the city, and Thecla to be burnt.

So the governor arose, and went immediately into the theatre; and all the people went forth to see the dismal sight.

But Thecla, just as a lamb in the wilderness looks every way to see his shepherd, looked around for Paul;

And as she was looking upon the multitude, she saw the Lord Jesus in the likeness of Paul, and said to herself, Paul is come to see me in my distressed circumstances. And she fixed her eyes upon him; but he instantly ascended up to heaven, while she looked on him.

Then the young men and women brought wood and straw for the burning of Thecla; who, being brought naked to the stake, extorted tears from the governor, with surprise beholding the greatness of her beauty.

And when they had placed the wood in order, the people commanded her to go upon it; which she did, first making the sign of the cross.

Then the people set fire to the pile; though the flame was exceeding large, it did not touch her, for God took compassion on her, and caused a great eruption from the earth beneath, and a cloud from above to pour down great quantities of rain and hail;

Insomuch that by the rupture of the earth, very many were in great danger, and some were killed, the fire was extinguished, and Thecla preserved.

CHAPTER VI.

Paul with Onesiphorus in a cave. Thecla discovers Paul; proffers to follow him: he exhorts her not for fear of fornication.

IN the mean time Paul, together with Onesiphorus, his wife and children, was keeping a fast in a certain cave, which was in the road from Iconium to Daphne.

THE LOST BOOKS OF THE BIBLE

And when they had fasted for several days, the children said to Paul, Father, we are hungry, and have not wherewithal to buy bread; for Onesiphorus had left all his substance to follow Paul with his family.

Then Paul, taking off his coat, said to the boy, Go, child, and buy bread, and bring it hither.

But while the boy was buying the bread, he saw his neighbour Thecla and was surprised, and said to her. Thecla, where are you going?

She replied, I am in pursuit of Paul, having been delivered from the flames.

The boy then said, I will bring you to him, for he is under great concern on your account, and has been in prayer and fasting these six days.

When Thecla came to the cave, she found Paul upon his knees praying and saying, O holy Father, O Lord Jesus Christ, grant that the fire may not touch Thecla; but be her helper, for she is thy servant.

Thecla then standing behind him, cried out in the following words: O sovereign Lord, Creator of heaven and earth, the Father of thy beloved and holy Son, I praise thee that thou hast preserved me from the fire, to see Paul again.

Paul then arose, and when he saw her, said, O God, who searchest the heart, Father of my Lord Jesus Christ, I praise thee that thou hast answered my prayer.

And there prevailed among them in the cave an entire affection to each other; Paul, Onesiphorus, and all that were with them being filled with joy.

They had five loaves, some herbs and water, and they solaced each other in reflections upon the holy works of Christ.

Then said Thecla to Paul, If you be pleased with it, I will follow you whithersoever you go.

He replied to her, Persons are now much given to fornication, and you being handsome, I am afraid lest you should meet with greater temptation than the former, and should not withstand, but be overcome by it.

Thecla replied, Grant me only the seal of Christ, and no temptation shall affect me.

Paul answered, Thecla, wait with patience, and you shall receive the gift of Christ.

CHAPTER VII.

Paul and Thecla go to Antioch. Alexander, a magistrate, falls in love with Thecla: kisses her by force: she resists him: is carried before the governor, and condemned to be thrown to wild beasts.

THEN Paul sent back Onesiphorus and his family to their own home, and taking Thecla along with him, went for Antioch;

101

And as soon as they came into the city, a certain Syrian, named Alexander, a magistrate, in the city, who had done many considerable services for the city during his magistracy, saw Thecla and fell in love with her, and endeavoured by many rich presents to engage Paul in his interest.

But Paul told him, I know not the woman of whom you speak, nor does she belong to me.

But he being a person of great power in Antioch, seized her in the street and kissed her; which Thecla would not bear, but looking about for Paul, cried out in a distressed loud tone, Force me not, who am a stranger; force me not, who am a servant of God; I am one of the principal persons of Iconium, and was obliged to leave that city because I would not be married to Thamyris.

Then she laid hold on Alexander, tore his coat, and took his crown off his head, and made him appear ridiculous before all the people.

But Alexander, partly as he loved her, and partly being ashamed of what had been done, led her to the governor, and upon her confession of what she had done,' he condemned her to be thrown among the beasts.

CHAPTER VIII.

Thecla entertained by Trifina; brought out to the wild beasts; a she-lion licks her feet. Trifina upon a vision of her deceased daughter, adopts Thecla, who is taken to the amphitheatre again.

WHICH when the people saw, they said: The judgments passed in this city are unjust. But Thecla desired the favour of the governor, that her chastity might not be attacked, but preserved till she should be cast to the beasts.

The governor then inquired, Who would entertain her; upon which a certain very rich widow, named Trifina, whose daughter was lately dead, desired that she might have the keeping of her; and she began to treat her in her house as her own daughter.

At length a day came, when the beasts were to be brought forth to be seen; and Thecla was brought to the amphitheatre, and put into a den in which was an exceeding fierce she-lion, in the presence of a multitude of spectators.

Trifina, without any surprise, accompanied Thecla, and the she-lion licked the feet of Thecla. The title written which denotes her crime, was, Sacrilege. Then the woman cried out, O God, the judgments of this city are unrighteous.

After the beasts had been shewn, Trifina took Thecla home with her, and they went to bed; and behold, the daughter of Trifina, who was dead, appeared to her mother, and said; Mother, let the young woman, Thecla, be reputed by you as your daughter in my stead; and desire her that she should pray for me, that I may be translated to a state of happiness.

Upon which Trifina, with a mournful air, said, My daughter Falconilla has appeared to me, and ordered me to receive you in her room; wherefore I desire, Thecla, that you would pray for my daughter, that she may be translated into a state of happiness, and to life eternal.

When Thecla heard this, she immediately prayed to the Lord, and said: O Lord God of heaven and earth, Jesus Christ, thou Son of the Most High, grant that her daughter Falconilla may live forever. Trifina hearing this groaned again, and said: O unrighteous judgments! O unreasonable wickedness! that such a creature should (again) be cast to the beasts!

On the morrow, at break of day, Alexander came to Trifina's house, and said: The governor and the people are waiting; bring the criminal forth.

But Trifina ran in so violently upon him, that he was affrighted, and ran away. Trifina was one of the royal family; and she thus expressed her sorrow, and said; Alas! I have trouble in my house' on two accounts, and there is no one who will relieve me, either under the loss of my daughter, or my being unable to save Thecla. But now, O Lord God, be thou the helper of Thecla thy servant.

While she was thus engaged, the governor sent one of his own officers to bring Thecla. Trifina took her by the hand, and, going with her, said: I went with Falconilla to her grave, and. now must go with Thecla to the beasts.

When Thecla heard this, she weeping prayed, and said: O Lord God, whom I have made my confidence and refuge, reward Trifina for her compassion to me, and preserving my chastity.

Upon this there was a great noise in the amphitheatre; the beasts roared, and the people cried out, Bring in the criminal.

But the woman cried out, and said: Let the whole city suffer for such crimes; and order all of us, O governor, to the same punishment. O unjust judgment! O cruel sight!

Others said, Let the whole city be destroyed for this vile action. Kill us all, O governor. O cruel sight! O unrighteous judgment.

CHAPTER IX.

Thecla thrown naked to the wild beasts; they all refuse to attack her; throws herself into a pit of water. other wild beasts refuse her. Tied to wild bulls. Miraculously saved. Released. Entertained by Trifina.

THEN Thecla was taken out of the hand of Trifina, stripped naked, had a girdle put on, and thrown into the place appointed for fighting with the beasts: and the lions and the bears were let loose upon her.

But a she-lion, which was of all the most fierce, ran to Thecla, and fell down at her feet. Upon which the multitude of women shouted aloud.

Then a she-bear ran fiercely towards her; but the she-lion met the bear, and tore it to pieces.

Again, a he-lion, who had been wont to devour men, and which belonged to

Alexander, ran towards her; but the she-lion encountered the he-lion, and they killed each other.

Then the women were under a greater concern, because the she-lion, which had helped Thecla, was dead.

Afterwards they brought out many other wild beasts; but Thecla stood with her hands stretched towards heaven, and prayed; and when she had done praying, she turned about, and saw a pit of water, and said, Now it is a proper time for me to be baptized.

Accordingly she threw herself into the water, and said, In thy name, O my Lord Jesus Christ, I am this last day baptized. The women and the people seeing this, cried out, and said, Do not throw yourself into the water. And the governor himself cried out, to think that the fish (sea-calves) were like to devour so much beauty.

Notwithstanding all this, Thecla threw herself into the water, in the name of our Lord Jesus Christ.

But the fish (sea-calves,) when they saw the lighting and fire, were killed, and swam dead upon the surface of the water, and a cloud of fire surrounded Thecla, so that as the beasts could not come near her, so the people could not see her nakedness.

Yet they turned other wild beasts upon her; upon which they made a very mournful outcry; and some of them scattered spikenard, others cassia, others amomus (a sort of spikenard, or the herb of Jerusalem, or ladies-rose) others ointment; so that the quantity of ointment was large, in proportion to the number of people; and upon this all the beasts lay as though they had been fast asleep, and did not touch Thecla.

Whereupon Alexander said to the Governor, I have some very terrible bulls; let us bind her to them. To which the governor, with concern, replied, You may do what you think fit.

Then they put a cord round Thecla's waist, which bound also her feet, and with it tied her to the bulls, to whose privy-parts they applied red-hot irons, that so they being the more tormented, might more violently drag Thecla about, till they had killed her.

The bulls accordingly tore about, making a most hideous noise; but the flame which was about Thecla, burnt off the cords which were fastened to the members of the bulls, and she stood in the middle of the stage, as unconcerned as if she had not been bound.

But in the mean time Trifina, who sat upon one of the benches, fainted away and died; upon which the whole city was under a very great concern.

And Alexander himself was afraid, and desired the governor, saying: I entreat you, take compassion on me and the city, and release this woman, who has fought with the beasts; lest, both you and I, and the whole city be destroyed

For if Caesar should have any account of what has passed now, he will certainly immediately destroy the city, because Trifina, a person of royal extract, and a relation of his, is dead upon her seat.

Upon this the governor called Thecla from among the beasts to him, and said to her, Who art thou? and what are thy circumstances, that not one of the beasts will touch thee?

Thecla replied to him; I am a servant of the living God; and as to my state, I am a believer on Jesus Christ his Son, in whom God is well pleased; and for that reason none of the beasts could touch me.

He alone is the way to eternal salvation, and the foundation of eternal life. He is a refuge to those who are in distress; a support to the afflicted, hope and defence to those who are hopeless; and, in a word, all those who do not believe on him, shall not live, but suffer eternal death.

When the govern or heard these things, he ordered her clothes to be brought, and said to her put on your clothes.

Thecla replied: May that God who clothed me when I was naked among the beasts, in the day of judgment clothe your soul with the robe of salvation. Then she took her clothes, and put them on; and the governor immediately published an order in these words; I release to you Thecla the servant of God.

Upon which the women cried out together with a loud voice, and with one accord gave praise unto God, and said; There is but one God, who is the God of Thecla; the one God who delivered Thecla.

So loud were their voices that the whole city seemed to be shaken; and Trifina herself heard the glad tidings, and arose again, and ran with the multitude to meet Thecla; and embracing her, said: Now I believe there shall be a resurrection of the dead; now I am persuaded that my daughter is alive. Come therefore home with me, my daughter Thecla, and I will make over all that I have to you.

So Thecla went with Trifina, and was entertained there a few days, teaching her the word of the Lord, whereby many young women were converted; and there was great joy in the family of Trifina.

But Thecla longed to see Paul, and inquired and sent everywhere to find him; and when at length she was informed that he was at Myra, in Lycia, she took with her many young men and women; and putting on a girdle, and dressing herself in the habit of a man, she went to him to Myra in Lycia, and there found Paul preaching the word of God; and she stood by him among the throng.

CHAPTER X.

Thecla visits Paul. Visits Onesiphorus. Visits her mother. Who repulses her. Is tempted by the devil. Works miracles.

BUT it was no small surprise to Paul when he saw her and the people with her; for he imagined some fresh trial was coming upon them;

Which when Thecla perceived, she said to him: I have been baptized, O Paul; for he who assists you in preaching, has assisted me to baptize.

Then Paul took her, and led her to the house of Hermes; and Thecla related to Paul all that had befallen her in Antioch, insomuch that Paul exceedingly wondered, and all who heard were confirmed in the faith, and prayed for Trifina's happiness.

Then Thecla arose, and said to Paul, I am going to Iconium. Paul replied to her: Go, and teach the word of the Lord.

But Trifina had sent large sums of money to Paul, and also clothing by the hands of Thecla, for the relief of the poor.

So Thecla went to Iconium. And when she came to the house of Onesiphorus, she fell down upon the floor where Paul had sat and preached, and, mixing tears with her prayers, she praised and glorified God in the following words:

O Lord the God of this house, in which I was first enlightened by thee; O Jesus, son of the living God, who wast my helper before the governor, my helper in the fire, and my helper among the beasts; thou alone art God forever and ever. Amen.

Thecla now (on her return) found Thamyris dead, but her mother living. So calling her mother, she said to her: Theoclia, my mother, is it possible for you to be brought to a belief, that there is but one Lord God, who dwells in the heavens? If you desire great riches, God will give them to you by me; if you want your daughter again, here I am.

These and many other things she represented to her mother, (endeavouring) to persuade her (to her own opinion). But her mother Theoclia gave no credit to the things which were said by the martyr Thecla.

So that Thecla perceiving she discoursed to no purpose, signing her whole body with the sign (of the cross), left the house and went to Daphine; and when she came there, she went to the cave, where she had found Paul with Onesiphorus, and fell down on the ground; and wept before God.

When she departed thence, she went to Seleucia, and enlightened many in the knowledge of Christ.

And a bright cloud conducted her in her journey.

And after she had arrived at Seleucia she went to a place out of the city, about the distance of a furlong, being afraid of the inhabitants, because they were worshippers of idols.

And she was led (by the cloud) into a mountain called Calamon, or Rodeon. There she abode many years, and underwent a great many grievous temptations of the devil, which she bore in a becoming manner, by the assistance which she had from Christ.

At length certain gentlewomen hearing of the virgin Thecla, went to her, and were instructed by her in the oracles of God, and many of them abandoned this world, and led a monastic life with her.

Hereby a good report was spread everywhere of Thecla, and she wrought several (miraculous) cures, so that all the city and adjacent countries brought their sick to that mountain, and before they came as far as the door of the cave, they were instantly cured of whatsoever distemper they had.

The unclean spirits were cast out, making a noise; all received their sick made whole, and glorified God, who had bestowed such power on the virgin Thecla;

Insomuch that the physicians of Seleucia were now of no more account, and lost all the profit of their trade, because no one regarded them; upon which they were filled with envy, and began to contrive what methods to take with this servant of Christ.

CHAPTER XI.

Is attempted to be ravished, escapes by a rock opening, and closing miraculously.

THE devil then suggested bad advice to their minds; and being on a certain day met together to consult, they reasoned among each other thus: The virgin is a priestess of the great goddess Diana, and whatsoever she requests from her, is granted, because she is a virgin, and so is beloved by all the gods.

Now then let us procure some rakish fellows, and after we have made them sufficiently drunk, and given them a good sum of money, let us order them to go and debauch this virgin, promising them, if they do it, a larger reward.

(For they thus concluded among themselves, that if they be able to debauch her, the gods will no more regard her, nor Diana cure the sick for her.)

They proceeded according to this resolution, and the fellows went to the mountain, and as fierce as lions to the cave, knocking at the door.

The holy martyr Thecla, relying upon the God in whom she believed, opened the door, although she was before apprized of their design, and said to them, Young men, what is your business?

They replied, Is there any one within, whose name is Thecla? She answered, What would you have with her? They said, We have a mind to lie with her.

The blessed Thecla answered: Though I am a mean old woman, I am the servant of my Lord Jesus Christ; and though you have a vile design against me, ye shall not be able to accomplish it. They replied: It is impossible but we must be able to do with you what we have a mind.

And while they were saying this, they laid hold on her by main force, and would have ravished her. Then she with the (greatest) mildness said to them: Young men have patience, and see the glory of the Lord.

And while they held her, she looked up to heaven and said; O God most reverend, to whom none can be likened; who makest thyself glorious over thine enemies; who didst deliver me from the fire, and didst not give me up to Thamyris, didst not give me up to Alexander; who deliveredst me from the wild beasts; who didst preserve me in the deep waters; who hast everywhere been my helper, and hast glorified thy name in me;

Now also deliver me from the hands of these wicked and unreasonable men, nor suffer them to debauch my chastity which I have hitherto preserved for thy honour; for I love thee and long for thee, and worship thee, O Father, Son, and Holy Ghost, for evermore. Amen.

Then came a voice from heaven, saying, Fear not, Thecla, my faithful servant, for I am with thee. Look and see the place which is opened for thee: there thy eternal abode shall be; there thou shalt receive the beatific vision.

The blessed Thecla observing, saw the rock opened to as large a degree as that a man might enter in; she did as she was commanded, bravely fled from the vile crew, and went into the rock, which instantly so closed, that there was not any crack visible where it had opened.

The men stood perfectly astonished at so prodigious a miracle, and had no power to detain the servant of God; but only, catching hold of her veil, or hood, they tore off a piece of it;

And even that was by the permission of God, for the confirmation of their faith who should come to see this venerable place, and to convey blessings to those in succeeding ages, who should believe on our Lord Jesus Christ from a pure heart.

Thus suffered that first martyr and apostle of God, and virgin, Thecla; who came from Iconium at eighteen years of age; afterwards, partly in journeys and travels, and partly in a monastic life in the cave, she lived seventy-two years; so that she was ninety years old when the Lord translated her.

Thus ends her life.

The day which is kept sacred to her memory, is the twenty-fourth of September, to the glory of the Father, and the Son, and the Holy Ghost, now and for evermore. Amen.

THE FIRST EPISTLE OF CLEMENT TO THE CORINTHIANS.

Clement was a disciple of Peter, and afterwards Bishop of Rome. Clemens Alexandrinus calls him an apostle. Jerome says he was an apostolical man, and Rufinus that he was almost an apostle. Eusebius calls this the wonderful Epistle of St. Clement, and says that it was publicly read in the assemblies of the primitive church. It is included in one of the ancient collections of the Canon Scripture. Its genuineness has been much questioned, particularly by Photius, patriarch of Constantinople in the ninth century, who objects that Clement speaks of worlds beyond the ocean; that he has not written worthily of the divinity of Christ; and that to prove the possibility of a future resurrection, he introduces the fabulous story of the phoenix's revival from its own ashes. To the latter objection, Archbishop Wake replies that the generality of the ancient Fathers have made use of the same instance in proof of the same point; and asks if St. Clement really believed that there was such a bird, and that it did revive out of the cinders of the body after burning, where was the great harm either in giving credit to such a wonder, or, believing it, to make such a use as he here does of it?—The present is the Archbishop's translation from the ancient Greek copy of the Epistle, which is at the end of the celebrated Alexandrine MS. of the Septuagint and New Testament, presented by Cyril, patriarch of

Alexandria, to King Charles the First, now in the British Museum. The Archbishop, in prefacing his translation, esteems it a great blessing that this "Epistle" was at last so happily found out for the increase and confirmation both of our faith and our charity.

CHAPTER I.

He commends them for their excellent order and piety in Christ, before their schism broke out.

THE Church of God which is at Rome, to the Church of God which is at Corinth, elect, sanctified by the will of God, through Jesus Christ our Lord: grace and peace from the Almighty God, by Jesus Christ be multiplied unto you.

Brethren, the sudden and unexpected dangers and calamities that have fallen upon us, have, we fear, made us the more slow in our consideration of those things which you inquired of us:

As also of that wicked and detestable sedition, so unbecoming the elect of God, which a few heady and self-willed men have fomented to such a degree of madness, that your venerable and renowned name, so worthy of all men to be beloved, is greatly blasphemed thereby.

For who that has ever been among you has not experimented the firmness of your faith, and its fruitfulness in all good works; and admired the temper and moderation of your religion in Christ; and published abroad the magnificence of your hospitality, and thought you happy in your perfect and certain knowledge of the Gospel?

For ye did all things without respect of persons and walked according to the laws of God; being subject to those who had the rule over you, and giving the honour that was fitting to the aged among you.

Ye commanded the young men to think those things that were modest and grave.

The women ye exhorted to do all things with an unblameable and seemly, and pure conscience; loving their own husbands, as was fitting: and that keeping themselves within the bounds of a due obedience, they should order their houses gravely, with all discretion.

Ye were all of you humble minded, notboasting of any thing: desiring rather to be subject than to govern; to give than to receive; being content with the portion God hath dispensed to you;

And hearkening diligently to his word, ye were enlarged in your bowels, having his suffering always before your eyes.

Thus a firm, and blessed and profitable peace was given unto you; and an unsatiable desire of doing good; and a plentiful effusion of the Holy Ghost was upon all of you.

And being full of good designs, ye did with great readiness of mind, and with a religious confidence stretch forth your hands to God Almighty; beseeching him to be merciful unto you, if in any thing ye had unwillingly sinned against him.

Ye contended day and night for the whole brotherhood; that with compassion and a good conscience, the number of his elect might be saved.

Ye were sincere, and without offence towards each other; not mindful of injuries; all sedition and schism was an abomination unto you.

Ye bewailed every one his neighbour's sins, esteeming their defects your own.

Ye were kind one to another without grudging; being ready to every good work. And being adorned with a conversation altogether virtuous and religious, ye did all things in the fear of God; whose commandments were written upon the tables of your heart.

CHAPTER II.

How their divisions began.

ALL honour and enlargement was given unto you; and so was fulfilled that which is written, my beloved did eat and drink, he was enlarged and waxed fat, and he kicked.

From hence came emulation, and envy, and strife, and sedition; persecution and disorder, war and captivity.

So they who were of no renown, lifted up themselves against the honourable; those of no reputation, against those who were in respect; the foolish against the wise; the young men against the aged.

Therefore righteousness and peace are departed from you, because every one hath forsaken the fear of God; and is grown blind in his faith; nor walketh by the rule of God's commandments nor liveth as is fitting in Christ:

But every one follows his own wicked lusts: having taken up an unjust and wicked envy, by which death first entered into the world.

CHAPTER III.

Envy and emulation the original of all strife and disorder. Examples of the mischiefs they have occasioned.

FOR thus it is written, And in process of time it came to pass that Cain brought of the fruit of the ground an offering unto the Lord. And Abel, he also brought of the firstlings of his flock, and of the fat thereof:

And the Lord had respect unto Abel, and to his offering. But unto Cain and unto his offering he had not respect. And Cain was very sorrowful, and his countenance fell.

And the Lord said unto Cain, Why art thou sorrowful? And why is thy countenance fallen? If thou shalt offer aright, but not divide aright, hast thou not sinned? Hold thy peace: unto thee shall be his desire, and thou shalt rule over him.

And Cain said unto Abel his brother, Let us go down into the field. And it came to pass, as they were in the field, that Cain rose up against Abel his brother, and slew him.

Ye see, brethren, how envy and emulation wrought the death of a brother. For this our father Jacob fled from the face of his brother Esau.

It was this that caused Joseph to be persecuted even unto death, and to come into bondage. Envy forced Moses to flee from the face of Pharaoh king of Egypt, when he heard his own countrymen ask him, Who made thee a Judge, and a ruler over us? Wilt thou kill me as thou didst the Egyptian yesterday?

Through envy Aaron and Miriam were shut out of the camp, from the rest of the congregation seven days.

Emulation sent Dathan and Abiram quick into the grave because they raised up a sedition against Moses the servant of God.

For this Davidwas not only hated of strangers, but was persecuted even by Saul the king of Israel.

Butnot to insist upon antient examples, let us come to those worthies that have been nearest to us; and take the brave examples of our own age.

Through zeal and envy, the most faithful and righteouspillars of the church have been persecuted even to the most grievous deaths.

Let us set before our eyes the holy Apostles; Peter by unjust envy underwent not one or two, but many sufferings; til at last being martyred, he went to the place of glory that was due unto him.

For the same cause did Paul in like manner receive the reward of his patience. Seven times he was in bonds; he was whipped, was stoned; he preached both in the East and in the West; leaving behind him the glorious report of his faith:

And so having taught the whole world righteousness, and for that end travelled even to the utmost bounds of the West; he at last suffered martyrdom by the command of the governors,

And departed out of the world, and went unto his holy place; being become a most eminent pattern of patience unto all ages.

To these Holy Apostles were joined a very great number of others, who having through envy undergone in like manner many pains and torments, have left a glorious example to us.

For this not only men but women have been persecuted: and having suffered very grievous and cruel punishments, have finished the course of their faith with firmness; and though weak in body, yet received a glorious reward.

This has alienated the minds even of women from their husbands; and changed what was once said by our father Adam; This is now bone of my bone, and flesh of my flesh.

In a word, envy and strife, have overturned whole cities, and rooted out great nations from off the earth.

CHAPTER IV.

He exhorts them to live by the rules, and repent of their divisions, and they shall be forgiven.

THESE things, beloved, we write unto you, not only for your instruction, but also for our own remembrance.

For we are all in the same lists, and the same combat is prepared for us all.

Wherefore let us lay aside all vain and empty cares; and let us come up to the glorious and venerable rule of our holy calling.

Let us consider what is good, and acceptable and well-pleasing in the sight of him that made us.

Let us look steadfastly to the blood of Christ, and see how precious his blood is in the sight of God: which being shed for our salvation, has obtained the grace of repentance for all the world.

Let us search into all the ages that have gone before us; and let us learn that our Lord has in every one of them still given place for repentance to all such as would turn to him.

Noah preached repentance; and as many as hearkened to him were saved. Jonah denounced destruction against the Ninevites:

Howbeit they repenting of their sins, appeased God by their prayers: and were saved, though they were strangers to the covenant of God.

Hence we find how all the ministers of the grace of God have spoken by the Holy Spirit of repentance. And even the Lord of all has himself declared with an oath concerning it;

As I live, saith the Lord, I desire not the death of a sinner, but that he should repent. Adding farther this good sentence, saying: Turn from your iniquity, O house of Israel.

Say unto the children of my people, Though your sins should reach from earth to heaven; and though they shall be redder than scarlet, and blacker than sackcloth; yet if ye shall turn to me with all your heart, and shall call me father, I will hearken to you, as to a holy people.

And in another place he saith on this wise: Wash ye, make you clean; put away the evil of your doings from before mine eyes; cease to do evil, learn to do well; seek judgment, relieve the oppressed, judge the fatherless, plead for the widow.

Come now and let us reason together, saith the Lord: though your sins be as scarlet, they shall be as white as snow; though they he red as crimson, they shall be as wool.

If ye he willing and obedient, ye shall eat the good of the land; but if ye refuse and rebel, ye shall be devoured with the sword; for the mouth of the Lord hath spoken it.

These things has God established by his Almighty will, desiring that all his beloved should come to repentance.

CHAPTER V.

He sets before them the examples of holy men, whose piety is recorded in the Scriptures.

WHEREFORE let us obey his excellent and glorious will; and imploring his mercy and goodness, let us fall down upon our faces before him, and cast ourselves upon his mercy; laying aside all vanity, and contention, and envy which leads unto death.

Let us look up to those who have the most perfectly ministered to his excellent glory. Let us take Enoch for our example; who being found righteous in obedience, was translated, and his death was not known.

Noah being proved to be faithful, did by his ministry preach regeneration to the world; and the Lord saved by him all the living creatures, that went with one accord into the ark.

Abraham, who was called God's friend, was in like manner found faithful; inasmuch as he obeyed the commands of God.

By obedience he went out of his own country, and from his own kindred, and from his father's house: that so forsaking a small country, and a weak affinity, and a little house, he might inherit the promises of God.

For thus God said unto him; get thee out of thy country, and from thy kindred, and from thy father's house, unto a land that I will show thee.

And I will make thee a great nation, and will bless thee, and make thy name great, and thou shalt be blessed. And I will bless them that bless thee, and curse them that curse thee; and in thee shall all families of the earth be blessed.

And again when he separated himself from Lot, God said unto him; Lift up now thine eyes, and look from the place where thou art northward and southward and eastward and westward for all the land which thou seest, to thee will I give it, and to thy seed for ever.

And I will make thy seed as the dust of the earth, so that if a man can number the dust of the earth, then shall thy seed also be numbered.

And again he saith: and God brought forth Abraham, and said unto him; Look now toward heaven, and tell the stars, if thou be able to number them: so shall thy seed be.

And Abraham believed God, and it was counted to him for righteousness.

Through faith and hospitality, he had a son given him in his old age; and through obedience he offered him up in sacrifice to God, upon one of the mountains which God showed unto him.

CHAPTER VI.

And particularly such as have been eminent for their kindness and charity to their neighbours.

BY hospitality and godliness was Lot saved out of Sodom, when all the country round about was destroyed by fire and brimstone:

The Lord thereby making it manifest, that he will not forsake those that trust in him; but will bring the disobedient to punishment and correction.

For his wife who went out with him, being of a different mind, and not continuing in the same obedience, was for that reason set forth for an example, being turned into a pillar of salt unto this day.

That so all men may know, that those who are double minded, and distrustful of the power of God, are prepared for condemnation, and to be a sign to all succeeding ages.

By faith and hospitality was Rahab the harlot saved. For when the spies were sent by Joshua the son of Nun, to search out Jericho and the king of Jericho knew that they were come to spy out his country; he sent men to take them, so that they might be put to death.

Rahab therefore being hospitable, received them, and hid them under the stalks of flax, on the top of her house.

And when the messengers that were sent by the king came unto her, and asked her, saying, There came men unto thee to spy out the land, bring them forth, for so hath the king commanded: She answered, The two men whom ye seek came unto me, but presently they departed, and are gone: Not discovering them unto them.

Then she said to the spies, I know that the Lord your God has given this city into your hands; for the fear of you is fallen upon all that dwell therein. When, therefore, ye shall have taken it ye shall save me and my father's house.

And they answered her, saying, It shall be as thou hast spoken to us. Therefore, when thou shalt know that we are near thou shalt gather all thy family together upon the housetop, and they shall be saved: but all that shall be found without thy house, shall be destroyed.

And they gave her moreover a sign: that she should hang out of her house a scarlet rope; sheaving thereby, that by the blood of our Lord, there should be redemption to all that believe and hope in God. Ye see, beloved, how there was not only faith, but prophecy too in this woman.

CHAPTER VII.

What rules are given for this purpose.

LET us, therefore, humble ourselves, brethren, laying aside all pride, and boasting, and foolishness, and anger: And let us do as it is written.

For thus saith the Holy Spirit; Let not the wise man glory in his wisdom, nor the strong man in his strength, nor the rich man in his riches; but let him that glorieth, glory in the Lord, to seek him, and to do judgment and justice.

Above all, remembering the words of the Lord Jesus, which he spake concerning equity and long suffering, saying,

Be ye merciful and ye shall obtain mercy; forgive, and ye shall be forgiven: as ye do, so shall it be done unto you: as ye give, so shall it be given unto you: as ye judge, so shall ye be judged; as ye are kind to others so shall God be kind to you: with what measure ye mete, with the same shall it be measured to you again.

By this command, and by these rules, let us establish ourselves, that so we may always walk obediently to his holy words; being humble minded:

For so says the Holy Scripture; upon whom shall I look, even upon him that is poor and of a contrite spirit, and that trembles at my word.

It is, therefore, just and righteous, men and brethren, that we should become obedient unto God, rather than follow such as through pride and sedition, have made themselves the ring-leaders of a detestable emulation.

For it is not an ordinary harm that we shall do ourselves but rather a very great danger that we shall run, if we shall rashly give up ourselves to the wills of men who promote strife and seditions, to turn us aside from that which is fitting.

But let us be kind to one another, according to the compassion and sweetness of him that made us.

For it is written, The merciful shall inherit the earth; and they that are without evil shall be left upon it: but the transgressors shall perish from off the face of it.

And again he saith, I have seen the wicked in great power and spreading himself like the cedar of Libanus. I passed by, and lo! he was not; I sought his place, but it could not be found.

Keep innocently, and do the thing that is right, for there shall be a remnant to the peaceable man.

Let us, therefore, hold fast to those who religiously follow peace; and not to such as only pretend to desire.

For he saith in a certain place, This people honoureth me with their lips, but their heart is far from me.

And again, They bless with their mouths, but curse in their hearts.

And again he saith, They loved him with their mouths, and with their tongues they lied to him. For their heart was not r right with him, neither were they, faithful in his covenant.

Let all deceitful lips become dumb, and the tongue that speaketh proud things. Who have said, with our tongue will we prevail; our lips are our own, who is Lord over us.

For the oppression of the poor, for the sighing of the needy, now will I arise saith the Lord; I will set him in safety, I will deal confidently with him.

CHAPTER VIII.

He advises them to be humble; and that from the examples of Jesus and of holy men in all ages.

FOR Christ is theirs who are humble, and not who exalt themselves over his flock. The sceptre of the majesty of God, our Lord Jesus Christ, came not in the shew of pride and arrogance, though he could have done so; but with humility as the Holy Ghost had before spoken concerning him.

For thus he saith, Lord, who hath believed our report, and to whom is the arm of the Lord revealed? For he shall grow up before him as a tender plant, and as a root out of a dry ground.

He hath no form or comeliness, and when we shall see him, there is no beauty that we should desire him.

He is despised and rejected of men; a man of sorrows and acquainted with grief.

And we hid, as it were, our faces from him; he was despised, and we esteemed him not.

Surely he hath born our griefs, and carried our sorrows: yet we did esteem him stricken, smitten of God, and afflicted.

But he was wounded for our transgressions; he was bruised for our iniquities; the chastisement of our peace was upon him; and with his stripes we are healed.

All we like sheep have gone astray; we have turned every one to his own way, and the Lord hath laid on him the iniquity of us all.

He was oppressed, and he was afflicted, yet he opened not his mouth: he is brought as a lamb to the slaughter; and as a sheep before her shearers is dumb, so he openeth not his mouth.

He was taken from prison, and from judgment; and who shall declare his generation? For he was cut off out of the land of the living, for the transgressions of my people was he stricken.

And he made his grave with the wicked, and with the rich in his death; because he had done no violence, neither was any deceit in his mouth.

Yet it pleased the Lord to bruise him, he hath put him to grief; when thou shalt make his soul an offering for sin, he shall see his seed, he shall prolong his days; and the pleasure of the Lord shall prosper in his hand.

He shall see of the travail of his soul and shall be satisfied; by his knowledge shall my righteous servant justify many: for he shall bear their iniquities.

Therefore will I divide him a portion with the great, and he shall divide the spoil with the strong; because he hath poured out his soul into death; and he was numbered with the transgressors, and he bare the sin of many, and made intercession for the transgressors.

And again he himself saith, I am a worm and no man, a reproach of men, and despised of the people. All they that see me laugh me to scorn; they shoot out their lips, they shake their heads, saying: He trusted in the Lord that he would deliver him, let him deliver him seeing he delighted in him.

Ye see, beloved, what the pattern is that has been given to us. For if the Lord thus humbled himself, what should we do who are brought by him under the yoke of his grace?

Let us be followers of those who went about in goat-skins and sheep-skins; preaching the coming of Christ.

Such were Elias, and Elisaeus, and Ezekiel the prophets. And let us add to these such others as have received the like testimony.

Abraham has been greatly witnessed of; having been called the friend of God. And yet he steadfastly beholding the glory of God, says with all humility, I am dust and ashes.

Again of Job it is thus written, That he was just and without blame, true; one that served God, and abstained from all evil. Yet he accusing himself, says, No man is free from pollution, no not though he should live but one day.

Moses was called faithful in all God's House; and by his conduct the Lord punished Israel by stripes and plagues.

And even this man, though thus greatly honoured, spake not greatly of himself; but when the oracle of God was delivered to him out of the bush he said, Who am I, that thou dost send me? I am of a slender voice, and a slow tongue.

And again he saith, I am as the smoke of the pot.

And what shall we say of David, so highly testified of in the Holy Scriptures? To whom God said I have found a man after my own heart, David the son of Jesse, with my holy oil have I anointed him.

But yet be himself saith unto God, Have mercy upon me, O God, according to thy loving kindness; according unto the multitude of thy tender mercies, blot out my transgressions.

Wash me thoroughly from mine iniquity, and cleanse me from my sin! For I acknowledge my transgressions, and my sin is ever before me.

Against Thee only have I sinned, and done this evil in thy sight, that thou mightest be justified when thou speakest, and be clear when thou judgest.

Behold I was shapen in iniquity, and in sin did my mother conceive me.

Behold, thou desireth truth in the inward parts; and in the hidden part thou shalt make me to know wisdom.

Purge me with hyssop and I shall be clean, wash me and I shall be whiter than snow.

Make me to hear joy and gladness, that the bones which thou hast broken may rejoice.

Hide thy face from my sins, and blot out all mine iniquities.

Create in me a clean heart O God; and renew a right spirit within me.

Cast me not away from thy presence, and take not thy holy spirit from me.

Restore unto me the joy of thy salvation, and uphold me with thy free spirit.

Then I will teach transgressors thy ways, and sinners shall be converted unto thee.

Deliver me from blood-guiltiness, O God, thou God of my salvation, and my tongue shall sing aloud of thy righteousness.

O Lord open thou my lips, and my mouth shall show forth thy praise.

For thou desirest not sacrifice, else would I give it; thou delightest not in burnt offerings.

The sacrifices of God are a broken spirit, a broken and a contrite heart, O God, thou wilt not despise.

CHAPTER IX.

He again persuades them to compose their divisions.

THUS has the humility and godly fear of these great and excellent men, recorded in the Scriptures, through obedience, made not only us, but also the generations before us better; even as many as have received his holy oracles with fear and truth.

Having therefore so many, and such great and glorious examples, let us return to that peace which was the mark that from the beginning was set before us;

Let us look up to the Father and Creator of the whole world; and let us hold fast to his glorious and exceeding gifts and benefits of peace.

Let us consider and behold with the eyes of our understanding his long-suffering will; and think how gentle and patient he is towards his whole creation.

The heavens moving by his appointment, are subject to him in peace.

Day and night accomplish the courses that he has allotted unto them, not disturbing one another.

The sun and moon, and all the several companies and constellations of the stars, run thecourses that he has appointed to them in concord, without departing in the least from them.

The fruitful earth yields its food plentifully in due season both to man and beast, and to all animals that are upon it, according to his will; not disputing, nor altering any thing of what was ordered by him.

So also the unfathomable and unsearchable floods of the deep, are kept in by his command;

And the conflux of the vast sea, being brought together by his order into its several collections, passes not the bounds that he has set to it;

But as he appointed it, so it remains. For he said, Hitherto shalt thou come, and thy floods shall be broken within thee.

The ocean, unpassable to mankind, and the worlds that are beyond it, are governed by the same commands of their great master.

Spring and summer, autumn and winter, give place peaceably to each other.

The several quarters of the winds fulfil their work in their seasons, without offending one another.

The ever-flowing fountains, made both for pleasure and health, never fail to reach out their breasts to support the life of men.

Even the smallest creatures live together in peace and concord with each other.

All these has the Great Creator and Lord of all, commanded to observe peace and concord; being good to all.

But especially to us who flee to his mercy through our Lord Jesus Christ; to whom be glory and majesty for ever and ever. Amen.

CHAPTER X.

He exhorts them to obedience, from the consideration of the goodness of God, and of his presence in every place.

TAKE heed, beloved, that his many blessings be not to us to condemnation; except we shall walk worthy of him, doing with one consent what is good and pleasing in his sight.

The spirit of the Lord is a candle, searching out the inward of the belly.

Let us therefore consider how near he is to us; and how that none of our thoughts, or reasonings which we frame with in ourselves, are hid from him.

It is therefore just that we should not forsake our rank, by doing contrary to his will.

Let us choose to offend a few foolish and inconsiderate men, lifted up and glorying in their own pride, rather than God.

Let us reverence our Lord Jesus Christ whose blood was given for us.

Let us honour those who are set over us; let us respect the aged that are amongst us; and let us instruct the younger men, in the discipline and fear of the LORD.

Our wives let us direct to do that which is good.

Let them show forth a lovely habit of purity in all their conversation; with a sincere affection of meekness.

Let the government of their tongues be made manifest by their silence.

Let their charity be without respect of persons alike towards all such as religiously fear God.

Let your children be bred up in the instruction of Christ:

And especially let them learn how great a power humility has with God; how much a pure and holy charity avails with him; how excellent and great his fear is; and how it will save all such as turn to him with holiness in a pure mind.

For he is the searcher of the thoughts and counsels of the heart; whose breath is in us, and when he pleases he can take it from us.

CHAPTER XI.

Of faith, and particularly what we are to believe as to the resurrection.

BUT all these things must be confirmed by the faith which is in Christ; for so he himself bespeaks us by the Holy Ghost.

Come ye children and hearken unto me, and I will teach you the fear of the Lord. What man is there that desireth life, and loveth to see good days?

Keep thy tongue from evil, and thy lips that they speak no guile.

Depart from evil and do good; seek peace and ensue it.

The eyes of the Lord are upon the righteous, and his ears are open unto their prayers.

But the face of the Lord is against them that do evil, to cut off the remembrance of them from the earth.

The righteous cried, and the Lord heard him, and delivered him out of all his troubles.

Many are the troubles of the wicked; but they that trust in the Lord, mercy shall encompass them about.

Our all-merciful and beneficent Father hath bowels of compassion towards them that fear him; and kindly and lovingly bestows his graces upon all such as come to him with a simple mind.

Wherefore let us not waver, neither let us have any doubt in our hearts, of his excellent and glorious gifts.

Let that be far from us which is written, Miserable are the double-minded, and those who are doubtful in their hearts.

Who say these things have we heard, and our fathers have told us these things. But behold we are grown old, and none of them has happened unto us.

O ye fools! consider the trees: take the vine for an example. First it sheds its leaves; then it buds; after that it spreads its leaves; then it flowers; then come the sour grapes; and after them follows the ripe fruit. Ye see how in a little time the fruit of the tree comes to maturity.

Of a truth, yet a little while and his will shall suddenly be accomplished.

The Holy Scripture itself bearing witness, That He shall quickly come and not tarry, and that the Lord shall suddenly come to his temple, even the holy ones whom ye look for.

Let us consider, beloved, how the Lord does continually shew us, that there shall be a future resurrection; of which he has made our Lord Jesus Christ the first fruits, raising him from the dead.

Let us contemplate, beloved, the resurrection that is continually made before our eyes.

Day and night manifest a resurrection to us. The night lies down, and the day arises: main the day departs, and the night comes on.

Let us behold the fruits of the earth. Every one sees how the seed is sown. The sower goes forth, and casts it upon the earth; and the seed which when it was sown fell upon the earth dry and naked, in time dissolves.

And from the dissolution, the great power of the providence of the Lord raises it again; and of one seed many arise, and bring forth fruit.

CHAPTER XII.

The Resurrection further proved.

LET us consider that wonderful type of the resurrection which is seen in the Eastern countries; that is to say, in Arabia.

There is a certain bird called a Phoenix; of this there is never but one at a time: and that lives five hundred years. And when the time of its dissolution draws near, that it must die, it makes itself a nest of frankincense, and myrrh, and other spices into which when its time is fulfilled it enters and dies.

But its flesh putrifying, breeds a certain worm, which being nourished with the juice of the dead bird brings forth feathers; and when it is grown to a perfect state, it takes up the nest in which the bones of its parents lie, and carries it from Arabia into Egypt, to a city called Heliopolis:

And flying in open day in the sight of all men, lays it upon the altar of the sun, and so returns from whence it came.

The priests then search into the records of the time; and find that it returned precisely at the end of five hundred years.

And shall we then think it to be any very great and strange thing for the Lord of all to raise up those that religiously him in the assurance of good faith, when even by a bird he shews us the greatness of his power to fulfil his promise?

For he says in a certain place, Thou shalt raise me up, and I shall confess unto thee.

And again I laid me down and slept, and awaked, because thou art with me.

And again, Job says, Thou shalt raise up this flesh of mine, that has suffered all these things.

Having therefore this hope, let us hold fast to him who is faithful in all his promises, and righteous in all his judgments; who has commanded us not to lie: how much more will he not himself lie?

For nothing is impossible with God but to lie.

Let his faith then be stirred up again in us; and let us consider that all things are nigh unto him.

By the word of his power he made all things; and by the same word he is able (whenever he will), to destroy them.

Who shall say unto him, what dost thou? or who shall resist the power of his strength?

When, and as he pleased, he will do all things; and nothing shall pass away of all that has been determined by him.

All things are open before him; nor can anything be hid from his council.

The heavens declare the glory of God, and the firmament sheweth his handy work. Day unto day uttereth speech, and night unto night sheweth knowledge. There is no speech nor language where their voice is not heard.

CHAPTER XIII.

It is impossible to escape the vengeance of God, if we continue in sin.

SEEING then all things are seen and heard by God; let us fear him, and let us lay aside our wicked works which proceed from ill desires; that through his mercy we may be delivered from the condemnation to come.

For whither can any of us flee from his mighty hand? Or what world shall receive any of those who run away from him?

For thus saith the Scripture in a certain place, Whither shall I flee from thy Spirit, or where shall I hide myself from thy presence?

If I ascend up into heaven, thou art there; if I shall go to the utmost part of the earth, there is thy right hand: If I shall make my bed in the deep, thy Spirit is there.

Whither then shall any one go; or whither shall he run from him that comprehends all things?

Let us therefore come to him with holiness of heart, lifting up chaste and undefiled hands unto him; loving our gracious and merciful Father, who has made us to partake of his election.

For so it is written, When the Most High divided the nations, when he separated the sons of Adam, he set the bounds of the nations, according to the number of his angels; his people Jacob became the portion of the Lord, and Israel the lot of his inheritance.

And in another place he saith, Behold the Lord taketh unto himself a nation, out of the midst of the nations, as a man taketh the first-fruits of his flower; the Most Holy shall come out of that nation.

CHAPTER XIV.

How we must live that we may please God.

WHEREFORE we being a part of the Holy One, let us do all those things that pertain unto holiness:

Fleeing all evil-speaking against one another; all filthy and impure embraces, together with all drunkenness, youthful lusts, abominable concupiscences, detestable adultery, and execrable pride.

For God, saith he, resisteth the proud, but giveth grace to the humble.

Let us therefore hold fast to those to whom God has given His grace.

And let us put on concord, being humble, temperate; free from all whispering and detraction; and justified by our actions, not our words.

For he saith, Doth he that speaketh and heareth many things, and that is of a ready tongue, suppose that he is righteous? Blessed is he that is born of a woman, that liveth but a few days: use not therefore much speech.

Let our praise be of God, not of ourselves; for God hateth those that commend themselves.

Let the witness of our good actions be given to us of others, as it was given to the holy men that went before us.

Rashness, and arrogance, and confidence, belong to them who are accursed of God: but equity, and humility, and mildness, to such as are blessed by him.

Let us then lay hold of his blessing, and let us consider what are the ways by which we may attain unto it.

THE LOST BOOKS OF THE BIBLE

Let us look back upon those things that have happened from the beginning.

For what was our father Abraham blessed? Was it not because that through faith he wrought righteousness and truth?

Isaac being fully persuaded of what he knew was to come, cheerfully yielded himself up for a sacrifice. Jacob with humility departed out of his own country, fleeing from his brother, and went unto Laban and served him; and so the sceptre of the twelve tribes of Israel was given unto him.

Now what the greatness of this Gift was, will plainly appear, if we shall take the pains distinctly to consider all the parts of it.

For from him came the priests and Levites, who all ministered at the altar of God.

From him came our Lord Jesus Christ according to the flesh.

From him came the kings, and princes, and rulers in Judah.

Nor were the rest of his tribes in any small glory: God having promised that thy seed (says he) shall be as the stars of heaven.

They were all therefore greatly glorified, not for their own sake, or for their own works, or for the righteousness that they themselves wrought, but through his will.

And we also being called by the same will in Christ Jesus, are not justified by ourselves, neither by our own wisdom, or knowledge, or piety, or the works which we have done in the holiness of our hearts:

But by that faith by which God Almighty has justified all men from the beginning; to whom be glory for ever and ever. Amen.

CHAPTER XV.

We are justified by faith; yet this must not lessen our care to live well, nor our pleasure in it.

WHAT shall we do therefore, brethren? Shall we be slothful in well-doing, and lay aside our charity? God forbid that any such thing should be done by us.

But rather let us hasten with all earnestness and readiness of mind, to perfect every good work. For even the Creator and Lord of all things himself rejoices in his own works.

By his Almighty power he fixed the heavens, and by his incomprehensible wisdom he adorned them.

He also divided the earth from the water, with which it is encompassed; and fixed it as a secure tower, upon the foundation of his own will.

He also by his appointment, commanded all the living creatures that are upon it, to exist.

So likewise the sea, and all the creatures that are in it; having first created them, he enclosed them therein by his power.

And above all, he with his holy and pure hands, formed man, the most excellent, and, as to his understanding, truly the greatest of all other creatures, the character of his own image.

For so God says, Let us make man in our image, after our own likeness So God created man, male and female created he them.

And having thus finished all these things, he commended all that he had made, and blessed them, and said, increase and multiply.

We see how all righteous men have been adorned with good works: Wherefore even the Lord himself, having adorned himself with his works, rejoiced.

Having therefore such an example, let us without delay, fulfil his will; and with all our strength, work the work of righteousness.

CHAPTER XVI.

This enforced from the examples of the holy angels, and from the exceeding greatness of that reward which God has prepared for us.

THE good workman with confidence receives the bread of his labour; but the sluggish and lazy cannot look him in the face that set him on work.

We must therefore be ready and forward in well doing; for from him are all things.

And thus he foretells us, behold the Lord cometh, and his reward is with him, even before his face, to render to every one according to his work.

He warns us therefore beforehand, with all his heart to this end, that we should not be slothful and negligent in well doing.

Let our boasting, therefore, and our confidence be in God: let us submit ourselves to his will. Let us consider the whole multitude of his angels, how ready they stand to minister unto his will.

As saith the scripture, thousands of thousands stood before him and ten thousand times ten thousand ministered unto him. And they cried, saying, Holy, holy, holy is the Lord of Sabaoth: The whole earth is full of his glory.

Wherefore let us also, being conscientiously gathered together in concord with one another; as it were with one mouth, cry earnestly unto him, that he would make us partakers of his great and glorious promises.

For he saith, Eye hath not seen, nor ear heard, neither have entered into the heart of man, the things which God has prepared for them that wait for him.

CHAPTER XVII.

We must attain unto this reward by faith and obedience, which we must carry on in an orderly pursuing of the duties of our several stations, without envy or contention.

The necessity of different orders among men. We have none of us anything but what we received of God: whom therefore we ought in every condition thankfully to obey.

HOW blessed and wonderful, beloved, are the gifts of God.

Life in immortality! brightness in righteousness! truth in full assurance! faith in confidence! temperance in holiness!

And all this has God subjected to our understandings:

What therefore shall those things be which he has prepared for them that wait for him?

The Creator and Father of spirits, the Most Holy; he only knows both the greatness and beauty of them.

Let us therefore strive with all earnestness, that we may be found in the number of those that wait for him, that so we may receive the reward which he has promised.

But how, beloved, shall we do this? We must fix our minds by faith towards God, and seek those things that are pleasing and acceptable unto him.

We must act conformably to his holy will; and follow the way of truth, casting off from us all unrighteousness and iniquity, together with all covetousness, strife, evil manners, deceit, whispering, detractions; all hatred of God, pride and boasting; vainglory and ambition;

For they that do these things are odious to God; and not only they that do them, but also all such as approve of those that do them.

For thus saith the Scripture, But unto the wicked, God said, What hast thou to do to declare my statute, or that thou shouldst take my covenant in the mouth? Seeing that thou hatest instruction, and castest my words behind thee.

When thou sawest a thief, then thou consentedst with him; and hast been partaker with adulterers. Thou givest thy mouth to evil, and thy tongue frameth deceit. Thou sittest and speakest against thy brother; thou slanderest thine own mother's son.

These things hast thou done and I kept silence; thou thoughtest that I was altogether such a one as thyself: but I will reprove thee, and set them in order before thine eyes.

Now consider this ye that forget God, lest I tear you in pieces, and there be none to deliver.

Whoso offereth praise, glorifieth me: and to him that disposeth his way aright, will I shew the salvation of God.

This is the way, beloved, in which we may find our Saviour, even Jesus Christ the high-priest of all our offerings, the defender and helper of our weakness.

By him we look up to the highest heavens; and behold, as in a glass, his spotless and most excellent visage.

By him are the eyes of our hearts opened; by him our foolish and darkened understanding rejoiceth to behold his wonderful light.

By him would God have us to taste the knowledge of immortality: who being the brightness of his glory, is by so much greater than the angels, as he has by inheritance obtained a more excellent name than they.

For so it is written, who maketh his angels spirits, and his ministers a flame of fire:

But to his son, thus saith the Lord, Thou art my Son, today have I begotten thee.

Ask of me, and I will give thee the heathen for thy inheritance, and the utmost parts of the earth for thy possession.

And again he saith unto him, Sit thou on my right hand until I make thine enemies my footstool.

But who are his enemies? even the wicked, and such who oppose their own wills to the will of God.

Let us therefore march on, men and brethren, with all earnestness in his holy laws.

Let us consider those who fight under our earthly governors: How orderly, how readily, and with what exact obedience they perform those things that are commanded them.

All are not generals, nor colonels, nor captains, nor inferior officers:

But every one in his respective rank does what is commanded him by the king, and those who have the authority over him.

They who are great, cannot subsist without those that are little; nor the little without the great.

But there must be a mixture in all things, and then there will be use and profit too.

Let us, for example, take our body: the head without the feet is nothing, neither the feet without the head.

And even the smallest members of our body are yet both necessary and useful to the whole body.

But all conspire together, and are subject to one common use, namely, the preservation of the whole body.

Let therefore our whole body be saved in Christ Jesus; and let every one be subject to his neighbour, according to the order in which he is placed by the gift of God.

Let not the strong man despise the weak; and let the weak see that he reverence the strong.

Let the rich man distribute to the necessity of the poor: and let the poor bless God, that he has given one unto him, by whom his want may be supplied.

Let the wise man shew forth his wisdom, not in words, but in good works.

Let him that is humble, not bear witness to himself, but let him leave it to another to bear witness of him.

Let him that is pure in the flesh, not grow proud of it, knowing that it was from another that he received the gift of continence.

Let us consider therefore, brethren, whereof we are made; who, and what kind of men we came into the world, as it were out of a sepulchre, and from outer darkness.

He that made us, and formed us, brought us into his own world; having presented us with his benefits, even before we were born.

Wherefore, having received all these things from him, we ought in everything to give thanks unto him; to whom be glory for ever and ever. Amen.

CHAPTER XVIII.

From whence he exhorts them to do everything orderly in the Church, as the only way to please God.

FOOLISH and unwise men who have neither prudence nor learning may mock and deride us; being willing to set up themselves in their own conceits;

But what can a mortal man do? Or what strength is there in him that is made out of the dust?

For it is written, there was no shape before mine eyes; only I heard a sound and a voice.

For what? Shall man be pure before the Lord? Shall he be blameless in his works?

Behold, he trusteth not in his servants; and his angels he chargeth with folly.

Yes, the heaven is not clean in his sight, how much less they that dwell in houses of clay; of which also we ourselves were made?

He smote them as a moth: and from morning even unto the evening they endure not. Because they were not able to help themselves, they perished; he breathed upon them and they died, because they had no wisdom.

Call now if there be any that will answer thee; and to which of the angels wilt thou look?

For wrath killeth the foolish man, and envy slayeth him that is in error.

I have seen the foolish taking root, but lo, their habitation was presently consumed.

Their children were far from safety, they perished at the gates of those who were lesser than themselves; and there was no man to help them.

For what was prepared for them, the righteous did eat: and they shall not be delivered from evil.

Seeing then these things are manifest unto us, it will behoove us, to take care that looking into the depths of the divine knowledge, we do all things in order, whatsoever our Lord has commanded us to do.

And particularly, that we perform our offerings and service to God, at their appointed seasons: for these he has commanded to be done, not rashly and disorderly, but at certain determinate times and hours.

And therefore he has ordained by his supreme will and authority, both where, and by what persons, they are to be performed; that so all things being piously done unto all well-pleasing, they may be acceptable unto him.

They therefore who make their offerings at the appointed seasons, are happy and accepted: because that obeying the commandments of the Lord, they are free from sin.

And the same care must be had of the persons that minister unto him.

For the chief-priest has his proper services; and to the priests their proper place is appointed; and to the Levites appertain their proper ministries: and the layman is confined within the bounds of what is commanded to laymen.

Let every one of you therefore, brethren, bless God in his proper station, with a good conscience, and with all gravity, not exceeding the rule of his service that is appointed to him.

The daily sacrifices are not offered everywhere; nor the peace-offerings, nor the sacrifices appointed for sins and transgressions; but only at Jerusalem: nor in any place there, but only at the altar before the temple; that which is offered being first diligently examined by the high-priest and the other minister we before mentioned.

They therefore who do anything which is not agreeable to His will are punished with death.

Consider, brethren, that by how much the better knowledge God has vouchsafed unto us by so much the greater danger are we exposed to.

CHAPTER XIX.

The orders of Ministers in Christ's Church established by the Apostles according to Christ's command, after the example of Moses. Therefore they who have been duly placed in the ministry according to their order cannot without great sin be put out of it.

THE Apostles have preached to us from the Lord Jesus Christ; Jesus Christ from God.

Christ therefore was sent by God, the Apostles by Christ; so both were orderly sent, according to the will of God.

For having received their command, and being thoroughly assured by the resurrection of our Lord Jesus Christ; and convinced by the word of God, with the fulness of the Holy Spirit, they went abroad, publishing, That the kingdom of God was at hand.

And thus preaching through countries and cities, they appointed the first fruits of their conversion to be bishops and ministers over such as should afterwards believe, having first proved them by the Spirit.

Nor was this any new thing: seeing that long before it was written concerning bishops and deacons.

For thus saith the Scripture, in a certain place: I will appoint their overseers in righteousness, and their ministers in faith.

And what wonder if they, to whom such a work was committed by God in Christ, established such officers as we before mentioned; when even that blessed and faithful servant in all his house, Moses, set down in the Holy Scriptures all things that were commanded him.

Whom also all the rest of the prophets followed, bearing witness with one consent to those things that were appointed by him.

For he, perceiving an emulation to arise among the tribes concerning the priesthood, and that there was a strife about it, which of them should be adorned with that glorious name; commanded their twelve captains to bring to him twelve rods; every tribe being written upon its rod, according to its name.

And he took them and bound them together, and sealed them with the seals of the twelve princes of the tribes; and laid them up in the tabernacle of witness, upon the table of God.

And when he had shut the door of the tabernacle he sealed up the keys of it, in like manner as he had done the rods; and said unto them, Men and brethren, whichsoever tribe shall have its rod blossom, that tribe has God chosen to perform the office of a priest, and to minister unto him in holy things.

And when the morning was come, he called together all Israel, six hundred thousand men; and shewed to the princes their seals; and opened the tabernacle of witness; and brought forth the rods.

And the rod of Aaron was found not only to have blossomed, but also to have fruit upon it.

What think you, beloved? Did not Moses before know what should happen?

Yes verily: but to the end there might be no division, nor tumult in Israel, he did in this manner, that the name of the true and only God might be glorified, to him be honour for ever and ever, Amen.

So likewise our Apostles knew by our Lord Jesus Christ, that there should contentions arise, upon account of the ministry.

And therefore having a perfect fore-knowledge of this, they appointed persons, as we have before said, and then gave direction, how, when they should die, other chosen and approved men should succeed in their ministry.

Wherefore we cannot think that those may justly be thrown out of their ministry, who were either appointed by them, or afterwards chosen by other eminent men, with the consent of the whole church; and who have with all lowliness and innocency ministered to the flock of Christ, in peace, and without self-interest, and were for a long time commended by all.

For it would be no small sin in us, should we cast off those from their ministry who holily and without blame fulfil the duties of it.

Blessed are those priests, who having finished their course before these times have obtained a fruitful and perfect dissolution: for they have no fear, lest any one should turn them out of the place which is now appointed for them.

But we see how you have put out some, who lived reputably among you, from the ministry, which by their innocence they had adorned.

CHAPTER XX.

He exhorts them to peace from examples out of the Holy Scriptures, particularly from St. Paul's exhortation to them.

YE are contentious, brethren, and zealous for things that pertain not unto salvation.

Look into the Holy Scriptures, which are the true words of the Holy Ghost. Ye know that there is nothing unjust or counterfeit written in them.

There you shall not find that righteous men were ever cast off by such as were good themselves.

They were persecuted, but it was by the wicked and unjust.

They were cast into prison; but they were cast in by those that were unholy.

They were stoned; but it was by transgressors.

They were killed; but by accursed men, and such as had taken up an unjust envy against them.

And all these things they underwent gloriously.

For what shall we say, brethren? Was Daniel cast into the den of lions, by men fearing God? Ananias, Azarius, and Misael, were they cast into the fiery furnace by men, professing the excellent and glorious worship of the Most High? God forbid.

What kind of persons then were they that did these things? They were men abominable, full of all wickedness; who were incensed to so great a degree, as to bring those into sufferings, who with a holy and unblameable purpose of mind worshipped God: not knowing that the Most High is the protector and defender of all such as with a pure conscience serve his holy name: to whom be glory for ever and ever, Amen.

But they who with a full persuasion have endured these things, and are made partakers of glory and honour: and are exalted and lifted up by God in their memorial throughout all ages, Amen.

Wherefore it will behoove us also, brethren, to follow such examples as these; for it is written, Hold fast to such as are holy; for they that do so shall be sanctified.

And again in another place he saith, With the pure thou shalt be pure, (and with the elect thou shalt be elect), but with the perverse man thou shalt be perverse.

Let us therefore join ourselves to the innocent and righteous; for such are the elect of God.

Wherefore are there strifes, and anger, and divisions, and schisms, and wars, among us?

Have we not all one God, and one Christ? Is not one spirit of grace poured out upon us all? Have we not one calling in Christ?

Why then do we rend and tear in pieces the members of Christ; and raise seditious against our own body? And are come to such a height of madness, as to forget that we were members one of another?

Remember the words of our Lord Jesus, how he said, Wo to that man, (by whom offences come) It were better for him that he had never been born, than that he should have offended one of my elect. It were better for him, that a millstone should be tied about his neck, and he should be cast into the sea, than that he should offend one of my little ones.

Your schism has perverted many, has discouraged many: it has caused diffidence in many, and grief in us all. And yet your sedition continues still.

Take the epistle of the blessed Paul the Apostle into your hands; What was it that he wrote to you at his first preaching the Gospel among you?

Verily he did by the spirit admonish you concerning himself, and Cephas, and Apollos, because that even then ye had begun to fall into parties and factions among yourselves.

Nevertheless your partiality then led you into a much less sin: forasmuch as ye placed your affections upon Apostles, men of eminent reputation in the church; and upon another, who was greatly tried and approved of by them.

But consider, we pray you, who are they that have now led you astray; and lessened the reputation of that brotherly love that was so eminent among you?

It is a shame, my beloved, yea, a very great shame, and unworthy of your Christian profession, to hear that the most firm and ancient church of the Corinthians should, by one or two persons, be led into a sedition against its priests.

And this report is come not only to us, but to those also that differ from us.

Insomuch that the name of the Lord is blasphemed through your folly; and even ye yourselves are brought into danger by it.

Let us therefore with all haste put an end to this sedition; and let us fall down before the Lord, and beseech Him with tears that He would be favourably reconciled to us, and restore us again to a seemly and holy course of brotherly love.

For this is the gate of righteousness, opening unto life: as it is written, Open unto me the gates of righteousness; I will go in unto them and will praise the Lord. This is the gate of the Lord, the righteous shall enter into it.

Although therefore many gates are opened, yet this gate of righteousness is that gate in Christ at which blessed are they that enter in, and direct their way in holiness and righteousness, doing all things without disorder.

Let a man be faithful, let him be powerful in the utterance of knowledge: let him be wise in making an exact judgment of words; let him be pure in all his actions.

But still by how much the more he seems to be above others by reason of these things, by so much the more will it behoove him to be humble-minded; and to seek what is profitable to all men, and not his own advantage.

CHAPTER XXI.

The value which God puts upon love and unity: the effects of a true charity, which is the gift of God, and must be obtained by prayer.

HE that has the love that is in Christ, let him keep the commandments of Christ.

For who is able to express the obligation of the love of God? What man is sufficient to declare, and is fitting, the excellency of its beauty?

The height to which charity leads is inexpressible.

Charity unites us to God; charity covers the multitude of sins: charity endures all things, is long-suffering in all things.

There is nothing base and sordid in charity; charity lifts not itself up above others; admits of no divisions; is not seditious; but does all things in peace and concord.

By charity were all the elect of God made perfect: Without it nothing is pleasing and acceptable in the sight of God.

Through charity did the Lord join us unto himself; whilst for the love that he bore towards us, our Lord Jesus Christ gave his own blood for us, by the will of God; his flesh for our flesh; his soul, for our souls.

Ye see, beloved, how great and wonderful a thing charity is: and how that no expressions are sufficient to declare its perfection.

But who is fit to be found in it? Even such only as God shall vouchsafe to make so.

Let us therefore pray to him, and beseech him, that we may be worthy of it; that so we may live in charity; being , without human propensities, without respect of persons.

All the ages of the world, from Adam, even unto this day, are passed away; but they who have been made perfect in love, have by the grace of God obtained a place among the righteous; and shall be made manifest in the judgment of the kingdom of Christ.

For it is written, Enter into thy chambers for a little space, till my anger and indignation shall pass away: And I will remember the good day, and will raise you up out of your graves.

Happy then shall we be, beloved, if we shall have fulfilled the commandments of God, in the unity of love; that so, through love, our sins may be forgiven us.

For so it is written, Blessed are they whose iniquities are forgiven, and whose sins are covered. Blessed is the man to whom the Lord imputeth no sin, and in whose mouth there is no guile.

Now this blessing is fulfilled in those who are chosen by God through Jesus Christ our Lord, to whom be glory for ever and ever. Amen.

CHAPTER XXII.

He exhorts such as have been concerned in these divisions to repent, and return to their unity, confessing their sin to God, which he enforces from the example of Moses, and of many among the heathen, and of Judith and Esther among the Jews.

LET us therefore, as many as have transgressed by any of the suggestions of the adversary, beg God's forgiveness.

And as for those who have been the heads of the sedition and faction among you, let them look to the common end of our hope.

For as many as are endued with fear and charity, would rather they themselves should fall into trials than their neighbours: And choose to be themselves condemned, rather than that the good and just charity delivered to us, should suffer.

For it is seemly for a man to confess wherein he has transgressed.

And not to harden his heart, as the hearts of those were hardened, who raised up sedition against Moses the servant of God; whose punishment was manifest unto all men; for they went down alive into the grave, death swallowed them up.

Pharaoh and his host, and all the rulers of Egypt, their chariots also and their horsemen, were for no other cause drowned, in the bottom of the Red Sea, and perished; but because they hardened their foolish hearts, after so many signs done in the land of Egypt, by Moses the servant of God.

Beloved, God is rot indigent of any thing; nor does he demand any thing of us, but that we should confess our sins unto him.

For so says the Holy David, I will confess unto the Lord, and it shall please him better than a young bullock that hath horns and hoof. Let the poor see it and be glad.

And again he saith, Offer unto God the sacrifice of praise, and pay thy vows unto the Most Highest. And call upon me in the day of trouble, and I will deliver thee, and thou shalt glorify me. The sacrifice of God is a broken spirit.

Ye know, beloved, ye know full well the Holy Scriptures; and have thoroughly searched into the oracles of God: call them therefore to your remembrance.

For when Moses went up into the mount, and tarried there forty days and forty nights in fasting and humiliation; God said unto him, Arise, Moses, and get thee down quickly from hence, for thy people whom thou broughtest out of the land of Egypt, have committed wickedness: they have soon transgressed the way that I commanded them, and have made to themselves graven images.

And the Lord said unto him, I have spoken unto thee several times, saying I have seen this people, and behold it is a stiffnecked people: let me therefore destroy them, and put out their name from under heaven. And I will make unto thee a great and a wonderful nation, that shall be much larger than this.

But Moses said, Not so, Lord; Forgive now this people their sin; or if thou wilt not, blot me also out of the book of! the living. O admirable charity! O insuperable perfection! The servant speaks freely to his Lord; He beseeches him either to forgive the people, or to destroy him together with them.

Who is there among you that is generous? Who that is compassionate? Who that has any charity? Let him say, if this sedition, this contention, and these schisms, be upon my account, I am ready to depart; to go away whithersoever you please; and do whatsoever ye shall command me: Only let the flock of Christ be in peace, with the elders that are set over it.

He that shall do this, shall get to himself a very great honour in the Lord; and there is no place but what will be ready to receive him: For the earth is the Lord's and the fulness thereof.

These things they who have their conversation towards God not to be repented of, both have done and will always be ready! to do.

Nay and even the Gentiles themselves have given us! examples of this kind.

For we read, How many kings and princes, in times of pestilence, being warned by their oracles, have given up themselves unto death: that by their own blood, they might deliver their country from destruction.

Others have forsaken their cities, so that they might put an end to the seditions of them.

We know how many among ourselves, have given up themselves unto bonds, that thereby they might free others from them.

Others have sold themselves into bondage that they might feed their brethren with the price of themselves.

And even many women, being strengthened by the grace of God, have done many glorious and manly things on such occasions.

The blessed Judith, when her city was besieged, desired the elders, that they would suffer her to go into the camp of their enemies: and she went out exposing herself to danger for the love she bore to her country and her people that were besieged; and the Lord delivered Holofernes into the hands of a woman.

Nor did Esther, being perfect in faith, expose herself to any less hazard, for the delivery of the twelve tribes of Israel, in danger of being destroyed. For, by fasting and humbling herself, she entreated the Great Maker of all things, the God of spirits; so that beholding the humility of her soul, he delivered the people, for whose sake she was in peril.

CHAPTER XXIII.

The benefit of mutual advice and correction. He entreats them to follow that which is here given to them.

WHEREFORE let us also pray for such as are fallen into sin. That being endued with humility and moderation, they may submit not unto us, but to the will of God.

For by this means they shall obtain a fruitful and perfect remembrance, with mercy, both in our prayers to God, and in our mention of them before his saints.

Let us receive correction, at which no man ought to repine.

Beloved, the reproof and the correction which we exercise towards one another, is good, and exceeding profitable: for it unites us the more closely to the will of God.

For so says the Holy Scripture, The Lord corrected me, but he did not deliver me over unto death. For whom the Lord loveth he chasteneth, and scourgeth every son whom he receiveth.

The righteous, saith he, shall instruct me in mercy and reprove me; but let not oil of sinners make fat my head.

And again he saith, Happy is the man whom God correcteth; therefore despise not thou the chastening of the Almighty.

For he maketh sore and bindeth up; he woundeth and his hands make whole.

He shall deliver thee in six troubles; yea in seven there shall no evil touch thee. In famine he shall redeem thee from death; and in war from the power of the sword.

Thou shalt be hid from the scourge of the tongue; neither shalt thou be afraid of destruction when it cometh.

Thou shalt laugh at the wicked and sinners; neither shalt thou be afraid of the beasts of the earth. The wild beast shall be at peace with thee.

Then shalt thou know that thy house shall be in peace; and the habitation of thy tabernacle shall not err. Thou shalt know also that thy seed shall be great and thy offspring as the grass of the earth.

Thou shalt come to thy grave as the ripe corn, that is taken in due time; like as a shock of corn cometh in, in its season.

Ye see, beloved, how there shall be a defence to those that are corrected of the Lord. For being a good instructor, he is willing to admonish us by his holy discipline.

Do ye therefore who laid the first foundation of this sedition, submit yourselves unto your priests; and be instructed unto repentance, bending the knees of your hearts.

Learn to be subject, laying aside all proud and arrogant boasting of your tongues.

For it is better for you to be found little, and approved, in the sheepfold of Christ, than to seem to yourselves better than others, and be cast out of his fold.

For thus speaks the excellent and all virtuous wisdom, Behold I will pour out the word of my spirit upon you, I will make known my speech unto you.

Because I called and ye would not hear, I stretched out my words and ye regarded not.

But ye have set at nought all my counsel, and would none of my reproof. I will also laugh at your calamity, and mock when your fear cometh.

When your fear cometh as desolation, and your destruction as a whirlwind, when distress and anguish cometh upon you.

Then shall ye call upon me, but I will not hear you: the wicked shall seek me, but they shall not find me. For that they hated knowledge, and did not seek the fear of the Lord.

They would not hearken unto my counsel: they despised all my reproof. Therefore shall they eat of the fruit of their own ways; and be filled with their own wickedness.

* * *

CHAPTER XXIV.

Recommends there to God. Desires speedily to hear that this Epistle has had a good effect upon them. Conclusion.

NOW God, the inspector of all things, the Father of Spirits, and the Lord of all flesh, who hath chosen our Lord Jesus Christ, and us by him, to be his peculiar people;

Grant to every soul of man that calleth upon his glorious and holy name, faith, fear, peace, long-suffering, patience, temperance, holiness and sobriety, unto all well-pleasing in his sight; through our High-Priest and Protector Jesus Christ, by whom be glory, and majesty, and power, and honour, unto him now and for ever more. Amen.

The messengers whom we have sent unto you, Claudius, Ephebus, and Valerios Bito, with Fortunatus, send back to us again with all speed in peace, and with joy, that they may the sooner acquaint us with your peace and concord, so much prayed for and desired by us; and that we may rejoice in your good order.

THE LOST BOOKS OF THE BIBLE

The Grace of our Lord Jesus Christ be with you, and with all that are anywhere called by God through him: To whom be honour and glory, and might and majesty, and eternal dominion, by Christ Jesus, from everlasting to everlasting. Amen.

THE SECOND EPISTLE OF CLEMENT TO THE CORINTHIANS.

[Archbishop Wake is the translator of this Second Epistle, which he says was not of so great reputation among the primitive Fathers as the first. He defends it notwithstanding; and in answer to those who objected to Clement's First Epistle, that it did not duly honour the Trinity, the Archbishop refers to this as containing proof of the writer's fulness of belief on that point.]

CHAPTER I.

That we ought to value our salvation; and to skew that we do, by a sincere obedience.

BRETHREN, we ought so to think of Jesus Christ as of God: as of the judge of the living, and the dead; nor should we think any less of our salvation.

For if we think meanly of him, we shall hope only to receive some small things from him.

And if we do so; we shall sin; not considering from whence we have been called, and by whom, and to what place; and how much Jesus Christ vouchsafed to suffer for our sakes.

What recompense then shall we render unto him? Or what fruit that may be worthy of what he has given to us?

For indeed how great are those advantages which we owe to him in relation to our holiness? He has illuminated us: as a father, he has called us his children; he has saved us who were lost and undone.

What praise shall we give to him? Or what reward that may be answerable to those things which we have received?

We were defective in our understandings; worshipping stones and wood; gold, and silver, and brass, the works of men's hands; and our whole life was nothing else but death.

Wherefore being encompassed with darkness, and having such a mist before our eyes, we have looked up, and through his will have laid aside the cloud wherewith we were surrounded.

For he had compassion upon us, and being moved in his bowels towards us, he saved us; having beheld in us much error, and destruction; and seen that we had no hope of salvation, but only through him.

For he called us who were not; and was pleased from nothing to give us being.

CHAPTER II.

That God had before prophesied by Isaiah, that the Gentiles should be saved. That this ought to engage such especially to live well; without which they will still miscarry.

REJOICE, thou barren, that bearest not, break forth and cry thou that travailest not; for she that is desolate hath many more children than she that hath an husband.

In that he said, Rejoice thou barren that bearest not, he spake of us: for our church was barren before that children were given unto it.

And again; when he said, Cry thou that travailest not; he implied thus much: That after the manner of women in travail, we should not cease to put up our prayers unto God abundantly.

And for what follows, because she that is desolate hath more children than she that hath an husband: it was therefore added, because our people which seem to have been forsaken by God, now believing in him, are become more than they who seemed to have God.

And another Scripture saith, I came not to call the righteous but sinners (to repentance). The meaning of which is this: that those who were lost must be saved.

For that is, indeed, truly great and wonderful, not to confirm those things that are yet standing, but those which are falling.

Even so did it seem good to Christ to save what was lost; and when he came into the world, he saved many, and called us who were already lost.

Seeing then he has shewed so great mercy towards us; and chiefly for that, we who are alive, do now no longer sacrifice to dead Gods, nor pay any worship to them, but have by him been brought to the knowledge of the Father of truth.

Whereby shall we shew that we do indeed know him, but by not denying him by whom we have come to the knowledge of him?

For even he himself saith, Whosoever shall confess me before men, him will I confess before my Father. This therefore is our reward if we shall confess him by whom we have been saved.

But, wherein must we confess him?—Namely, in doing those things which he saith, and not disobeying his commandments: by worshipping him not with our lips only, but with all our heart, and with all our mind. For he saith in Isaiah: This people honoureth me with their lips, but their heart is far from me.

Let us then not only call him Lord; for that will not save us. For he saith: Not every one that saith unto me Lord, Lord, shall be saved, but he that doeth righteousness.

Wherefore, brethren, let us confess him by our works; by loving one another; in not committing adultery, not speaking evil against each other, not envying one another; but by being temperate, merciful, good.

Let us also have a mutual sense of one another's sufferings; and not be covetous of money: but let us, by our good works, confess God, and not by those that are otherwise.

Also let us not fear men: but rather God. Wherefore, if we should do such wicked things, the Lord hath said: Though ye should be joined unto me, even in my very bosom, and not keep my commandments, I would cast you off, and say unto you: Depart from me; I know not whence you are, ye workers of iniquity.

CHAPTER III.

That whilst we secure the other world, we need not fear what can befall us in this. That if we follow the interests of this present world, we cannot escape the punishment of the other. Which ought to bring us to repentance and holiness, 14 and that presently: because in this world is the only time for repentance.

WHEREFORE, brethren, leaving willingly for conscience sake our sojourning in this world, let us do the will of him who has called us, and not fear to depart out of this world.

For the Lord saith, Ye shall be as sheep in the midst of wolves. Peter answered and said, What if the wolves shall tear in pieces the sheep? Jesus said unto Peter, Let not the sheep fear the wolves after death: And ye also fear not those that kill you, and after that have no more that they can do unto you; but fear him who after you are dead, has power to cast both soul and body into hell-fire.

For consider, brethren, that the sojourning of this flesh in the present world, is but little, and of a short continuance, but the promise of Christ is great and wonderful, even the rest of the kingdom that is to come, and of eternal life.

What then must we do that we may attain unto it?—We must order our conversation holily and righteously, and look upon all the things of this world as none of ours, and not desire them. For, if we desire to possess them we fall from the way of righteousness.

For thus saith the Lord, No servant can serve two masters. If therefore we shall desire to serve God and Mammon it will be without profit to us. For what will it profit, if one gain the whole world, and lose his own soul?

Now this world and that to come are two enemies. This speaketh of adultery and corruption, of covetousness and deceit; but renounces these things.

We cannot, therefore, be the friends of both; but we must resolve by forsaking the one, to enjoy the other. And we think it is better to hate the present things, as little, short-lived, and corruptible, and to love those which are to come, which are truly good and incorruptible.

For, if we do the will of Christ, we shall find rest: but if not, nothing shall deliver us from eternal punishment if we shall disobey his commands. For even thus saith the Scripture in the prophet Ezekiel, If Noah, Job, and Daniel should rise up, they shall not deliver their children in captivity.

Wherefore, if such righteous men are not able by their righteousness to deliver their children; how can we hope to enter into the kingdom of God, except we keep our baptism holy and undefiled? Or who shall be our advocate, unless we shall be found to have done what is holy and just?

Let us, therefore, my brethren, contend with all earnestness, knowing that our combat is at hand; and that many go long voyages to encounter for a corruptible reward.

And yet all are not crowned, but they only that labour much, and strive gloriously. Let us, therefore, so contend, that we may all be crowned. Let us run in the straight road, the race that is incorruptible: and let us in great numbers pass unto it, and strive that we may receive the crown. But and if we cannot all be crowned, let us come as near to it as we are able.

Moreover, we must consider, that he who contends in a corruptible combat, if he be found doing anything that is not fair, is taken away and scourged, and cast out of the lists. What think ye then that he shall suffer, who does anything that is not fitting in the combat of immortality?

Thus speaks the prophet concerning those who keep not their seal; Their worm shall not die, and their fire shall not be quenched; and they shall be for a spectacle unto all flesh.

Let us therefore repent, whilst we are yet upon the earth: for we are as clay in the hand of the artificer. For as the potter if he make a vessel, and it be turned amiss in his hands, or broken, again forms it anew; but if he have gone so far as to throw it into the furnace of fire, he can no more bring any remedy to it.

So we, whilst we are in this world, should repent with our whole heart for whatsoever evil we have done in the flesh; while we have yet the time of repentance, that we may be saved by the Lord.

For after we shall have departed out of this world, we shall no longer be able to confess our sins or repent in the other.

Wherefore, brethren, let us doing the will of the Father, and keeping our flesh pure, and observing the commandments of the Lord, lay hold on eternal life: for the Lord saith in the gospel, If ye have not kept that which was little, who will give you that which is great?—For I say unto you, he that is faithful in that which is least, is faithful also in much.

This, therefore, is what he saith; keep your bodies pure, and your seal without spot, that ye may receive eternal life.

CHAPTER IV.

We shall rise, and be judged in our bodies; therefore we must live well in them, that we ought, for our own interest, to live well; though few seem to mind what really is for their advantage, and not deceive ourselves: seeing God will certainly judge us, and render to all of us according to our works.

AND let not any one among you say, that this very flesh is not judged, neither raised up. Consider, in what were you saved; in what did you look up, if not whilst you were in this flesh.

We must, therefore, keep our flesh as the temple of God. For in like manner as ye were called in the flesh ye shall also come to judgment in the flesh. Our one Lord Jesus Christ, who has saved us, being first a spirit, was made flesh, and so called us; even so we also shall in this flesh receive the reward.

Let us, therefore, love one another, that we may attain unto the kingdom of God. Whilst we have time to be healed, let us deliver up ourselves to God our physician, giving our reward unto him.

And what reward shall we give?—Repentance out of a pure heart. For he knows all things before hand, and searches out our very hearts.

Let us, therefore, give praise unto him: not only with our mouths, but with all our souls; that he may receive us as children. For so the Lord hath said; They are my brethren, who do the will of my father.

Wherefore, my brethren, let us do the will of the Father, who hath called us, that we may live. Let us pursue virtue, and forsake wickedness, which leadeth us into sins; and let us flee all ungodliness, that evils overtake us not.

For, if we shall do our diligence to live well, peace shall follow us. And yet how hard is it to find a man that does this? For almost all are led by human fears, choosing rather the present enjoyments, than the future promise.

For they know not how great a torment the present enjoyments bring with them; nor what delights the future promise

And if they themselves only did this, it might the more easily be endured; but now they go on to infect innocent souls with their evil doctrines; not knowing that both themselves, and those that hear them, shall receive a double condemnation.

Let us, therefore, serve God with a pure heart, and we shall be righteous: but if we shall not serve him because we do not believe the promise of God, we shall be miserable.

For thus saith the prophet; Miserable are the double minded who doubt in their heart, and say, these things we have heard, even in the time of our fathers, but we have seen none of them, though we have expected them from day to day.

O ye fools! compare yourselves to a tree; take the vine for an example. First it sheds its leaves, then it buds, then come the sour grapes, then the ripe fruit; even so my people have borne its disorders and afflictions, but shall hereafter receive good things.

Wherefore my brethren, let us not doubt in our minds, but let us expect with hope, that we may receive our reward; for he is faithful, who has promised he will render to every one a reward according to his works.

If, therefore, we shall do what is just in the sight of God we shall enter into his kingdom, I and shall receive the promises; Which neither eye has seen, nor ear heard, nor have entered into the heart of man.

Wherefore let us every hour expect the kingdom of God in love and righteousness; because we know not the day of God's appearing.

CHAPTER V.

A FRAGMENT.

Of the Lord's kingdom.

* * For the Lord himself, being asked by a certain person, When his kingdom should come? answered, When two shall be one, and that which is without as that which is within; and the male with the female, neither male nor female.

Now two are one, when we speak the truth to each other, and there is (without hypocrisy) one soul in two bodies:

And that which is without as that which is within;—He means this: he calls the soul that which is within, and the body that which is without. As therefore thy body appears, so let thy soul be seen by its good works.

And the male with the female neither male nor female;—He means this; he calls our anger the male, our concupiscence the female.

When therefore a man is come to such a pass that he is subject neither to the one nor the other of these (both of which, through the prevalence of custom, and an evil education, cloud and darken the reason,)

But rather, having dispelled the mist arising from them, and being full of shame, shall by repentance have united both his soul and spirit in the obedience of reason; then, as Paul says, there is in us neither male nor female

THE GENERAL EPISTLE OF BARNABAS.

[Barnabas was a companion and fellow-preacher with Paul. This Epistle lays a greater claim to canonical authority than most others. It has been cited by Clemens Alexandrinus, Origen, Eusebius, and Jerome, and many ancient Fathers. Cotelerius affirms that Origen and Jerome esteemed it genuine and canonical; but Cotelerius himself did not believe it to be either one or the other; on the contrary, he supposes it was written for the benefit of the Ebionites (the christianized Jews,) who were tenacious of rites and ceremonies. Bishop Fell feared to own expressly what he seemed to be persuaded of, that it ought to be treated with the same respect as several of the books of the present canon. Dr. Bernard, Savilian professor at Oxford, not only believed it to be genuine, but that it was read throughout, in the churches at Alexandria, as the canonical scriptures were. Dodwell supposed it to have been published before the Epistle of Jude, and the writings of both the Johns. Vossius, Dupuis, Dr. Cane, Dr. Mill, Dr. S. Clark, Whiston, and Archbishop Wake also esteemed it genuine: Menardus, Archbishop Laud, Spanheim, and others, deemed it apocryphal.]

CHAPTER I.

THE LOST BOOKS OF THE BIBLE

Preface to the Epistle.

ALL happiness to you my sons and daughters, in the name of our Lord Jesus Christ, who loved us, in peace.

Having perceived abundance of knowledge of the great and excellent laws of God to be in you, I exceedingly rejoice in your blessed and admirable souls, because ye have so worthily received the grace which was grafted in you.

For which cause I am full of joy, hoping the rather to he saved; inasmuch as I truly see a spirit infused into you, from the pure fountain of God:

Having this persuasion, and being fully convinced thereof, because that since I have begun to speak unto you, I have had a more than ordinary good success in the way of the law of the Lord which is in Christ.

For which cause brethren, I also think verily that I love you above my own soul: because that therein dwelleth the greatness of faith and charity, as also the hope of that life which is to come.

Wherefore considering this, that if I shall take care to communicate to you a part of what I have received, it shall turn to my reward, that I have served such good souls; I gave diligence to write in a few words unto you; that together with your faith, knowledge also may be perfect.

There are therefore three things ordained by the Lord; the hope of life; the beginning and the completion of it.

For the Lord hath both declared unto us, by the prophets those things that are past; and opened to us the beginnings of those that are to come.

Wherefore, it will behoove us, as he has spoken, to come more holily, and nearer to his altar.

I therefore, not as a teacher, but as one of you, will endeavour to lay before you a few things by which you may, on many accounts, become the more joyful.

CHAPTER II.

That God has abolished the legal sacrifices to introduce the spiritual righteousness of the Gospel.

SEEING then the days are exceeding evil, and the adversary has got the power of this present world we ought to give the more diligence to inquire into the righteous judgments of the Lord.

Now the assistants of our faith are fear and patience; our fellow-combatants, long-suffering and continence.

Whilst these remain pure in what relates unto the Lord, wisdom, and understanding, and science, and knowledge, rejoice together with them.

For God has manifested to us by all the prophets, that he has no occasion for our sacrifices, or burnt-offerings, or oblations: saying thus; To what purpose is the multitude of your sacrifices unto me, saith the Lord.

I am full of the burnt-offerings of rams, and the fat of fed beasts; and I delight not in the blood of bullocks, or of he-goats

When ye come to appear before me; who hath required this at your hands? Ye shall no more tread my courts.

Bring no more vain oblations, incense is an abomination unto me; your new moons and sabbaths; the calling of assemblies I cannot away with, it is iniquity, even the solemn meeting; your new moons and your appointed feasts my soul hateth.

These things therefore hath God abolished, that the new law of our Lord Jesus Christ, which is without the yoke of any such necessity, might have the spiritual offering of men themselves.

For so the Lord saith again to those heretofore; Did I at all command your fathers when they came out of the land of Egypt concerning burnt-offerings of sacrifices?

But this I commanded them, saying, Let none of you imagine evil in your hearts against his neighbour, and love no false oath.

Forasmuch then as we are not without understanding, we ought to apprehend the design of our merciful Father. For he speaks to us, being willing that we who have been in the same error about the sacrifices, should seek and find how to approach unto him.

And therefore he thus bespeaks us, The sacrifice of God (is a broken spirit,) a broken and contrite heart God will not despise.

Wherefore brethren, we ought the more diligently to inquire after these things that belong to our salvation, that the adversary may not have any entrance into us, and deprive us of our spiritual life.

Wherefore he again speaketh to them, concerning these things; Ye shall not fast as ye do this day, to make your voice to be heard on high.

Is it such a fast that I have chosen? a day for a man to afflict his soul? Is it to bow down his head like a bulrush, and to spread sackcloth and ashes under him? Wilt thou call this a fast, and an acceptable day to the Lord?

But to us he saith on this wise. Is not this the fast that I have chosen, to loose the bands of wickedness, to undo the heavy burdens, and to let the oppressed go free; and that ye break every yoke?

Is it not to deal thy bread to the hungry, and that thou bring the poor that are cast out to thy house? When thou seest the naked that thou cover him, and that thou hide not thyself from thine own flesh.

Then shall thy light break forth as the morning, and thy health shall spring forth speedily; and thy righteousness shall go before thee, the glory of the Lord shall be thy reward.

THE LOST BOOKS OF THE BIBLE

Then shalt thou call and the Lord shall answer; thou shalt cry and he shall say, Here I am. If thou put away from the midst of thee the yoke, the putting forth of the finger, and speaking vanity; and if thou draw out thy soul to the hungry; and satisfy the afflicted soul.

In this therefore brethren, God has manifested his foreknowledge and love for us; because the people which he has purchased to his beloved Son were to believe in sincerity; and therefore he has shewn these things to all of us, that we should not run as proselytes to the Jewish law.

CHAPTER III.

The prophecies of Daniel, concerning the ten kings, and the coming of Christ.

WHEREFORE it is necessary that searching diligently into those things which are near to come to pass, we should write to you what may serve to keep you whole.

To which end let us flee from every evil work and hate the errors of the present time, that we may be happy in that which is to come:

Let us not give ourselves the liberty of disputing with the wicked and sinners; lest we should chance in time to become like unto them.

For the consummation of sin is come, as it is written, as the prophet Daniel says. And for this end the Lord hath shortened the times and the days, that his beloved might hasten his coming to his inheritance.

For so the prophet speaks; There shall ten kings reign in the heart, and there shall rise last of all another little one, and he shall humble three kings.

And again Daniel speaks in like manner concerning the kingdoms; and I saw the fourth beast dreadful and terrible, and strong exceedingly; and it had ten horns. I considered the horns, and behold there came up among them another little horn, before which were three of the first horns plucked up by the roots.

We ought therefore to understand this also: And I beseech you as one of your own brethren, loving you all beyond my own life, that you look well to yourselves, and be not like to those who add sin to sin, and say: That their covenant is ours also. Nay, but it is ours only: for they have for ever lost that which Moses received.

For thus saith the Scripture: And Moses continued fasting forty days and forty nights in the Mount; and he received the covenant from the Lord, even the two tables of stone, written by the hand of God.

But having turned themselves to idols they lost it; as the Lord also said to Moses; Moses, go down quickly, for thy people which thou hast brought forth out of Egypt, have corrupted themselves, and turned aside from the way which I commanded them. And Moses cast the two tables out of his hands: and their covenant was broken; that the love of Jesus might be sealed in your hearts, unto the hope of his faith.

Wherefore let us give heed unto the last times. For all the time past of our life, and

146

our faith will profit us nothing; unless we continue to hate what is evil, and to withstand the future temptations. So the Son of God tells us; Let us resist all iniquity and hate it.

Wherefore consider the works of the evil way. Do not withdraw yourselves from others, as if you were already justified; but coming altogether into one place, inquire what is agreeable to and profitable for the beloved of God. For the Scripture saith; Wo unto them that are wise in their own eyes, and prudent in their sight.

Let us become spiritual, a perfect temple to God. As much as in us lies let us meditate upon the fear of God; and strive to the utmost of our power to keep his commandments; that we may rejoice in his righteous judgments.

For God will judge the world without respect of persons: and every one shall receive according to his works.

If a man shall be good, his righteousness shall go before him; if wicked, the reward of his wickedness shall follow him.

Take heed therefore lest sitting still, now that we are called, we fall asleep in our sins; and the wicked one getting the dominion over us, stir us up, and shut us out of the kingdom of the Lord.

Consider this also: although you have seen so great signs and wonders done among the people of the Jews, yet this notwithstanding the Lord hath forsaken them.

Beware therefore, lest it happen to us; as it is written. There may be many called, but few chosen.

CHAPTER IV.

That Christ was to suffer: proved from the prophecies concerning him.

FOR this cause did our Lord vouchsafe to give up his body to destruction, that through the forgiveness of our sins we might be sanctified; that is, by the sprinkling of his blood.

Now for what concerns the things that are written about him, some belong to the people of the Jews, and some to us.

For thus saith the Scripture: He was wounded for our transgressions, he was bruised for our iniquities, and by his blood we are healed. He was led as a lamb to the slaughter, and as a sheep before his shearers is dumb, so he opened not his mouth.

Wherefore we ought the more to give thanks unto God, for that he hath both declared unto us what is passed, and not suffered us to be without understanding of those things that are to come.

But to them he saith; The nests are not unjustly spread for the birds.

This he spake, because a man will justly perish, if having the knowledge of the way of truth, he shall nevertheless not refrain himself from the way of darkness.

And for this cause the Lord was content to suffer for our souls, although he be the

THE LOST BOOKS OF THE BIBLE

Lord of the whole earth; to whom God said before the beginning of the world, Let us make man after our own image and likeness.

Now how he suffered for us, seeing it was by men that he underwent it, I will shew you.

The prophets having received from him the gift of prophecy, spake before concerning him:

But he, that he might abolish death, and make known the resurrection from the dead, was content, as it was necessary, to appear in the flesh, that he might make good the promise before given to our fathers, and preparing himself a new people, might demonstrate to them whilst he was upon earth, that after the resurrection he would judge the world.

And finally teaching the people of Israel, and doing many wonders and signs among them, he preached to them, and shewed the exceeding great love which he bare towards them.

And when he chose his apostles, which were afterwards to publish his Gospel, he took men who had been very great sinners; that thereby he might plainly shew, That he came not to call the righteous but sinners to repentance.

Then he clearly manifested himself to be the Son of God. For had he not come in the flesh, how should men have been able to look upon him, that they might be saved?

Seeing if they beheld only the sun, which was the work of his hands, and shall hereafter cease to be, they are not able to endure steadfastly to look against the rays of it.

Wherefore the Son of God came in the flesh for this cause, that he might fill up the measure of their iniquity, who have persecuted his prophets unto death. And for the same reason also he suffered.

For God hath said of the stripes of his flesh, that they were from them. And, I will smite the shepherd, and the sheep of the flock shall be scattered.

Thus he would suffer, because it behooved him to suffer upon the cross.

For thus one saith, prophesying concerning him; Spare my soul from the sword. And again, Pierce my flesh from thy fear.

And again, the congregation of wicked doers rose up against me, (They have pierced my hands and my feet).

And again he saith, I gave my back to the smiters, and my face I set as an hard rock.

CHAPTER V.

The subject continued.

AND when he had fulfilled the commandment of God, What says he? Who will

148

contend with me? Let him stand against me: or who is he that will me? Let him draw near to the servant of the Lord. Wo be to you! Because ye shall all wax old as a garment, the moth shall eat you up.

And again the prophet adds, He is put for a stone for stumbling. Behold I lay in Zion for a foundation, a precious stone, a choice corner stone; an honourable stone. And what follows? And he that hopeth in him shall live for ever.

What then? Is our hope built upon a stone? God forbid. But because the Lord hath hardened his flesh against sufferings, he saith, I have put me as a firm rock.

And again the prophet adds; The stone which the builders refused has become the head of the corner. And again he saith; This is the great and wonderful day which the Lord hath made. I write these things the more plainly to you that ye may understand: For indeed I could be content even to die for your sakes.

But what saith the prophet again? The counsel of the wicked encompassed me about. They came about me, as bees about the honey-comb: and, Upon my vesture they cast lots.

Forasmuch then as our Saviour was to appear in the flesh and suffer, his passion was hereby foretold.

For thus saith the prophet against Israel: Wo be to their soul, because they have taken wicked counsel against themselves, saying, let us lay snares for the righteous, because he is unprofitable to us.

Moses also in like manner speaketh to them; Behold thus saith the Lord God; Enter ye into the good land of which the Lord hath sworn to Abraham, and Isaac, and Jacob, that he would give it you, and possess it; a land flowing with milk and honey.

Now what the spiritual meaning of this is, learn; It is as if it had been said, Put your trust in Jesus, who shall be manifested to you in the flesh. For man is the earth which suffers: forasmuch as out of the substance of the earth Adam was formed.

What therefore does he mean when he says, Into a good land flowing with milk and honey? Blessed be our Lord, who has given us wisdom, and a heart to understand his secrets. For so says the prophet, Who shall understand the hard sayings of the Lord? But he that is wise, and intelligent, and that loves his Lord.

Seeing therefore he has renewed us by the remission of our sins, he has put us into another frame, that we should have souls like those of children, forming us again himself by the spirit.

For thus the Scripture saith concerning us, where it introduceth the Father speaking to the Son; Let us make man after our likeness and similitude; and let them have dominion over the beasts of the earth, and over the fowls of the air, and the fish of the sea.

And when the Lord saw the man which he had formed, that behold he was very good; he said, Increase and multiply, and replenish the earth. And this he spake to his son.

I will now shew you, how he made us a new creature, in the latter days.

The Lord saith; Behold I will make the last as the first. Wherefore the prophet thus spake, Enter into the land flowing with milk and honey, and have dominion over it.

Wherefore ye see how we are again formed anew; as also he speaks by another prophet; Behold saith the Lord, I will take from them, that is, from those whom the spirit of the Lord foresaw, their hearts of stone, and I will put into them hearts of flesh.

Because he was about to be made manifest in the flesh and to dwell in us.

For, my brethren, the habitation of our heart is a holy temple unto the Lord. For the Lord saith again. In what place shall I appear before the Lord my God, and be glorified?

He answers I will confess unto thee in the congregation in the midst of my brethren; and will sing unto thee in the church of the saints.

Wherefore we are they whom he has brought into that good land.

But what signifies the milk and honey? Because as the child is nourished first with milk, and then with honey; so we being kept alive by the belief of his promises, and his word, shall live and have dominion over the land.

For he foretold above, saying, increase and multiply, and have dominion over the fishes, etc.

But who is there that is now able to have this dominion over the wild beasts, or fishes, or fowls of the air? For you know that to rule is to have power, that a man should be set over what he rules.

But forasmuch as this we have not now, he tells us when we shall have it; namely, when we shall become perfect, that we may be made the inheritors of the covenant of the Lord.

CHAPTER VI.

The scape-goat an evident type of this.

UNDERSTAND then my beloved children, that the good God hath before manifested all things unto us, that we might know to whom we ought always to give thanks and praise.

If therefore the Son of God whet is the Lord of all, and shall come to judge both the quick and dead, hath suffered, that by his stripes we might live: let us believe that the Son of God could not have suffered but for us. But being crucified, they gave him vinegar and gall to drink.

Hear therefore how the priests of the temple did foreshew this also: the Lord by his command which was written, declared that whosoever did not fast the appointed fast he should die the death: because he also was himself one day to offer up his body for our sins; that so the type of what was done in Isaac might be fulfilled, who was offered upon the altar.

THE LOST BOOKS OF THE BIBLE

What therefore is it that he says by the prophet? And let them eat of the goat which is offered in the day of the fast for all their sins. Hearken diligently (my brethren,) and all the priests, and they only shall eat the inwards not washed with vinegar.

Why so? because I know that when I shall hereafter offer my flesh for the sins of a new people, ye will give me vinegar to drink mixed with gall; therefore do ye only eat, the people fasting the while, and lamenting in sackcloth and ashes.

And that he might foreshew that he was to suffer for them, hear then how he appointed it.

Take, says he, two goats, fair and alike, and offer them, and let the high priest take one of them for a burnt offering. And what must be done with the other? Let it says he be accursed.

Consider how exactly this appears to have been a type of Jesus. And let all the congregation spit upon it, and prick it; and put the scarlet wool about its head, and thus let it be carried forth into the wilderness.

And this being done, he that was appointed to convey the goat, led it into the wilderness, and took away the scarlet wool, and put it upon a thorn bush, whose young sprouts when we find them in the field we are wont to eat: so the fruit of that thorn only is sweet.

And to what end was this ceremony? Consider; one was offered upon the altar, the other was accursed.

And why was that which was accursed crowned? Because they shall see Christ in that day having a scarlet garment about his body; and shall say: Is not this he whom we crucified; having despised him, pierced him, mocked him? Certainly, this is he, who then said, that he was the Son of God.

As therefore he shall be then like to what he was on earth, so were the Jews heretofore commanded, to take two goats fair and equal. That when they shall see (our Saviour) hereafter coming (in the clouds of heaven), they may be amazed at the likeness of the goats.

Wherefore ye here again see a type of Jesus who was to suffer for us.

But what then signifies this. That the wool was to be put into the midst of the thorns?

This also is a figure of Jesus, sent out to the church. For as he who would take away the scarlet wool must undergo many difficulties, because that thorn was very sharp, and with difficulty get it: So they, says Christ, that will see me, and come to my kingdom, must through many afflictions and troubles attain unto me.

CHAPTER VII.

The red heifer, another type of Christ.

BUT what type do ye suppose it to have been, where it is commanded to the people of Israel, that grown persons in whom sins are come to perfection, should offer an heifer,

151

and after they had killed it should burn the same.

But then young men should take up the ashes and put them in vessels; and tie a piece of scarlet wool and hyssop upon a stick, and so the young men should sprinkle every one of the people, and they should be clear from their sins.

Consider how all these are delivered in a figure to us.

This heifer is Jesus Christ; the wicked men that were to offer it are those sinners who brought him to death: who afterwards have no more to do with it; the sinners have no more the honour of handling of it:

But the young men that performed the sprinkling, signified those who preach to us the forgiveness of sins and the purification of the heart, to whom the Lord gave authority to preach his Gospel: being at the beginning twelve, to signify the tribes, because there were twelve tribes of Israel.

But why were there three young men appointed to sprinkle? To denote Abraham, and Isaac, and Jacob, because they were great before God.

And why was the wool put upon a stick? Because the kingdom of Jesus was founded upon the cross; and therefore they that put their trust in him, shall live for ever.

But why was the wool and hyssop put together? To signify that in the kingdom of Christ there shall be evil and filthy days, in which however we shall be saved; and because he that has any disease in the flesh by some filthy humours is cured by hyssop.

Wherefore these things being thus done, are to us indeed evident, but to the Jews they are obscure; because they hearkened not unto the voice of the Lord.

CHAPTER VIII.

Of the circumcision of the ears; and how in the first institution of circumcision Abraham, mystically foretold Christ by name.

AND therefore the Scripture again speaks concerning our ears, that God has circumcised them, together with our hearts For thus saith the Lord by the holy prophets: By the hearing of the ear they obeyed me.

And again, whey who are afar off, shall hear and understand what things I have done. And again, Circumcise your hearts, saith the Lord.

And again he saith, Hear O Israel! For thus saith the Lord thy God. And again the Spirit of God prophesieth, saying: Who is there that would live for ever, let him hear the voice of my Son.

And again, Hear, O Heaven and give ear O Earth! Because the Lord has spoken these things for a witness.

And again he saith Hear the word of the Lord, ye princes of the people. And again Hear O Children! The voice of one crying in the wilderness.

Wherefore he has circumcised our ears that we should hear his word, and believe. But as for that circumcision, in which the Jews trust, it is abolished. For the circumcision of which God spake, was not of the flesh;

But they have transgressed his commands, because the evil one hath deceived them. For thus God bespeaks them; Thus saith the Lord your God (Here I find the new law) Sow not among thorns; but circumcise yourselves to the Lord your God. And what doth he mean by this saying? Hearken unto your Lord.

And again he saith, Circumcise the hardness of your heart, and harden not your neck. And again, Behold, saith the Lord, all the nations are uncircumcised, (they have not lost their fore-skin): but this people is uncircumcised in heart.

But you will say the Jews were circumcised for a sign. And so are all the Syrians and Arabians, and all the idolatrous priests: but are they therefore of the covenant of Israel? And even the Egyptians themselves are circumcised.

Understand therefore, children, these things more fully, that Abraham, who was the first that brought in circumcision, looking forward in the Spirit to Jesus, circumcised, having received the mystery of three letters.

For the Scripture says that Abraham circumcised three hundred and eighteen men of his house. But what therefore was the mystery that was made known unto him?

Mark, first the eighteen, and next the three hundred. For the numeral letters of ten and eight are I H. And these denote Jesus.

And because the cross was that by which we were to find grace; therefore he adds, three hundred; the note of which is T (the figure of his cross). Wherefore by two letters he signified Jesus, and by the third his cross.

He who has put the engrafted gift of his doctrine within us, knows that I never taught to any one a more certain truth; but I trust that ye are worthy of it.

CHAPTER IX.

That the commands of Moses concerning clean and unclean beasts, &c., were all designed for a spiritual signification.

BUT why did Moses say Ye shall not eat of the swine, neither the eagle nor the hawk; nor the crow; nor any fish that has not a scale upon him?—answer, that in the spiritual sense, he comprehended three doctrines, that were to be gathered from thence.

Besides which he says to them in the book of Deuteronomy, And I will give my statutes unto this people. Wherefore it is not the command of God that they should not eat these things; but Moses in the spirit spake unto them.

Now the sow he forbade them to eat; meaning thus much; thou shalt not join thyself to such persons as are like unto swine; who whilst they live in pleasure, forget their God; but when any want pinches them, then they know the Lord; as the sow when she is full knows not her master; but when she is hungry she makes a noise; and being again fed, is silent.

Neither, says he, shalt thou eat the eagle, nor the hawk, nor the kite, nor the crow; that is thou shalt not keep company with such kind of men as know not how by their labour and sweat to get themselves food: but injuriously ravish away the things of others; and watch how, to lay snares for them; when at the same time they appear to live in perfect innocence.

(So these birds alone seek not food for themselves, but) sitting idle seek how they may eat of the flesh others have provided; being destructive through their wickedness.

Neither, says he, shalt thou eat the lamprey, nor the polypus, nor the cuttle-fish; that is, thou shalt not be like such men, by using to converse with them; who are altogether wicked and adjudged to death. For so those fishes are alone accursed, and wallow in the mire, nor swim as other fishes, but tumble in the dirt at the bottom of the deep.

But he adds, neither shalt thou eat of the hare. To what end?—To signify this to us; Thou shalt not be an adulterer; nor liken thyself to such persons. For the hare every year multiplies the places of its conception; and so many years as it lives, so many it has.

Neither shalt thou eat of the hyena; that is, again, be not an adulterer, nor a corruptor of others; neither be like to such. And wherefore so?—Because that creature every year changes its kind, and is sometimes male and sometimes female.

For which cause also he justly hated the weasel; to the end that they should not be like such persons who with their mouths commit wickedness by reason of their uncleanness; nor join themselves with those impure women, who with their mouths commit wickedness. Because that animal conceives with its mouth.

Moses, therefore, speaking as concerning meats, delivered indeed three great precepts to them in the spiritual signification of those commands. But they according to the desires of the flesh, understood him as if he had only meant it of meats.

And therefore David took aright the knowledge of his threefold command, saying in like manner.

Blessed is the man that hath not walked in the counsel of the ungodly; as the fishes before mentioned in the bottom of the deep in darkness.

Nor stood in the way of sinners, as they who seem to fear the Lord, but yet sin, as the sow.

And hath not sat in the seat of the scorners; as those birds who sit and watch that they may devour.

Here you have the law concerning meat perfectly set forth, and according to the true knowledge of it.

But, says Moses, ye shall eat all that divideth the hoof, and cheweth the cud. Signifying thereby such an one as having taken his food, knows him that nourisheth him; and resting upon him, rejoiceth in him.

And in this he spake well, having respect to the commandment. What, therefore, is it that he says?—That we should hold fast to them that fear the Lord; with those who meditate on the command of the word which they have received in their heart; with those that declare the righteous judgments of the Lord, and keep his commandments;

In short, with those who know that to meditate is a work of pleasure, and therefore exercise themselves in the word of the Lord.

But why might they eat those that clave the hoof?—Because the righteous liveth in this present world; but his expectation is fixed upon the other. See, brethren, how admirably Moses commanded these things.

But how should we thus know all this, and understand it? We, therefore, understanding aright the commandments, speak as the Lord would have us. Wherefore he has circumcised our ears and our hearts, that we might know these things.

CHAPTER X.

Baptism and the Cross of Christ foretold in figures under the law.

LET us now inquire whether the Lord took care to manifest anything beforehand concerning water and the cross.

Now for the former of these, it is written to the people of Israel how they shall not receive that baptism which brings to forgiveness of sins; but shall institute another to themselves that cannot.

For thus saith the prophet: Be astonished, O Heaven! and let the earth tremble at it, because this people have done two great and wicked things; they have left me, the fountain of living water, and have digged for themselves broken cisterns, that can hold no water.

Is my holy mountain a Zion, a desolate wilderness? For ye shall be as a young bird when its nest is taken away.

And again the prophet saith, I will go before thee, and will make plain the mountains, and will break the gates of brass, and will snap in sunder the bars of iron; and will give thee dark, and hidden, and invisible treasures, that they may know that I am the Lord God.

And again: He shall dwell in the high den of the strong rock. And then, what follows in the same prophet? His water is faithful; ye shall see the king with glory, and your soul shall learn the fear of the Lord.

And again he saith in another prophet: He that does these things; shall be like a tree, planted by the currents of water, which shall give its fruit in its season. Its leaf also shall not wither, and whatsoever he doth it shall prosper.

As for the wicked it is not so with them; but they are as the dust which the wind scattereth away from the face of the earth.

Therefore the ungodly shall not stand in the judgment, neither the sinners in the council of the righteous. For the Lord knoweth the way of the righteous and the way of the ungodly shall perish.

Consider how he has joined both the cross and the water together.

For thus he saith: Blessed are they who put their trust in the cross, descend into the water; for they shall have their reward in due time; then, saith he, will I give it them.

But as concerning the present time, he saith, their leaves shall not fall; meaning thereby that every word that shall go out of your mouth, shall through faith and charity be to the conversion and hope of many.

In like manner doth another prophet speak. And the land of Jacob was the praise of all the earth; magnifying thereby the vessel of his spirit.

And what follows?—And there was a river running on the right hand, and beautiful trees grew up by it; and he that shall eat of them shall live for ever. The signification of which is this: that we go down into the water full of sins and pollutions; but come up again, bringing forth fruit; having in our hearts the fear and hope which is in Jesus, by the spirit. And whosoever shall eat of them shall live for ever.

That is, whosoever shall hearken to those who call them, and shall believe, shall live for ever.

CHAPTER XI.

The subject continued.

IN like manner he determines concerning the cross in another prophet, saying: And when shall these things be fulfilled?

The Lord answers; When the tree that has fallen shall rise, and when blood shall drop down from the tree. Here you have again mention made, both of the cross, and of him that was to be crucified upon it.

And yet farther he saith by Moses; (when Israel was fighting with, and beaten by, a strange people; to the end that God might put them in mind how that for their sins they were delivered unto death) yea, the holy spirit put it into the heart of Moses, to represent both the sign of the cross, and of him that was to suffer; that so they might know that if they did not believe in him, they should be overcome for ever.

Moses therefore piled up armour upon armour in the middle of a rising ground, and standing up high above all of them, stretched forth his arms, and so Israel again conquered.

But no sooner did he let down his hands, but they were again slain. And why so?— To the end they might know, that except they trust in him they cannot be saved.

And in another prophet, he saith, I have stretched out my hands all the day long to a people disobedient, and speaking against my righteous way.

And again Moses makes a type of Jesus, to show that he was to die, and then that he, whom they thought to be dead, was to give life to others; in the type of those that fell in Israel.

For God caused all sorts of serpents to bite them, and they died; forasmuch as by a serpent transgression began in Eve: that so he might convince them that for their transgressions they shall be delivered into the pain of death.

Moses then himself, who had commanded them, saying, Ye shall not make to yourselves any graven or molten image, to be your God; yet now did so himself, that he might represent to them the figure of the Lord Jesus.

For he made a brazen serpent, and set it up on high, and called the people together by a proclamation; where being come, they entreated Moses that he would make an atonement for them, and pray that they might be healed.

Then Moses spake unto them, saying: when any one among you shall be bitten, let him come unto the serpent that is set upon the pole; and let him assuredly trust in him, that though he be dead, yet he is able to give life, and presently he shall be saved; and so they did. See therefore how here also you have in this the glory of Jesus; and that in him and to him are all things.

Again; What says Moses to Jesus the son of Nun, when he gave that name unto him, as being a prophet that all the people might hear him alone, because the father did manifest all things concerning his son Jesus, in Jesus the Son of Nun; and gave him that name when he sent him to spy out the land of Canaan; he said: Take a book in thine hands, and write what the Lord saith: Forasmuch as Jesus the Son of God shall in the last days cut off by the roots all the house of Amalek. See here again Jesus, not the son of man, but the Son of God, made manifest in a type and in the flesh.

But because it might hereafter be said, that Christ was the Son of David; therefore David fearing and well knowing the errors of the wicked, saith; the Lord saith unto my Lord, sit thou on my right hand until I make thine enemies thy footstool.

And again Isaiah speaketh on this wise. The Lord said unto Christ my Lord, I have laid hold on his right hand, that the nations should obey before him, and I will break the strength of kings.

Behold, how doth David and Isaiah call him Lord, and the Son of God.

CHAPTER XII.

The promise of God not made to the Jews only, but to the Gentiles also, and fulfilled to us by Jesus Christ.

BUT let us go yet farther, and inquire whether this people be the heir, or the former; and whether the covenant be with us or with them.

And first, as concerning the people, hear now what the Scripture saith.

Isaac prayed for his wife Rebekah, because she was barren; and she conceived. Afterwards Rebekah went forth to inquire of the Lord.

And the Lord said unto her; There are two nations in thy womb, and two people shall come from thy body; and the one shall have power over the other, and the greater shall serve the lesser. Understand here who was Isaac; who Rebekah; and of whom it was foretold, this people shall be greater than that.

And in another prophecy Jacob speaketh more clearly to his son Joseph saying; Behold the Lord hath not deprived me of seeing thy face, bring me thy sons that I may bless them. And he brought unto his father Manasseh and Ephraim, desiring that he should bless Manasseh, because he was the elder.

Therefore Joseph brought him to the right hand of his father Jacob. But Jacob by the spirit foresaw the figure of the of the people that was to come.

And what saith the Scripture? And Jacob crossed his hands, and put his right hand upon Ephraim, his second, and the younger son, and blessed him. And Joseph said unto Jacob; Put thy right hand upon the head of Manasseh, for he is my first-born son. And Jacob said unto Joseph; I know it, my son, I know it; but the greater shall serve the lesser; though he also shall be blessed.

Ye see of whom he appointed it, that they should be the first people, and heirs of the covenant.

If therefore God shall have yet farther taken notice of this by Abraham too; our understanding of it will then be perfectly established.

What then saith the Scripture to Abraham, when he believed, and it was imputed unto him for righteousness? Behold I have made thee a father of the nations, which without circumcision believe in the Lord.

Let us therefore now inquire whether God has fulfilled the covenant, which he sware to our fathers, that he would give this people? Yes, verily, he gave it: but they were not worthy to receive it by reason of their sins.

For thus saith the prophet: And Moses continued fasting in mount Sinai, to receive the covenant of the Lord with the people, forty days and forty nights.

And he received of the Lord two tables written with the finger of the Lord's hand in the Spirit. And Moses when he had received them brought them down that he might deliver them to the people.

And the Lord said unto Moses; Moses, Moses, get thee down quickly, for the people which thou broughtest out of the land of Egypt have done wickedly.

And Moses understood that they had again set up a molten image: and he cast the two tables out of his hands; and the tables of the covenant of the Lord were broken. Moses therefore received them, but they were not worthy.

Now then learn how we have received them. Moses, being a servant, took them; but the Lord himself has given them unto us, that we might be the people of his inheritance, having suffered for us.

He was therefore made manifest; that they should fill up the measure of their sins, and that we being made heirs by him, should receive the covenant of the Lord Jesus.

And again the prophet saith; Behold, I have set thee for a light unto the Gentiles, to be the saviour of all the ends of the earth, saith the Lord the God who hath redeemed thee.

Who for that very end was prepared, that by his own appearing he might redeem our hearts, already devoured by death, and delivered over to the irregularity of error, from darkness; and establish a covenant with us by his word.

For so it is written that the father commanded him by delivering us from darkness, to prepare unto himself a holy people.

Wherefore the prophet saith: I the Lord thy God have called thee in righteousness, and I will take thee by thy hand and will strengthen thee. And give thee for a covenant of the people, for a light of the Gentiles. To open the eyes of the blind, to bring out the prisoners from the prison, and them that sit in darkness out of the prison house.

Consider therefore from whence we have been redeemed. And again the prophet saith: The spirit of the Lord is upon me, because he hath anointed me: he hath sent me to preach glad tidings to the lowly; to heal the broken in heart; to preach remission to the captives, and sight unto the blind; to proclaim the acceptable year of the Lord, and the day of restitution; to comfort all that mourn.

CHAPTER XIII.

That the sabbath of the Jews was but a figure of a more glorious sabbath to come, and their temple, of the spiritual temples of God.

FURTHERMORE it is written concerning the sabbath, in the Ten Commandments, which God spake in the Mount Sinai to Moses, face to face; Sanctify the sabbath of the Lord with pure hands, and with a clean heart.

And elsewhere he saith; If thy children shall keep my sabbaths, then will I put my mercy upon them.

And even in the beginning of the creation he makes mention of the sabbath. And God made in six days the works of his hands; and he finished them on the seventh day, and he rested the seventh day, and sanctified it.

Consider, my children, what that signifies, he finished them in six days. The meaning of it is this; that in six thousand years the Lord God will bring all things to an end.

For with him one day is a thousand years; as himself testifieth, saying, Behold this day shall be as a thousand years. Therefore, children, in six days, that is, in six thousand years, shall all things be accomplished.

And what is that he saith, And he rested the seventh day: he meaneth this; that when his Son shall come, and abolish the season of the Wicked One, and judge the ungodly; and shall change the sun and the moon, and the stars; then he shall gloriously rest in that seventh day.

He adds lastly; Thou shalt sanctify it with clean hands and a pure heart. Wherefore we are greatly deceived if we imagine that any one can now sanctify that day which God has made holy, without having a heart pure in all things.

Behold therefore he will then truly sanctify it with blessed rest, when we (having received the righteous promise, when iniquity shall be no more, all things being renewed by the Lord) shall be able to sanctify it, being ourselves first made holy.

Lastly, he saith unto them: Your new moons and you: sabbaths I cannot bear them. Consider what he means by it; the sabbaths, says he, which ye now keep are not acceptable unto me, but those which I have made; when resting from all things I shall begin the eighth day, that is, the beginning of the other world.

For which cause we observe the eighth day with gladness, in which Jesus rose from the dead; and having manifested himself to his disciples, ascended into heaven.

It remains yet that I speak to you concerning the temple how these miserable men being deceived have put their trust in the house, and not in God himself who made them, as if it were the habitation of God.

For much after the same manner as the Gentiles, they consecrated him in the temple.

But learn therefore how the Lord speaketh, rendering the temple vain: Who has measured the heaven with a span, and the earth with his hand? Is it not I? Thus saith the Lord, Heaven is my throne, and the earth is my footstool. What is the house that ye will build me? Or what is the place of my rest? Know therefore that all their hope is vain.

And again he speaketh after this manner: Behold they that destroy this temple, even they shall again build it up. And so it came to pass; for through their wars it is now destroyed by their enemies; and the servants of their enemies built it up.

Furthermore it has been made manifest, how both the city and the temple, and the people of Israel should be given up. For the Scripture saith; And it shall come to pass in the last days, that the Lord will deliver up the sheep of his pasture, and their fold, and their tower into destruction. And it is come to pass, as the Lord hath spoken.

Let us inquire therefore, whether there be any temple of God? Yes there is; and that there, where himself declares that he would both make and perfect it. For it is written; And it shall be that as soon as the week shall be completed, the temple of the Lord shall be gloriously built in the name of the Lord.

I find therefore that there is a temple. But how shall it be built in the name of the Lord? I will shew you.

Before that we believed in God, the habitation of our heart was corruptible, and feeble, as a temple truly built with hands.

For it was a house full of idolatry, a house of devils; inasmuch as there was done in it whatsoever was contrary unto God. But it shall be built in the name of the Lord.

Consider, how that the temple of the Lord shall be very gloriously built; and by what means that shall be, learn.

Having received remission of our sins, and trusting in the name of the Lord, we are become renewed, being again created as it were from the beginning. Wherefore God truly dwells in our house, that is, in us.

But how does he dwell in us? The word of his faith, the calling of his promise, the wisdom of his righteous judgments, the commands of his doctrine; he himself prophesies within us, he himself dwelleth in us, and openeth to us who were in bondage of death the gate of our temple, that is, the mouth of wisdom, having given repentance unto us; and by this means has brought us to be an incorruptible temple.

He therefore that desires to be saved looketh not unto the man, but unto him that dwelleth in him, and speaketh by him; being struck with wonder, forasmuch as he never either heard him speaking such words out of his mouth, nor ever desired to hear them.

This is that spiritual temple that is built unto the Lord.

CHAPTER XIV.

Of the way of light; being a summary of what a Christian is to do, that he may be happy for ever.

AND thus, I trust, I have declared to you as much, and with as great simplicity as I could, those things which make for your salvation, so as not to have omitted anything that might be requisite thereunto.

For should I speak further of the things that now are, and of those that are to come, you would not yet understand them, seeing they lie in parables. This therefore shall suffice as to these things.

Let us now go on to the other kind of knowledge and doctrine There are two ways of doctrine and power; the one of light, the other of darkness.

But there is a great deal of difference between these two ways: for over one are appointed the angels of God, the leaders of the way of light; over the other, the angels of Satan. And the one is the Lord from everlasting to everlasting; the other is the prince of the time of unrighteousness.

Now the way of light is this, if any one desires to attain to the place that is appointed for him, and will hasten thither by his works. And the knowledge that has been given to us for walking in it, to this effect: Thou shalt love him that made thee: thou shalt glorify him that hath redeemed thee from death.

Thou shalt be simple in heart, and rich in the spirit. Thou shalt not cleave to those that walk in the way of death. Thou shalt hate to do anything that is not pleasing unto God. Thou shalt abhor all dissimulation. Thou shalt not neglect any of the commands of the Lord.

THE LOST BOOKS OF THE BIBLE

Thou shalt not exalt thyself, but shalt be humble. Thou shalt not take honour to thyself. Thou shalt not enter into any wicked counsel against thy neighbour. Thou shalt not be over-confident in thy heart.

Thou shalt not commit fornication, nor adultery. Neither shalt thou corrupt thyself with mankind. Thou shalt not make use of the word of God, to any impurity.

Thou shalt not accept any man's person, when thou reprovest any one's faults. Thou t shalt be gentle. Thou shalt be quiet. Thou shalt tremble at the words which thou hast heard. Thou shalt not keep any hatred in thy heart against thy brother. Thou shalt not entertain any doubt whether it shall be or not.

Thou shalt not take the name of the Lord in vain. Thou shalt love thy neighbour above thy own soul.

Thou shalt not destroy thy conceptions before they are brought forth; nor kill them after they are born.

Thou shalt not withdraw thy hand from thy son, or from thy daughter; but shall teach them from their youth the fear of the Lord.

Thou shalt not covet thy neighbour's goods; neither shalt thou be an extortioner. Neither shall thy heart be joined to proud men; but thou shalt be numbered among the righteous and the lowly. Whatever events shall happen unto thee, thou shalt receive them as good.

Thou shalt not he double-minded, or double-tongued; for a double tongue is the snare of death. Thou shalt be subject unto the Lord and to inferior masters as to the representatives of God, in fear and reverence.

Thou shalt not be bitter in thy commands towards any of thy servants that trust in God; lest thou chance not to fear him who is over both; because he came not to call any with respect of persons, but whomsoever the spirit had prepared.

Thou shalt communicate to thy neighbour of all thou hast; thou shalt not call anything thine own: for if ye partake in such things as are incorruptible, how much more should you do it in those that are corruptible?

Thou shalt not be forward to speak; for the mouth is the snare of death. Strive for thy soul with all thy might. Reach not out thine hand to receive, and withhold it not when thou shouldest give.

Thou shalt love, as the apple of thine eye, every one that speaketh unto thee the Word of the Lord. Call to thy remembrance, day and night, the future judgment.

Thou shalt seek out every day the persons of the righteous: and both consider and go about to exhort others by the, word, and meditate how thou mayest save a soul.

Thou shalt also labour with thy hands to give to the poor, that thy sins may be forgiven thee. Thou shalt not deliberate whether thou shouldst give: nor, having given, murmur at it.

Give to every one that asks: so shalt thou know who is the good rewarder of thy gifts.

Keep what thou hast received; thou shalt neither add to it nor take from it.

Let the wicked be always thy aversion. Thou shalt judge righteous judgment. Thou shalt never cause divisions; but shalt make peace between those that are at variance, and bring them together.

Thou shalt confess thy sins; and not come to thy prayer with an evil conscience.

This is the way of light.

CHAPTER XV.

Of the way of darkness; that is, what kind of persons shall be for ever cast out of the kingdom of God.

BUT the way of darkness is crooked and full of cursing. For it is the way of eternal death, with punishment; in which they that walk meet those things that destroy their own souls.

Such are; idolatry, confidence, pride of power, hypocrisy, double-mindedness, adultery, murder, rapine, pride, transgression, deceit, malice, arrogance, witchcraft, covetousness, and the want of the fear of God.

In this walk those who are the persecutors of them that are good; haters of truth; lovers of lies; who know not the reward of righteousness, nor cleave to any thing that is good.

Who administer not righteous judgment to the widow and orphan; who watch for wickedness, and not for the fear of the Lord:

From whom gentleness and patience are far off; who love vanity, and follow after rewards; having no compassion upon the poor; nor take any pains for such as are heavy laden and oppressed.

Ready to evil speaking, not knowing him that made them; murderers of children; corrupters of the creatures of God; that turn away from the needy; oppress the afflicted; are the advocates of the rich, but unjust judges of the poor; being altogether sinners.

It is therefore fitting that learning the just commands of the Lord, which we have before mentioned, we should walk in them. For he who does such things shall be glorified in the kingdom of God.

But he that chooses the other part, shall be destroyed, together with his works. For this cause there shall be both a resurrection, and a retribution.

I beseech those that are in high estate among you, (if so be you will take the counsel which with a good intention I offer to you,) you have those with you towards whom you may do good; do not forsake them.

For the day is at hand in which all things shall be destroyed, together with the wicked one. The Lord is near, and his reward is with him.

I beseech you, therefore, again, and again, be as good lawgivers to one another; continue faithful counsellors to each other; remove from among you all hypocrisy.

And may God, the Lord of all the world give you wisdom, knowledge, counsel, and understanding of his judgments in patience.

Be ye taught of God; seeking what it is the Lord requires of you, and doing it; that ye may be saved in the day of judgment.

And if there be among you any remembrance of what is good, think of me; meditating upon these things, that both my desire and my watching for you may turn to a good account.

I beseech you; I ask it as a favour of you; whilst you are in this beautiful tabernacle of the body, be wanting in none of these things; but without ceasing seek them, and fulfil every command. For these things are fitting and worthy to be done.

Wherefore I have given the more diligence to write unto you, according to my ability, that you might rejoice. Farewell, children, of love and peace.

The Lord of glory and of all grace, be with your spirit, Amen.

The end of the Epistle of Barnabas, the Apostle, and fellow-traveller of St. Paul the Apostle.

THE EPISTLE OF IGNATIUS TO THE EPHESIANS.

OF THE EPISTLES OF IGNATIUS.

[The Epistles of Ignatius are translated by Archbishop Wake from the text of Vossius. He says that there were considerable differences in the editions; the best for a long time extant containing fabrications, and the genuine being altered and corrupted. Archbishop Usher printed old Latin translations of them at Oxford, in 1644. At Amsterdam, two years afterwards, Vossius printed six of them, in their ancient and pure Greek; and the seventh greatly amended from the ancient Latin version, was printed at Paris, by Ruinart, in 1689, in the Acts and Martyrdom of Ignatius, from a Greek uninterpolated copy. These are supposed to form the collection that Polycarp made of the Epistles of Ignatius, mentioned by Irenaeus, Origen, Eusebius, Jerome, Athanasius, Theodoret, and other ancients; but many learned men have imagined all of them to be apocryphal. This supposition, the piety of Archbishop Wake, and his persuasion of their utility to the faith of the church, will not permit him to entertain; hence he has taken great pains to render the present translation acceptable, by adding numerous readings and references to the Canonical Books.]

CHAPTER I.

Commends them for sending Onesimus, and other members of the church to him. 8 Exhorts them to unity, by a due subjection to their bishop.

IGNATIUS, who is also called Theophorus, to the church which is at Ephesus in

Asia; most deservedly happy; being blessed through the greatness and fulness of God the Father, and predestinated before the world began, that it should be always unto an enduring and unchangeable glory; being united and chosen through his true passion, according to the will of the Father, and Jesus Christ our God; all happiness, by Jesus Christ, and his undefiled grace.

I have heard of your name much beloved in God; which ye have very justly attained by a habit of righteousness, according to the faith and love which is in Jesus Christ our Saviour.

How that being followers of God, and stirring up yourselves by the blood of Christ ye have perfectly accomplished the work that was con-natural unto you.

For hearing that I came bound from Syria, for the common name and hope, trusting through your prayers to fight with beasts at Rome; so that by suffering I may become indeed the disciple of him who gave himself to God, an offering and sacrifice for us; (ye hastened to see me). I received, therefore, in the name of God, your whole multitude in Onesimus.

Who by inexpressible love is ours, but according to the flesh is your bishop; whom I beseech you, by Jesus Christ, to love; and that you would all strive to be like unto him. And blessed be God, who has granted unto you, who are so worthy of him, to enjoy such an excellent bishop.

For what concerns my fellow servant Burrhus, and your most blessed deacon in things pertaining to God; I entreat you that he may tarry longer, both for yours, and your bishop's honour.

And Crocus also worthy both our God and you, whom I have received as the pattern of your love, has in all things refreshed me, as the Father of our Lord Jesus Christ shall also refresh him; together with Onesimus, and Burrhus, and Euclus, and Fronto, in whom I have, as to your charity, seen all of you. And may I always, have joy of you, if I shall be worthy of it.

It is therefore fitting that you should by all means glorify Jesus Christ who hath glorified you: that by a uniform obedience ye may be perfectly joined together, in the same mind, and in the same judgment: and may all speak the same things concerning everything.

And that being subject to your bishop, and the presbytery, ye may be wholly and thoroughly sanctified.

These things I prescribe to you, not as if I were somebody extraordinary: for though I am bound for his name, I am not yet perfect in Christ Jesus. But now I begin to learn, and I speak to you as fellow disciples together with me.

For I ought to have been stirred up by you, in faith, in admonition, in patience, in long-suffering; but forasmuch as charity suffers me not to be silent towards you, I have first taken upon me to exhort you, that ye would all run together according to the will of God.

For even Jesus Christ, our inseparable life, is sent by the will of the Father; as the bishops, appointed unto the utmost bounds of the earth, are by the will of Jesus Christ.

Wherefore it will become you to run together according to the will of your bishop, as also ye do.

For your famous presbytery, worthy of God, is fitted as exactly to the bishop, as the strings are to the harp.

Therefore in your concord and agreeing charity, Jesus Christ is sung; and every single person among you makes up the chorus:

That so being all consonant in love, and taking up the song of God, ye may in a perfect unity with one voice, sing to the Father by Jesus Christ; to the end that he may both hear you, and perceive by your works, that ye are indeed the members of his son.

Wherefore it is profitable for you to live in an unblameable unity, that so ye may always have a fellowship with God.

CHAPTER II.

The benefit of subjection.The bishop not to be respected the less because he is not forward in exacting it: warns them against heretics; bidding them cleave to Jesus, whose divine and human nature is declared; commends them for their care to keep themselves front false teachers; and shews them the way to God.

FOR if I in this little time have had such a familiarity with your bishop, I mean not a carnal, but spiritual acquaintance with him; how much more must I think you happy who are so joined to him, as the church is to Jesus Christ, and Jesus Christ to the Father; that so all things may agree in the same unity?

Let no man deceive himself; if a man be not within the altar, he is deprived of the bread of God. For if the prayers of one or two be of such force, as we are told; how much more powerful shall that of the bishop and the whole church be?

He therefore that does not come together in the same place with it, is proud, and has already condemned himself. For it is written, God resisteth the proud. Let us take heed therefore, that we do not set ourselves against the bishop, that we may be subject to God.

The more any one sees his bishop silent, the more let him revere him. For whomsoever the master of the house sends to be over his own household, we ought in like manner to receive him, as we would do him that sent him. It is therefore evident that we ought to look upon the bishop, even as we would do upon the Lord himself.

And indeed Onesimus himself does greatly commend your good order in God: that you all live according to the truth, and that no heresy dwells among you. For neither do ye hearken to any one more than to Jesus Christ speaking to you in truth.

For some there are who carry about the name of Christ in deceitfulness, but do things unworthy of God; whom ye must flee, as ye would do so many wild beasts. For they are ravening dogs, who bite secretly: against whom ye must guard yourselves, as men hardly to be cured.

There is one physician, both fleshly and spiritual; made and not made; God incarnate; true life in death; both of Mary and of God; first , then impassible; even Jesus Christ our Lord.

Wherefore let no man deceive you; as indeed neither are ye deceived. being wholly the servants of God. For inasmuch as there is no contention nor strife among you, to trouble you, ye must needs live according to God's will. My soul be for yours; and I myself the expiatory offering for your church of Ephesus, so famous throughout the world.

They that are of the flesh cannot do the works of the spirit; neither they that are of the spirit the works of the flesh. As he that has faith cannot be an infidel; nor he that is an infidel have faith. But even those things which ye do according to the flesh are spiritual; forasmuch as ye do all things in Jesus Christ.

Nevertheless I have heard of some who have passed by you, having perverse doctrine; whom ye did not suffer to sow among you; but stopped your ears, that ye might not receive those things that were sown by them; as becoming the stones of the temple of the Father, prepared for his building; and drawn up on high by the Cross of Christ, as by an engine.

Using the Holy Ghost as the rope: your faith being your; and your charity the way that leads unto God.

Ye are therefore, with all your companions in the same journey, full of God; his spiritual temples, full of Christ, full of holiness: adorned in all things with the commands of Christ.

In whom also I rejoice that I have been thought worthy by this present epistle to converse, and joy together with you; that with respect to the other life, ye love nothing but God only.

CHAPTER III.

Exhorts them to prayer; to be unblameable. To be careful of salvation; frequent in public devotion; and to live in charity.

PRAY also without ceasing for other men: for there is hope of repentance in them, that they may attain unto God. Let them therefore at least be instructed by your works, if they will be no other way.

Be ye mild at their anger; humble at their boasting; to their blasphemies return your prayers: to their error, your firmness in the faith: when they are cruel, be ye gentle; not endeavouring to imitate their ways.

Let us be their brethren in all kindness and moderation, but let us be followers of the Lord; for who was ever more unjustly used? More destitute? More despised?)

That so no herb of the devil may be found in you: but ye may remain in all holiness and sobriety both of body and spirit, in Christ Jesus.

The last times are come upon us: let us therefore be very reverent and fear the long-suffering of God, that it be not to us e unto condemnation.

For let us either fear the wrath that is to come, or let us love the grace that we at present enjoy: that by the one, or other, of these we may be found in Christ Jesus, unto true life.

Besides him, let nothing be worthy of you; for whom also I bear about these bonds, those spiritual jewels, in which I would to God that I might arise through your prayers.

Of which I entreat you to make me always partaker, that I may be found in the lot of the Christians of Ephesus, who have always agreed with the Apostles, through the power of Jesus Christ.

I know both who I am, and to whom I write; I, a person condemned: ye, such as have obtained mercy: I, exposed to danger; ye, confirmed against danger.

Ye are the passage of those that are killed for God; the companions of Paul in the mysteries of the Gospel; the Holy, the martyr, the deservedly most happy Paul: at whose feet may I be found, when I shall have attained unto God; who throughout all his epistle, makes mention of you in Christ Jesus.

Let it be your care therefore to come more fully together, to the praise and glory of God. For when ye meet fully together in the same place, the powers of the devil are destroyed, and his mischief is dissolved by the unity of their faith.

And indeed, nothing is better than peace, by which all war both spiritual and earthly is abolished.

Of all which nothing is hid from you, if ye have perfect faith and charity in Christ Jesus, which are the beginning and end of life.

For the beginning is faith; the end is charity. And these two joined together, are of God: but all other things which concern a holy life are the consequences of these.

No man professing a true faith, sinneth; neither does he who has charity hate any.

The tree is made manifest by its fruit; so they who profess themselves to be Christians are known by what they do.

For Christianity is not the work of an outward profession; but shows itself in the power of faith, if a man be found faithful unto the end.

It is better for a man to hold his peace, and be; than to say he is a Christian and not to be.

It is good to teach; if what he says he does likewise.

There is therefore one master who spake, and it was done; and even those things which he did without speaking, are worthy of the Father.

He that possesses the word of Jesus is truly able to hear his very silence, that he may be perfect; and both do according to what he speaks, and be known by those things of which he is silent.

There is nothing hid from God, but even our secrets are nigh unto him.

Let us therefore do all things, as becomes those who have God dwelling in them; that we may be his temples, and he may be our God: as also he is, and will manifest himself before our faces, by those things for which we justly love him.

CHAPTER IV.

To have a care for the Gospel. The virginity of Mary, the incarnation, and the death of Christ, were hid front the Devil. How the birth of Christ was revealed. Exhorts to unity.

BE not deceived, my brethren: those that corrupt families inherit adultery, shall not inherit the kingdom of God.

If therefore they who do this according to the flesh, have suffered death; how much more shall he die, who by his wicked doctrine corrupts the faith of God, for which Christ was crucified?

He that is thus defiled, shall depart into unquenchable fire, and so also shall he that hearkens to him.

For this cause did the Lord suffer the ointment to be poured on his head; that he might breathe the breath of immortality unto his church.

Be not ye therefore anointed with the evil savour of the doctrine of the prince of this world: let him not take you captive from the life that is set before you.

And why are we not all wise, seeing we have receive the knowledge of God, which is Jesus Christ? Why do we suffer ourselves foolishly to perish; not considering the gift which the Lord has truly sent to us?

Let my life be sacrificed for the doctrine of the cross; which is indeed a scandal to the unbelievers, but to us is salvation and life eternal.

Where is the wise man? Where is the disputer? Where is the boasting of those who are called wise?

For our God Jesus Christ was according to the dispensation of God conceived in the womb of Mary, of the seed of David, by the Holy Ghost; he was born and baptized, that through his passion he might purify water, to the washing away of sin.

Now the Virginity of Mary, and he who was born of her, was kept in secret from the prince of this world; as was also the death of our Lord: three of the mysteries the most spoken of throughout the world, yet done in secret by God.

How then was our Saviour manifested to the world? A star shone in heaven beyond all the other stars, and its light was inexpressible, and its novelty struck terror into men's minds. All the rest of the stars, together with the sun and moon, were the chorus to this star; but that sent out its light exceedingly above them all.

And men began to be troubled to think whence this new star came so unlike to all the others.

Hence all the power of magic became dissolved; and every bond of wickedness was destroyed: men's ignorance was taken away; and the old kingdom abolished; God himself appearing in the form of a man, for the renewal of eternal life.

From thence began what God had prepared: from thenceforth things were disturbed; forasmuch as he designed to abolish death.

But if Jesus Christ shall give me grace through your prayers, and it be his will, I purpose in a second epistle which I will suddenly write unto you to manifest to you more fully the dispensation of which I have now begun to speak, unto the new man, which is Jesus Christ; both in his faith, and charity; in his suffering, and in his resurrection.

Especially if the Lord shall make known unto me, that ye all by name come together in common in one faith, and in one Jesus Christ; who was of the race of David according to the flesh; the Son of man, and Son of God; obeying your bishop and the presbytery with an entire affection; breaking one and the same bread, which is the medicine of immortality; our antidote that we should not die, but live forever in Christ Jesus.

My soul be for yours, and theirs whom ye have sent to the glory of God, even unto Smyrna; from whence also I write to you; giving thanks unto the Lord and loving Polycarp even as I do you. Remember me, as Jesus Christ does remember you.

Pray for the church which is in Syria, from whence I am carried bound to Rome; being the least of all the faithful which are there, as I have been thought worthy to be found to the glory of God.

Fare ye well in God the Father, and in Jesus Christ, our common Hope. Amen.

To the Ephesians.

THE EPISTLE OF IGNATIUS TO THE MAGNESIANS.

CHAPTER I.

Mentions the arrival of Damon, their bishop, and others, whom he exhorts them to reverence, notwithstanding he was a young man.

IGNATIUS who is also called Theophorus; to the blessed (church) by the grace of God the Father in Jesus Christ our Saviour: in whom I salute the church which is at Magnesia near the Maeander: and wish it all joy in God the Father and in Jesus Christ.

When I heard of your well ordered love and charity in God, being full of joy, I desired much to speak unto you in the faith of Jesus Christ.

For having been thought worthy to obtain a most excellent name, in the bonds which I carry about, I salute the churches; wishing in them a union both of the body and spirit of Jesus Christ, our eternal life: as also of faith and charity, to which nothing is pre-

THE LOST BOOKS OF THE BIBLE

ferred: but especially of Jesus and the Father in whom if we undergo all the injuries of the prince of this pre sent world, and escape, we shall enjoy God.

Seeing then I have been judged worthy to see you, by Damas your most excellent bishop; and by your very worthy presbyters, Bassus and Apollonius; and by my fellow-servant Sotio, the deacon;

In whom I rejoice, forasmuch as he is the subject unto his bishop as to the grace of God, and to the presbytery as to the law of Jesus Christ; I determined to write unto you.

Wherefore it will become you also not to use your bishop too familiarly upon the account of his youth; but to yield all reverence to him according to the power of God the Father; as also I perceive that your holy presbyters do: not considering is age, which indeed to appearance is young; but as becomes those who are prudent in God, submitting to him, or rather not to him, but to the Father of our Lord Jesus Christ, the bishop of us all.

It will therefore behoove you with all sincerity, to obey your bishop; in honour him whose pleasure it is that ye should do so.

Because he that does not do so, deceives not the bishop whom he sees, but affronts him that is invisible. For whatsoever of this kind is done, it reflects not upon man, but upon God, who knows the secrets of our hearts.

It is therefore fitting, that we should not only be called Christians, but be so.

As some call indeed their governor, bishop; but yet do all things without him.

But I can never think that such as these have a good conscience, seeing that they are not gathered together thoroughly according to God's commandment.

CHAPTER II.

That as all must die, he exhorts them to live orderly and in unity.

SEEING then all things have an end, there are these two indifferently set before us, death and life: and every one shall depart unto his proper place.

For as there are two sorts of coins, the one of God, the other of the world; and each of these has its proper inscription engraven upon it; so also is it here.

The unbelievers are of this world; but the faithful, through charity, have the character of God the Father by Jesus Christ: by whom if we are not readily disposed to die after the likeness of his passion, his life is not in us.

Forasmuch, therefore, as I have in the persons before mentioned seen all of you in faith and charity; I exhort you that ye study to do all things in divine concord:

Your bishop presiding in the place of God; your presbyters in the place of the council of the Apostles; and your deacons most dear to me being entrusted with the ministry of Jesus Christ; who was the Father before all ages, and appeared in the end to us.

171

Wherefore taking the same holy course, see that ye all reverence one another: and let no one look upon his neighbour after the flesh; but do ye all mutually love each other in Jesus Christ.

Let there be nothing that may be able to make a division among you; but be ye united to your bishop, and those who preside over you, to be your pattern and direction in the way to immortality.

As therefore the Lord did nothing without the Father, being united to him; neither by himself nor yet by his Apostles, so neither do ye do anything without your bishop and presbyters:

Neither endeavour to let anything appear rational to yourselves apart;

But being come together into the same place have one common prayer; one supplication; one mind; one hope; one in charity, and in joy undefiled.

There is one Lord Jesus Christ, than whom nothing is better. Wherefore come ye all together as unto one temple of God; as to one altar, as to one Jesus Christ; who proceeded from one Father, and exists in one, and is returned to one.

CHAPTER III.

He cautions them against false opinions. Especially those of Ebion and the Judaizing Christians.

BE not deceived with strange doctrines; nor with old fables which are unprofitable. For if we still continue to live according to the Jewish law, we do confess ourselves not to have received grace. For even the most holy prophets lived according to Christ Jesus.

And for this cause were they persecuted, being inspired by his grace, to convince the unbelievers and disobedient that there is one God who has manifested himself by Jesus Christ his Son; who is his eternal word, not coming forth from silence, who in all things pleased him that sent him.

Wherefore if they who were brought up in these ancient laws came nevertheless to the newness of hope: no longer observing sabbaths, but keeping the Lord's day in which also our life is sprung up by him, and through his death, whom yet some deny:

(By which mystery we have been brought to believe and therefore wait that we may be found the disciples of Jesus Christ, our only master:)How shall we be able to live different from him whose disciples the very prophets themselves being, did by the spirit expect him as their master.

And therefore he whom they justly waited for, being come, raised them up from the dead.

Let us not then be insensible of his goodness; for should he have dealt with us according to our works, we had not no had a being.

Wherefore being become his disciples, let us learn to live according to the rules of Christianity; for whosoever is called by any other name besides this, he is not of God.

Lay aside therefore the old and sour and evil leaven; and be ye changed into the new leaven, which is Jesus Christ.

Be ye salted in him, lest any one among you should be corrupted; for by your savour ye shall be judged.

It is absurd to name Jesus Christ, and to Judaize. For the Christian religion did not embrace the Jewish, but the Jewish the Christian; that so every tongue that believed might be gathered together unto God.

These things, my beloved, I write unto you; not that I know of any among you that lie under this error; but as one of the least among you, I am desirous to forewarn you, that ye fall not into the snares of false doctrine.

But that ye be fully instructed in the birth, and suffering, and resurrection of Jesus Christ, our hope; which was accomplished in the time of the government of Pontius Pilate, and that most truly and certainly and from which God forbid that any among you should be turned aside.

CHAPTER IV.

Commends their faith and piety; exhorts them to persevere; desires their prayers for himself and the church at Antioch.

MAY I therefore have joy of you in all things, if I shall be worthy of it. For though I am bound, yet I am not worthy to be compared to one of you that are at liberty.

I know that ye are not puffed up; for ye have Jesus Christ in your hearts.

And especially when I commend you, I know that ye are ashamed, as it is written, The just man condemneth himself.

Study therefore to be confirmed in the doctrine of our Lord, and of his Apostles; that so whatever ye do, ye may prosper both in body and spirit, in faith and charity, in the Son, and in the Father and in the Holy Spirit: in the beginning, and in the end.

Together with your most worthy bishop, and the well-wrought spiritual crown of your presbytery, and your deacons, which are according to God.

Be subject to your bishop, and to one another, as Jesus Christ to the Father, according to the flesh: and the Apostles both to Christ, and to the Father, and to the Holy Ghost: that so ye may be united both in body and spirit.

Knowing you to be full of God, I have the more briefly exhorted you.

Be mindful of me in your prayers, that I may attain unto God, and of the Church that is in Syria, from which I am not worthy to be called.

For I stand in need of your joint prayers in God, and of your charity, that the church which is in Syria may be thought worthy to be nourished by your church.

THE LOST BOOKS OF THE BIBLE

The Ephesians from Smyrna salute you, from which place I write unto you: (being present here to the glory of God, in like manner as you are,) who have in all things refreshed me, together with Polycarp, the bishop of the Smyrnaeans.

The rest of the churches in the honour of Jesus Christ, salute you.

Farewell, and be ye strengthened in the concord of God: enjoying his inseparable spirit, which is Jesus Christ.

To the Magnesians.

THE EPISTLE OF IGNATIUS TO THE TRALLIANS.

CHAPTER I.

Acknowledges the coming of their bishop. Commends them for their subjection to their bishop, priests, and deacons; and exhorts them to continue in it: is afraid even of his over-great desire to suffer, lest it should be prejudicial to him.

IGNATIUS, who is also called Theophorus, to the holy church which is at Tralles in Asia: beloved of God the Father of Jesus Christ, elect and worthy of God, having peace through the flesh and blood, and passion of Jesus Christ our hope, in the resurrection which is by him: which also I salute in its fulness, continuing in the apostolical character, wishing all joy and happiness unto it.

I have heard of your blameless and constant disposition through patience, which not only appears in your outward conversation, but is naturally rooted and grounded in you.

In like manner as Polybius your bishop has declared unto me, who came to me to Smyrna, by the will of God and Jesus Christ, and so rejoiced together with me in my bonds for Jesus Christ, that in effect I saw your whole church in him.

Having therefore received testimony of your good will towards me for God's sake, by him; I seemed to find you, as also I knew that ye were the followers of God.

For whereas ye are subject to your bishop as to Jesus Christ, ye appear to me to live not after the manner of men, but according to Jesus Christ; who died for us, that so believing in his death, ye might escape death.

It is therefore necessary, that as ye do, so without your bishop, you should do nothing: also be ye subject to your presbyters, as to the Apostles of Jesus Christ our hope; in whom if we walk, we shall be found in him.

The deacons also, as being the ministers of the mysteries of Jesus Christ, must by all means please ye. For they are not the ministers of meat and drink, but of the church of God. Wherefore they must avoid all offences, as they would do fire.

In like manner let us reverence the deacons as Jesus Christ; and the bishop as the father; and the presbyters as the Sanhedrim of God, and college of the Apostles.

Without these there is no church. Concerning all which I am persuaded that ye think after the very same manner: for I have received, and even now have with me, the pattern of your love, in your bishop.

Whose very look is instructive; and whose mildness powerful: whom I am persuaded, the very Atheists themselves cannot but reverence.

But because I have a love towards you, I will not write any more sharply unto you about this matter, though I very well might; but now I have done so; lest being a condemned man, I should seem to prescribe to you as an Apostle.

I have great knowledge in God; but I refrain myself, lest I should perish in my boasting.

For now I ought the more to fear; and not to hearken to those that would puff me up.

For they that speak to me, in my praise, chasten me.

For I indeed desire to suffer, but I cannot tell whether I am worthy so to do.

[*20] And this desire, though to others it does not appear, yet to myself it is for that very reason the more violent. I have, therefore, need of moderation; by which the prince of this world is destroyed.

Am I not able to write to you of heavenly things?—But I fear lest I should harm you, who are yet but babes in Christ: (excuse me this care;) and lest per chance being not able to receive them, ye should be choken with them.

For even I myself, although I am in bonds, yet am not therefore able to understand heavenly things:

As the places of the angels, and the several companies of them, under their respective princes; things visible and invisible; but in these I am yet a learner.

For many things are wanting to us, that we come not short of God.

CHAPTER II.

Warns them against heretics, exhorts them to humility and unity, briefly sets before them the true doctrine concerning Christ.

I EXHORT you therefore, or rather not I, but the love of Jesus Christ; that ye use none but Christian nourishment; abstaining from pasture which is of another kind, I mean heresy.

For they that are heretics, confound together the doctrine of Jesus Christ, with their own poison: whilst they seem worthy of belief:

As men give a deadly potion mixed with sweet wine; which he who drinks of, does with the treacherous pleasure sweetly drink in his own death.

Wherefore guard yourselves against such persons. And that you will do if you are not puffed up; but continue inseparable from Jesus Christ our God, and from your bishop, and from the commands of the Apostles.

He that is within the altar is pure; but he that is without, that is, that does anything without the bishop, the presbyters, and deacons, is not pure in his conscience.

Not that I know there is any thing of this nature among you; but I fore-arm you, as being greatly beloved by me, foreseeing the snares of the devil.

Wherefore putting on meekness, renew yourselves in faith, that is, the flesh of the Lord; and in charity, that is, the blood of Jesus Christ.

Let no man have any grudge against his neighbour. Give no occasion to the Gentiles; lest by means of a few foolish men, the whole congregation of God be evil spoken of.

For woe to that man through whose vanity my name is blasphemed by any.

Stop your ears therefore, as often as any one shall speak contrary to Jesus Christ; who was of the race of David, of the Virgin Mary.

Who was truly born and did eat and drink; was truly persecuted under Pontius Pilate; was truly crucified and dead; both those in heaven and on earth, being spectators of it.

Who was also truly raised from the dead by his Father. after the same manner as he will also raise up us who believe in him by Christ Jesus; without whom we have no true life.

But if, as some who are Atheists, that is to say infidels, pretend, that he only seemed to suffer: (they themselves only seeming to exist) why then am I bound?—Why do I desire to fight with beasts?—Therefore do I die in vain: therefore I will not speak falsely against the Lord.

Flee therefore these evil sprouts which bring forth deadly fruit; of which if any one taste, he shall presently die.

For these are not the plants of the Father; seeing if they were, they would appear to be the branches of the cross, and their fruit would be incorruptible; by which he invites you through his passion, who are members of him.

For the head cannot be without its members, God having promised a union, that is himself.

CHAPTER III.

He again exhorts to unity: and desires their prayers for himself and for his church at Antioch.

I SALUTE you from Smyrna, together with the churches of God that are present with me; who have refreshed me in all things, both in the flesh and in the spirit.

My bonds, which I carry about me for the sake of Christ, beseeching him that I may attain unto God) exhort you, that you continue in concord among yourselves and in prayer with one another.

For it becomes every one of you, especially the presbyters, to refresh the bishop, to the honour of the Father of Jesus Christ and of the Apostles.

I beseech you, that you hearken to me in love; that I may not by those things which I write, rise up in witness against you.

Pray also for me; who through the mercy of God stand in need of your prayers, that I may be worthy of the portion which I am about to obtain that I be not found a reprobate.

The love of those who are at Smyrna and Ephesus salute you. Remember in your prayers the church of Syria, from which I am not worthy to be called, being one of the least of it.

Fare ye well in Jesus Christ; being subject to your bishop as to the command of God; and so likewise to the presbytery.

Love every one his brother with an unfeigned heart. My soul be your expiation, not only now, but when I shall have attained unto God; for I am yet under danger.

But the Father is faithful in Jesus Christ, to fulfil both mine and your petition; in whom may ye be found unblamable.

To the Trallians.

THE EPISTLE OF IGNATIUS TO THE ROMANS.

CHAPTER I.

He testifies his desire to see, and his hopes of suffering for Christ, which he earnestly entreats them not to prevent, but to pray for him, that God would strengthen him to the combat.

IGNATIUS, who is also called Theophorus, to the church which has obtained mercy from the majesty of the Most High Father, and his only begotten Son Jesus Christ; beloved, and illuminated through the will of who willeth all things which are according to the love of Jesus Christ our God which also presides in the place of the region of the Romans; and which I salute in the name of Jesus Christ (as being) united both in flesh and spirit to all his commands, and filled with the grace of God; (all joy) in Jesus Christ our God.

Forasmuch as I have at last obtained through my prayers to God, to see your faces, which I much desired to do; being bound in Jesus Christ, I hope ere long to salute you, if it shall be the will of God to grant me to attain unto the end I long for.

For the beginning is well disposed, if I shall but have grace, without hindrance, to receive what is appointed for me.

But I fear your love, lest it do me an injury. For it is easy for you to do what you please; but it will be hard for me to attain unto God, if you spare me.

But I would not that ye should please men, but God whom also ye do please. For neither shall I hereafter have such an opportunity of going unto God; nor will you if ye shall now be silent, ever be to a better work. For if you shall be silent in my behalf, I shall be made partaker of God.

But if you shall love my body, I shall have my course again to run. Wherefore ye cannot do me a greater kindness, than to suffer me to be sacrificed unto God, now that the altar is already prepared:

That when ye shall be gathered together in love, ye may give thanks to the Father through Christ Jesus; that he has vouchsafed to bring a bishop of Syria unto you, being called from the east unto the west.

For it is good for me to set from the world, unto God; that I may rise again unto him.

Ye have never envied any one; ye have taught other. I would therefore that ye should now do those things yourselves, which in your instructions you have prescribed to others.

Only pray for me, that God would give me both inward and outward strength, that I may not only say, but will; nor be only called a Christian, but be found one.

For if I shall be found a Christian, I may then deservedly be called one; and be thought faithful, when I shall no longer appear to the world.

Nothing is good, that is seen.

For even our God, Jesus Christ, now that he is in the Father, does so much the more appear.

A Christian is not a work of opinion; but of greatness of mind, (especially when he is hated by the world.)

CHAPTER II.

Expresses his great desire and determination to suffer martyrdom.

I WRITE to the churches, and signify to them all, that am willing to die for God, unless hinder me.

I beseech you that you shew not an unseasonable good will towards me. Suffer me to be food to the wild beasts; by whom I shall attain unto God.

For I am the wheat of God; and I shall be ground by the teeth of the wild beasts, that I may be found the pure bread of Christ.

Rather encourage the beasts, that they may become my sepulchre; and may leave nothing of my body; that being dead I mazy not be troublesome to any.

Then shall I be truly the disciple of Jesus Christ, when the world shall not see so much as my body, Pray therefore unto Christ for me, that by these instruments I may be made the sacrifice of God.

I do not, as Peter and Paul, command you. They were Apostles, I a condemned man; they were free, but I am even to this day a servant:

But if I shall suffer, I shall then become the freeman of Jesus Christ, and shall rise free. And now, being in bonds, I learn, not to desire anything.

From Syria even unto Rome, I fight with beasts both by sea and land; both night and day: being bound to ten leopards, that is to say, to such a band of soldiers; who, though treated with all manner of kindness, are the worse for it.

But I am the more instructed by their injuries; yet am I not therefore justified.

May I enjoy the wild beasts that are prepared for me; which also I wish may exercise all their fierceness upon me.

And whom for that end I will encourage, that they may be sure to devour me, and not serve me as they have done some, whom out of fear they have not touched. But, and if they will not do it willingly, I will provoke them to it.

Pardon me in this matter; I know what is profitable for me. Now I begin to be a disciple. Nor shall anything move me, whether visible or invisible, that I may attain to Jesus Christ.

Let fire, and the cross; let the companies of wild beasts; let breakings of bones and tearing of members; let the shattering in pieces of the whole body, and all the wicked torments of the devil come upon me; only let me enjoy Jesus Christ.

All the ends of the world, and the kingdoms of it, will profit me nothing: I would rather die for Jesus Christ, than rule to the utmost ends of the earth. Him I seek who died for us; him I desire, that rose again for us. This is the gain that is laid up for me.

Pardon me, my brethren, ye shall not hinder me from living. Nor seeing I desire to go to God, may you separate me from him, for the sake of this world; nor reduce me by any of the desires of it. Suffer me to enter into pure light: Where being come, I shall be indeed the servant of God.

Permit me to imitate the passion of my God. If any one has him within himself, let him consider what I desire; and let him have compassion on me, as knowing how I am straightened.

CHAPTER III.

Further expresses his desire to suffer.

THE prince of this world would fain carry me away, and corrupt my resolution towards my God. Let none of you therefore help him: Rather do ye join with me, that is, with God.

Do not speak with Jesus Christ, and yet covet the world. Let not any envy dwell with you; No not though I myself when I shall be come unto you, should exhort you to it, yet do not ye hearken to me; but rather believe what I now write to you.

For though I am alive, at the writing this, yet my desire is to die. My love is crucified; (and the fire that is within me does not desire any water; but being alive and springing within me, says,) Come to the Father.

I take no pleasure in the food of corruption, nor in the pleasures of this life.

I desire the bread of God which is the flesh of Jesus Christ, (of the seed of David; and the drink that I long for) is his blood, which is incorruptible love.

I have no desire to live any longer after the manner of men, neither shall I, if you consent. Be ye therefore willing, that ye yourselves also may be pleasing to God. I exhort you in a few words; I pray you believe me.

Jesus Christ will shew you that I speak truly. My mouth is without deceit, and the Father hath truly spoken by it. Pray therefore for me, that I may accomplish what I desire.

I have not written to you after the flesh, but according to the will of God. If I shall suffer, ye have loved me; but if I shall be rejected, ye have hated me.

Remember in your prayers the church of Syria, which now enjoys God for its shepherd instead of me: Let Jesus Christ only oversee it, and your charity.

But I am even ashamed to be reckoned as one of them: For neither am I worthy, being the least among them, and as one born out of due season. But through mercy I have obtained to be somebody, if I shall get unto God.

My spirit salutes you; and the charity of the churches that have received me in the name of Jesus Christ; not as a passenger. For even they that were not near to me in the way, have gone before me to the next city to meet me.

These things I write to you from Smyrna, by the most worthy of the church of Ephesus.

There is now with me, together with many others, Crocus, most beloved of me. As for those which are come from Syria, and are gone before me to Rome, to the glory of God, I suppose you are not ignorant of them.

Ye shall therefore signify to them, that I draw near, for they are all worthy both of God and of you: Whom it is fit that you refresh in all things.

This have I written to you, the day before the ninth of the calends of September. Be strong unto the end, in the patience of Jesus Christ.

To the Romans.

THE EPISTLE OF IGNATIUS TO THE PHILADELPHIANS.

CHAPTER I.

Commends their bishop whom they had sent unto him, warns them against divisions and schism.

IGNATIUS, who is also called Theophorus, to the church of God the Father, and our Lord Jesus Christ, which is at Philadelphia in Asia; which has obtained mercy, being fixed in the concord of God, and rejoicing evermore in the passion of our Lord, and being fulfilled in all mercy through his resurrection: Which also I salute in the blood of Jesus Christ, which is our eternal and undefiled joy; especially if they are at unity with the bishop, and presbyters who are with him, and the deacons appointed according to the mind of Jesus Christ; whom he has settled according to his own will in all firmness by his Holy Spirit:

Which bishop I know obtained that great ministry among you, not of himself, neither by men, nor out of vain glory; but by the love of God the Father, and our Lord Jesus Christ.

Whose moderation I admire; who by his silence is able to do more than others with all their vain talk. For he is fitted to the commands, as the harp to its strings.

Wherefore my soul esteems his mind towards God most happy, knowing it to be fruitful in all virtue, and perfect; full of constancy, free from passion, and according to all the moderation of the living God.

Wherefore as becomes the children both of the light and of truth; flee divisions and false doctrines; but where your shepherd is, there do ye, as sheep, follow after.

For there are many wolves who seem worthy of belief with a false pleasure lead captive those that run in the course of God; but in the concord they shall find no place.

Abstain therefore from evil herbs which Jesus does not dress; because such are not the plantation of the Father. Not that I have found any division among you, but rather all manner of purity.

For as many as are of God, and of Jesus Christ, are also with their bishop. And as many as shall with repentance return into the unity of the church, even these shall also be the servants of God, that they may live according to Jesus.

Be not deceived, brethren; if any one follows him that makes a schism in the church, he shall not inherit the kingdom of God. If any one walks after any other opinion, he agrees not with the passion of Christ.

Wherefore let it be your endeavour to partake all of the same holy eucharist.

For there is but one flesh of our Lord Jesus Christ; and one cup in the unity of his blood; one altar;

As also there is one bishop, together with his presbytery, and the deacons my fellow-servants: that so whatsoever ye do, ye may do it according to the will of God.

CHAPTER II.

Desires their prayers, and to be united but not to Judaize.

MY brethren, the love I have towards you makes me the more large; and having a great joy in you, I endeavour to secure you against danger; or rather not I, but Jesus Christ; in whom being bound I the more fear, as being yet only on the way to suffering.

But your prayer to God shall make me perfect, that I may attain to that portion, which by God's mercy is allotted to me: Fleeing to the Gospel as to the flesh of Christ; and to the Apostles as to the presbytery of the church.

Let us also love the prophets, forasmuch as they also have led us to the Gospel, and to hope in Christ, and to expect him.

In whom also believing they were saved in the unity of Jesus Christ; being holy men, worthy to be loved, and had in wonder;

Who have received testimony from Jesus Christ, and are numbered in the Gospel of our common hope.

But if any one shall preach the Jewish law unto you, hearken not unto him; for it is better to receive the doctrine of Christ from one that has been circumcised, than Judaism from one that has not.

But if either the one, or other, do not speak concerning Christ Jesus, they seem to me to be but as monuments and sepulchres of the dead, upon which are written only the names of men.

Flee therefore the wicked arts and snares of the prince of this world; lest at any time being oppressed by his cunning ye grow cold in your charity. But come all together into the same place with an undivided heart.

And I bless my God that I have a good conscience towards you, and that no one among you has whereof to boast either openly or privately, that I have been burthensome to him in much or little.

And I wish to all among whom I have conversed, that it may not turn to a witness against them.

For although some would have deceived me according to the flesh, yet the spirit, being from God, is not deceived; for it knows both whence it comes and whither it goes, and reproves the secrets of the heart.

I cried whilst I was among you; I spake with a loud voice: attend to the bishop, and to the presbytery, and to the deacons.

Now some supposed that I spake this as foreseeing the division that should come among you.

But he is my witness for whose sake I am in bonds that I knew nothing from any man. But the spirit spake, saying on this wise: Do nothing without the bishop:

Keep your bodies as the temples of God: Love unity; Flee divisions; Be the followers of Christ, as he was of his Father.

I therefore did as became me, as a man composed to unity. For where there is division, and wrath, God dwelleth not.

But the Lord forgives all that repent, if they return to the unity of God, and to the council of the bishop.

For I trust in the grace of Jesus Christ that he will free you from every bond.

Nevertheless I exhort you that you do nothing out of strife, but according to the instruction of Christ.

Because I have heard of some who say; unless I find it written in the originals, I will not believe it to be written in the Gospel. And when I said, It is written; they answered what lay before them in their corrupted copies.

But to me Jesus Christ is instead of all the uncorrupted monuments in the world; together with those undefiled monuments, his cross, and death, and resurrection, and the faith which is by him; by which I desire, through your prayers, to be justified.

The priests indeed are good; but much better is the High Priest to whom the Holy of Holies has been committed; and who alone has been entrusted with the secrets of God.

He is the door of the Father; by which Abraham, and Isaac, and Jacob, and all the prophets, enter in; as well as the Apostles, and the church.

And all these things tend to the unity which is of God. Howbeit the Gospel has some. what in it far above all other dispensations; namely, the appearance of our Saviour, the Lord Jesus Christ, his passion and resurrection.

For the beloved prophets referred to him; but the gospel is the perfection of incorruption. All therefore together are good, if ye believe with charity.

CHAPTER III.

Informs them he had heard that the persecution was stopped at Antioch, and directs them to send a messenger hitherto to congratulate with the church.

NOW as concerning the church of Antioch which is in Syria, seeing I am told that through your prayers and the bowels which ye have towards it in Jesus Christ, it is in peace; it will become you, as the church of God, to ordain some deacon to go to them thither as the ambassador of God; that he may rejoice with them when they meet together, and glorify God's name.

Blessed be that man in Jesus Christ, who shall be found worthy of such a ministry; and ye yourselves also shall be glorified.

Now if you be willing, it is not impossible for you to do this for the grace of God; as also the other neighbouring churches have sent them, some bishops, some priests and deacons.

As concerning Philo the deacon of Cilicia, a most worthy man, he still ministers unto me in the word of God: together with Rheus of Agathopolis, a singular good person, who has followed me even from Syria, not regarding his life: These also bear witness unto you.

And I myself give thanks to God for you that you receive them as the Lord shall receive you. But for those that dishonoured them, may they be forgiven through the grace of Jesus Christ.

The charity of the brethren that are at Troas salutes you: from whence also I now write by Burrhus, who was sent together with me by those of Ephesus and Smyrna, for respect sake.

May our Lord Jesus Christ honour them; in whom they hope, both in flesh, and soul, and spirit; in faith, in love, in unity. Farewell in Christ Jesus our common hope.

THE EPISTLE OF IGNATIUS TO THE SMYRNAEANS.

CHAPTER I.

Declares his joy for their firmness in the Gospel. Enlarges on the person of Christ, against such as pretend that Christ did not really suffer.

IGNATIUS, who is also called Theophorus, to the church of God the Father, and of the beloved Jesus Christ, which God hath mercifully blessed with every good gift; being filled with faith and charity, so that this is wanting in no gift; most worthy of God, and fruitful in saints: the church which is at Smyrna in Asia; all joy, through his immaculate spirit, and the word of God.

I glorify God, even Jesus Christ, who has given you such wisdom.

For I have observed that you are settled in an immovable faith, as if you were nailed to the cross of our Lord Jesus Christ, both in the flesh and in the spirit; and are confirmed in love through the blood of Christ; being fully persuaded of those things which relate unto our Lord.

Who truly was of the race of David according to the flesh, but the Son of God according to the will and power of God; truly born of the Virgin, and baptized of John; that so all righteousness might be fulfilled by him.

He was also truly crucified by Pontius Pilate, and Herod the Tetrarch, being nailed for us in the flesh; by the fruits of which we are, even by his most blessed passion.

That he might set up a token for all ages through his resurrection, to all his holy and faithful servants, whether they be Jews or Gentiles, in one body of his church.

Now all these things he suffered for us that we might be saved. And he suffered truly, as he also truly raised up himself: And not, as some unbelievers say, that he only seemed to suffer, they themselves only seeming to be.

And as they believe so shall it happen unto them; when being divested of the body they shall become mere spirits.

But I know that even after his resurrection he was in the flesh; and I believed that he is still so.

And when he came to those who were with Peter, he said unto them, Take, handle

THE LOST BOOKS OF THE BIBLE

me, and see that I am not an incorporeal daemon. And straightway they felt and believed; being convinced both by his flesh and spirit.

For this cause they despised death, and were found to be above it.

But after his resurrection he did eat and drink with them, as he was flesh; although as to his Spirit he was united to the Father.

CHAPTER II.

Exhorts them against heretics.The danger of their doctrine.

NOW these things, beloved, put you in mind of, not questioning but that you yourselves also believe that they are so.

But I arm you before-hand against certain beasts in the shape of men whom you must not only not receive, but if it be possible must not meet with.

Only you must pray for them, that if it be the will of God they may repent; which yet will be very hard. But of this our Lord Jesus Christ has the power, who is our true life.

For if all these things were done only in shew by our Lord, then do I also seem only to be bound.

And why have I given up myself to death, to the fire, to the sword, to wild beasts!

But now the nearer I am to the sword, the nearer I am to God: when I shall come among the wild beasts, I shall come to God.

Only in the name of Jesus Christ, I undergo all, to suffer together with him; he who was made a perfect man strengthening me.

Whom some not knowing, do deny; or rather have been denied by him, being the advocates of death, rather than of the truth. Whom neither the prophecies, nor the law of Moses have persuaded; nor the Gospel itself even to this day, nor the sufferings of every one of us.

For they think also the same things of us. For what does a man profit me, if he shall praise me, and blaspheme my Lord; not confessing that he was truly made man?

Now he that doth not say this, does in effect deny him, and is in death. But for the names of such as do this, they being unbelievers, I thought it not fitting to write them unto you.

Yea, God forbid that I should make any mention of them, till they shall repent to a true belief of Christ's passion, which is our resurrection.

Let no man deceive himself; both the things which are in heaven and the glorious angels, and princes, whether visible or invisible, if they believe not in the blood of Christ, it shall be to them to condemnation.

He that is able to receive this, let him receive it. Let no man's place or state in the world puff him up: that which is worth all his faith and charity, to which nothing is to be

185

preferred.

But consider those who are of a different opinion from us, as to what concerns the grace of Jesus Christ which is come unto us, how contrary they are to the design of God.

They have no regard to charity, no care of the widow, the fatherless, and the oppressed; of the bond or free, of the hungry or thirsty.

They abstain from the eucharist, and from the public offices; because they confess not the eucharist to be the flesh of our Saviour Jesus Christ; which suffered for our sins, and which the Father of his goodness, raised again from the dead.

And for this cause contradicting the gift of God, they die in their disputes: but much better would it be for them to receive it, that they might one day rise through it.

It will therefore become you to abstain from such persons; and not to speak with them neither in private nor in public.

But to hearken to the prophets, and especially to the Gospel, in which both Christ's passion is manifested unto us, and his resurrection perfectly declared.

But flee all divisions, as the beginning of evils.

CHAPTER III.

Exhorts them to follow their bishop and pastors; but especially their bishop. Thanks them for their kindness, and acquaints them with the ceasing of the persecution at Antioch.

SEE that ye all follow your bishop, as Jesus Christ, the Father; and the presbytery, as the Apostles. And reverence the deacons, as the command of God.

Let no man do anything of what belongs to the church separately from the bishop.

Let that eucharist be looked upon as well established, which is either offered by the bishop, or by him to whom the bishop has given his consent.

Wheresoever the bishop shall appear, there let the people also be: as where Jesus Christ is, there is the Catholic church.

It is not lawful without the bishop, neither to baptize, nor to celebrate the Holy Communion; but whatsoever he shall approve of, that is also pleasing unto God; that so whatever is done, may be sure and well done.

For what remains, it is very reasonable that we should repent whilst there is yet time to return unto God.

It is a good thing to have a due regard both to God, and to the bishop: he that honours the bishop, shall be honoured of God. But he that does anything without his knowledge, ministers unto the devil.

Let all things therefore abound to you in charity; seeing that ye are worthy.

Ye have refreshed me in all things; so shall Jesus Christ you. Ye have loved me both when I was present with you, and now being absent, ye cease not to do so.

May God be your reward, from whom whilst ye undergo all things, ye shall attain unto him.

Ye have done well in that ye have received Philo, and Rheus Agathopus, who followed me for the word of God, as the deacons of Christ our God.

Who also gave thanks unto the Lord for you, forasmuch as ye have refreshed them in all things. Nor shall any thing that you have done be lost to you.

My soul be for yours, and my bonds which ye have not despised, nor been ashamed of. Wherefore neither shall Jesus Christ, our perfect faith, be ashamed of you.

Your prayer is come to the church of Antioch which is in Syria. From whence being sent bound with chains becoming God, I salute the churches; being not worthy to be called from thence, as being the least among them.

Nevertheless by the will of God I have been thought worthy of this honour; not for that I think I have deserved it, but by the grace of God.

Which I wish may be perfectly given unto me, that through your prayers I may attain unto God.

And therefore that your work may be fully accomplished both upon earth and in heaven; it will be fitting, and for the honour of God, that your church appoint some worthy delegate, who being come as far as Syria, may rejoice together with them that they are in peace; and that they are again restored to their former state, and have again received their proper body.

Wherefore I should think it a worthy action, to send some one from you with an epistle, to congratulate with them their peace in God; and that through your prayers they have now gotten to their harbor.

For inasmuch as ye are perfect yourselves, you ought to think those things that are perfect. For when you are desirous to do well, God is ready to enable you thereunto.

The love of the brethren that are at Troas salute you; from whence I write to you by Burrhus whom you sent with me, together with the Ephesians your brethren; and who has in all things refreshed me.

And I would to God that all would imitate him, as being a pattern of the ministry of God. May his grace fully reward him.

I salute your very worthy bishop, and your venerable presbytery; and your deacons, my fellow-servants; and all of you in general, and every one in particular, in the name of Jesus Christ, and in his flesh and blood; in his passion and resurrection both fleshly and spiritually; and in the unity of God with you.

Grace be with you, and mercy, and peace, and patience, for evermore.

I salute the families of my brethren, with their wives and children; and the virgins that are called widows. Be strong in the power of the Holy Ghost. Philo, who is present with me salutes you.

I salute the house of Tavias, and pray that it may be strengthened in faith and charity, both of flesh and spirit.

I salute Alce my well-beloved, together with the incomparable Daphnus, and Eutechnus, and all by name.

Farewell in the grace of God.

To the Smyrnaeans from Troas.

THE EPISTLE OF IGNATIUS TO POLYCARP.

CHAPTER I.

Blesses God for the firm establishment of Polycarp in the faith, and gives him particular directions for improving it.

IGNATIUS, who is also called Theophorus, to Polycarp, bishop of the church which is at Smyrna; their overseer, but rather himself overlooked by God the Father, and the Lord Jesus Christ: all happiness.

Having known that thy mind towards God, is fixed as it were upon an immovable rock; I exceedingly give thanks, that I have been thought worthy to behold thy blessed face, in which may I always rejoice in God.

Wherefore I beseech thee by the grace of God with which thou art clothed, to press forward in thy course, and to exhort all others that they may be saved.

Maintain thy place with all care both of flesh and spirit: Make it thy endeavour to preserve unity, than which nothing is better. Bear with all men, even as the Lord with thee.

Support all in love, as also thou dost. Pray without ceasing: ask more understanding than what thou already hast. Be watchful, having thy spirit always awake.

Speak to every one according as God shall enable thee. Bear the infirmities of all, as a perfect combatant; where the labour is great, the gain is the more.

If thou shalt love the good disciples, what thank is it? But rather do thou subject to thee those that are mischievous, in meekness.

Every wound is not healed with the same plaster: if the accessions of the disease be vehement, modify them with soft remedies: be in all things wise as a serpent, but harmless as a dove.

For this cause thou art composed of flesh and spirit; that thou mayest modify those things that appear before thy face.

And as for those that are not seen, pray to God that he would reveal them unto thee, that so thou mayest be wanting in nothing, but mayest abound in every gift.

The times demand thee, as the pilots the winds; and he that is tossed in a tempest, the haven where he would be; that thou mayst attain unto God.

Be sober as the combatant of God: the crown proposed to thee is immortality, and eternal life; concerning which thou art also fully persuaded. I will be thy surety in all things, and my bonds, which thou hast loved.

Let not those that seem worthy of credit, but teach other doctrines, disturb thee. Stand firm and immovable, as au anvil when it is beaten upon.

It is the part of a brave combatant to be wounded, and yet overcome. But especially we ought to endure all things for God's sake, that he may bear with us.

Be every day better than other: consider the times; and expect him, who is above all time, eternal, invisible, though for our sakes made visible: impalpable, and impassable, yet for us subjected to sufferings; enduring all manner of ways for our salvation.

CHAPTER II.

Continues his advice, and teaches him how to advise others. Enforces unity and subjection to the bishop.

LET not the widows be neglected: be thou after God, their guardian.

Let nothing be done without thy knowledge and consent; neither do thou anything but according to the will of God; as also thou dost, with all constancy.

Let your assemblies be more full: inquire into all by name.

Overlook not the men and maid servants; neither let them be puffed up: but rather let them be the more subject to the glory of God, that they may obtain from him a better liberty.

Let them not desire to be set free at the public cost, that they be not slaves to their own lusts.

Flee evil arts; or rather, make not any mention of them.

Say to my sisters, that they love the Lord; and be satisfied with their own husbands, both in the flesh and spirit.

In like manner, exhort my brethren, in the name of Jesus Christ, that they love their wives, even as the Lord the Church.

If any man can remain in a virgin state, to the honour of the flesh of Christ, let him remain without boasting; but if he boast, he is undone. And if he desire to be more taken notice of than the bishop he is corrupted.

But it becomes all such as are married, whether men or women to come together with the consent of the bishop, that so their marriage may be according to godliness, and not in lust.

Let all things be done to the honour of God.

Hearken unto the bishop, that God also may hearken unto you. My soul be security for them that submit to their bishop, with their presbyters and deacons. And may my portion be together with theirs in God.

Labour with one another; contend together, run together, suffer together; sleep together, and rise together; as the stewards, and assessors, and ministers of God.

Please him under whom ye war, and from whom ye receive your wages. Let none of you be found a deserter; but let your baptism remain, as your arms; your faith, as your helmet; your charity, as your spear; your patience, as your whole armour.

Let your works be your charge, that so you may receive a suitable reward. Be longsuffering therefore towards each other in meekness: as God is towards you.

Let me have joy of you in all things.

CHAPTER III.

Greets Polycarp on the peace of the church at Antioch: and desires him to write to that and other churches.

NOW forasmuch as the church of Antioch in Syria, is, as I am told, [one word illegible.—JBH] through your prayers; I also have been the more comforted and without care in God; if so be that by suffering, I shall attain unto God; that through your prayers I may be found a disciple of Christ.

It will be very fit, O most worthy Polycarp, to call a select council, and choose some one whom ye particularly love, and who is patient of labour; that he may be the messenger of God; and that going unto Syria, he may glorify your incessant love, to the praise of Christ.

A Christian has not the power of himself: but must be always at leisure for God's service. Now this work is both God's and your's: when ye shall have perfected it.

For I trust through the grace of God that ye are ready to every good work that is fitting for you in the Lord.

Knowing therefore your earnest affection for the truth, I have exhorted you by these short letters.

But forasmuch as I have not been able to write to all the churches, because I must suddenly sail from Troas to Neapolis; (for so is the command of those to whose pleasure I am subject;) do you write to the churches that are near you, as being instructed in the will of God, that they also may do in like manner.

Let those that are able send messengers; and let the rest send their letters by those who shall be sent by you: that you may be glorified to all eternity, of which you are worthy.

I salute all by name, particularly the wife of Epitropus, with all her house and children. I salute Attalus my well-beloved.

I salute him who shall be thought worthy to be sent by you into Syria. Let grace be ever with him, and with Polycarp who sends him.

I wish you all happiness in our God, Jesus Christ; in whom continue, in the unity and protection of God.

I salute Alce my well-beloved. Farewell in the Lord.

To Polycarp.

THE EPISTLE OF POLYCARP TO THE PHILIPPIANS.

[The genuineness of this Epistle is controverted, but implicitly believed by Archbishop Wake, whose translation is below. There is also a translation by Dr. Cave, attached to his Life of Polycarp.]

CHAPTER I.

Commends the Philippians for their respect to those who suffered for the Gospel; and for their own faith.

POLYCARP, and the presbyters that are with him, to the church of God which is at Philippi: mercy unto you and peace from God Almighty; and the Lord Jesus Christ, our Saviour, be multiplied.

I rejoiced greatly with you in our Lord Jesus Christ, that ye received the images of a true love, and accompanied, as it is behooved you, those who were in bonds, becoming saints; which are the crowns of such as are truly chosen by God and our Lord:

As also that the root of the faith which was preached from ancient times, remains firm in you to this day; and brings forth fruit to our Lord Jesus Christ, who suffered himself to be brought even to the death for our sins.

Whom God hath raised up, having loosed the pains of death, whom having not seen, ye love; in whom though now ye see him not, yet believing ye rejoice with joy unspeakable and full of glory.

Into which many desire to enter; knowing that by grace ye are saved; not by works, but by the will of God through Jesus Christ.

Wherefore girding up the loins of your minds; serve the Lord with fear, and in truth: laying aside all empty and vain speech, and the error of many; believing in him that raised up our Lord Jesus Christ from the dead, and hath given him glory and a throne at his right hand.

To whom all things are made subject, both that are in heaven, and that are in earth; whom every living creature shall worship; who shall come to be the judge of the quick and dead.: whose blood God shall require of them that believe in him.

But he that raised up Christ from the dead, shall also raise up us in like manner, if we do his will and walk according to his commandments; and love those things which he loved:

Abstaining from all unrighteousness; inordinate affection, and love of money; from evil speaking; false witness; not rendering evil for evil, or railing for railing, or striking for striking, or cursing for cursing.

But remembering what the Lord has taught us saying, Judge not, and ye shall not be judged; forgive and ye shall be forgiven; be ye merciful, and ye shall obtain mercy; for with the same measure that ye mete withal, it shall be measured to you again.

And again, that blessed are the poor, and they that are persecuted for righteousness' sake; for theirs is the kingdom of God.

CHAPTER II.

Exhorts to Faith, Hope, and Charity. Against covetousness, and as to the duties of husbands, wives, widows, deacons, young men, virgins, and presbyters.

THESE things, my brethren, I took not the liberty of myself to write unto you concerning righteousness, but you yourselves before encouraged me to it.

For neither can I, nor any other such as I am, come up to the wisdom of the blessed and renowned Paul: who being himself in person with those who then lived, did with all exactness and soundness teach the word of truth; and being gone from you wrote an epistle to you.

Into which if you look, you will be able to edify yourselves in the faith that has been delivered unto you; which is the mother of us all; being followed with hope, and led on by a general love, both towards God and towards Christ, and towards our neighbour.

For if any man has these things he has fulfilled the law of righteousness: for he that has charity is far from all sin.

But the love of money is the root of all evil. Knowing therefore that as we brought nothing into this world, so neither may we carry any thing out; let us arm ourselves with the armour of righteousness.

And teach ourselves first to walk according to the commandments of the Lord; and then your wives to walk likewise according to the faith that is given to them; in charity, and in purity; loving their own husbands with all sincerity, and all others alike with all temperance; and to bring up their children in the instruction and fear of the Lord.

The widows likewise teach that they be sober as to what concerns the faith of the Lord: praying always for all men; being far from all detraction, evil speaking, false witness; from covetousness, and from all evil.

Knowing that they are the altars of God, who sees all blemishes, and from whom nothing is hid; who searches out the very reasonings, and thoughts, and secrets of our hearts.

Knowing therefore that God is not mocked, we ought to walk worthy both of his command and of his glory.

Also the deacons must be blameless before him, as the ministers of God in Christ, and not of men. Not false accusers; not double tongued; not lovers of money; but moderate in all things; compassionate, careful; walking according to the truth of the Lord, who was the servant of all.

Whom if we please in this present world we shall also be made partakers of that which is to come, according as he has promised to us, that he will raise us from the dead; and that if we shall walk worthy of him, we shall also reign together with him, if we believe.

In like manner the younger men must be unblameable in all things; above all, taking care of their purity, and to restrain themselves from all evil. For it is good to be cut off from the lusts that are in the world; because every such lust warreth against the spirit: and neither fornicators, nor effeminate, nor abusers of themselves with mankind, shall inherit the kingdom of God; nor they who do such things as are foolish and unreasonable.

Wherefore ye must needs abstain from all these things, being subject to the priests and deacons, as unto God and Christ.

The virgins admonish to walk in a spotless and pure conscience.

And let the elders be compassionate and merciful towards all; turning them from their errors; seeking out those that are weak; not forgetting the widows, the fatherless, and the poor; but always providing what is good both in the sight of God and man.

Abstaining from all wrath, respect of persons, and unrighteous judgment: and especially being free from all covetousness.

Not easy to believe any thing against any; not severe in judgment; knowing that we are all debtors in point of sin.

If therefore we pray to the Lord that he would forgive us, we ought also to forgive others; for we are all in the sight of our Lord and God; and must all stand before the judgment seat of Christ; and shall every one give an account of himself.

Let us therefore serve him in fear, and with all reverence as both himself hath commanded; and as the Apostles who have preached the Gospel unto us, and the prophets who have foretold the coming of our Lord have taught us.

Being zealous of what is good; abstaining from all offence, and from false brethren; and from those who bear the name of Christ in hypocrisy; who deceive vain men.

CHAPTER III.

As to faith in our Saviour Christ: his nature and sufferings, the resurrection and judgment. Exhorts to prayer and steadfastness in the faith, from the examples of Christ, and Apostles and saints, and exhorts to carefulness in all well-doing.

FOR whosoever does not confess that Jesus Christ is come in the flesh, he is Antichrist: and whoever does not confess his suffering upon the cross, is from the devil.

And whosoever perverts the oracles of the Lord to his own lusts; and says that there shall neither be any resurrection, nor judgment, he is the first-born of Satan.

THE LOST BOOKS OF THE BIBLE

Wherefore leaving the vanity of many, and their false doctrines; let us return to the word that was delivered to us from the beginning; Watching unto prayer; and persevering in fasting.

With supplication beseeching the all seeing God not to lead us into temptation; as the Lord hath said, The spirit is truly willing, but the flesh is weak.

Let us therefore without ceasing hold steadfastly to him who is our hope, and the earnest of our righteousness, even Jesus Christ; Who his own self bare our sins in his own body on the tree: who did no sin, neither was guile found in his mouth. But suffered all for us that we might live through him.

Let us therefore imitate his patience; and if we suffer for his name, let us glorify him; for this example he has given us by himself, and so have we believed.

Wherefore I exhort all of you that ye obey the word of righteousness, and exercise all patience; which ye have seen set forth before our eyes, not only in the blessed Ignatius, and Zozimus, and Rufus; but in others among yourselves; and in Paul himself, and the rest of the Apostles:

Being confident of this, that all, these have not run in vain; but in faith and righteousness, and are gone to the place that was due to them from the Lord; with whom they also suffered.

For they loved not this present world; but him who died, and was raised again by God for us.

Stand therefore in these things, and follow the example of the Lord; being firm and immutable in the faith, lovers of the brotherhood, lovers of one another: companions together in the truth, being kind and gentle towards each other, despising none.

When it is in your power to do good, defer it not, for charity delivered from death.

Be all of you subject one to another, having your conversation honest among the Gentiles; that by your good works, both ye yourselves may receive praise, and the Lord may not be blasphemed through you. But wo be to him by whom the name of the Lord is blasphemed.

Therefore teach all men sobriety; in which do ye also exercise yourselves.

CHAPTER IV.

Valens, a presbyter, having fallen into the sin of covetousness, he exhorts them against it.

I AM greatly afflicted for Valens, who was once a presbyter among you; that he should so little understand the place that was given to him in the church. Wherefore I admonish you that ye abstain from covetousness; and that ye be chaste, and true of speech.

Keep yourselves from all evil. For he that in these things cannot govern himself how shall he be able to prescribe them to another?

If a man does not keep himself from covetousness, he shall be polluted with idolatry and be judged as if he were a Gentile.

But who of you are ignorant of the judgment of God? Do we not know that the saints shall judge the world, as Paul teaches?

But I have neither perceived nor heard any thing of this kind in you, among whom the blessed Paul laboured; and who are named in the beginning of his Epistle.

For he glories of you in all the churches who then only knew God; for we did not then know him. Wherefore, my brethren, I am exceedingly sorry both for him, and for his wife; to whom God grant a true repentance.

And be ye also moderate upon this occasion; and look not upon such as enemies, but call them back as suffering, and erring members, that ye may save your whole body: for by so doing, ye shall edify your own selves.

For I trust that ye are well exercised in the Holy Scriptures, and that nothing is hid from you; but at present it is not granted unto me to practice that which is written, Be angry and sin not; and again, Let not the sun go down upon your wrath.

Blessed be he that believeth and remembereth these things; which also I trust you do.

Now the God and Father of our Lord Jesus Christ; and he himself who is our everlasting high-priest, the Son of God, even Jesus Christ, build you up in faith and in truth and in all meekness and lenity; in patience and long-suffering, in forbearance and chastity.

And grant unto you a lot and portion among his saints; and us with you, and to all that are under the heavens, who shall believe in our Lord Jesus Christ, and in his Father who raised him from the dead.

Pray for all the saints: pray also for kings, and all that are in authority; and for those who persecute you, and hate you, and for the enemies of the cross; that your fruit may be manifest in all; and that ye may be perfect in Christ.

Ye wrote to me, both ye, and also Ignatius, that if any one went from hence into Syria, he should bring your letters with him; which also I will take care of, as soon as I shall have a convenient opportunity; either by myself, or him whom I shall send upon your account.

The Epistles of Ignatius which he wrote unto us, together with what others of his have come to our hands, we have sent to you, according to your order; which are subjoined to this epistle.

By which we may be greatly profited; for they treat of faith and patience, and of all things that pertain to edification in the Lord Jesus.

1 What you know certainly of Ignatius, and those that are with him signify to us.

If These things have I written unto you by Crescens, whom by this present epistle

I have recommended to you, and do now again commend.

For he has had his conversation without blame among us; and I suppose also with you.

Ye will also have regard unto his sister when she shall come unto you.

Be ye safe in the Lord Jesus Christ; and in favour with all yours. Amen.

THE SHEPHERD OF HERMAS.

[This book is thus entitled, because it was composed by Hermas, brother to Pius, bishop of Rome; and because the Angel, who bears the principal part in it, is represented in the form and habit of a shepherd. Irenaeus quotes it under the very name of Scripture. Origen thought it a most useful writing and that it was divinely inspired; Eusebius says, that, though it was not esteemed canonical, it was read publicly in the churches, which is corroborated by Jerome; and Athanasius cites it, calls it a most useful work, and observes, that though it was not strictly canonical, the Fathers appointed it to be read for direction and confirmation in faith and piety. Jerome, notwithstanding this, and that he applauded it in his catalogue of writers, in his comments upon it afterwards, terms it apocryphal and foolish. Tertullian praised it when a Catholic, and abused it when a Montanist. Although Gelasius ranks it among the apocryphal books, it is found attached to some of the most ancient MS. of the New Testament; and Archbishop Wake, believing it the genuine work of an apostolic Father, preserves it to the English reader by the following translation, in which he has rendered the books not only more exact, but in greater purity than they had before appeared. The Archbishop procured Dr. Grabe to entirely collate the old Latin version with an ancient MS. in the Lambeth library; and the learned prelate himself still further improved the whole from a multitude of fragments of the original Greek never before used for that purpose.]

THE FIRST BOOK OF HERMAS, WHICH IS CALLED HIS VISIONS.

VISION I.

Against filthy and proud thoughts, also the neglect of Hermas in chastising his children.

HE who had bred me up sold a certain young maid at Rome; whom when I saw many years after, I remembered her, and began to love her as a sister. It happened some time afterwards, that I saw her washing in the river Tyber; and I reached out my hand unto her, and brought her out of the river.

And when I saw her I thought with myself, saying, How happy should I be if I had such a wife, both for beauty and manners. This I thought with myself; nor did I think any more. But not long after, as I was walking and musing on these thoughts, I began to honour this creature of God, thinking with myself; how noble and beautiful she was.

And when I had walked a little, I fell asleep. And the spirit caught me away, and carried me through a certain place toward the right-hand, through which no man could pass. It was a place among rocks, very steep, and unpassable for water.

When I was past this place, I came into a plain; and there falling down upon my knees, I began to pray unto the Lord, and to confess my sins.

And as I was praying, the heaven was opened, and I saw the woman which I had coveted, saluting me from heaven, and saying, Hermas, hail! and I looking upon her, answered, Lady, what dost thou do here? She me, I am taken up hither to accuse thee of sin before the Lord.

Lady, said I, wilt thou convince me? No, said she: but hear the words which I am about to speak unto thee. God who dwelleth in heaven, and hath made all things out of nothing, and hath multiplied them for his holy church's sake, is angry with thee because thou hast sinned against me.

And I answering said unto her, Lady, if I have sinned against thee, tell me where, or in what place, or when did I ever speak an unseemly or dishonest word unto thee?

Have I not always esteemed thee as a lady? Have I not always reverenced thee as a sister? Why then dost thou imagine these wicked things against me?

Then she, smiling upon me, said: the desire of naughtiness has risen up in thy heart. Does it not seem to thee to be an ill thing for a righteous man to have an evil desire rise up in his heart?

It is indeed a sin, and that a very great one, to such a one; for a righteous man thinketh that which is righteous. And whilst he does so, and walketh uprightly, he shall have the Lord in heaven favorable unto him in all his business.

But as for those who think wickedly in their hearts, they take to themselves death and captivity; and especially those who love this present world, and glory in their riches, and regard not the good things that are to come; their souls wander up and down, and know not where to fix.

Now this is the case of such as are double-minded, who trust not in the Lord, and despise and neglect their own life.

But do thou pray unto the Lord, and he will heal thy sins, and the sins of thy whole house, and of all his saints.

As soon as she had spoken these words the heavens were shut, and I remained utterly swallowed up with sadness and fear; and said within myself, if this be laid against me for sin, how can I be saved?

Or how shall I ever be able to entreat the Lord for my many and great sins? With what words shall I beseech him to be merciful unto me?

As I was thinking over these things, and meditating in myself upon them, behold a chair was set over against me of the whitest wool, as bright as snow.

And there came an old woman in a bright garment, having a book in her hand, and sat alone, and saluted me, saying, Hermas, hail! and I being full of sorrow, and weeping, answered, Hail, Lady!

And she said unto me, Why art thou sad, Hermas, who wert wont to be patient, and modest, and always cheerful? I answered, and said to her, Lady, a reproach has been laid to my charge by an excellent woman, who tells me, that I have sinned against her.

She replied, Far be any such thing from the servant of God. But it may be the desire of her has risen up in thy heart. For indeed such a thought maketh the servants of God guilty of sin.

Nor ought such a detestable thought to be in the servant of God: nor should he who is approved by the Spirit desire that which is evil; but especially Hermas, who contains himself from all wicked lusts, and is full of all simplicity, and of great innocence.

Nevertheless the Lord is not so much angry with thee for thine own sake, as upon the account of thy house, which has committed wickedness against the Lord, and against their parents.

And for that out of thy fondness towards thy sons, thou hast not admonished thy house, but hast permitted them to live wickedly; for this cause the Lord is angry with thee: but he will heal all the evils that are done in thy house. For through their sins and iniquities, thou art wholly consumed in secular affairs.

But now the mercy of God hath taken compassion upon thee, and upon thine house, and hath greatly comforted thee. Only as for thee, do not wander, but be of an even mind, and comfort thy house.

As the workman bringing forth his work, offers it to whomsoever he pleaseth; so shalt thou by teaching every day what is just cut off a great sin. Wherefore cease not to admonish thy sons, for the Lord knows that they will repent with all their heart, and they shall be written in the book of life.

And when she had said this, she added unto me; Wilt thou hear me read?—I answered her, Lady, I will.

Hear then, said she; and opening the book she read, gloriously, greatly, and wonderfully, such things as I could not keep in my memory. For they were terrible words, such as no man could bear.

Howbeit I committed her last words to my remembrance; for they were but few, and of great use to us.

Behold the mighty Lord, who by his invisible power, and with his excellent wisdom made the world, and by his glorious counsel beautified his creature, and with the word of his strength fixed the heaven, and founded the earth upon the waters; and by this powerful virtue established his Holy Church, which he hath blessed.

Behold he will remove the heavens, and the mountains, the hills, and the seas; and all things shall be made plain for his elect; that he may render unto them the promise which he has promised, with much honour and joy; if so be that they shall keep the commandments of God, which they have received with great faith.

And when she had made an end of reading, she rose out of the chair; and behold four young men came, and carried the chair to the east.

And she called me unto her, and touched my breast, and said unto me, Did my reading please thee? I answered, Lady, these last things please me; but what went before was severe and hard.

She said unto me, these last things are for the righteous, but the foregoing for the revolters and heathen.

And as she was talking with me, two men appeared, and took her upon their shoulders and went to the east where the chair was.

And she went cheerfully away; and as she was going, said unto me, Hermas, be of good cheer.

VISION II.

Again, of his neglect in correcting his talkative wife; and of his lewd sons.

AS I was on the way to Cuma, about the same time that I went the year before, I began to call to mind the vision I formerly had. And again the spirit carried me away, and brought me into the same place, in which I had been the year before.

And when I was come into the place, I fell down upon my knees, and began to pray unto the Lord, and to glorify his name, that he had esteemed me worthy, and had manifested unto me my former sins.

And when I arose from prayer, behold I saw over against me the old woman whom I had seen the last year, walking and reading in a certain book.

And she said unto me, Canst thou tell these things to the elect of God? I answered and said unto her, Lady, I cannot retain so many things in my memory, but give me the book, and I will write them down.

Take it, says she, and see that thou restore it again to me.

As soon as I had received it, I went aside into a certain place of the field, and transcribed every letter, for I found no syllables.

And as soon as I had finished what was written in the book, the book was suddenly caught out of my hand, but by whom I saw not.

After fifteen days, when I had fasted, and entreated the Lord with all earnestness, the knowledge of the writing was revealed unto me. Now the writing was this:

Thy seed, O Hermas! hath sinned against the Lord, and have betrayed their parents, through their great wickedness. And they have been called the betrayers of their parents, and have gone on in their treachery.

And now have they added lewdness to their other sins, and the pollutions of their naughtiness: thus have they filled up the measure of their iniquities. But do thou upbraid thy sons with all these words; and thy wife, which shall be thy sister; and let her learn to refrain her tongue, with which she calumniates.

And when she shall hear these things, she will refrain herself, and shall obtain mercy.

And they also shall be instructed, when thou shalt have reproached them with these words, which the Lord has commanded to be revealed unto thee.

Then shall their sins be forgiven, which they have heretofore committed, and the sins of all the saints who have sinned even unto this day; if they shall repent with all their hearts, and remove all doubts out of their hearts.

For the Lord hath sworn by his glory concerning his elect, having determined this very time, that if any one shall even now sin, he shall not be saved.

For the repentance of the righteous has its end; the days of repentance are fulfilled to all the saints; but to the heathen, there is repentance even unto the last day.

Thou shalt therefore say to those who are over the church; that they order their ways in righteousness, that they may fully receive the promise with much glory.

Stand fast therefore ye that work righteousness and continue to do it, that your departure may be with the holy angels.

Happy are ye, as many as shall endure the great trial that is at hand, and whosoever shall not deny his life.

For the Lord hath sworn by his Son, that whoso denieth his Son and him, being afraid of his life, he will also deny him in the world that is to come.

But those who shall never deny him, he will of his exceeding great mercy be favourable unto them.

But thou, O Hermas! remember not the evils which thy sons have done, neither neglect thy sister, but take care that they amend of their former sins.

For they will be instructed by this doctrine, if thou shalt not be mindful of what they have done wickedly.

For the remembrance of evils worketh death, but the forgetting of them life eternal.

But thou, O Hermits! hast undergone a great many worldly troubles for the offences of thy house, because thou hast neglected them, as things that did not belong unto thee; and thou art wholly taken up with thy great business.

Nevertheless, for this cause shalt thou be saved, that thou hast not departed from the living God, and thy simplicity and singular continency shall preserve thee, if thou shalt continue in them.

Yea, they shall save all such as do such things, and walk in innocence and simplicity.

They who are of this kind shall prevail against all impiety, and continue until life eternal.

Happy are all they that do righteousness, they shall not be consumed for ever.

But thou wilt say, Behold there is a great trial coming. If it seem good to thee, deny him again.

The Lord is nigh to them that turn to him, as it is written in the book of Heldam and Modal, who prophesied to the people of Israel in the wilderness.

Moreover, brethren, it was revealed to me, as I was I sleeping, by a very goodly young man, saying unto me, What thinkest thou of that old woman from whom thou receivedst the book; who is she? I answered, a Sybil.

Thou art mistaken, said he, she is not. I replied, Who is she then, sir? He answered me, It is the church of God.

And I said unto him, Why then does she appear old? She is therefore, said he, an old woman, because she was the first of all the creation, and the world was made for her.

After this I saw a vision at home in my own house, and the old woman whom I had seen before, came to me and asked me, whether I had yet delivered her book to the elders of the church? And I answered, that I had not yet.

She replied, Thou hast well done, for I have certain words more to tell thee But when I shall have finished all the words, they shall be clearly understood by the elect.

And thou shalt write two books, and send one to Clement and one to Grapte. For Clement shall send it to the foreign cities, because it is permitted to him so to do: but Grapte shall admonish the widows and orphans.

But thou shalt read in this city with the elders of the church.

VISION III.

Of the building of the church triumphant, and of the several sorts of reprobates.

THE vision which I saw, brethren, was this.

When I had often fasted and prayed unto the Lord, that he would manifest unto me the revelation, which he had promised by the old woman to shew unto me; the same night she appeared unto me, and said unto me:

Because thou dost thus afflict thyself, and art so desirous to know all things, come into the field, where thou wilt, and about the sixth hour, I will appear unto thee, and shew thee what thou must see.

I asked her, saying: Lady, into what part of the field? She answered, wherever thou wilt, only choose a good and a private place. And before I began to speak and tell her the place, she said unto me: I will come where thou wilt.

I was therefore, brethren, in the field, and I observed the hours and came into the place where I had appointed her to come.

And I beheld a bench placed; it was a linen pillow, and over it spread a covering of fine linen.

When I saw these things ordered in this manner, and that there was nobody in the place, I began to be astonished, and my hair stood on end, and a kind of horror seized me; for I was alone.

But, being come to myself, and calling to mind the glory of Gad, and taking courage, I fell down upon my knees, and began again to confess my sins as before.

And whilst I was doing this, the old woman came thither with the six young men whom I had seen before, and stood behind me as I was praying, and heard me praying and confessing my sins unto the Lord.

And touching me, she said: Leave off to pray now only for thy sins; pray also for righteousness, that thou mayest receive part of her in thy house.

And she lifted me up from the place, and took me by the hand, and brought me to the seat; and said to the young men; go, and build.

As soon as they were departed, and we were alone, she said unto me: sit here. I answered her: Lady, let those who are elder sit first. She replied, Sit down as I bid you.

And when I would have sat on the right side, she suffered me not, but made a sign to me with her hand, that I should sit on the left.

As I was therefore musing, and full of sorrow, that she would not suffer me to sit on the right side, she said unto me, Hermes, why art thou sad?

The place which is on the right hand is theirs who have already attained unto God, and have suffered for his name-sake. But there is yet a great deal remaining unto thee, before thou Banat sit with them.

But continue as thou doest in thy sincerity, and thou shalt sit with them: as all others shall that do their works, and shall bear what they have borne.

I said to her: Lady, I would know what it is that they have suffered? Hear then, said she: wild beasts, scourgings, imprisonments, and crosses for his name-sake.

For this cause the right hand of holiness belongs to them, and to all others as many as shall suffer for the name of God; but the left belongs to the rest.

Howbeit the gifts and the promises belong to both, to them on the right, and to those on the left hand; only that sitting on the right hand they have some glory above the others.

But thou art desirous to sit on the right hand with them, and yet thy defects are many. But thou shalt be purged from thy defects, as also all who doubt not shall be cleansed from all the sins which they have committed unto this day.

And when she had said this she would have departed.

Wherefore, falling down before her feet, I began to entreat her, for the Lord's sake, hat she would shew me the vision which she had promised.

Then she again took me by the hand, and lifted me up, and made me sit upon the seat on the left side; and holding up a certain bright wand, said unto me, Seest thou that great thing? I replied, Lady, I see nothing.

She answered, Dost thou not see over against thee a great tower, which is built upon the water, with bright square stones?

For the tower was built upon a square by these six young men that came with her.

But many thousand of other men brought stones; some drew them out of the deep, others carried them from the ground, and gave them to the six young men. And they took them and built.

As for those stones which were drawn out of the deep, they put them all into the building; for they were polished, and their squares exactly answered one another, and so one was joined in such wise to the other, that there was no space to be seen where they joined, insomuch that the whole tower appeared to be built as it were of one stone.

But as for the other stones that were taken off from the ground, some of them they rejected, others they fitted into the building.

As for those which were rejected, some they cut out, and cast them at a distance from the tower; but many others of them lay round about the tower, which they made no use of in the building.

For some of these were rough, others had clefts in them, others were white and round, not proper for the building of the tower.

But I saw the other stones cast afar off from the tower, and falling into the highway, and yet not continuing in the way, but were rolled from the way into a desert place.

Others I saw falling into the fire and burning; others fell near the water, yet could not roll themselves into it, though very desirous to fall into the water.

And when she had shewed me these things she would have departed: but I said to her, Lady, what doth it profit me to see these things, and not underw stand what they mean?

She answered and said unto me: You are very cunning, in that you are desirous to know those things which relate to the tower. Yea, said I, Lady, that I may declare them unto the brethren, and they may rejoice, and hearing these things may glorify God with great glory.

Then she said, Many indeed shall hear them, and when they shall have heard them, some shall rejoice, and others weep. And yet even these, if they shall repent, shall rejoice too.

Hear therefore what I shall say concerning the parable of the tower, and after this be no longer importunate with me about the revelation.

For these revelations have an end, seeing they are fulfilled. But thou dost not leave off to desire revelations, for thou art very urgent.

As for the tower which thou seest built, it is myself, namely the church, which have appeared to thee both now and heretofore. Wherefore ask what thou wilt concerning the tower, and I will reveal it unto thee, that thou mayst rejoice with the saints.

I said unto her, Lady, because thou hast thought me once worthy to receive from thee the revelation of all these things, declare them unto me.

She answered me, Whatsoever is fit to be revealed unto thee shall be revealed: only let thy heart be with the Lord, and doubt not, whatsoever thou shalt see.

I asked her, Lady, why is the tower built upon the water? She replied, I said before to thee that thou wert very wise to inquire diligently concerning the building, therefore thou shalt find the truth.

Hear therefore why the tower is built upon the water: because your life is and shall be saved by water. For it is founded by the word of the almighty and honourable name, and is supported by the invisible power and virtue of God.

And I answering, said unto her, These things are very admirable; but, lady, who are those six young men that build?

They are, said she, the angels of God, which were first appointed, and to whom the Lord has delivered all his creatures, to frame and build them up, and to rule over them. For by these the building of the tower shall be finished.

And who are the rest who bring them stones?

They also are the holy angels of the Lord; but the other are more excellent than these. Wherefore when the whole building of the tower shall be finished, they shall all feast together beside the tower, and shall glorify God, because the structure of the tower is finished.

I asked her, saying, I would know the condition of the stones, and the meaning of them, what it is?

She answering, said unto me, Art thou better than all others that this should be revealed unto thee? For others are both before thee, and better than thou art, to whom these visions should be made manifest.

Nevertheless, that the name of God may he glorified, it has been, and shall be revealed unto thee, for the sake of those who are doubtful, and think in their hearts whether these things are so or not.

Tell them that all these things are true, and that there is nothing in them that is not true; but all are firm and truly established.

Hear now then concerning the stones that are in the building.

The square and white stones which agree exactly in their joints, are the apostles, and bishops, and doctors, and ministers, who through the mercy of God have come in, and governed, and taught and ministered holily and modestly to the elect of God, both they that have fallen asleep, and which yet remain; and have always agreed with them, and have had peace within themselves, and have heard each other.

For which cause their joints exactly meet together in the building of the tower.

They which are drawn out of the deep and put into the building, and whose joints agree with the other stones which are already built, are those which are already fallen asleep, and have suffered for the sake of the Lord's name.

And what are the other stones, lady, that are brought from the earth? I would know what are they.

She answered, They which lie upon the ground and are not polished, are those which God has approved, because they have walked in the law of the Lord, and directed their ways in his commandments.

They which are brought and put in the building of the tower, are the young in faith and the faithful. And these are admonished by the angels to do well because that iniquity is not found in them.

But who are those whom they rejected, and laid beside the tower?

They are such as have sinned and are willing to repent; for which cause they are not cast far from the tower, because they will be useful for the building, if they shall repent.

They therefore that are yet to repent, if they shall repent, shall become strong in the faith; that is, if they repent now, whilst the tower is building. For if the building shall be finished there will then be no place for them to be put in, but they shall be rejected; for he only has this privilege who shall now be out into the tower.

But would you know who they are that were cut out, and cast afar off from the tower? Lady, said I, I desire it.

They are the children of iniquity, who believed only in hypocrisy, but departed not from their evil ways; for this cause they shall not be saved, because they are not of any use in the building by reason of their sins.

Wherefore they are cut out, and cast afar off, because of the anger of the Lord, and because they have provoked him to anger against them.

As for the great number of other stones which thou hast seen placed about the tower, but not put into the buildings; those which are rugged, are they who have known the truth, but have not continued in it, nor been joined to the saints, and therefore are unprofitable.

Those that have clefts in them, are they that keep up discord in their hearts against each other, and live not in peace; that are friendly when present with their brethren, but as soon as they are departed from one another, their wickedness still continues in their hearts: these are the clefts which are seen in those stones.

Those that are maimed and short, are they who have believed indeed, but still are in great measure full of wickedness: for this cause they are maimed and not whole.

But what are the white and round stones, lady, and which are not proper for the building of the tower?

She answering said unto me: How long wilt thou continue foolish and without understanding, asking everything and discerning nothing?

They are such as have faith indeed, but have withal the riches of this present world. When therefore any troubles arise, for the sake of their riches and traffic, they deny the Lord.

I answering, said unto her, When therefore will they be profitable to the Lord? When their riches shall be cut away, says she, in which they take delight, then they will be profitable unto the Lord for his building.

For as a round stone, unless it be cut away, and cast somewhat off, its bulk cannot be made square, so they who are rich in this world, unless their riches be pared off, cannot be made profitable unto the Lord.

Learn this from thy own experience; when thou wert rich, thou wast unprofitable; but now thou art profitable, and fit for the life which thou hast undertaken; for thou also once wast one of those stones.

As for the rest of the stones which thou sawest cast afar off from the tower, and running in the way, and tumbled out of the way into desert places, they are such as have believed indeed, but through their doubting have forsaken the true way, thinking that they could find a better. But they wander and are miserable, going into desolate ways.

Then for those stones which fell into the fire and were burnt, they are those who have for ever departed from the living God; nor doth it ever come into their hearts to repent, by reason of the affection which they bear to their lusts and wickednesses which they commit.

And what are the rest which fell by the water, and could not roll into the water?

They are such as have heard the word, and were willing to be baptized in the name of the Lord; but considering the great holiness which the truth requires, have withdrawn themselves, and walked again after their wicked lusts.

Thus she finished the explication of the tower.

But I being still urgent, asked her, Is there repentance allowed to all those stones which are thus cast away. and were not suitable to the building of the tower; and shall they find place in this tower?

They may repent, said she, but they cannot come into this tower; but they shall be placed in a much lower rank, and this after that they shall have been afflicted, and fulfilled the days of their sins.

And for this cause they shall be removed, because they have received the word of righteousness: and then they shall be translated from their afflictions, if they shall have a true sense in their hearts of what they have done amiss.

But if they shall not have this sense in their hearts, they shall not be saved by reason of the hardness of their hearts.

When therefore I had done asking her concerning all these things, she said unto me, Wilt thou see somewhat else? And being desirous of seeing it, I became very cheerful of countenance.

She therefore looking back upon me, and smiling a little, said unto me, Seest thou seven women about the tower? Lady, said I, I see them.

This tower, replied she, is supported by them, according to the command of the Lord: hear therefore the effects of them.

The first of them, which holds fast with her hand, is called Faith, by her the elect shall be saved. The next, which is girt up, and looks manly, is named Abstinence: she is the daughter of Faith.

Whosoever therefore shall follow her shall be happy in all his life, because he shall abstain from all evil works, believing that if he shall contain himself from all concupiscence, he shall be the heir of eternal life. And what, lady, said I, are the other five?

They are, replied she, the daughters of one another. The first of them is called Simplicity; the next Innocence; the third Modesty; then Discipline; and the last of all is Charity. When therefore thou shalt have fulfilled the works of their mother, thou shalt be able to do all things.

Lady, said I, I would know what particular virtue every one of these has.

Hear then, replied she; they have equal virtues, and their virtues are knit together, and follow one another as they were born.

From Faith proceeds Abstinence; from Abstinence, Simplicity; from Simplicity, Innocence; from Innocence, Modesty; from Modesty, Discipline and Charity. Therefore the works of these are holy, and chaste, and right.

Whoever therefore shall serve these, and hold fast to their works, he shall have his dwelling in the tower with the saints of God.

Then I asked her concerning the times, whether the end were now at hand;

But she cried out with a loud voice, saying, O foolish man! Dost thou not see the tower yet a building? When therefore the tower shall be finished, and built, it shall have an end; and indeed it shall soon be accomplished.

But do not ask me any more questions. What has been said may suffice thee and all the saints for the refreshment of your spirits. For these things have not been revealed to thee only, but that thou mayest make them manifest unto all.

For therefore, O Hermes, after three days thou must understand these words which I begin to speak unto thee, that thou mayest speak them in the ears of the saints; that when they shall have heard and done them, they may be cleansed from their iniquities, and thou together with them.

Hear me therefore, O my sons I have bred you up in much simplicity, and innocency, and modesty for the love of God, which has dropped down upon you in righteousness, that you should be sanctified and justified from all sin and wickedness; but ye will not cease from your evil doings.

Now therefore hearken unto me, and have peace one with another, and visit one another, and receive one another, and do not enjoy the creatures of God alone.

Give freely to them that are in need. For some by too free feeding contract an infirmity in their flesh, and do injury to their bodies; whilst the flesh of others who have not food, withers away, because they want sufficient nourishment, and the bodies are consumed.

Wherefore this intemperance is hurtful to you, who have, and do not communicate to them that want. Prepare for the judgment that is about to come upon you.

Ye that are the more eminent, search out them that are hungry, whilst the tower is yet unfinished. For when the tower shall be finished, ye shall be willing to do good, and shall not find any place in it.

Beware, therefore, ye that glory in your riches, lest perhaps they groan who are in want, and their sighing come up unto God, and ye be shut out with your goods without the gate of the tower.

Behold I now warn you who are set over the church, and love the highest seats, be not ye like unto those that work mischief.

And they indeed carry about their poison in boxes, but ye contain your poison and infection in your hearts, and will not purge them, and mix your sense with a pure heart, that ye may find mercy with the Great King.

Take heed, my children, that your dissensions deprive you not of your lives. How will ye instruct the elect of God, when ye yourselves want correction? Wherefore admonish one another, and be at peace among yourselves, that I, standing before your father, may give an account for you unto the Lord.

And when she had made an end of talking with me, the six young men that built, came and carried her to the tower; and four others took up the seat on which she sate, and they also went away again to the tower. I saw not the faces of these, for their backs were towards me.

As she was going away, I asked her, that she would reveal to me what concerned the three forms, in which she had appeared unto me.

But she answering said unto me, concerning these things thou must ask some other, that they may be revealed unto thee.

Now, brethren, in the first vision the last year, she appeared unto me exceeding old, and sitting in a chair.

In another vision, she had indeed a youthful face, but her flesh and hair were old; but she talked with me standing, and was more cheerful than the first time.

In the third vision, she was in all respects much younger, and comely to the eye; only she had the hair of an aged person; yet she looked cheerful, and sate upon a seat.

I was therefore very sad concerning these things, until I might understand the vision.

Wherefore I saw the same old woman in a vision of the night saying unto me, All prayer needeth humiliation. Fast, therefore, and thou shalt learn from the Lord that which thou dost ask. I fasted therefore one day.

The same night a young man appeared to me and said, Why dost thou thus often desire Revelations in thy prayers? Take heed that by asking many things, thou hurt not the body. Let these Revelations suffice thee.

Canst thou see more notable Revelations than those which thou hast already received?

I answered and said unto him, Sir, I only ask this one thing upon the account of the three figures of the old woman that appeared to me, that the Revelation may be complete.

He answered me, You are not without understanding, but your doubts make you so; forasmuch as you have not your heart with the Lord.

I replied and said, But we shall learn these things more carefully from you.

Hear then, says he, concerning the figures about which you inquire.

And first, in the first vision she appeared to thee in the shape of an old woman sitting in a chair, because your old spirit was decayed, and without strength, by reason of your infirmities, and the doubtfulness of your heart.

For as they who are old have no hope of renewing themselves, nor expect any thing but their departure; so you being weakened through your worldly affairs gave yourself up to sloth, and cast not away your solicitude from yourself upon the Lord: and your sense was confused, and you grow old in your sadness.

But, sir, I would know why she sate upon a chair?

He answered, because every one that is weak sitteth upon a chair by reason of his infirmity, that his weakness may be upheld. Behold therefore the figure of the first vision.

In the second vision you saw her standing, and having a youthful face, and more cheerful than her former; but her flesh and her hair were ancient. Hear, said he, this parable also.

When any one grows old, he despairs of himself by reason of his infirmity and poverty, and expects nothing but the last day of his life.

But on a sudden an inheritance is left to him, and he hears of it, and rises; and being become cheerful, he puts on new strength. And he now no longer sits down, but stands, and is delivered from his former sorrow; and sits not, but acts manfully.

So you, having heard the Revelation which God revealed unto you because God had compassion upon you, and renewed your spirit, both laid aside your infirmities, and strength came to you, and you grew strong in the faith; and God, seeing your strength, rejoiced.

For this cause he shewed you the building of the tower, and will shew other things unto you, if you shall have peace with all your heart among each other.

But in the third vision you saw her yet younger, fair and cheerful, and of a serene countenance.

For as if some good news comes to him that is sad, he straightway forgets his sadness, and regards nothing else but the good news which he has heard; and for the rest he is comforted, and his spirit is renewed through the joy which he has received: even so you have been refreshed in your spirit by seeing these good things.

And for that you saw her sitting upon a bench, it denotes a strong position; because a bench has four feet and stands strongly. And even the world itself is upheld by the four elements.

They therefore that repent perfectly, shall be young; and they that turn from their sins with their whole heart, shall be established.

And now you have the Revelation fully, ask no more to have any thing farther revealed unto you.

But if any thing be to be revealed, it shall be made manifest unto you.

VISION IV.

Of the trial and tribulation that is about to come upon men.

I SAW a vision, brethren, twenty days after the former vision; a representation of the tribulation that is at hand. I was walking in the field way.

Now from the public way to the place whither I went is about ten furlongs; it is a way very little frequented:

And as I was walking alone I entreated the Lord that he would confirm the Revelations which he had shewed unto me by his holy Church:

And would grant repentance to all his servants who had been offended, that his great and honourable name might be glorified, and because he thought me worthy to whom he might shew his wonders, and, that I might honour him, and give thanks unto him.

And behold somewhat like a voice answered me; Doubt not, Hermas. Wherefore I began to think, and say within myself; why should I doubt, seeing I am thus settled by the Lord, and have seen such glorious things?

I had gone but a little farther, brethren, when behold I saw a dust rise up to heaven. I began to say within myself, is there a drove of cattle coming, that raises such a dust?

It was about a furlong off from me. And behold I saw the dust rise more and more, insomuch that I began to suspect that there was somewhat extraordinary in it.

And the sun shone a little: and behold I saw a great beast, as it were a whale; and fiery locusts came out of his mouth. The height of the beast was about a hundred feet, and he had a head like a large earthen vessel.

I began to weep, and to pray unto the Lord that he would deliver me from it. Then I called to mind the word which I had heard; Doubt not, Hermas.

Wherefore, brethren, putting on a divine faith, and remembering who it was that had taught me great things, I delivered myself bodily unto the beast.

Now the beast came on in such a manner, as if it could at once have devoured a city.

I came near unto it, and the beast extended its whole bulk upon the ground, and put forth nothing but its tongue, nor once moved itself till I had quite passed by it.

Now the beast had upon its head four colours; first black, then a red and bloody colour, then a golden, and then a white.

After that I had passed by it, and was gone forward about thirty feet, behold there met me a certain virgin, well adorned as if she had been just come out of her bride chamber, all in white, having on white shoes, and a veil down her face, and covered with shining hair.

Now I knew by my former visions that it was the church, and thereupon grew the more cheerful. She saluted me saying, Hail, O Man! I returned the salutation, saying, Lady, Hail!

She answering said unto me, Did nothing meet you, O man? I replied, Lady, there met me such a beast, as seemed able to devour a whole people; but by the power of God, and through his singular mercy, I escaped it.

Thou didst escape it well, said she, because thou didst cast thy whole care upon God, and opened thy heart unto him, believing that thou couldst be safe by no other than by his great and honourable name.

For this cause the Lord sent his angel, who is over the beast, whose name is Hegrin, and stopped his mouth, that he should not devour thee. Thou hast escaped a great trial through thy faith, and because thou didst not doubt for such a terrible beast.

Go therefore, and relate to the elect of God the great things that he hath done for thee. And thou shalt say unto them, that this beast is the figure of the trial that is about to came.

If therefore, ye shall have prepared yourselves, ye may escape it, if your heart be pure and without spot; and if ye shall serve God all the rest of your days without complaint.

Cast all your cares upon the Lord, and he will direct them. Believe in God, ye doubtful, because he can do all things; he can both turn away his wrath from you, and send you help and security.

Woe to the doubtful, to those who shall hear these words, and shall despise them: it had been better for them that they had not been born.

Then I asked her concerning the four colours which the beast had upon its head. But she answered me saying; Again thou art curious in that thou asketh concerning these things. But I said to her, Lady, shew me what they are.

Hear, said she; The black which thou sawest denotes the world in which you dwell. The fiery and bloody colour signifies that this age must be destroyed by fire and blood.

The golden part are ye, who have escaped out of it. For as gold is tried by the fire, and is made profitable, so are ye also in like manner tried who dwell among the men of this world.

They therefore, that shall endure to the end, and be proved by them shall be purged. And as gold, by this trial, is cleansed and loses its dross, so shall ye also cast away all sorrow and trouble, and be made pure for the building of the tower.

But the white colour denotes the time of the world which is to come, in which the elect of God shall dwell: because the elect of God shall be pure and without spot until life eternal.

Wherefore do not thou cease to speak these things in the ears of the saints. Here ye have the figure of the great tribulation that is about to come; which, if you please shall be nothing to you. Keep therefore in mind the things that I have said unto you.

When she had spoken thus much, she departed; but I saw not whither she went. But suddenly I heard a noise, and I turned back, being afraid, for I thought that the beast was coming toward me.

THE SECOND BOOK OF HERMAS, CALLED HIS COMMANDS.

Introduction.

WHEN I had prayed at home, and was sat down upon the bed, a certain man came in to me with a reverend look, in the habit of a shepherd, clothed with a white cloak, having his bag upon his back, and his staff in his hand, and saluted me.

I returned his salutation, and immediately he sat down by me, and said unto me, I am sent by that venerable messenger, that I should dwell with thee all the remaining days of thy life.

But I thought that he was come to try me, and said unto him, Who are you? For I know to whom I am committed. He said unto me, Do you not know me? I answered no. I am, said he, that shepherd to whose care you are delivered.

Whilst he was yet speaking, his shape was changed; and when I knew that it was he to whom I was committed, I was ashamed, and a sudden fear came upon me, and I was utterly overcome with sadness, because I had spoken so foolishly unto him.

But he said unto me, Be not ashamed, but receive strength in thy mind, through the commands which I am about to deliver unto thee. For, said he, I am sent to shew unto thee all those things again, which thou hast seen before, but especially such of them as may be of most use unto thee.

And first of all write my Commands and Similitudes, the rest thou shalt so write as I shall shew unto thee. But I therefore bid thee first of all write my Commands and Similitudes, that by often reading of them thou mayest the more easily keep them in memory.

Whereupon I wrote his Commands and Similitudes, as he bade me.

Which things if when you have heard, ye shall observe to do them, and shall walk according to them, and exercise yourselves in them with a pure mind, ye shall receive from the Lord those things which he has promised unto you.

But if having heard them ye shall not repent, but shall still go on to add to your sins, ye shall be punished by him.

All these things that Shepherd, the angel of repentance, commanded me to write.

COMMAND I.

Of believing in one God.

FIRST of all believe that there is one God who created and framed all things of nothing into a being.

He comprehends all things, and is only immense, not to be comprehended by any.

Who can neither be defined by any words, nor conceived by the mind.

Therefore believe in him; and fear him; and fearing him abstain from all evil.

Keep these things, and cast all lust and iniquity far from thee, and put on righteousness, and thou shalt live to God, if thou shalt keep this commandment.

COMMAND II.

That we must avoid detraction, and do our alms-deeds with simplicity.

HE said unto me, Be innocent and without disguise; so shalt thou be like an infant who knows no malice which destroys the life of man.

Especially see that thou speak evil of none, nor willingly hear any one speak evil of any.

For if thou observest not this, thou also who hearest shalt be partaker of the sin of him that speaketh evil, by believing the slander, and thou also shalt have sin, because thou believed-est him that spoke evil of thy brother.

THE LOST BOOKS OF THE BIBLE

Detraction is a pernicious thing; an inconstant, evil spirit; that never continues in peace, but is always in discord. Wherefore refrain thyself from it, and keep peace ever more with thy brother.

Put on an holy constancy, in which there are no sins, but all is full of joy; and do good of thy labours.

Give without distinction to all that are in want, not doubting to whom thou givest.

But give to all, for God will have us give to all, of all his own gifts. They therefore that receive shall give an account to God, both wherefore they received and for what end.

And they that receive without a real need, shall give an account for it; but he that gives shall be innocent.

For he has fulfilled his duty as he received it from God; not making any choice to whom he should give, and to whom not. And this service he did with simplicity and to the glory of God.

Keep therefore this command according as I have delivered it unto thee; that thy repentance may be found to be sincere, and that good may come to thy house; and have a pure heart.

COMMAND III.

Of avoiding lying, and the repentance of Hermas for his dissimulation.

MOREOVER he said unto me, love truth; and let all the speech be true which proceeds out of thy mouth.

That the spirit which the Lord hath given to dwell in thy flesh may be found true towards all men; and the Lord be glorified, who hath given such a spirit unto thee: because God is true in all his words, and in him there is no lie.

They therefore that lie, deny the Lord, and become robbers of the Lord, not rendering to God what they received from him.

For they received the spirit free from lying: If therefore they make that a liar, they defile what was committed to them by the Lord, and become deceivers.

When I heard this, I wept bitterly; and when he saw me weeping, he said unto me, Why weepest thou? And I said, Because, sir, I doubt whether I can be saved?

He asked me, Wherefore? I replied, because sir, I never spake a true word in my life; but always lived in dissimulation, and affirmed a lie for truth to all men; and no man contradicted me, but all gave credit to my words. How then can I live, seeing I have done in this, manner?

And he said unto me, Thou thinkest well and truly. For thou oughtest, as the servant of God, to have walked in the truth, and not have joined an evil conscience with the spirit of truth, nor have grieved the holy and true Spirit of God.

And I replied unto him, sir, I never before hearkened so diligently to these things. He answered, Now thou hearest them: Take care from henceforth, that even those things which thou hast formerly spoken falsely for the sake of thy business, may, by thy present truth receive credit.

For even those things may be credited, if for the time to come thou shalt speak the truth; and by so doing thou mayest attain unto life.

And whosoever shall hearken unto this command, and do it, and shall depart from all lying, he shall live unto God.

COMMAND IV.

Of putting away one's wife for adultery.

FURTHERMORE, said he, I command thee, that thou keep thyself chaste; and that thou suffer not any thought of any other marriage, or of fornication, to enter into thy heart: for such a thought produces great sin.

But be thou at all times mindful of the Lord, and thou shalt never sin. For if such an evil thought should arise in thy heart, thou shouldest be guilty of a great sin; and they who do such things follow the way of death.

Look therefore to thyself, and keep thyself from such a thought; for where chastity remains in the heart of a righteous man, there an evil thought ought never to arise.

And I said unto him, Sir, suffer me to speak a little to you. He bade me say on. And I answered, Sir, if a man that is faithful in the Lord shall have a wife, and shall catch her in adultery; doth a man sin that continues to live still with her?

And he said unto me, As long as he is ignorant of her sin, he commits no fault in living with her; but if a man shall know his wife to have offended, and she shall not repent of her sin, but go on still in her fornication, and a man shall continue nevertheless to live with her, he shall become guilty of her sin, and partake with her in her adultery.

And I said unto him, What therefore is to be done, if the woman continues on in her sin? He answered, Let her husband put her away, and let him continue by himself. But if he shall put away his wife, and marry another he also doth commit adultery.

And I said, What if the woman that is so put away, shall repent, and be willing to return to her husband, shall she not be received by him? He said unto me, Yes; and if her husband shall not receive her, he will sin, and commit a great offence against himself; but he ought to receive the offender, if she repents; only not often.

For to the servants of God there is but one repentance. And for this cause a man that putteth away his wife ought not to take another, because she may repent.

This act is alike both in the man and in the woman. Now they commit adultery, not only who pollute their flesh, but who also make an image. If therefore a woman perseveres in any thing of this kind, and repents not, depart from her, and live not with her, otherwise thou also shalt be partaker of her sin.

But it is therefore commanded that both the man and the woman should remain unmarried because such persons may repent.

Nor do I in this administer any occasion for the doing of these things; but rather that whoso has offended, should not offend any more.

But for their former sins, God who has the power of healing will give a remedy; for he has the power of all things.

I asked him again and said, Seeing the Lord hath thought me worthy that thou shouldest dwell with me continually, speak a few words unto me, because I understand nothing, and my heart is hardened through my former conversation; and open my understanding because I am very dull, and apprehend nothing at all.

And he answering said unto me, I am the minister of repentance, and give understanding to all that repent. Does it not seem to thee to be a very wise thing to repent? Because he that does so gets great understanding.

For he is sensible that he hath sinned and done wickedly in the sight of the Lord, and he remembers within himself that he has offended, and repents and does no more wickedly, but does that which is good, and humbles his soul and afflicts it, because he has offended. You see therefore that repentance is great wisdom.

And I said unto him, For this cause, sir, I inquire diligently into all things, because I am a sinner, that I may know what I must do that I may live; because my sins are many.

And he said unto me, Thou shalt live if thou shalt keep these my commandments. And whosoever shall hear and do these commands shall live unto God.

And I said unto him, I have even now heard from certain teachers, that there is no other repentance beside that of baptism; when we go down into the water, and receive the forgiveness of our sins; and that after that, we must sin no more, but live in purity.

And he said unto me, Thou has been rightly informed. Nevertheless seeing now thou inquirest diligently into all things, I will manifest this also unto thee: yet not so as to give any occasion of sinning either to those who shall hereafter believe, or to those who have already believed in the Lord.

For neither they who have newly believed, or who shall hereafter believe, have any repentance of sins, but forgiveness of them.

But as to those who have been called to the faith, and since that are fallen into any gross sin, the Lord hath appointed repentance, because God knoweth the thoughts of all men's hearts, and their infirmities, and the manifold wickedness of the devil, who is always contriving something against the servants of God, and maliciously lays snares for them.

Therefore our merciful Lord had compassion towards his creature, and appointed that repentance, and gave unto me the power of it. And therefore I say unto thee, if any one after that great and holy calling shall be tempted by the devil and sin, he has one repentance. But if he shall often sin and repent it shall not profit such a one; for he shall hardly live unto God.

And I said, Sir, I am restored again to life since I have thus diligently hearkened to these commands. For I perceive that if I shall not hereafter add any more to my sins, I shall be saved.

And he said, Thou shalt be saved: and so shall all others, as many as shall observe these commandments.

And again I said unto him, Sir, seeing thou hearest me patiently shew me yet one thing more. Tell me, saith he, what it is.

And I said, If a husband or a wife die, and the party which survives marry again, does he sin in so doing? He that marries says he, sins not: howbeit, if he shall remain single, he shall thereby gain to himself great honour before the Lord.

Keep therefore thy chastity and modesty, and thou shalt live unto God. Observe from henceforth those things which I speak with thee, and command thee to observe, from the time that I have been delivered unto thee, and dwell in thy house.

So shall thy former sins be forgiven, if thou shalt keep these my commandments. And in like manner shall alt others be forgiven, who shall observe these my commandments.

COMMAND V.

Of the sadness of the heart, and of patience.

BE patient, says he, and longsuffering; so shalt thou have dominion over all wicked works, and shalt fulfil all righteousness.

For if thou shalt be patient, the Holy Spirit which dwelleth in thee shall be pure, and not be darkened by any evil spirit; but being full of joy shall be enlarged, and feast in the body in which it dwells, and serve the Lord with joy, and in great peace.

But if any anger shall overtake thee, presently the Holy Spirit which is in thee will be straightened and seek to depart from thee.

For he is choked by the evil spirit, and has not the liberty of serving the Lord as he would for he is grieved by anger. When, therefore, both these spirits dwell together, it is destructive to a man.

As if one should take a little wormwood, and put it into a vessel of honey, the whole honey would be spoiled; and a great quantity of honey is corrupted by a very little wormwood, and loses the sweetness of honey, and is no longer acceptable to its Lord because the whole honey is made bitter, and loses its use.

But if no wormwood be put into the honey, it is sweet and profitable to its Lord. Thus is forbearance sweeter than honey, and profitable to the Lord who dwelleth in it.

But anger is unprofitable. If therefore anger shall be mixed with forbearance, the soul is distressed, and its prayer is not profitable with God.

And I said unto him, Sir, I would know the sinfulness of anger, that I may keep myself from it. And he said unto me, Thou shalt know it; and if thou shalt not keep thyself from it, thou shalt lose thy hope with all thy house. Wherefore depart from it.

For I the messenger of righteousness am with thee; and all that depart from it, as many as shall repent with all their hearts, shall live unto God; and I will be with them, and will keep them all.

For all such as have repented have been justified by the most holy messenger, who is a minister of salvation.

And now, says he, hear the wickedness of anger; how evil and hurtful it is, and how it overthrows the servants of God; for it cannot hurt those that are full of faith because the power of God is with them; but it overthrows the doubtful, and those that are destitute of faith.

For as often as it sees such men, it casts itself into their hearts; and so a man or woman is in bitterness for nothing, for the things of life, or for sustenance, or for a vain word, if any should chance to fall in; or by reason of any friend, or for a debt, or for any other superfluous things of the like nature.

For these things are foolish, and superfluous, and vain to the servants of God. But equanimity is strong, and forcible; and of great power, and sitteth in great enlargement; is cheerful, rejoicing in peace; and glorifying God at all times with meekness.

And this long-suffering dwells with those that are full of faith. But anger is foolish, and light, and empty. Now bitterness is bred through folly; by bitterness, anger; by anger, fury. And this fury arising from so many evil principles, worketh a great and incurable sin.

For when all these things are in the same man in which the Holy Spirit dwells, the vessel cannot contain them, but runs over: and because the Spirit being tender cannot tarry with the evil one; it departs and dwells with him that is meek.

When, therefore, it is departed from the man in whom it dwelt; that man becomes destitute of the Holy Spirit, and is afterwards filled with wicked spirits, and is blinded with evil thoughts. Thus doth it happen to all angry men.

Wherefore depart thou from anger and put on equanimity, and resist wrath; so thou shalt be found with modesty and chastity by God. Take good heed therefore that thou neglect not this commandment.

For if thou shalt obey this command, then shalt thou also be able to observe the other commandments, which I shall command thee.

Wherefore strengthen thyself now in these commands, that thou mayest live unto God. And whosoever shall observe these commandments shall live unto God.

COMMAND VI.

That every man has two angels, and of the suggestions of both.

I COMMANDED thee, said he, in my first commandments, that thou shouldst keep faith and fear, and repentance. Yes, Sir, said I.

He continued: But now I will shew thee the virtues of these commands, that thou mayest know their effects; how they are prescribed alike to the just and unjust.

Do thou therefore believe the righteous, but give no credit to the unrighteous. For righteousness keepeth the right way, but unrighteousness the wicked way.

Do thou therefore keep the right way, and leave that which is evil. For the evil way has not a good end, but hath many stumbling-blocks; it is rugged and full of thorns, and leads to destruction; and it is hurtful to all such as walk in it.

But they who go in the right way, walk with evenness, and without offence; because it is not rough nor thorny.

Thou seest therefore how it is best to walk in this way. Thou shalt therefore go, says he, and all others, as many as believe in God with all their heart, shall o through it.

And now, says he; understand first of all what belongs to faith. There are two angels with man; one of righteousness, the other of iniquity.

And I said unto him: Sir, how shall I know that there are two such angels with man? Hear says he, and understand.

The angel of righteousness, is mild and modest, and gentle, and quiet. When therefore, he gets into thy heart, immediately he talks with thee of righteousness, of modesty, of chastity, of bountifulness, of forgiveness, of charity, and piety.

When all these things come into thy heart, know then that the angel of righteousness is with thee. Wherefore hearken to this angel and to his works.

Learn also the works of the angel of iniquity. He is first of all bitter, and angry, and foolish; and his works are pernicious, and overthrow the servants of God. When therefore these things come into thy heart; thou shalt know by his works, that this is the angel of .

And I said unto him, Sir, how shall I understand these things? Hear says he, and understand. When anger overtakes thee, or bitterness, know that he is in thee:

As also, when the desire of many things, and of the best meats and of drunkenness; when the love of what belongs to others, pride, and much speaking and ambition, and the like things, come upon thee.

When therefore these things arise in thy heart, know that the angel of iniquity is with thee. Seeing therefore thou knowest his works, depart from them all, and give no credit to him: because his works are evil, and become not the servants of God.

Here therefore thou hast the works of both these angels. Understand now and believe the angel of righteousness, because his instruction is good.

For let a man be never so happy; yet if the thoughts of the other angel arise in his heart, that man or woman must needs sin.

But let man or woman be never so wicked, if the works of the angel of righteousness come into his heart, that man or woman must needs do some good.

Thou seest therefore how it is good to follow the angel of righteousness. If therefore thou shall follow him, and submit to his works, thou shalt live unto God. And as many as shall submit to his work, shall live also unto God.

COMMAND VII.

That we must fear God, but not the Devil.

FEAR God, says he, and keep his commandments. For if thou keepest his commandments thou shalt be powerful in every work, and all thy works shall be excellent. For by fearing God, thou shalt do every thing well.

This is that fear with which thou must be affected that thou mayest be saved. But fear not the devil: for if thou fearest the Lord, thou shalt have dominion over him; because there is no power in him.

Now if there be no power in him, then neither is he to be feared. But he in whom there is excellent power, he is to be feared: for every one that has power, is to be feared. But he that has no power is despised by every one.

Fear the works of the devil, because they are evil. For by fearing the Lord, thou wilt fear and not do the works of the devil, but keep thyself from them.

There is therefore a twofold fear; if thou wilt not do evil, fear the Lord and thou shalt not do it. But if thou wilt do good, the fear of the Lord is strong, and great and glorious.

Wherefore, fear God and thou shalt live: and whosoever shall fear him, and keep his commandments, their life is with the Lord. But they who keep them not, neither is life in them.

COMMAND VIII.

That we must flee from evil, and do good.

I HAVE told thee, said he, that there are two kinds of creatures of the Lord, and that there is a two-fold abstinence. From some things therefore thou must abstain, and from others not.

I answered, Declare to me, sir, from what I must abstain, and from what not. Hearken, said he. Keep thyself from evil, and do it not; but abstain not from good, but do it. For if thou shalt abstain from what is good, and not do it, thou shalt sin. Abstain therefore from all evil, and thou shalt know all righteousness.

I said, What evil things are they from which I must abstain? Hearken, said he: from adultery, from drunkenness, from riots, from excess of eating, from daintiness and dishonesty, from pride, from fraud, from lying, from detraction, from hypocrisy, from remembrance of injuries, and from all evil speaking.

For these are the works of iniquity, from which the servant of God must abstain. For he that cannot keep himself from these things, cannot live unto God.

But hear, said he, what follows of these kind of things: for indeed many more there are from which the servant of God must abstain. From theft, and cheating; from false witness, from covetousness, from boasting, and all other things of the like nature.

Do these things seem to thee to be evil or not? Indeed they are very evil to the servants of God. Wherefore the servant of God must abstain from all these works.

Keep thyself therefore from them, that thou mayest live unto God, and be written among those that abstain from them. And thus have I shown thee what things thou must avoid: now learn from what thou must not abstain.

Abstain not from any good works, but do them. Hear, said he, what the virtue of those good works is which thou must do, that thou mayest be saved. The first of all is faith; the fear of the Lord; charity; concord; equity; truth; patience; chastity.

There is nothing better than these things in the life of man; who shall keep and do these things in their life. Hear next what follow these.

To minister to the widows; not to despise the fatherless and poor; to redeem the servants of God from necessity; to be hospitable; (for in hospitality there is sometimes great fruit) not to be contentious, but be quiet.

To be humble above all men; to reverence the aged; to labour to be righteous; to respect the brotherhood; to bear affronts; to be long-suffering; not to cast away those that have fallen from the faith, but to convert them, and make them be of good cheer; to admonish sinners; not to oppress those that are our debtors; and all other things of a like kind.

Do these things seem to thee to be good or not? And I said, What can be better than these words? Live then, said he, in these commandments, and do not depart from them. For if thou shalt keep all these commandments, thou shalt live unto God. And all they that shall keep these commandments shall live unto God.

COMMAND IX.

That we must ask of God daily; and without doubting.

AGAIN he said unto me; remove from thee all doubting; and question nothing at all, when thou askest anything of the Lord; saying within thyself: how shall I be able to ask anything of the Lord and receive it, seeing I have so greatly sinned against him?

Do not think thus, but turn unto the Lord with all thy heart, and ask of him without doubting, and thou shalt know the mercy of the Lord; how that he will not forsake thee, but will fulfil the request of thy soul.

For God is not as men, mindful of the injuries he has received; but he forgets injuries, and has compassion upon his creature.

Wherefore purify thy heart from all the vices of this present world; and observe the commands I have before delivered unto thee from God; and thou shalt receive whatsoever good things thou shalt ask, and nothing shall be wanting unto thee of all thy petitions; if thou shalt ask of the Lord without doubting.

But they that are not such, shall obtain none of those things which they ask. For they that are full of faith ask all things with confidence, and receive from the Lord, because they ask without doubting. But he that doubts, shall hardly live unto God, except he repent.

Wherefore purify thy heart from doubting, and put on faith, and trust in God, and thou shalt receive all that thou shalt ask. But and if thou shouldest chance to ask somewhat and not (immediately) receive it, yet do not therefore doubt, because thou hast not presently received the petition of thy soul.

For it may be thou shalt not presently receive it for thy trial, or else for some sin which thou knowest not. But do not thou leave off to ask, and then thou shalt receive. Else if thou shalt cease to ask, thou must complain of thyself, and not of God, that he has not given unto thee what thou didst desire.

Consider therefore this doubting, how cruel and pernicious it is; and how it utterly roots out many from the faith, who were very faithful and firm. For this doubting is the daughter of the devil, and deals very wickedly with the servants of God.

Despise it therefore, and thou shalt rule over it on every occasion. Put on a firm and powerful faith: for faith promises all things and perfects all things. But doubting will not believe, that it shall obtain anything, by all that it can do.

Thou seest therefore, says he, how faith cometh from above, from God; and hath great power. But doubting is an earthly spirit, and proceedeth from the devil, and has no strength.

Do thou therefore keep the virtue of faith, and depart from doubting, in which is no virtue, and thou shalt live unto God. And all shall live unto God, as many as do these things.

COMMAND X.

Of the sadness of the heart; and that we must take heed not to grieve the spirit of God that is in us.

PUT all sadness far from thee; for it is the sister of doubting and of anger. How, sir, said I, is it the sister of these? for sadness, and anger, and doubting, seem to me to be very different from one another.

And he answered: Art thou without sense that thou dost not understand it? For sadness is the most mischievous of all spirits, and the worst to the servants of God: It destroys the spirits of all men, and torments the Holy Spirit; and again, it saves.

THE LOST BOOKS OF THE BIBLE

Sir, said I, I am very foolish, and understand not these things. I cannot apprehend how it can torment, and yet save. Hear, said he, and understand. They who never sought out the truth, nor inquired concerning the majesty of God, but only believed, are involved in the affairs of the heathen.

And there is another lying prophet that destroys the minds of the servants of God; that is of those that are doubtful, not of those that fully trust in the Lord. Now those doubtful persons come to him, as to a divine spirit, and inquire of him what shall befall them.

And this lying prophet having no power in him of the divine Spirit, answers them according to their demands, and fills their souls with promises according as they desire. Howbeit that prophet is vain, and answers vain things to those who are themselves vain.

And whatsoever is asked of him by vain men, he answers them vainly. Nevertheless he speaketh some things truly. For the devil fills him with his spirit, that he may overthrow some of the righteous.

Whosoever therefore are strong in the faith of the Lord, and have put on the truth: they are not joined to such spirits, but depart from them. But they that are doubtful, and often repenting like the heathens, consult them, and heap up to themselves great sin, serving idols.

As many therefore as are such, inquire of them upon every occasion; worship idols; and are foolish, and void of the truth.

For every spirit that is given from God needs not to be asked; but having the power of divinity speaks all things of itself; because he comes from above, from the power of God.

But he that being asked speaks according to men's desires, and concerning many other affairs of the present world, understands not the things which relate unto God. For these spirits are darkened through such affairs, and corrupted and broken.

As good vines if they are neglected, are oppressed with weeds and thorns, and at last killed by them; so are the men who believe such spirits.

They fall into many actions and businesses, and are void of sense, and when they think of things pertaining unto God, they understand nothing at all: but if at any time they chance to hear anything concerning the Lord, their thoughts are upon their business.

But they that have the fear of the Lord, and search out the truth concerning God, having all their thoughts towards the Lord; apprehend whatsoever is said to them, and forthwith understand it, because they have the fear of the Lord in them.

For where the spirit of the Lord dwells, there is also much understanding added. Wherefore join thyself to the Lord, and thou shalt understand all things.

Learn now, O unwise man! how sadness troubleth the Holy Spirit, and how it saves. When a man that is doubtful is engaged in any affair, and does not accomplish it by reason of his doubting, this sadness enters into him, and grieves the Holy Spirit, and makes him sad.

Again, anger when it overtakes any man for any business he is greatly moved; and then again sadness entereth into the heart of him, who was moved with anger, and he is troubled for what he hath done, and repenteth, because he hath done amiss.

This sadness therefore seemeth to bring salvation, because he repenteth of his evil deed. But both the other things, namely, doubting and sadness, such as before was mentioned, vex the spirit: doubting, because his work did not succeed: and sadness, because he angered the Holy Spirit.

Remove therefore sadness from thyself, and afflict not the Holy Spirit which dwelleth in thee, lest he entreat God, and depart from thee. For the spirit of the Lord which is given to dwell in the flesh, endureth no such sadness.

Wherefore clothe thyself with cheerfulness, which has always favour with the Lord, and thou shalt rejoice in it. For every cheerful man does well; and relishes those things that are good, and despises sadness.

But the sad man does always wickedly. First, he doth wickedly, because he grieveth the Holy Spirit, which is given to man, being of a cheerful nature. And again he does ill, because he prays with sadness unto the Lord, and maketh not a first thankful acknowledgment unto him of former mercies, and obtains not of God what he asks.

For the prayer of a sad man has not always efficacy to come up to the altar of God. And I said unto him, Sir, why has not the prayer of a sad man virtue to come up to the altar of God? because, said he, that sadness remaineth in his heart.

When therefore a man's prayer shall be accompanied with sadness, it will not suffer his requests to ascend pure to the altar of God. For as wine when it is mingled with vinegar, has not the sweetness it had before; so sadness being mixed with the Holy Spirit, suffers not a man's prayer to be the same as it would be otherwise.

Wherefore cleanse thyself from sadness, which is evil, and thou shalt live unto God. And all others shall live unto God, as many as shall lay aside and put on cheerfulness.

COMMAND XI.

That the spirits and prophets are to be tried by their works; and of a twofold spirit.

HE shewed me certain men sitting upon benches, and one sitting in a chair: and he said unto me seest thou who sit upon the benches? Sir, said I, I see them. He answered, They are the faithful; and he who sits in the chair is an earthly spirit.

For he cometh not into the assembly of the faithful, but avoids it. But he joins himself to the doubtful and empty; and prophesies to them in corners and hidden places; and pleases them by speaking according to all the desires of their hearts.

For he placing himself among empty vessels, is not broken, but the one fitteth the other. But when he cometh into the company of just men, who are full of the spirit of God, and they pray unto the Lord; that man is emptied because that earthly spirit flies from him, and he is dumb, and cannot speak anything.

As if in a store-house you shall stop up wine or oil; and among those vessels shall place an empty jar; and shall afterwards come to open it, you shall find it empty as you stopped it up: so those empty prophets when they come among the spirits of the just, are found to be such as they came.

I said, How then shall a man be able to discern them? Consider what I am going to say considering both kinds of men; and as I speak unto thee so shalt thou prove the prophet of God, and the false prophet.

And first try the man who hath the spirit of God; because the spirit which is from above is humble, and quiet; and departs from all wickedness; and from the vain desires of the present world; and makes himself more humble than all men; and answers to none when he is asked; nor to every one singly: for the Spirit of God doth not speak to a man when he will, but when God pleases.

When therefore a man who hath the Spirit of God shall come into the church of the righteous, who have the faith of God, and they pray unto the Lord; then the holy angel of God fills that man with the blessed Spirit, and he speaks in the congregation as he is moved of God.

Thus therefore is the spirit of God known, because whosoever speaketh by the Spirit of God, speaketh as the Lord will.

Hear now concerning the earthly spirit, which is empty and foolish, and without virtue. And first of all the man who is supposed to have the Spirit, (whereas he hath it not in reality), exalteth himself, and desires to have the first seat, and is wicked, and full of words.

And spends his time in pleasure, and in all manner of voluptuousness; and receives the reward of his divination; which if he receives not, he does not divine.

Should the Spirit of God receive reward and divine? It doth not become a prophet of God so to do.

Thus you see the life of each of these kind of prophets. Wherefore prove that man by his life and works, who says that he hath the Holy Spirit. And believe the Spirit which comes from God, and has power as such. But believe not the earthly and empty spirit, which is from the devil, in whom there is no faith nor virtue.

Hear now the similitude which I am about to speak unto thee. Take a stone, and throw it up towards heaven; or take a spout of water, and mount it up thitherward; and see if thou canst reach unto heaven.

Sir, said I, how can this be done? For neither of those things which you have mentioned, are possible to be done. And he answered, Therefore as these things cannot be done, so is the earthly spirit without virtue, and without effect.

Understand yet farther the power which cometh from above, in this similitude. The grains of hail that drop down are exceedingly small; and yet when they fall upon the head of a man, how do they cause pain to it?

THE LOST BOOKS OF THE BIBLE

And again; consider the droppings of a house: how the little drops falling upon the earth, work a hollow in the stones.

So in like manner the least things which come from above, and fall upon the earth, have great force. Wherefore join thyself to this spirit, which has the power; and depart from the other which is empty.

COMMAND XII.

Of a two fold desire: that the commands of God are not impossible: and that the devil is not to be feared by them that believe.

AGAIN he said unto me; remove from thee all evil desires, and put on good and holy desires. For having put on a good desire, thou shalt hate that which is evil, and bridle it as thou wilt. But an evil desire is dreadful and hard to be tamed.

It is very horrible and wild: and by its wildness consumes men. And especially if a servant of God shall chance to fall into it, except he be very wise, he is ruined by it. For it destroys those who have not the garment of a good desire: and are engaged in the affairs of this present world; and delivers them unto death.

Sir, said I, what are the works of an evil desire, which bring men unto death? Shew them to me, that I may depart from them. Hear said he, by what works an evil desire bringeth the servants of God unto death.

First of all, it is an evil desire to covet another man's wife; or for a woman to covet another's husband; as also to desire the dainties of riches: and multitude of superfluous meats; and drunkenness; and many delights.

For in much delicacy there is folly; and many pleasures are needless to the servants of God. Such lusting therefore is evil and pernicious, which brings to death the servants of God. For all such lusting is from the devil.

Whosoever therefore shall depart from all evil desires, shall live unto God; but they that are subject unto them shall die for ever. For this evil lusting is deadly. Do thou therefore put on the desire of righteousness, and being armed with the fear of the Lord, resist all wicked lusting.

For this fear dwelleth in good desires; and when evil coveting shall see thee armed with the fear of the Lord, and resisting it, it will fly far from thee, and not appearing before thee, but be afraid of thy armour.

And thou shalt have the victory, and be crowned for it; and shalt attain to that desire which is good; and shalt give the victory which thou hast obtained unto God, and shalt serve him in doing what thou thyself wouldest do.

For if thou shalt serve good desires, and be subject to them; thou shalt be able to get the dominion over thy wicked lustings; and they shall be subject to thee as thou wilt.

And I said, Sir, I would know how to serve that desire which is good? Hearken, saith he, Fear God and put thy trust in him, and love truth, and righteousness, and do that which is good.

If thou shalt do these things, thou shalt be an approved servant of God; and shalt serve him: and all others who shall in like manner serve a good desire shall live unto God.

And when he had fulfilled these twelve commands, he said unto me, Thou hast now these commands, walk in them; and exhort those that hear them that repent, and that they keep their repentance pure all the remaining days of their life.

And fulfil diligently this ministry which I commit to thee, and thou shalt receive great advantage by it; and shalt find favour with all such as shall repent, and shall believe thy words. For I am with thee, and will force them to believe.

And I said unto him, Sir, those commands are great and excellent, and able to cheer the heart of that man that shall be able to keep them. But, Sir, I cannot tell, whether they can be observed by any man?

He answered, Thou shalt easily keep these commands, and they shall not be hard: howbeit, if thou shalt suffer it once to enter into thy heart that they cannot be kept by any one, thou shalt not fulfil them.

But now I say unto thee if thou shalt not observe these commands, but shall neglect them, thou shalt not be saved, nor thy children, nor thy house; because thou hast judged that these cannot be kept by man.

These things he spake very angrily unto me, insomuch that he greatly affrighted me. For he changed his countenance, so that a matt could not bear his anger.

And when he saw me altogether troubled and confounded, he began to speak more moderately and cheerfully, saying, O foolish, and without understanding!

Unconstant, not knowing the majesty of God how great and wonderful he is; who created the world for man, and hath made every creature subject unto him: and given him all power, that he should be able to fulfil all these commands.

He is able, said he, to fulfil all these commands, who ha the Lord in his heart: but they who have the Lord only in their mouths, and their heart is hardened, and they are far from the Lord; to such persons these commands are hard and difficult.

Put therefore, ye that are empty and light in the faith, the Lord your God in your hearts and ye shall perceive how that nothing is more easy than these commands, nor more pleasant, nor more gentle and holy.

And turn yourselves to the Lord your God, and forsake the devil and his pleasures, because they are evil, and bitter, and impure. And fear not the devil, because he has no power over you.

For I am with you, the messenger of repentance, who have the dominion over him. The devil doth indeed affright men; but his terror is vain. Wherefore fear him not, and he will flee from you.

And I said unto him; Sir, hear me speak a few words unto you. He answered, Say on: A man indeed desires to keep the commandments of God: and there is no one but what prays unto God, that he may be able to keep his commandments.

But the devil is hard, and by his power rules over the servants of God. And he said He cannot rule over the servants of God, who trust in him with all their hearts.

The devil may strive, but he cannot overcome them.

For if ye resist him, he will floe away with confusion from you. But they that are not full in the faith, fear the devil, as if he had some great power. For the devil tries the i servants of God and if he finds them empty, he destroys them.

For as man, when he fills up vessels with good wine, and among them puts a few vessels half full, and comes to try and taste of the vessels, doth not try those that are full, because ho knows that they are good; but tastes those that are half full, lest they should grow sour; (for vessels half full soon grow sour, and lose the taste of wine:) so the devil comes to the servants of God to try them.

They that are full of faith resist him stoutly, and he departs from them, because he finds no place where to enter into them: then he goes to those that are not full of faith, and because he has place of entrance, he goes into them, and does what he will with them, and they become his servants.

But I, the messenger of repentance, say unto you, fear not the devil, for I am sent unto you, that I may he with you, as many as shall repent with your whole heart, and that I may confirm you in the faith.

Believe therefore, ye who by reason of your transgressions have forgot God, and your own salvation; and adding to your sins have made your life very heavy.

That if ye shall turn to the Lord with your whole hearts, and shall serve him according to his will; he will heal you of your former sins, and ye shall have dominion over all the works of the devil.

Be not then afraid in the least of his threatenings, for they are without force, as the nerves of a dead man. But hearken unto me, and fear the Lord Almighty, who is able to save and to destroy you; and keep his commands, that ye may live unto God.

And I said unto him; Sir, I am now confirmed in all the commands of the Lord whilst that you are with me, and I know that you will break all the power of the devil.

And we also shall overcome him, if we shall be able, through the help of the Lord, to keep these commands which you have delivered.

Thou shalt keep them, said he, if thou shalt purify thy heart towards the Lord. And all they also shall keep them who shall cleanse their hearts from the vain desires of the present world, and shall live unto God.

THE THIRD BOOK OF HERMAS, WHICH IS CALLED HIS SIMILITUDES.

SIMILITUDE I.

That seeing we have no abiding city in this world, we ought to look after that which is to come.

AND he said unto me; Ye know that ye who are the servants of the Lord, live here as in a pilgrimage; for your city is far off from this city.

If, therefore, ye know your city in which ye are to dwell, why do ye here buy estates, and provide yourselves with delicacies, and stately buildings, and superfluous houses? For he that provides himself these things in this city, does not think of returning into his own city.

O foolish, and doubtful, and wretched man; who understandest not that all these things belong to other men, and are under the power of another. For the Lord of this city saith unto thee; Either obey my laws, or depart out of my city.

What therefore shalt thou do who art subject to a law in thine own city? Canst thou for thy estate, or for any of those things which thou hast provided, deny thy law? But if thou shalt deny it, and wilt afterwards return into thy own city, thou shalt not be received, but shall be excluded thence.

See therefore, that like a man in another country, thou procure no more to thyself than what is necessary, and sufficient for thee? and be ready, that when the God or Lord of this city shall drive thee out of it, thou mayst oppose his law, and go into thine own city; where thou mayst with all cheerfulness live according to thine own law with no wrong.

Take heed therefore ye that serve God, and have him in your hearts: work ye the works of God, being mindful both of his commands and of his promises, which he has promised; and be assured that he will make them good unto you; if ye shall keep his commandments.

Instead therefore of the possessions that ye would otherwise purchase, redeem those that are in want from their necessities, as every one is able; justify the widows; judge the cause of the fatherless; and spend your riches and your wealth in such works as these.

For, for this end has God enriched you, that ye might fulfil these kind of services. It is much better to do this, than to buy lands or houses; because all such things shall perish with this present time.

But what ye shall do for the name of the Lord, ye shall find in your city, and shall have joy without sadness or fear. Wherefore covet not the riches of the heathen; for they are destructive to the servants of God.

But trade with your own riches which you possess, by which ye may attain unto everlasting joy.

And do not commit adultery, nor touch any other man's wife, nor desire her; but covet that which is thy own business, and thou shalt be saved.

SIMILITUDE II.

As the vine is supported by the elm, so is the rich man helped by the prayers of the poor.

AS I was walking into the field, and considered the elm and the vine, and thought with myself of their fruits, an angel appeared unto me, and said unto me; What is it that thou thinkest upon thus long within thyself?

And I said unto him, Sir, I think of this vine and this elm because their fruits are fair. And he said unto me; These two trees are set for a pattern to the servants of God.

And I said unto him, Sir, I would know in what the pattern of these trees which thou mentionest, does consist. Hearken, saith he; seest thou this vine and this elm; Sir, said I, I see them,

This vine, saith he, is fruitful, but the elm is a tree without fruit. Nevertheless this vine unless it were set by this elm, and supported by it, would not bear much fruit; but lying along upon the ground, would bear but ill fruit, because it did not hang upon the elm; whereas, being supported upon the elm, it bears fruit both for itself and for that.

See, therefore, how the elm gives no less, but rather more fruit, than the vine. How, Sir, said I, does it bear more fruit than the vine? Because, said he, the vine being supported upon the elm gives both much and good fruit; whereas, if it lay along upon the ground, it would bear but little, and that very ill too.

This similitude, therefore, is set forth to the servants of God; and it represents the rich and poor man. I answered, Sir, make this manifest unto me. Hear, said he; the rich man has wealth; howbeit towards the Lord he is poor; for he is taken up about his riches, and prays but little to the Lord; and the prayers which he makes are lazy and without force.

When, therefore, the rich man reaches out to the poor those things which he wants, the poor man prays unto the Lord for the rich; and God grants unto the rich man all good things, because the poor man is rich in prayer; and his requests have great power with the Lord.

Then the rich man ministers all things to the poor, because he perceives that he is heard by the Lord: and he the more willingly and without doubting, affords him what he wants, and takes care that nothing be lacking to him.

And the poor man gives thanks unto the Lord for the rich; because they do both their work from the Lord.

With men therefore, the elm is not thought to give any fruit; and they know not neither understand that its company being added to the vine, the vine bears a double increase, both for itself and for the elm.

Even so the poor praying unto the Lord for the rich, are heard by him; and their riches are increased, because they minister to the poor of their wealth. They are therefore both made partakers of each other's good works.

Whosoever, therefore, shall do these things, he shall not be forsaken by the Lord, but shall be written in the book of life.

Happy are they who are rich, and perceive themselves to be increased: for he that is sensible of this, will be able to minister somewhat to others.

SIMILITUDE III.

As the green trees in the winter cannot be distinguished from the dry; so neither can the righteous from the wicked in this present world.

AGAIN he showed me many trees whose leaves were shed, and which seemed to me to be withered, for they were all alike. And he said unto me, Seest thou these trees? I said, Sir, I see that they look like dry trees.

He answering, said unto me; These trees are like unto the men who live in the present world. I replied: Sir, why are they like unto dried trees? Because, said he, neither the righteous, nor unrighteous, are known from one another; but all are alike in this present world.

For this world is as the winter to the righteous men, because they are not known, but dwell among sinners.

As in the winter all the trees having lost their leaves, are like dry trees; nor can it be discerned which are dry and which are green: so in this present world neither the righteous nor wicked are discerned from each other; but they are all alike.

SIMILITUDE IV.

As in the summer the living trees are distinguished from the dry by their fruit and green leaves; so in the world to come the righteous shall be distinguished from the unrighteous by their happiness.

AGAIN he showed me many other trees, of which some had leaves, and others appeared dry and withered. And he said unto me, Seest thou these trees? I answered, Sir, I see them; .and some are dry, and others full of leaves.

These trees, saith he, which are green, are the righteous which shall possess the world to come. For the world to come, is the summer to the righteous; but to sinners it is the winter.

When, therefore, the mercy of the Lord shall shine forth, then they who serve God shall be made manifest, and plain unto all. For as in the summer the fruit of every tree is shown and made manifest, so also the works of the righteous shall be declared and made manifest, and they shall be restored in that world merry and joyful.

For the other kind of men, namely the wicked, like the trees which thou sawest dry, shall as such be found dry and without fruit in that other world; and like dry wood shall be burnt; and it shall be made manifest that they have done evil all the time of their life;

And they shall be burnt because they have sinned and have not repented of their sins. And also all the other nations shall be burnt, because they have not acknowledged

THE LOST BOOKS OF THE BIBLE

God their Creator.

Do thou therefore bring forth good fruit, that in the summer thy fruit may be known; and keep thyself from much business, and thou shalt not offend. For they who are involved in much business, sin much; because they are taken up with their affairs, and serve not God.

And how can a man that does not serve God, ask anything of God, and receive it? But they who serve him, ask and receive what they desire.

But, if a man has only one thing to follow, he may serve God, because his mind is not taken off from God but he serves him with a pure mind.

If, therefore, thou shalt do this, thou mayest have fruit in the world to come; and all, as many as shall do in like manner, shall bring forth fruit.

SIMILITUDE V.

Of a true fast, and the rewards of it, also of the cleanliness of the body.

AS I was fasting, and sitting down in a certain mountain, and giving thanks unto God for all the things that he had done unto me; behold I saw the shepherd, who was wont to converse with me, sitting by me, and saying unto me: What has brought thee hither thus early in the morning? I answered, Sir, today I keep a station.

He answered, What is a station? I replied, it is a fast. He said, What is that fast? I answered, I fast, as I have been wont to do. Ye know not, said he, what it is to fast unto God; nor is this a fast which ye fast, profiting nothing with God.

Sir, said I, what makes you speak thus? He replied, I speak it, because this is not the true fast which you think that you fast; but I will show you what that is which is a complete fast, and acceptable unto God.

Hearken, said he, The Lord does not desire such a needless fast: for by fasting in this manner, thou advancest nothing in righteousness.

But the true fast is this: Do nothing wickedly in thy life, but serve God with a pure mind; and keep his commandments and walk according to his precepts, nor suffer any wicked desire to enter into the mind.

But trust in the Lord, that if thou dost these things, and fearest him, and abstaineth from every evil work, thou shalt live unto God.

If thou shalt do this, thou shalt perfect a great fast, and an acceptable one unto the Lord.

Hearken unto the similitude which I am about to propose unto thee, as to this matter.

A certain man having a farm, and many servants, planted a vineyard in a certain part of his estate for his posterity:

And taking a journey into a far country, chose one of his servants which he thought

THE LOST BOOKS OF THE BIBLE

the most faithful and approved, and delivered the vineyard into his care; commanding him that he should take up the vines. Which if he did, and fulfilled his command, he promised to give him his liberty. Nor did he command him to do anything more; and so went into a far country.

And after that servant had taken that charge upon him, he did whatsoever his lord commanded him. And when he had staked the vineyard, and found it to be full of weeds, he began to think with himself, saying;

I have done what my lord commanded me, I will now dig this vineyard, and when it is digged, it will be more beautiful; and the weeds being pulled up, it will bring forth more fruit and not be choked by the weeds.

So setting about this work he digged it, and plucked up all the weeds that were in it; and so the vineyard became very beautiful and prosperous, not being choked with weeds.

After some time the lord of the vineyard comes and goes into the vineyard, and when he saw that it was handsomely staked and digged, and the weeds plucked up that were in it, and the vines flourishing, he rejoiced greatly at the care of his servant.

And calling his son whom he loved, and who was to be his heir, and his friends with whom he was wont to consult; he tells them what he had commanded his servant to do, and what his servant had done more; and they immediately congratulated that servant, that he had received so full a testimony from his lord.

Then he said to them, I indeed promised this servant his liberty, if he observed the command which I gave him; and he observed it, and besides has done a good work to my vineyard, which has exceedingly pleased me.

Wherefore, for this work which he hath done, I will make him my heir together with my son, because that when he saw what was good, he neglected it not, but did it.

This design of the lord both his son and his friends approved, namely, that his servant should be heir together with his son.

Not long after this, the master of the family calling together his friends, sent from his supper several kinds of food to that servant.

Which when he had received, he took so much of them as was sufficient for himself, and divided the rest among his fellow servants.

Which when they had received, they rejoiced; and wished that he might find yet greater favour with his lord, for what he had done to them.

When his lord heard all these things, he was again filled with great joy; and calling again his friends and his son together, he related to them what his servant had done with the meats which he had sent unto them.

They therefore so much the more assented to the master of the household; and he ought to make that servant his heir together with his son.

I said unto him, Sir, I know not these similitudes, neither can I understand them, unless you expound them unto me. I will, says he, expound all things unto thee whatsoever I have talked with thee, or shewn unto thee.

Keep the commandments of the Lord and thou shalt be approved, and shalt be written in the number of those that keep his commandments. But if besides those things which the Lord hath commanded, thou shalt add some good thing; thou shalt purchase to thyself a greater dignity, and be in more favour with the Lord than thou shouldst otherwise have been.

If therefore thou shalt keep the commandments of the Lord, and shalt add to them these stations, thou shalt rejoice; but especially if thou shalt keep them according to my commands.

I said unto him, Sir, whatsoever thou shalt command me, I will observe; for I know that thou wilt be with me. I will, said he, be with thee who hast taken up such a resolution; and I will be with all those who purpose in like manner.

This fast, saith he, whilst thou dost also observe the commandments of the Lord, is exceeding good. Thus shalt there. fore thou keep it.

First of all, take heed to thyself, and keep thyself from every wicked act, and from every filthy word, and from every hurtful desire; and purify thy mind from all the vanity of this present world. If thou shalt observe these things, this fast shall be right.

Thus therefore do. Having performed what is before written, that day on which thou fastest thou shalt taste nothing at all but bread and water; and computing the quantity of food which thou art wont to eat upon other days, thou shalt lay aside the expense which thou shouldest have made that day, and give it unto the widow, the fatherless, and the poor.

And thus thou shalt perfect the humiliation of thy soul; that he who receives of it may satisfy his soul, and his prayer come up to the Lord God for thee.

If therefore thou shalt thus accomplish thy fast, as I command thee, thy sacrifice shall be acceptable unto the Lord, and thy fast shall be written in his book.

This station, thus performed, is good and pleasing, and acceptable unto the Lord. These things if thou shalt observe with thy children and with all thy house, thou shalt be happy.

And whosoever when they hear these things, shall do them, they also shall be happy; and whatsoever they shall ask of the Lord they shall receive it.

And I prayed him that he would expound unto me the similitude of the farm, and the Lord, and of the vineyard, and of the servant that had staked the vineyard; and of the weeds that were plucked out of the vineyard; and of his son and his friends which he took into council with him. For I understand that that was a similitude.

He said unto me, Thou art very bold in asking: for thou oughtest not to ask any thing; because if it be fitting to shew it unto thee, it shall be shewed unto thee.

THE LOST BOOKS OF THE BIBLE

I answered him; Sir, whatsoever thou shalt shew me, without explaining it unto me, I shall in vain see it, if I do not understand what it is. And if thou shalt propose any similitudes, and not expound them, I shall in vain hear them.

He answered me again, saying: Whosoever is the servant of God, and has the Lord in his heart, he desires understanding of him, and receives it; and he explains every similitude, and understands the words of the Lord which need an inquiry.

But they that are lazy and slow to pray, doubt to seek from the Lord; although the Lord be of such an extraordinary goodness, that without ceasing he giveth all things to them that ask of him.

Thou therefore who art strengthened by that venerable messenger, and hast received such a powerful gift of prayer; seeing thou art not slothful, why dost thou not now ask understanding of the Lord, and receive it?

I said unto him; seeing I have thee present, it is necessary that I should seek it of thee, and ask thee; for thou showest all things unto me, and speakest to me when thou art present.

But if I should see or hear these things when thou wert not present, I would then ask the Lord that he would shew them unto me.

And he replied, I said a little before that thou wert subtle and bold, in that thou asketh the meaning of these similitudes.

But because thou still persistest, I will unfold to thee this parable which thou desirest, that thou mayest make it known unto all men.

Hear therefore, said he, and understand. The farm before mentioned denotes the whole earth. The Lord of the farm is he who created and finished all things, and gave virtue unto them.

His son is the Holy Spirit: the servant is the Son of God: the vineyard is the people whom he saves. The stakes are the messengers which are set over them by the Lord, to support his people. The weeds that are plucked up out of the vineyard, are the sins which the servants of God had committed.

The food which he sent him from his supper, are the commands which he gave to his people by his Son. The friends whom he called to counsel with him, are the holy angels whom he first created. The absence of the master of the household, is the time that remains unto his coming.

I said unto him, Sir, all these things are very excellent, and wonderful, and good. But, continued I, could I or any other man besides though never so wise, have understood these things?

Wherefore now, sir, tell me, what I ask. He replied, ask me what thou wilt. Why, said I, is the Son of God in this parable, put in the place of a servant?

Hearken, he said; the Son of God is not put in the condition of a servant, but in great power and authority. I said unto him 'how, sir? I understand it not.'

Because, said he, the Son set his over those whom the Father delivered unto him, to keep every one of them; but he himself labored very much, and suffered much, that he might blot out their offences.

For no vineyard can be digged without much labour and pains. Wherefore having blotted out the sins of his people, he shewed to them the paths of life, giving them the law which he had received of the Father.

You see, said he, that he is the Lord of his people, having received all power from his Father. But why the Lord did take his Son into counsel, about dividing the inheritance, and the good angels, hear now.

That Holy Spirit, which was created first of all, he placed in the body in which God should dwell; namely, in a chosen body, as it seemed good to him. This body therefore into which the Holy Spirit was brought, served that Spirit, walked rightly and purely in modesty; nor ever defiled that Spirit.

Seeing therefore the body at all times obeyed the Holy Spirit, and laboured rightly and chastely with him, nor faltered at any time; that body being wearied conversed indeed servilely, but being mightily approved to God with the Holy Spirit, was accepted by him.

For such a stout course pleased God, because he was not defiled in the earth, keeping the Holy Spirit. He called therefore to counsel his Son, and the good angels, that there might be some place of standing given to this body which had served the Holy Spirit without blame; lest it should seem to have lost the reward of its service.

For every pure body shall receive its reward; that is found without spot, in which the Holy Spirit has been appointed to dwell. And thus you have now the exposition of this parable also.

Sir, said I, I now understand your meaning, since I have heard this exposition. Hearken further, said he: keep this thy body clean and pure, that the Spirit which shall dwell in it may bear witness unto it, and be judged to have been with thee.

Also take heed that it be not instilled into thy mind that this body perishes, and thou abuse it to any lust. For if thou shalt defile thy body, thou shalt also at the same time defile the Holy Spirit; and if thou shalt defile the Holy Spirit, thou shalt not live.

And I said, What if through ignorance this should have been already committed, before a man heard these words; How can he attain unto salvation, who has thus defiled his body?

He replied, As for men's former actions which through ignorance they have committed, God only can afford a remedy unto them; for all the power belongeth unto him.

But now guard thyself; and seeing God is almighty and merciful, he will grant a remedy to what thou hast formerly done amiss, if for the time to come thou shalt not defile thy body and spirit;

For they are companions together, and the one cannot be defiled but the other will be so too. Keep therefore both of them pure, and thou shalt live unto God.

SIMILITUDE VI.

Of two sorts of voluptuous men, and of their death, defection, and of the continuance of their pains.

AS I was sitting at home, and praising God for all the things which I had seen; and was thinking concerning the commands, that they were exceeding good, and great, and honest, and pleasant; and such as were able to bring a man to salvation; I said thus within myself; I shall be happy if I shall walk according to these commands, and whosoever shall walk in them shall live unto God.

Whilst I was speaking on this wise within myself, I saw him whom I had before been wont to see, sitting by me; and he spake thus unto me:

What doubtest thou concerning my commands which I have delivered unto thee? They are good, doubt not, but trust in the Lord, and thou shalt walk in them. For I will give thee strength to fulfil them.

These commands are profitable to those who shall repent of those sins which they have formerly committed; if for the time to come they shall not continue in them.

Whosoever therefore ye be that repent, cast away from you the naughtiness of the present world; and put on all virtue, and righteousness, and so shall ye be able to keep these commands; and not sin from henceforth any more.

For if ye shall keep yourselves from sin from the time to come, ye shall cut off a great deal of your former sins. Walk in my commands, and ye shall live unto God: These things have I spoken unto you.

And when he had said this, he added; let us go into the field, and I will show thee shepherds of sheep. I replied, sir, let us go.

And we came into a certain field, and there he showed me a young shepherd, finely arrayed, with his garments of a purple colour. And he fed large flocks; and his sheep were full of pleasure, and in much delight and cheerfulness; and they skipping, ran here and there.

And the shepherd took very great satisfaction in his flock; and the countenance of that shepherd was cheerful, running up and down among his flock.

Then the angel said unto me, Seest thou this shepherd? I answered, sir, I see him. He said unto me, this is the messenger of delight and pleasure. He therefore corrupts the minds of the servants of God, and turns them from the truth, delighting them with many pleasures, and they perish.

For they forget the commands of the living God, and live in luxury and in vain pleasures, and are corrupted by the evil angel, some of them even unto death; and others to a falling away.

I replied; I understand not what you mean, by saying unto death, and to a falling away. Hear, says he; all these sheep which thou sawest exceeding joyful, are such as have for ever departed from God, and given themselves up to the lusts of this present time.

To these therefore there is no return, by repentance unto life; because that to their other sins they have added this, that they have blasphemed the name of the Lord. These kind of men are ordained unto death.

But those sheep which thou sawest not leaping, but feeding in one place, are such as have in deed given themselves up to pleasures and delights; but have not spoken anything wickedly against the Lord.

These therefore are only fallen off from the truth, and so have yet hope laid up for them in repentance. For such a falling off hath some hope still left of a renewal; but they that are dead, are utterly gone forever.

Again we went a little farther forward; and he showed me a great shepherd, who had as it were a rustic figure, clad with a white goat's skin, having his bag upon his shoulder, and in his hand a stick full of knots, and very hard, and a whip in his other hand; and his countenance was stern and sour; enough to affright a man; such was his look.

He took from that young shepherd such sheep as lived in pleasures, but did not skip up and down; and drove them into a certain steep craggy place full of thorns and briars, insomuch that they could not get themselves free from them.

But being entangled in them, fed upon thorns and briars, and were grievously tormented with his whipping. For he still drove them on, and afforded them not any place or time to stand still.

When therefore I saw them so cruelly whipped and afflicted, I was grieved for them; because they were greatly tormented, nor had they any rest afforded them.

And I said unto the shepherd that was with me; Sir, who is this cruel and implacable shepherd, who is moved with no compassion towards these sheep? He answered, This shepherd is indeed one of the holy angels, but is appointed for the punishment of sinners.

To him therefore are delivered those who have erred from God, and served the lusts and pleasures of this world. For this cause he punishes them every one according to their deserts, with cruel and various kinds of pains.

Sir, said I, I would know, what kind of pains they are which every one undergoes? Hearken, said he; The several pains and torments are those which men every day undergo in their present lives. For some suffer losses; others poverty; others divers sicknesses. Some are unsettled; others suffer injuries from those that are unworthy; others fall under many other trials and inconveniences.

For many with an unsettled design aim at many things, and it profiteth them not; and they say that they have not success in their undertakings.

They do not call to their mind what they have done amiss, and they complain of the Lord. When therefore they shall have undergone all kind of vexation and inconvenience; then they are delivered over to me for good instruction, and are confirmed in the faith of the Lord, and serve the Lord all the rest of their days with a pure mind.

And when they begin to repent of their sins, then they call to mind their works which they have done amiss, and give honour to God, saying, That he is a just Judge, and they have deservedly suffered all things according to their deeds.

Then for what remains of their lives, they serve God with a pure mind; and have success in all their undertakings, and receive from the Lord whatever they desire.

And then they give thanks unto the Lord that they were delivered unto me; nor do they suffer any more cruelty.

I said unto him; Sir, I entreat you still to show me now one thing. What, said he, dost thou ask? I said unto him; Are they who depart from the fear of God, tormented for the same time that they enjoyed their false delight and pleasures? He answered me: They are tormented for the same time.

And I said unto him; They are then tormented but little; whereas they who enjoy their pleasures so as to forget God, ought to endure seven times as much punishment.

He answered me; Thou art foolish, neither understandest thou the efficacy of this punishment. I said unto him; Sir, if I understood it, I would not desire you to tell me.

Hearken, said he, and learn what the force of both is, both of the pleasure and of the punishment. An hour of pleasure is terminated within its own space; but one hour of punishment has the efficacy of thirty days. Whosoever therefore enjoys his false pleasure for one day, and is one day tormented; that one day of punishment is equivalent to a whole year's space.

Thus look how many days any one pursues his pleasures, so many years is he punished for it. You see therefore how that the time of worldly enjoyments is but short; but that of pain and torments a great deal more.

I replied; Sir, forasmuch as I do not understand at all these times of pleasure and pain;

entreat you that you would explain yourself more clearly concerning them. He answered me, saying; Thy foolishness still sticks unto thee.

Shouldst thou not rather purify thy mind, and serve God? Take heed, lest when thy time is fulfilled, thou be found still unwise. Hear then, as thou desirest, that thou mayest the more easily understand.

He that gives himself up one day to his pleasures and delights, and does whatsoever his soul desires, is full of great folly, nor understands what he does, but the day following forgets what he did the day before.

For delight and worldly pleasure are not kept in memory, by reason of the folly that is rooted in them. But when pain and torment befal a man a day, he is in effect troubled the whole year after; because his punishment continues firm in his memory.

Wherefore he remembers it with sorrow the whole year; and then calls to mind his vain pleasure and delight, and perceives that for the sake of that he was punished.

Whosoever therefore have delivered themselves over to such pleasures, are thus punished; because that when they had life, they rendered themselves liable to death.

I said unto him; Sir, what pleasures are hurtful? He answered; That is pleasure to every man which he doth willingly.

For the angry man, gratifying his passion, perceives pleasure in it; and so the adulterer and drunkard; the slanderer and liar; the covetous man and the defrauder; and whosoever commits anything like unto these, because he followeth his evil disposition, he receives a satisfaction in the doing of it.

All these pleasures and delights are hurtful to the servants of God. For these therefore they are tormented and suffer punishment.

There are also pleasures that bring salvation unto men. For many, when they do what is good, find pleasure in it, and are attracted by the delights of it.

Now this pleasure is profitable to the servants of God, and brings life to such men; but those hurtful pleasures, which were before mentioned, bring torments and punishment.

And whosoever shall continue in them, and shall not repent of what they have done, shall bring death upon themselves.

SIMILITUDE VII.

That they who repent, must bring forth fruits worthy of repentance.

AFTER a few days I saw the same person that before talked with me, in the same field, in which I had seen those shepherds. And he said unto me; What seekest thou?

Sir, said I, I came to entreat you that you would command the shepherd, who is the minister of punishment, to depart out of my house, because he greatly afflicts me.

And he answered, It is necessary for thee to endure inconveniences and vexations; for so that good angel hath commanded concerning thee, because he would try thee.

Sir, said I; What so great offence have I committed, that I should be delivered to this messenger? Hearken, said he: Thou art indeed guilty of many sins, yet not so many that thou shouldest be delivered to this messenger.

But thy house hath committed many sins and offences, and therefore that good messenger being grieved at their doings commanded that for some time thou shouldst suffer affliction; that they may both repent of what they have done, and may wash themselves from all the lusts of this present world.

When therefore they shall have repented, and be purified, then that messenger which is appointed over thy punishment, shall depart from thee.

I said unto him; Sir, if they have behaved themselves so as to anger that good angel, yet what have I done? He answered: They cannot otherwise be afflicted, unless thou, who art the head of the family, suffer.

For whatsoever thou shalt suffer, they must needs feel it; but as long as thou shalt stand well established, they cannot experience any vexation.

I replied; But, sir, behold they also now repent with all their hearts. I know, says he, that they repent with all their hearts; but dost thou therefore think that their offences who repent are immediately blotted out?

No, they are not presently; but he that repents must afflict his soul and shew himself humble in all his affairs, and undergo many and divers vexations.

And when he shall have suffered all things that were appointed for him; then perhaps he that made him, and formed all things besides, will be moved with compassion towards him, and afford him some remedy; and especially if he shall perceive his heart, who repents, to be pure from every evil work.

But at present it is expedient for thee, and for thy house, to be grieved; and it is needful that thou shouldest endure much vexation, as the angel of the Lord who committed thee unto me, has commanded.

Rather give thanks unto the Lord, that knowing what was to come, he thought thee worthy to whom he should foretell that trouble was coming upon thee, who art able to bear it.

I said unto him; Sir, be but thou also with me, and I shall easily undergo any trouble. I will, said he, be with thee; and I will entreat the messenger who is set over thy punishment, that he would moderate his afflictions towards thee.

And moreover thou shalt suffer adversity but for a little time; and then thou shalt again be restored to thy former state; only continue on in the humility of thy mind.

Obey the Lord with a pure heart; thou, and thy house, and thy children; and walk in the commands which I have delivered unto thee; and then thy repentance may be firm and pure.

And if thou shalt keep these things with thy house, thy inconveniences shall depart from thee.

And all vexation shall in like manner depart from all those, whosoever shall walk according to these commands.

SIMILITUDE VIII.

That there are many kinds of elect, and of repenting sinners: and how all of them shall receive a reward proportionable to the measure of their repentance and good works.

THE LOST BOOKS OF THE BIBLE

AGAIN he shewed me a low which covered the fields and the mountains, under whose shadow came all such as were called by the name of the Lord.

And by that willow stood an angel of the Lord very excellent and lofty; and did cut down boughs from that willow with a great hook; and reached out to the people that were under the shadow of that willow little rods, as it were about a foot long.

And when all of them had taken them, he laid aside his hook, and the tree continued entire, as I had before seen it. At which I wondered, and mused within myself.

Then that shepherd said unto me; Forbear to wonder that that tree continues whole, notwithstanding so many boughs have been cut off from it, but stay a little, for now it shall be shewn thee, what that angel means, who gave those rods to the people.

So he again demanded the rods of them, and in the same order that every one had received them, was he called to him, and restored his rod; which when he had received, he examined them.

From some he received them dry and rotten, and as it were touched with the moth; those he commanded to be separated from the rest and placed by themselves. Others gave in their rods dry indeed, but not touched with the moth: these also he ordered to be set by themselves.

Others gave in their rods half dry; these also were set apart. Others gave in their rods half dry and cleft; these too were set by themselves. Others brought in their rods half dry and half green, and these were in like manner placed by themselves.

Others delivered up their rods two parts green, and the third dry; and they too were set apart. Others brought their rods two parts dry, and the third green; and were also placed by themselves.

Others delivered up their rods less dry, (for there was but a very little, to wit, their tops dry) but they had clefts, and these were set in like manner by themselves. In the rods of others there was but a little green, and the rest dry; and these were set aside by themselves.

Others came, and brought their rods green as they had received them, and the greatest part of the people brought their rods thus; and the messenger greatly rejoiced at these, and they also were put apart by themselves.

Others brought in their rods not only green, but full of branches; and these were set aside, being also received by the angel with great joy. Others brought their rods green with branches, and those also some fruit upon them.

They who had such rods, were very cheerful; and the angel himself took great joy at them; nor was the shepherd that stood with me, less pleased with them.

Then the angel of the Lord commanded crowns to be brought: and the crowns were brought made of palms; and the angel crowned those men in whose rods he found the young branches with fruit; and commanded them to go into the tower.

He also sent those into the tower, in whose rods he found branches without fruit, giving a seal unto them. For they had the same garment, that is, one white as snow; with which he bade them go into the tower. And so he did to those who returned their rods green as he had received them; giving them a white garment, and so sent them away to go into the tower.

Having done this, he said to the shepherd that was with me, I go my way; but do thou send these within the walls, every one into the place in which be has deserved to dwell; examining first their rods, but examine them diligently that no one deceive thee. But and if any one shall escape thee, I will try them upon the altar. Having said this to the shepherd, he departed.

After he was gone, the shepherd said unto me: Let us take the rods from them, and plant them; if perchance they may grow green again. I said unto him; Sir, how can those dry rods ever grow green again?

He answered me; That tree is a willow, and always loves to live. If therefore these rods shall be planted, and receive a little moisture, many of them will recover themselves.

Wherefore I will try, and will pour water upon them, and if any of them can live, I will rejoice with him; but if not, at least by this means I shall be found not to have neglected my part.

Then he commanded me to call them; and they all came unto him, every one in the rank in which he stood, and gave him their rods; which having received, he planted every one of them in their several orders.

And after he had planted them all, he poured much water upon them, insomuch that they were covered with water, and did not appear above it. Then when he had watered them, he said unto me; Let us depart, and after a little time we will return and visit them.

For he who created this tree, would have all those live that received rods from it. And I hope now that these rods are thus watered, many of them receiving in the moisture, will recover.

I said unto him, Sir, tell me what this tree denotes? For I am greatly astonished, that after so many branches have been cut off, it seems still to be whole; nor does there any thing the less of it appear to remain, which greatly amazes me.

He answered, Hearken. This great tree which covers the plains and the mountains, and all the earth, is the law of God, published throughout the whole world.

Now this law is the Son of God, who is preached to all the ends of the earth. The people that stand under its shadow, are those which have heard his preaching, and believed.

The great and venerable angel which you saw, was Michael, who has the power over his people, and governs them. For he has planted the law in the hearts of those who have believed; and therefore he visits them to whom he has given the law, to see if they have kept it.

And he examines every one's rod; and of those, many that are weakened: for those rods are the law of the Lord. Then he discerns all those who have not kept the law, knowing the place of every one of them.

I said unto him, Sir, why did he send away some to the tower, and left others here to you? He replied, those who have transgressed the law, which they received from him, are left in my power, that they may repent of their sins: but they who fulfilled the law and kept it, are under his power.

But who then, said I, are those, who went into the tower crowned? He replied all such as having striven with the devil, have overcome him, are crowned: and they are those, who have suffered hard things, that they might keep the law.

But they who gave up their rods green, and with young branches, but without fruit, have indeed endured trouble for the same law, but have not suffered death; neither have they denied their holy law.

They who delivered up their rods green as they received them, are those who were modest and just, and have lived with a very pure mind, and kept the commandments of God.

The rest thou shalt know, when I shall have considered those rods which I have planted and watered.

After a few days we returned, and in the same place stood that glorious angel, and I stood by him, Then he said unto me; Gird thyself with a towel, and serve me.

And I girded myself with a clean towel, which was made of coarse cloth. And when he saw me girded, and ready to minister unto him, he said, Call those men whose rods have been planted, every one in his order as he gave them.

And he brought me into the field, and I called them all, and they all stood ready in their several ranks. Then he said unto them; let every one pluck up his rod, and bring it unto me. And first they delivered theirs, whose rods had been dry and rotten.

And those whose rods still continued so, he commanded to stand apart. Then they came whose rods had been dry but not rotten. Some of these delivered in their rods green; others dry and rotten, as if they had been touched by the moth.

Those who gave them up green, he commanded to stand apart; but those whose rods were dry and rotten, he caused to stand with the first sort. Then came they whose rods had been half dry, and cleft: many of these gave up their rods green, and uncleft.

Others delivered them up green with branches, and fruit upon the branches, like unto those who went crowned into the tower. Others delivered them up dry, but not rotten; and some gave them up as they were before, half dry, and cleft.

Every one of these he ordered to stand apart; some by themselves, others in their respective ranks.

Then came they whose rods had been green, but cleft. These delivered their rods altogether green, and stood in their own order. And the shepherd rejoiced at these, because they were all changed, and free from their clefts.

Then they gave in their rods, who had them half green and half dry. Of these some were found wholly green, others half dry; others green, with young shoots. And all these were sent away, every one to his proper rank.

Then they gave up their rods, who had them before two parts green, and the third dry. Many of those gave in their rods green; many half dry; the rest dry but not rotten. So these were sent away, each to his proper place.

Then came they who had before their rods two parts dry and the third green; many of these delivered up their rods half dry, others dry and rotten; others half dry and cleft; but few green. And all these were set every one in his own rank.

Then they reached in their rods, in which there was before but a little green, and the rest dry. Their rods were for the most part found green, having little boughs, with fruit upon them, and the rest altogether green.

And the shepherd upon sight of these rejoiced exceedingly, because he had found them thus; and they also went to their proper orders.

Now after he had examined all their rods, he said unto me I told thee that this tree loved life: thou seest how many have repented, and attained unto salvation. Sir, said I, I see it.

That thou mightest know, saith he, that the goodness and mercy of the Lord is great, and to be had in honour; who gave his spirit to them that were found worthy of repentance.

I answered, Sir, why then did not all of them repent? He replied, Those whose minds the Lord foresaw would be pure, and that they would serve him with all their hearts, to them he gave repentance.

But for those whose deceit and wickedness he beheld, and perceived that they would not truly return unto him; to them he denied any return unto repentance, lest they should again blaspheme his law with wicked words.

I said unto him; Now, Sir, make known unto me, what is the place of every one of those, who have given up their rods, and what their portion; that when they may have not kept their seal entire, but have wasted the seal which they received, shall hear and believe these things, they may acknowledge their evil deeds and repent;

And receiving again their seal from you, may give glory to God, that he was moved with compassion towards them, and sent you to renew their spirits.

Hearken, said he: they whose rods have been found dry and rotten, and as it were touched with the moth; are the deserters and the betrayers of the church.

Who with the rest of their crimes, have also blasphemed the Lord, and denied his name which had been called upon them. Therefore all these are dead unto God: and thou seest that none of them have repented, although they have heard my commands which thou hast delivered unto them. From these men therefore life is far distant.

They also who have delivered up their rods dry, but not rotten, have not been far from them. For they have been counterfeits, and brought in evil doctrines; and have perverted the servants of God: but especially those who had sinned; not suffering them to return unto repentance, but keeping them back by their false doctrines.

These therefore have hope; and thou seest that many of them have repented, since the time that thou hast laid my commands before them; and many more will yet repent. But they that shall not repent shall lose both repentance and life.

But they that have repented, their place is begun to be within the first walls, and some of them are even gone into the tower. Thou seest therefore, said he, that in the repentance of sinners there is life; but for those who repent not, death is prepared.

Hear now concerning those who gave in their rods half dry and full of clefts. Those whose rods were only half dry, are the doubtful; for they are neither living nor dead.

But they who delivered in their rods, not only half dry but also full of clefts, are both doubtful and evil speakers; who detract from those who are absent, and have never peace among themselves, and that envy one another.

Howbeit to those also repentance is offered; for thou seest that some of these have repented.

Now all those of this kind who have quickly repented, shall have a place in the tower; but they who have been more slow in their repentance, shall dwell within the walls; but they that shall not repent, but shall continue on in their wicked doings, shall die the death.

As for those who had their rods green, but yet cleft; they are such as were always faithful and good, but they had some envy and strife among themselves concerning dignity and pre-eminence.

Now all such are vain and without understanding, as contend with one another about these things.

Nevertheless, seeing they are otherwise good, if when they shall hear these commands they shall amend themselves, and shall at my persuasion suddenly repent; they shall at last dwell in the tower, as they who have truly and worthily repented.

But if any one shall again return to his dissension; he shall be shut out from the tower, and shall lose his life. For the life of those who keep the commandments of the Lord consists in doing what they are commanded; not in principality, or in any other dignity.

For by forbearance and humility of mind, men shall attain unto life; but by seditions and contempt of the law, they shall purchase death unto themselves.

They who in their rods had half dry and half green, are those who are engaged in many affairs of the world, and are not joined to the saints. For which cause half of them liveth, and half is dead.

Wherefore many of these since the time that they have heard my commands, have repented, and begun to dwell in the tower. But some of them have wholly fallen away; to these there is no more place for repentance.

For by reason of their present interests, they have blasphemed and denied God: and for this wickedness they have lost life. And of these many are still in doubt; these may yet return; and if they shall quickly repent, they shall have a place in the tower; but if they shall be more slow, they shall dwell within the walls; but if they shall not repent, they shall die.

As for those who had two parts of their rods green, and the third dry; they have by manifold ways denied the Lord. Of those many have repented, and found a place in the tower: and many have altogether departed from God. These have utterly lost life.

And some being in a doubtful state, have raised up dissensions: these may yet return, if they shall suddenly repent and not continue in their lusts; but if they shall continue in their evil doing they shall die.

They who gave in their rods two parts dry, and the other green; are those who have indeed been faithful, but withal rich and full of good things; and thereupon have desired to be famous among the heathen which are without, and have thereby fallen into great pride, and begun to aim at high matters, and to forsake the truth.

Nor were they joined to the saints, but lived with the heathen; and this life seemed the more pleasant to them. Howbeit they have not departed from God, but continued in the faith; only they have not wrought the works of faith.

Many therefore of these have repented, and begun to dwell in the tower. Yet others still living among the heathen people, and being lifted up with their vanities, have utterly fallen away from God, and followed the works and wickednesses of the heathen. These kind of men therefore are reckoned among strangers to the Gospel.

Others of these began to be doubtful in their minds; despairing by reason of their wicked doings ever to attain unto salvation: Others being thus made doubtful, did moreover stir up dissensions.

To these therefore, and to those who by reason of their doings are become doubtful, there is still hope of return; but they must repent quickly, that their place may be in the tower. But they that repent not, but continue still in their pleasures, are nigh unto death.

As for those who gave in their rods green, excepting their tops, which only were dry, and had clefts; these were always good, and faithful, and upright before God: nevertheless they sinned a little, by reason of their empty pleasures and trifling thoughts which they had within themselves.

Wherefore many of them when they heard my words, repented forthwith, and began to dwell in the tower. Nevertheless some grew doubtful, and others to their doubtful minds added dissensions. To these therefore there is still hope of return, because they were always good; but they shall not hardly be moved.

As for those, lastly, who gave in their rods dry, their tops only excepted, which alone were green: they are such as have believed indeed in God, but have lived in wickedness; yet without departing from God: having always willingly borne the name of the Lord; and readily received into their houses the servants of God.

Wherefore hearing these things they returned, and without delay repented, and lived in all righteousness. And some of them suffered death: others readily underwent many trials, being mindful of their evil doings.

And when he had ended his explications of all the rods, he said unto me, Go, and say unto all men that they repent, aid they shall live unto God: because the Lord being moved with great clemency hath sent me to preach repentance unto all.

Even unto those who by reason of their evil doings, deserve not to attain unto salvation. But the Lord will be patient, and keep the invitation that was made by his Son.

I said unto him, Sir, I hope that all when they shall hear these things, will repent. For I trust that everyone acknowledging his crimes, and taking up the fear of the Lord, will return unto repentance.

He said unto me, Whosoever shall repent with all their hearts, and cleanse themselves from all the evils that I have before mentioned, and not add anything more to their sins, shall receive from the Lord the cure of their former iniquities, if they shall not make any doubt of these commands, and shall live unto God.

But they that shall continue to add to their transgressions, and shall still converse with the lusts of the present world, shall condemn themselves unto death. But do thou walk in these commands, and whosoever shall walk in these, and exercise them rightly, shall live unto God.

And having shewed me all these things, he said; I will shew thee the rest in a few days.

SIMILITUDE IX.

The greatest mysteries of the militant and triumphant church which is to be built.

AFTER I had written the Commands and Similitudes of the Shepherd, the Angel of Repentance; he came unto me, and said to me, I will shew thee all those things which the Spirit spake with thee under the figure of the Church. For that Spirit is the Son of God.

And because thou wert weak in body, it was not declared unto thee by the angel, until thou wert strengthened by the Spirit, and increased in force, that thou mightest also see the angel.

For then indeed the building of the tower was very well and gloriously shewn unto thee by the church; nevertheless thou sawest all things shewn unto thee as it were by a virgin.

But now thou art enlightened by the angel, but yet by the same Spirit. But thou must consider all things diligently; for therefore am I sent into thy house by that venerable messenger, that when thou shalt have seen all things powerfully, thou mayest not be afraid as before.

And he led me to the height of a mountain in Arcadia, and we sat upon its top. And he showed me a great plain, and about it twelve mountains in different figures.

The first was black as soot. The second was smooth, without herbs. The third was full of thorns and thistles. The fourth had herbs half dried; of which the upper part was green, but that next the root was dry; and some of the herbs, when the sun grew hot, were dry.

The fifth mountain was very rugged; but yet had green herbs. The sixth mountain was full of clefts, some lesser, and some greater; and in these clefts grew grass, not flourishing, but which seemed to be withering

The seventh mountain had delightful pasture, and was wholly fruitful: and all kinds of cattle, and of the birds of heaven, fed upon it; and the more they fed of it, the more and better did the grass grow.

The eighth mountain was full of fountains, and from those fountains were watered all kinds of the creatures of God. The ninth mountain had no water at all, but was wholly destitute of it; and nourished deadly serpents, and destructive to men.

The tenth mountain was full of tall trees, and altogether shady: and under the shade of them lay cattle resting and chewing the cud.

The eleventh mountain was full of the thickest trees; and those trees seemed to be loaded with several sorts of fruits; that whosoever saw them could not choose but desire to eat of their fruit.

The twelfth mountain was altogether white, and of a most pleasant aspect, and itself gave a most excellent beauty to itself.

In the middle of the plain he showed me a huge white rock, which rose out of the plain, and the rock was higher than those mountains, and was square; so that it seemed capable of supporting the whole world.

It looked to me to be old, yet it had in it a new gate, which seemed to have been newly hewn out in it. Now that gate was bright beyond the sun itself; insomuch, that I greatly admired at its light.

About the gate stood twelve virgins; of which four that stood at the corners of the gate, seemed to me to be the chiefest, although the rest were also of worth: and they stood at the four parts of the gate.

It added also to the grace of those virgins, that they stood in pairs, clothed with linen garments, and decently girded, their right arms being at liberty, as if they were about to lift up some burthen; for so they were adorned, and were exceeding cheerful and ready.

When I saw this, I wondered with myself to see such great and noble things. And again I admired upon the account of those virgins, that they were so handsome and delicate; and stood with such firmness and constancy, as if they would carry the whole heaven.

And as I was thinking thus within myself, the shepherd said unto me: What thmkest thou within thyself, and art disquieted, and fillest thyself with care?

Do not seem to consider, as if thou wert wise, what thou doest not understand, but pray unto the Lord, that thou mayest have ability to understand it: what is to come thou canst not understand, but thou seest that which is before thee.

Be not therefore disquieted at those things which thou canst not see; but get the understanding of those which thou seest.

Forbear to be curious; and I will shew thee all things that I ought to declare unto thee; but first consider what yet remains.

And when he had said this unto me I looked up, and behold I saw six tall and venerable men coming; their countenances were all alike; and they called a certain multitude of men; and they who came at their call were also tall and stout.

And those six commanded them to build a certain tower over that gate. And immediately there began to be a great noise of those men running here and there about the gate, who were come together to build the tower.

But those virgins which stood about the gate perceived that the building of the tower was to be hastened by them. And they stretched out their hands, as if they were to receive somewhat from them to do.

Then those six men commanded, that they should lift up stones out of a certain deep place, and prepare them for the building of the tower. And there were lifted up ten white stones, square, and not cut round.

Then those six men called the ten virgins to them, and commanded them to carry all the stones that were to be put into the building and having carried them through the gate to deliver them to those that were about to build the tower.

Immediately the virgins began all of them together to lift up those stones, that were before taken out of the deep.

And they who also stood about the gate did carry stones in such a manner, that those stones which seemed to be the strongest were laid at the corners, the rest were put into the sides.

And thus they carried all the stones, and bringing them through the gate delivered them to the builders, as they had been commanded: who receiving them at their hands, built with them.

But this building was made upon that great rock, and over the gate; and by these the whole tower was supported. But the building of the ten stones filled the whole gate, which began to be made for the foundation of that tower.

After those ten stones did five and twenty others rise up out of the deep; and these were placed in the building of the same tower; being lifted up by those virgins, as the others had been before.

After these did five and thirty others rise up; and these were also in like manner fitted into the same work. Then forty other stones were brought up, and all these were added unto the building of that tower.

So there began to be four ranks in the foundation of that tower; and the stones ceased to rise out of the deep; and they also which built rested a little.

Again those six men commanded the multitude, that they should bring stones out of those twelve mountains to the building of the same tower.

So they cut out of all the mountains stones of divers colours, and brought them and gave them to the virgins; which when they had received they carried them, and delivered them into the building of the tower,

In which when they were built they became white, and different from what they were before; for they were all alike, and did change their former colours. And some were reached up by the men themselves, which when they came into the building, continued such as they were put in.

These neither became white, nor different from what they were before; because they were not carried by the virgins through the gate. Wherefore these stones were disagreeable in the building: which, when those six men perceived, they commanded them to be removed, and put again in the place from which they were brought.

And they said to those who brought those stones; Do not ye reach up to us any stones for this building, but lay them down by the tower, and these virgins may carry them and reach them to us.

For unless they shall be carried by these virgins through this gate, they cannot change their colours; therefore do not labour in vain.

So the building that day was done, howbeit the tower was not finished; for it was afterwards to be built, therefore now also there was some delay made of it.

And these six men commanded those that built to depart, and as it were to rest for some time; but they ordered those virgins that they should not depart from the tower; now they seemed to me to be left for the guarding of it.

When all were departed, I said unto that shepherd; Sir, why is not the building of the tower finished? Because it cannot, said he, be finished until its Lord comes, and approves of the building; that if he shall find any stones in it that are not good they may be changed; for this tower is built according to his will.

Sir, said I, I would know what the building of this tower signifies; as also I would be informed concerning this rock, and this gate.

And concerning the mountains, and the virgins, and the stones that did rise out of the deep, and were not cut, but put into the building just as they came forth; and why the ten stones were first laid in the foundation; then the twenty-five; then thirty-five; then forty?

Also concerning these stones that were put into the building, and again taken out, and carried back into their place? Fulfil, I pray, the desire of my soul as to all these things and manifest all unto me.

And he said unto me; If thou shalt not be dull, thou shalt know all, and shalt see all the other things that are about to happen in this tower; and shalt understand diligently all these similitudes.

And after a few days we came into the same place where we had sat before; and he said unto me, Let us go unto the tower; for the Lord of it will come and examine it.

So we came thither, and found none but those virgins there. And he asked them whether the Lord of that tower was come thither? And they replied, that he would be there presently to examine the building.

After a very little while I saw a great multitude of men coming, and in the middle of them a man so tall, that he surpassed the tower in height.

About him were those six, who before commanded in the building, and all the rest of those who had built that tower, and many others of great dignity: and the virgins that kept the tower ran to meet him, and kissed him, and began to walk near unto him.

But he examined the building with so much care that he handled every stone; and struck every one with a rod which he held in his hand:

Of which some being so struck turned black as soot; others were rough; some looked as if they had cracks in them; others seemed maimed: some neither black nor white; some looked sharp, and agreed not with the other stones, and others were full of spots.

These were the several kinds of those stones which were not found proper in the building; all which the Lord commanded to be taken out of the tower, and laid near it, and other stones to be brought and put in their places.

And they that built, asked him from which of the mountains he would have stones brought to put in the place of those that were laid aside. But he forbad them to bring any from the mountains, and commanded that they should take out of a certain field that was near.

So they digged in the field, and found many bright square stones, and some also that were round. Howbeit, all that were found in that field were taken away, and carried through the gate by those virgins; and those of them that were square were fitted and put into the places of those that were pulled out.

But the round ones were not put into the building, because they were hard, and it would have required too much time to cut them; but they were placed about the tower, as if they should hereafter be cut square, and put into the building; for they were very white.

When he who was chief in dignity, and lord of the whole tower saw this, he called to him the shepherd that was with me and gave him the stones that were rejected and laid about the tower and said unto him; cleanse these stones with all care, and fit them into the building of the tower, that they may agree with the rest; but those that will not suit with the rest, cast away afar off from the tower.

When he had thus commanded him, he departed, with all those that came with him to the tower: but those virgins still stood about the tower to keep it.

And I said unto that shepherd, How can these stones, seeing they have been rejected, return into the building of this tower? He replied; I will cut off the greatest part front these stones, and will add them to the building, and they will agree with the rest.

And I said, Sir, how will they be able to fill the same place, when they shall be so much cut away? He answered; They that shall be found too little shall be put into the middle of the building, and the greater shall be placed without, and keep them in.

When he had said thus unto me, he added; Let us go, and after three days we will return, and I will put these stones, being cleansed, into the tower.

For all these that are about the tower must be cleansed, lest the master of the house chance to come upon the sudden, and find those which are about the tower unclean; and be so exasperated, that these stones should never be put into the building of this tower, and I shall be looked upon to have been unmindful of my master's commands.

When therefore we came after three days to the tower, he said unto me; Let us examine all these stones, and let us see which of them may go into the building. I answered, Sir, let us see.

And first of all we begun to consider those which had been black; for they were found just such as they were when they were pulled out of the tower: wherefore he commanded them to be removed from the tower and put by themselves.

Then he examined those which had been rough; and commanded many of those to be cut round, and to be fitted by the virgins into the building of the tower; so they took them, and fitted them into the middle of the building; and he commanded the rest to be laid by with the black ones, for they also were become black.

Next he considered those which were full of cracks, and many of those also he ordered to be pared away, and so to be added to the rest of the building by the same virgins.

These were placed without because they were found entire; but the residue through the multitude of their cracks could not be reformed, and therefore were cast away from the building of the tower.

Then he considered those that had been maimed; many of these had cracks, and were become black; others were large clefts; these he commanded to be placed with those that were rejected.

But the rest being cleansed and reformed, he commanded to be put in the building. These therefore those virgins took up, and fitted into the middle of the building, because they were but weak.

After these he examined those which were found half white and half black; and many of those were now black; these also he ordered to be laid among those that were cast away.

The rest were found altogether white; those were taken up by the virgins, and fitted into the same tower: and these were put in the outside, because they were found entire; that so they might keep in those that were placed in the middle, for nothing was cut off from them.

Next he looked upon those which had been hard and sharp; but few of these were made use of, because they could not be cut, for they were found very hard: but the rest were formed, and fitted by the virgins into the middle of the building, because they were more weak.

Then he considered those which had spots; of these a few were found black, and these were carried to their fellows. The rest were white and entire; and they were fitted by the virgins into the building, and placed in the outside, by reason of their strength.

After this he came to consider those stones which were white and round: and he said unto me, What shall we do with these stones? I answered, Sir, I cannot tell.

He replied, Canst thou think of nothing then for these? I answered, Sir, I understand not this art; neither am I a stone-cutter, nor can I tell any thing.

And he said, seest thou not that they are very round? Now to make them square, I must cut off a great deal from them; howbeit, it is necessary that some of these should go into the building of the tower.

I answered; If it be necessary, why do you perplex yourself, and not rather choose, if you have any choice among them, and fit them into the building.

Upon this he chose out the largest and brightest, and squared them; which when he had done the virgins took them up, and placed them in the outside of the building.

And the rest that remained were carried back into the same field from which they were taken; howbeit, they were not cast away; because, said he, there is not yet a little wanting to this tower, which is to be built; and perhaps the Lord will have these stones fitted into this building, because they are exceeding white.

Then were there called twelve very stately women, clothed with a black garment, girded, and their shoulders free, and their hair loose. These seemed to me to be country women.

And the shepherd commanded them to take up those stones which were cast out of the building, and carry them back to the mountains out of which they were taken.

And they took them all up joyfully, and carried them back to their places from whence they had been taken.

When not one stone remained about the tower, he said unto me, Let us go about this tower, and see whether any thing be wanting to it.

We began therefore to go round about it; and when he saw that it was handsomely built, he began to be very glad; for it was so beautifully framed, that any one that had seen it must have been in love with the building:

For it seemed to be all but one stone, nor did a joint anywhere appear; but it looked as if it had all been cut out of one rock.

And when I diligently considered what a tower it was, I was extremely pleased: and he said unto me, Bring hither some lime and little shells, that I may fill up the spaces of those stones that were taken out of the building, and put in again; for all things about the tower must be made even.

And I did as he commanded me, and he said unto me, Be ready to help me, and this work will quickly be finished.

He therefore filled up the spaces of those stones, and commanded the place about the tower to be cleansed.

Then those virgins took besoms, and cleansed all the place around and took away all the rubbish, and threw water on; which being done, the place became delightful, and the tower beauteous.

Then he said unto me, All is now clean: if the Lord should come to finish the tower, he will find nothing whereby to complain of us.

When he had said this he would have departed. But I laid hold on his bag, and began to entreat him for the Lord's sake, that he would explain to me all things that he had shown me.

He said unto me, I have at present a little business; but I will suddenly explain all things unto thee. Tarry here for me till I come.

I said unto him, Sir, what shall I do here alone? He answered, Thou art not alone, seeing all these virgins are with thee.

I said, Sir, deliver me then unto them. Then he called them and said unto them, I commend this man unto you until I shall come.

So I remained with those virgins: now they were cheerful and courteous unto me; especially the four, which seemed to be the chiefest among them.

Then those virgins said unto me, that shepherd will not return hither to day. I said unto them, What then shall I do? They answered, Tarry for him till the evening, if perhaps he may come and speak with thee; but if not, yet thou shalt continue with us till he does coma.

I said unto them, I will tarry for him till evening; but if be comes not by that time, I will go home, and return hither again the next morning.

They answered me, Thou art delivered unto us, thou mayest not depart from us. I said, Where shall I tarry?

They replied, Thou shalt sleep with us as a brother, not as a husband: for thou art our brother, and we are ready from henceforth to dwell with thee; for thou art very dear to us.

Howbeit I was ashamed to continue with them. But she that seemed to be the chiefest amongst them, embraced me, and began to kiss me. And the rest when they saw that I was kissed by her, began also to kiss me as a brother; and led me about the tower, and played with me.

Some of them also sung psalms, others made up the chorus with them. But I walked about the tower with them, rejoicing silently, and seeming to myself to be grown young again.

When the evening came on, I would forthwith have gone home, but they withheld me, and suffered me not to depart. Wherefore I continued with them that night near the same tower.

So they spread their linen garments upon the ground; and placed me in the middle, nor did they anything else, only they prayed.

I also prayed with them without ceasing, nor less than they. Who when they saw me pray in that manner, rejoiced greatly; and I continued there with them till the next day.

And when we had worshipped God, then the shepherd came and said unto them: You have done no injury to this man. They answered, Ask him. I said unto him, Sir, I have received a great deal of satisfaction in that have remained with them.

And he said unto me, How thou sup? I answered, Sir, I feasted the whole night upon the words of the Lord. They received thee well then, said he; I said, Sir, very well.

He answered, Wilt thou now learn what thou didst desire? I replied, Sir, I will: and first I pray thee that thou shouldest shew me all things in the order that I asked them.

He answered, I will do all as thou wouldst have me, nor will I hide anything from thee.

First of all, Sir, said I, tell me, what this rock, and this gate denote? Hearken, said he; this rock, and this gate, are the Son of God. I replied, Sir, how can that be; seeing the rock is old, but the gate new.

Hear, said he, O foolish man! and understand. The Son of God is indeed more ancient than any creature; insomuch that he was in council with his Father at the creation of all things.

But the gate is therefore new, because he appeared in the last days in the fulness of time; that they who shall attain unto salvation, may by it enter into the kingdom of God.

You have seen, said he, those stones which were carried through the gate, how they were placed in the building of the tower; but that those which were not carried through the gate, were sent away into their own places?

I answered, Sir, I saw it. Thus, said he, no man shall enter into the kingdom of God, but he who shall take upon him the name of the Son of God.

For if you would enter into any city, and that city should w be encompassed with a wall, and had only one gate, could you n enter into that city except by that gate?

I answered, Sir, how could I do otherwise? As therefore, said he, there would be no other way of entering into that city but by its gate, so neither can any one enter into the kingdom of God, but only by the name of his Son, who is most dear unto him.

And he said unto me, Didst thou see the multitude of those that built that tower? Sir, said I, I saw it. He answered, All those are the angels, venerable in their dignity.

With those is the Lord encompassed as with a wall: but the gate is the Son of God, who is the only way of coming unto God. For no man shall go to God, but by his Son.

Thou sawest also, said he, the six men, and in the middle of them that venerable great man, who walked about the tower, and rejected the stones out of the tower?

Sir, said I, I saw them. He answered, that tall man was the Son of God: and those six were his angels of most eminent dignity, which stand about him on the right hand and on the left.

Of these excellent angels none comes in unto God without him. He added, Whosoever therefore shall not take upon him his name, he shall not enter into the kingdom of God.

Then I said, What is this tower? This, said he, is the church. And what, Sir, are these virgins? He said unto me, These are the holy spirits, for no man can enter into the kingdom of God, except these clothe him with their garment.

For it will avail thee nothing to take up the name of the Son of God, unless thou shalt also receive their garment from them. For these virgins are the powers of the Son of God. So shall a man in vain bear his name, unless he shall be also endued with his powers.

And he said unto me, sawest thou those stones that were cast away? They bore indeed the name, but put not on their garment. I said, Sir, what is their garment? Their very names, said he, are their garment.

Therefore whosoever beareth the name of the Son of God, ought to bear their names also; for the Son of God also himself beareth their names.

As for those stones, continued he, which being delivered by their hands, thou sawest remain in the building, they were clothed with their power; for which cause thou seest the whole tower of the same colour with the rock, and made as it were of one stone.

So also those who have believed in God by his Son, have put on his spirit. Behold there shall be one spirit, and one body, and one colour of their garments; and all they shall attain this, who shall bear the names of these virgins.

And I said, Sir, why then were those stones cast away which were rejected, seeing they also were carried through the gate, and delivered by the hands of these virgins into the building of this tower?

Seeing, said he, thou takest care to inquire diligently into all things, hear also concerning those stones which were rejected. All these received the name of the Son of God, and with that the power of these virgins.

Having therefore received these spirits, they were perfected, and brought into the number of the servants of God; and they began to be one body, and to have one garment, for they were endued with the same righteousness, which they alike exercised.

But after that they beheld those women which thou sawest clothed with a black garment, with their shoulders at liberty and their hair loose; they fixed their desires upon them, being tempted with their beauty; and were clothed with their power, and cast off the clothing of the virgins:

Therefore were they cast off from the house of God, and delivered to those women. But they that were not corrupted with their beauty, remained in the house of God. This, said he, is the signification of those stones which were rejected.

And I said, Sir, what if any of these men shall repent, and cast away their desire of those women, and be converted, and return to these virgins, and put on again their virtue; shall they not enter into the house of God?

They shall enter, said he, if they shall lay aside all the works of those women, and shall resume the power of these virgins, and shall walk in their works.

And for this cause there is a stop in the building, that if they shall repent, they may be added to the building of this tower; but if they shall not repent, that others may be built in their places, and so they may be utterly cast away.

For all these things I gave thanks unto the Lord, that being moved with mercy towards all those upon whom his name is called, he sent to us the angel of repentance to preside over us who have sinned against him; and that he has refreshed our spirits which were almost gone, and who had no hope of salvation, but are now refreshed to the renewal of life.

Then I said, Shew me now, Sir, why this tower is not built upon the ground, but upon a rock, and upon the gate? He replied, thou art foolish, and without understanding, therefore thou asketh this.

THE LOST BOOKS OF THE BIBLE

And I said, Sir, I must needs ask all things of you, because I understand nothing at all. For all your answers are great and excellent; and which a man can hardly understand.

Hear, said he: The name of the Son of God is great and without bounds, and the whole world is supported by it. If therefore, said I, every creature of God be sustained by his Son, why should he not support those also who have been invited by him, and who carry his name, and walk in his commandments?

Seest thou not, said he, that he doth support them, who with all their heart bear his' name? He therefore is their foundation, and gladly supports those who do not deny his name, but willingly bear it.

And I said: Sir, tell me the names of these virgins; and of those women that were clothed with the black garment.

Hear, said he, the names of those virgins which are the more powerful, and stand at the corners of the gate. These are their names:

The first is called Faith; the second Continence; the third, Power; the fourth, Patience; the rest which stand beneath these are, Simplicity, Innocence, Chastity, Cheerfulness, Truth, Understanding, Concord, Charity.

Whosoever therefore bear these names, and the names of the Son of God, shall enter into the kingdom of God.

Hear now, said he, the names of those women, which were clothed with the black garment. Of these, four are the principal: the first is Perfidiousness; the second, Incontinence; the third, Infidelity; the fourth, Pleasure.

And the rest which follow are called thus, Sadness, Malice, Lust, Anger, Lying, Foolishness, Pride, and Hatred. The servant of God, which carries these spirits, shall see indeed the kingdom of God, but he shall not enter into it.

But, Sir, what are those stones which were taken out of the deep and fitted into the building? The ten, said he, which were placed at the foundation, are the first age; the following five-and-twenty, the second, of righteous men.

The next thirty-five, are the prophets and ministers of the Lord. And the forty, are the Apostles and doctors of the preaching of the Son of God.

And I said, Sir, why did the virgins put even those stones into the building after they were carried through the gate? And he said, Because these first carried those spirits, and they departed not one from the one, neither the men from the spirits, nor the spirits from the men:

But the spirits were joined to those men even to the day of their death; who if they had not had these spirits with them, they could not have been useful to the building of this tower.

And I said, Sir, shew me this farther. He answered, What dost thou ask? Why did

259

these stones come out of the deep, and were placed into the building of this tower, seeing that they long ago carried those holy spirits.

It was necessary, said he, for them to ascend by water, that they might be at rest. For they could not otherwise enter into the kingdom of God, but by laying aside the mortality of their former life.

They therefore being dead, were nevertheless sealed with the seal of the Son of God, and so entered into the kingdom of God.

For before a man receives the name of the Son of God, he is ordained unto death; but when he receives that seal, he is freed from death, and assigned unto life.

Now that seal is the water of baptism, into which men go down under the obligation unto death, but come up appointed unto life.

Wherefore to those also was this seal preached, and they made use of it, that they might enter the kingdom of God.

And I said, Why then, sir, did these forty stones also ascend with them out of the deep, having already received that seal?

He answered, Because these Apostles and teachers, who preached the name of the Son of God, dying after they had received his faith and power, preached to them who were dead before; and they gave this seal to them.

They went down therefore into the water with them, and again came up. But these went down whilst they were alive, and came up again alive: whereas those who were before dead, went down dead, but came up alive;

Through these therefore they received life, and knew the Son of God: for which cause they came up with them, and were fit to come into the building of the tower; and were not cut, but put in entire; because they died in righteousness, and in great purity; only this seal was wanting to them.

Thus you have the explication of these things.

I answered: Sir, tell me now what concerns those mountains, why are they so different; some of one form, and some of another.

Hear, said he; These twelve mountains which thou seest, are twelve nations, which make up the whole world. Wherefore the Son of God is preached to them, by those whom he sent unto them.

But why, said I, are they different, and every one of a figure? He replied, Hearken. Those twelve nations which possess the whole world, are twelve people.

And as thou hast beheld these mountains different, so are they. I will therefore open to thee the meaning and actions of every mountain.

But first, sir, said I, shew me this; Seeing these mountains are so different, how have they agreed into the building of this tower; and been brought to one colour; and are no less bright than those that came out of the deep?

Because, replied he, all the nations which are under heaven, have heard and believed in the same one name of the Son of God by whom they are called.

Wherefore having received his seal, they have all been made partakers of the same understanding and knowledge; and their faith and charity have been the same; and they have carried the spirits of these virgins together with his name.

And therefore the building of this tower appeared to be of the same colour, and did shine like the brightness of the sun.

But after that they had thus agreed in one mind there began to be one body of them all; howbeit some of them polluted themselves, and were cast off from the kind of the righteous, and again returned to their former state, and became even worse than they were before.

How, said I, sir, were they worse who knew the Lord? He answered: If he who knows not the Lord liveth wickedly, the punishment of his wickedness attends him.

But he who has known the Lord, ought to abstain altogether from all wickedness, and more and more to be the servant of righteousness.

And does not he then seem to thee to sin more who ought to follow goodness, if he shall prefer the part of sin; than he who offends without knowing the power of God?

Wherefore these are indeed ordained unto death; but they who have known the Lord, and have seen his wonderful works, if they shall live wickedly, they shall be doubly punished, and shall die for ever.

As therefore thou hast seen that after the stones were cast out of the tower, which had been rejected; they were delivered to wicked and cruel spirits; and thou beheldest the tower so cleansed, as if it had all been made of one stone:

So the church of God, when it shall be purified: (the wicked and counterfeits, the mischievous and doubtful, and all that have behaved themselves wickedly in it, and committed divers kinds of sin, being cast out) shall become one body, and there shall be one understanding, one opinion, one faith, and the same charity.

And then shall the Son of God rejoice among them, and shall receive his people with a pure will.

And I said; Sir, all these things are great and honourable; but now shew unto me the effect and force of every mountain: that every soul which trusteth in the Lord, when it shall hear these things may honour his great, and wonderful, and holy name.

Hear, said he, the variety of these mountains, that is, of the twelve nations.

They who have believed of the first mountain, which is black, are those who have revolted from the faith; and spoken wicked things against the Lord; and betrayed the servants of God.

THE LOST BOOKS OF THE BIBLE

These are condemned to death, there is no repentance for them: and therefore they are black, because their kind is wicked.

Of the second mountain which was smooth, are the hypocrites, who have believed, and the teachers of naughtiness: and these are next to the foregoing, which have not in them the fruit of righteousness.

For as their mountain is barren and without fruit; so also such kind of men have indeed the name of Christians, but are empty of faith; nor is there any fruit of the truth in them.

Nevertheless there is room left to them for repentance, if they shall suddenly pursue it: but if they shall delay, they also shall be partakers of death with the foregoing kind.

I said, Sir, why is there room left to those for repentance, and not to the foregoing kind, seeing their sins are well nigh the same?

There is therefore, said he to these a return unto life by repentance, because they have not blasphemed against their Lord, nor betrayed the servants of God: but by their desire of gain have deceived men, leading them according to the lusts of sinners; wherefore they shall suffer for this thing.

Howbeit there is still left them room for repentance, because they have not spoken any thing wickedly against the Lord.

They who are of the third mountain which had thorns and brambles, are those who believed, but were some of them rich, others taken up with many affairs: the brambles are their riches: the thorns, those affairs in which they were engaged.

Now they who are entangled in much business, and in diversity of affairs, join not themselves to the servants of God, but wander, being called away by those affairs with which they are choked.

And so they which are rich, with difficulty yield themselves to the conversation of the servants of God; fearing lest anything should be asked of them. These therefore shall hardly enter into the kingdom of God.

For as men walk with difficulty bare-foot over thorns, even so these kind of men shall scarcely enter into the kingdom of God.

Nevertheless there is at. forded to all these a return unto repentance; if that they shall quickly return to it; that because in their former days they have neglected to work, in the time that is to come they may do some good.

If therefore having repented they shall do the works of righteousness, they shall live; but if they shall continue in their evil courses, they shall be delivered to those women that will take away their life.

As for the fourth mountain, which had many herbs, the upper part of which is green, but the roots dry, and some of which being touched with the heat of the sun are withered;

It denotes the doubtful, who have believed, and some others who carry the Lord in their tongues, but have him not in their heart: therefore their grass is dry, and without root; because they live only in words, but their works are dead.

These therefore are neither dead nor living, and withal are doubtful. For the doubtful are neither green nor dry; that is, neither dead nor alive.

For as the herbs dry away at the sight of the sun; so the doubtful as soon as they hear of persecution, and fear inconveniences, return to their idols, and again serve them, and are ashamed to bear the name of their Lord.

This kind of men then is neither dead nor alive; nevertheless these also may live, if they shall presently repent; but if not, they shall be delivered to those women, who shall take away their life.

As concerning the fifth mountain that is craggy, and yet has green grass: they are of this kind who have believed, and are faithful indeed, but believe with difficulty; and are bold, and self-conceited; that would be thought to know all things, but really know nothing.

Wherefore, by reason of this confidence, knowledge is departed from them; and a rash presumption is entered into them.

But they carry themselves high, and as prudent men; and though they are fools, yet would seem to be teachers.

Now by reason of this folly many of them, whilst they magnify themselves, are become vain and empty. For boldness and vain confidence is a very evil spirit.

Wherefore many of these are cast away; but others acknowledging their error, have repented, and submitted themselves to those who are knowing.

And to all the rest of this kind there is repentance allowed; forasmuch as they were not so much wicked as foolish, as void of understanding.

If these therefore shall repent, they shall live unto God; but if not, they shall dwell with those women, who shall exercise their wickedness upon them.

For what concerns the sixth mountain having greater and lesser clefts, they are such as have believed; but those in which were lesser clefts are they who have had controversies among themselves; and by reason of their quarrels languish in the faith;

Nevertheless many of these have repented, and so will the rest when they shall hear my commands; for their controversies are but small, and they will easily return unto repentance.

But those who have the greater clefts, will be as stiff stones, mindful of grudges and offences, and full of anger among themselves. These therefore are cast from the tower, and refused to be put into its building; for this kind of men shall hardly live.

Our God and Lord, who ruleth over all things, and has power over all his creatures, will not remember our offences, but is easily appeased by those who confess their sins: but man being languid, mortal, infirm, and full of sins, perseveres in his anger against man; as if it were in his power to save or destroy him.

But I, as the angel who am set over your repentance, admonish you, that whoso-ever among you has any such purpose he should lay it aside, and return unto repen-tance; and the Lord will heal your former sins, if you shall purge yourselves from this evil spirit; but if you shall not do it, ye shall be delivered to him unto death.

As for the seventh mountain in which the grass was green and flourishing, and the whole mountain faithful; and all kind of cattle fed upon the grass of it, and the more the grass was eaten so much the more it flourished:

They are such as believed, and were always good and upright; and without any differences among themselves, but still rejoiced in the servants of God, having put on the spirit of these virgins; and been always forward to shew mercy to all men, readily giving to all men of their labours without upbraiding, and without deliberation.

Wherefore the Lord seeing their simplicity and innocence, has increased them in the works of their hands, and given them grace in all their works.

But I, who am the angel appointed over your repentance, exhort you, that as many as are of this kind would continue in the same purpose, that your seed may not be rooted out forever.

For the Lord hath tried you, and written you into our number; and all your seed shall dwell with the Son of God; for ye are all of his spirit.

As concerning the eighth mountain in which were a great many springs, by which every kind of all the creatures of God was watered; they are such as have believed the Apostles which the Lord sent into all the world to preach;

And some of them being teachers have preached and taught purely and sincerely, and have not in the least yielded to any evil desires, but have constantly walked in righ-teousness and truth.

These therefore have their conversations among the angels.

Again; as for what concerns the ninth mountain which is desert, and full of ser-pents; they are such as have believed, but had many stains:

These are such ministers as discharge their ministry amiss; ravishing away the goods of the widows and fatherless; and serve themselves, not others, out of those things which they have received.

These, if they continue in this covetousness, have delivered themselves unto death, nor shall there be any hope of life for them. But if they shall be converted, and shall discharge their ministry sincerely, they may live.

As for those which were found rough, they are such as have denied the name of the Lord, and not returned again to the Lord, but have become savage and wild; not applying themselves to the servants of God; but being separated from them, have for a little carelessness lost their lives.

For as a vine that is forsaken in a hedge, and never dressed, perishes and is choked by the weeds, and in time becomes wild, and ceases to be useful to its lord; so this kind of men despairing of themselves, and being soured, have begun to be unprofitable to their Lord.

Howbeit to these there is, after all, repentance allowed, if they shall not be found from their hearts to have denied Christ; but if any of these shall be found to have denied him from his heart, I cannot tell whether such a one can attain unto life.

I say therefore that if any one hath denied, he should in these days return unto repentance; for it cannot be that any one who now denies the Lord, can afterwards attain unto salvation: nevertheless repentance is proposed unto them who have formerly denied.

But he who will repent must hasten on his repentance, before the building of this tower is finished: otherwise he shall be delivered by those women unto death.

But they that are maimed are the deceitful; and those who mix with one another, these are the serpents that you saw mingled in that mountain.

For as the poison of serpents is deadly unto men; so the words of such persons infect and destroy men. They are therefore maimed in their faith, by reason of that kind of life which they lead.

Howbeit some of them, having repented, have been saved, and so shall others of the same kind be also saved, if they shall repent; but if not, they shall die by those women whose power and force they possess.

For what concerns the tenth mountain, in which were the trees covering the cattle, they are such as have believed, and some of them have been bishops, that is, governors of the churches.

Others, are such stones as have not feignedly, but with a cheerful mind entertained the servants of God.

Then such as have been set over inferior ministries; and have protected the poor and the widows; and have always kept a chaste conversation: therefore they also are protected by the Lord.

Whosoever shall do on this wise, are honored with the Lord; and their place is among the angels, if they shall continue to obey the Lord even unto the end.

As to the eleventh mountain in which were trees loaded with several sorts of fruits, they are such as have believed, and suffered death, for the name of the Lord; and have endured with a ready mind, and have given up their lives with all their hearts.

And I said, Why then, sir, have all these fruit indeed, but yet some fairer than others?

Hearken, said he: Whosoever have suffered for the name of the Lord are esteemed honourable by the Lord; and all their offences are blotted out, because they have suffered death for the name of the Son of God.

Hear now, why their fruits are different, and some of them excel others, they who being brought before magistrates, and being asked, denied not the Lord, but suffered with a ready mind; these are more honourable with the Lord. The fruits therefore that are the most fair are these.

But they who were fearful and doubtful, and have deliberated with themselves whether they should confess or deny Christ, and yet have suffered; their fruits are smaller, because that this thought came into their hearts.

For it is a wicked and evil thought for a servant to deliberate whether he should deny his master. Take heed therefore ye who have such thoughts, that this mind continue not in you, and ye die unto God.

But ye who suffer death for his name sake, ought to honour the Lord, that he has esteemed you worthy to bear his name; and that you should be delivered from all your sins.

And why therefore do you not rather esteem yourselves happy? Yea think verily that if any one among you suffer, he performs a great work? For the Lord giveth you life, and ye understand it not. For your offences did oppress you; and if ye had not suffered for his name sake, ye had now been dead unto the Lord,

Wherefore I speak this unto you who deliberate whether ye should confess or deny him; confess that ye have the Lord for your God; lest at any time denying him, ye be delivered not into bonds.

For all nations punish their servants which deny their masters; what think you that the Lord will do unto you, who has the power of all things?

Remove therefore out of hearts these doubts, that ye may live forever unto God.

As for the twelfth mountain, which was white, they are such as have believed like sincere children, into whose thoughts there never came any malice, nor have they ever known what sin was, but have always continued in their integrity.

Wherefore this kind of men shall without all doubt inherit the kingdom of God; because they have never in any thing defiled the commandments of God, but have continued with sincerity in the same condition all the days of their life.

Whosoever therefore, said he, shall continue as children without malice; shall be more honourable than all those of whom I have yet spoken: for all such children are honoured by the Lord, and esteemed the first of all.

Happy therefore are ye who shall remove all malice from you, and put on innocence; because ye shall first see the Lord.

And after he had thus ended his explication of all the mountains, I said unto him, Sir, show me now also what concerns the stones that were brought out of the plain, and put into the tower in the room of those that were rejected:

As also concerning those round stones which were added into the building of the tower: and also of those who still continued round.

Hear now, says he, concerning those stones which were brought out of the plain into the building of the tower, and placed in the room of those that were rejected; they are the roots of that white mountain.

Wherefore because those who have believed of that mountain were very innocent; the lord of this tower commanded that they which were of the roots of this mountain should be placed into the building.

For he knew that if they were put into this building they would continue bright; nor would any of them any more be made black.

But if he had added on this manner from the rest of the mountains, he would almost have needed again to visit the tower and to cleanse it.

Now all these white stones are the young men who have believed, or shall believe; for they are all of the same kind. Happy is this kind, because it is innocent.

Hear now also concerning those round and bright stones: all these are of this white mountain. But they are therefore found round, because their riches have a little darkened them from the truth and dazzled their eyes:

Howbeit they have never departed from the Lord, nor has any wicked word proceeded out of their mouths; but all righteousness, and virtue, and truth.

When therefore the Lord saw their mind, and that they might adorn the truth; he commanded that they should continue good, and that their riches should be pared away:

For he would not have them taken wholly away, to the end they might do some good with that which was left, and live unto God; because they also are of a good kind.

Therefore was there a little cut off from them, and so they were put into the building of this tower.

As for the rest which continued still round, and were not found fit for the building of this tower, because they have not yet received the seal; they were carried back to their place, because they were found very round.

But this present world must be cut away from them, and the vanities of their riches; and then they will be fit for the kingdom of God. For they must enter into the kingdom of God, because God has blessed this innocent kind.

Of this kind therefore none shall fall away; for though any of them being tempted by the devil should offend, he shall soon return to his Lord God.

I the angel of repentance esteem you happy, whosoever are innocent as little children, because your portion is good and honourable with the Lord.

And I say unto all you who have received this seal; keep simplicity, and remember not the offences which are committed against you, nor continue in malice, or in bitterness, through the memory of offences.

But become one spirit, and provide remedies for these evil rents, and remove them from you; that the lord of the sheep may rejoice at it; for he will rejoice, if he shall find all whole.

But if any of these sheep shall be found scattered away, Wo shall be to the shepherds; but and if the shepherds themselves shall be scattered; what will they answer to the lord of the sheepfold? Will they say that they were troubled by the sheep? But they shall not be believed.

For it is an incredible thing that the shepherd should suffer by his flock; and he shall be the more punished for his lie.

Now I am the shepherd; and especially must give an account of you.

Wherefore take care of yourselves whilst the tower is yet building. The Lord dwells in those that love peace; for peace is beloved; but he is far off from the contentious, and those who are full of malice.

Wherefore restore unto him the spirit entire, as ye received it. For if thou shalt give unto a fuller a garment new and whole, thou wilt expect to receive it whole again; if therefore the fuller shall restore it unto thee torn, wouldest thou receive it?

Wouldst thou not presently be angry; and reproach him, saying; I gave my garment to thee whole; why hast thou rent it, and made it useless to me? Now it is of no use to me, by reason of the rent which thou hast made in it. Wouldst thou not say all this to a fuller, for the rent which he made in thy garment?

If therefore thou wouldst be concerned for thy garment, and complain that thou hadst not received it whole; what thinkest thou that the Lord will do, who gave his Spirit to thee entire, and thou hast rendered him altogether unprofitable, so that he can be of no use unto his Lord? For being corrupted by thee, he is no longer profitable to him.

Will not therefore the Lord do the same concerning his Spirit, by reason of thy deed? Undoubtedly, said I, he will do the same to all those whom he shall find to continue in the remembrance of injuries.

Tread not then under foot he said, his mercy; but rather honour him, because he is so patient with respect to your offences, and not like one of you; but repent, for that will be profitable for you.

All these things which are above written, I the shepherd, the angel of repentance, have shown and spoken to the servants of God.

If therefore ye shall believe and hearken to these words, and shall walk in them, and shall correct your ways, ye shall live. But if ye shall continue in malice, and in the remembrance of injuries, no such sinners shall live unto God.

All these things which were to be spoken by me I have thus delivered unto you.

Then the shepherd said unto me, Hast thou asked all things of me? I answered, Sir, I have.

Why, then, said he, hast thou not asked concerning the spaces of these stones that were put in the building, that I may explain that also unto thee? I answered, Sir, I forgot it. Hear, then, said he, concerning these also.

They are those who have now heard these commands, and have repented with all their hearts;

And when the Lord saw that their repentance was good and pure, and that they could continue in it, he commanded their former sins to be blotted out. For these spaces were their sins, and they are therefore made even that they might not appear.

SIMILITUDE X.

Of Repentance and alms-deeds.

AFTER that I had written this book, the angel which had delivered me to that shepherd, came into the house where I was and sat upon the bed, and that shepherd stood at his right hand.

Then he called me and said unto me; I delivered thee and thy house to this shepherd, that thou mightest be protected by him. I said, Yes, Lord.

If therefore, said he, thou wilt be protected from all vexations and from all cruelty, and have success in every good word and work; and have all virtue and righteousness; walk in those commands which he has given thee, and thou shalt have dominion over all sin.

For if thou keepest those commands, all the lust and pleasure of this present world shall be subject to thee; and success shall follow thee in every good undertaking.

Take therefore his gravity and modesty towards thee, and say unto all, that he is in great honour and renown with God, and is a prince of great authority and powerful in his office.

To him only is the power of repentance committed throughout the whole world. Does he not seem to thee to be of great authority?

But ye despise his goodness, and the modesty which he chews towards you.

I said unto him; Sir, ask him since the time that he came into my house whether I have done any thing disorderly, or have offended him in any thing?

I know, said he, that thou hast done nothing disorderly, neither wilt thou hereafter do any such thing; and therefore I speak these things with thee that thou mayest persevere; for he has given me a good account concerning thee,

But thou shalt speak these things to others, that they who either have repented, or shall repent, may be like-minded with thee; and he may give me as good an account of them also, and I may do the same unto the Lord.

I answered; Sir, I declare to all men the wonderful works of God; and I hope that all who love them and have before sinned, when they shall hear these things, will repent, and recover life.

Continue therefore, said he, in this ministry, and fulfil it. And whosoever shall do according to the commands of this shepherd, he shall live; and shall have great honour both here and with the Lord.

But they that shall not keep his commands, flee from their life, and are adversaries to it. And they that follow not his commands, shall deliver themselves unto death, and shall be every one guilty of his own blood.

But I say unto thee, keep these commandments, and thou shalt find a cure for all thy sins.

Moreover, I have sent these virgins to dwell with thee; for I have seen that they are very kind to thee. Thou shalt therefore have them for thy helpers, that thou mayest the better keep the commands which he hath given thee; for these commands cannot be kept without these virgins.

And I see how they are willing to be with thee; and I will also command them that they shall not all depart from thy house.

Only do thou purify thy house, for they will readily dwell in a clean house. For they are clean and chaste, and industrious; and all of them have grace with the Lord.

If therefore, thou shalt have thy house pure, they will abide with thee. But if it shall be never so little polluted, they will immediately depart from thy house: for these virgins cannot endure any manner of pollution.

I said unto him; Sir, I hope that I shall so please them, that they shall always delight to dwell in my house. And as he to whom you have committed me, makes no complaint of me; so neither shall they complain.

Then he said to that shepherd: I see that the servant of God will live and keep these commandments, and place these virgins in a pure habitation.

When he had said this, he delivered me again to that shepherd, and called the virgins, and said unto them; forasmuch as I see that ye will readily dwell in this man's house, I commend him and his house to you, that ye may not at all depart from his house. And they willingly heard these words.

Then he said unto me, Go on manfully in thy ministry; declare to all men the great things of God, and thou shalt find grace in this ministry.

And whosoever shall walk in these commands, shall live, and be happy in his life. But he that shall neglect them, shall not live, and shall be unhappy in his life.

Say unto all that whosoever can do well, cease not to exercise themselves in good works, for it is profitable unto them. For I would that all men should be delivered from the inconveniences they lie under.

For he that wants, and suffers inconveniences in his daily life, is in great torment and necessity. Whosoever therefore delivers such a soul from necessity, gets great joy unto himself.

For he that is grieved with such inconveniences is equally tormented, as if he were in chains. And many upon the account of such calamities, being not able to bear them, have chosen even to destroy themselves.

He therefore that knows the calamity of such a man, and does not free him from it, commits a great sin, and is guilty of his blood.

Wherefore exercise yourselves in good works, as many as have received ability from the Lord; lest whilst ye delay to do them, the building of the tower be finished; because for your sakes the building is stopped.

Except therefore ye shall make haste to do well, the tower shall be finished, and ye shall be shut out of it.

And after he had thus spoken with me, he rose up from the bed and departed, taking the shepherd and virgins with him.

Howbeit he said unto me that he would send back the shepherd and virgins unto my house. Amen.

LETTERS OF HEROD AND PILATE.

CONNECTING ROMAN HISTORY WITH THE DEATH OF CHRIST AT JERUSALEM.

[These letters occur in a Syriac MS., of the sixth or seventh century, in the British Museum. Dr. Tischendorf states in his Apocalypses Apocryphae (Prolegg. p. 56) that he has a copy of the same in Greek from a Paris MS., of which he says "scripture satis differt, non item argumentum." The letters are followed by a few extracts which seem to have been added by some copyist, although they are followed by the subscription to Pilate's letter. We suppose that by Justinus, we are to understand Justus of Tiberias of whom Josephus speaks as a historian of his tine. We cannot venture an opinion favorable to the genuineness of this extract, because Photius says Justus did not mention Christ. By Theodorus, we understand the Emperor Tiberius. The question and answer agree in sense with what is read in the "Anaphora," or response of Pilate.]

LETTER OF HEROD TO PILATE THE GOVERNOR.

HEROD TO PONTIUS PILATE THE GOVERNOR OF JERUSALEM: PEACE.

I AM in great anxiety. I write these things unto thee, that when thou hast heard them thou mayest be grieved for me. For as my daughter Herodias, who is dear to me, was playing upon a pool of water which had ice upon it, it broke under her, and all her body went down, and her head was cut off and remained on the surface of the ice. And behold, her mother is holding her head upon her knees in her lap, and my whole house is in great sorrow. For I, when I heard of the man Jesus, wished to come to thee, that I might see him alone, and hear his word, whether it was like that of the sons of men. And it is certain that because of the many evil things which were done by me to John the Baptist, and because I mocked the Christ, behold I receive the reward of righteousness, for I have shed much blood of others' children upon the earth. Therefore the judgments of God are righteous; for every man receives according to his thought. But since thou wast worthy to see that God-man, therefore it becometh you to pray for me.

My son Azbonius also is in the agony of the hour of death.

And I too am in affliction and great trial, because I have the dropsy; and am in great distress, because I persecuted the introducer of baptism by water, which was John. Therefore, my brother, the judgments of God are righteous.

And my wife, again, through all her grief for her daughter, is become blind in her left eye, because we desired to blind the Eye of righteousness. There is no peace to the doers of evil, saith the Lord. For already great affliction cometh upon the priests and upon the writers of the law; because they delivered unto thee the Just One. For this is the consummation of the world, that they consented that the Gentiles should become heirs. For the children of light shall be cast out, for they have not observed the things which were preached concerning the Lord, and concerning his Son. Therefore gird up thy loins, and receive righteousness, thou with thy wife remembering Jesus night and day; and the kingdom shall belong to you Gentiles, for we the (chosen) people have mocked the Righteous One.

Now if there is place for our request, O Pilate, because we were at one time in power, bury my household carefully; for it is right that we should be buried by thee, rather than by the priests, whom, after a little time, as the Scriptures say, at the coming of Jesus Christ, vengeance shall overtake.

Fare thee well, with Procla thy wife.

I send thee the earrings of my daughter and my own ring, that they may be unto thee a memorial of my decease. For already do worms begin to issue from my body, and lo, I am receiving temporal judgment, and I am afraid of the judgment to come. For in both we stand before the works of the living God; but this judgment, which is temporal, is for a time, while that to come is judgment for ever.

End of the Letter to Pilate the Governor.

LETTER OF PILATE TO HEROD.

PILATE TO HEROD THE TETRARCH: PEACE.

KNOW and see, that in the day when thou didst deliver Jesus unto me, I took pity on myself, and testified by washing my hands (that I was innocent), concerning him who rose from the grave after three days, and had performed thy pleasure in him, for thou didst desire me to be associated with thee in his crucifixion. But I now learn from the executioners and from the soldiers who watched his sepulchre that he rose from the dead. And I have especially confirmed what was told me, that he appeared bodily in

Galilee, to the same form, and with the same voice, and with the same doctrine, and with the sane disciples, not having changed in anything, but preaching with boldness his resurrection, and an everlasting kingdom.

And behold, heaven and earth rejoice; and behold, Procla my wife is believing in the visions which appeared unto her, when thou sentest that I should deliver Jesus to the people of Israel, because of the ill-will they had.

Now when Procla, my wife, heard that Jesus was risen, and had appeared in Galilee, she took with her Longinus the centurion and twelve soldiers, the same that had watched at the sepulchre, and went to greet the face of Christ, as if to a great spectacle, and saw him with his disciples.

Now while they were standing, and wondering, and gazing at him, he looked at them, and said to them, What is it? Do ye believe in me? Procla, know that in the covenant which God gave to the fathers, it is said that every body which had perished should live by means of my death, which ye have seen. And now, ye see that I live, whom ye crucified. And I suffered many things, till that I was laid in the sepulchre. But now, hear me, and believe in my Father—God who is in me. For I loosed the cords of death, and brake the gates of Sheol; and my coming shall be hereafter.

And when Procla my wife and the Romans heard these things, they came and told me, weeping; for they also were against him, when they devised the evils which they had done unto him. So that, I also was on the couch of my bed in affliction, and put on a garment of mourning, and took unto me fifty Romans with my wife and went into Galilee.

And when I was going in the way I testified these things; that Herod did these things by me, that he took counsel with me, and constrained me to arm my hands against him, and to judge him that judgeth all, and to scourge the Just One, Lord of the just. And when we drew nigh to him, O Herod, a great voice was heard from heaven, and dreadful thunder, and the earth trembled, and gave forth a sweet smell, like unto which was never perceived even in the temple of Jerusalem. Now while I stood in the way, our Lord saw me as he stood and talked with his disciples. But I prayed in my heart, for I knew that it was he whom ye delivered unto me, that he was Lord of created things and Creator of all. But we, when we saw him, all of us fell upon our faces before his feet. And I said with a loud voice, I have sinned, O Lord, in that I sat and judged thee, who avengest all in truth. And lo, I know that thou art God, the Son of God, and I beheld thy humanity and not thy divinity. But Herod, with the children of Israel, constrained me to do evil unto thee. Have pity, therefore, upon me, O God of Israel!

And my wife, in great anguish, said, God of heaven and of earth, God of Israel, reward me not according to the deeds of Pontius Pilate, nor according to the will of the children of Israel, nor according to the thought of the sons of the priests; but remember my husband in thy glory!

Now our Lord drew near and raised up me and my wife, and the Romans; and I looked at him and saw there were on him the scars of his cross. And he said, That which all the righteous fathers hoped to receive, and saw not—in thy time the Lord of Time, the

Son of Man, the Son of the Most High, who is for ever, arose from the dead, and is glorified on high by all that he created, and established for ever and ever.

1. Justinus, one of the writers that were in the days of Augustus and Tiberius and Gains, wrote in his third discourse: Now Mary the Galilaean, who bare the Christ that was crucified in Jerusalem, had not been with a husband. And Joseph did not abandon her; but Joseph continued in sanctity without a wife, he and his five sons by a former wife; and Mary continued without a husband.

2. Theodorus wrote to Pilate the Governor: Who was the man, against whom there was a complaint before thee, that he was crucified by the men of Palestine? If the many demanded this righteously, why didst thou not consent to their righteousness? And if they demanded this unrighteously, how didst thou transgress the law and command what was far from righteousness?

Pilate sent to him:—Because he wrought signs I did not wish to crucify him: and since his accusers said, He calleth himself a king, I crucified him.

3. Josephus saith: Agrippa, the king, was clothed in a robe woven with silver, and saw the spectacle in the theatre of Caesarea. When the people saw that his raiment flashed, they said to him, Hitherto we feared thee as a man: henceforth thou art exalted above the nature of mortals. And he saw an angel standing over him, and he smote him as unto death.

End of the Letter of Pilate to Herod.

THE EPISTLE OF PONTIUS PILATE, WHICH HE WROTE TO THE ROMAN EMPEROR CONCERNING OUR LORD JESUS CHRIST.

Pontius Pilate to Tiberius Caesar—Greeting:

UPON Jesus Christ, whom I fully made known to thee in my last, a bitter punishment hath at length been inflicted by the will of the people, although I was unwilling and apprehensive. In good truth, no age ever had or will have a man so good and strict. But the people made a wonderful effort, and all their scribes, chiefs and elders agreed to crucify this ambassador of truth, their own prophets, like the Sibyls with us, advising the contrary; and when he was hanged supernatural signs appeared, and in the judgment of philosophers menaced the whole world with ruin. His disciples flourish, not belying their master by their behavior and continence of life; nay, in his name they are most beneficent. Had I not feared a sedition might arise among the people, who were almost furious, perhaps this man would have yet been living with us. Although, being rather compelled by fidelity to thy dignity, than led by my own inclination, I did not strive with all my might to prevent the sale and suffering of righteous blood, guiltless of every accusation, unjustly, indeed, through the maliciousness of men, and yet, as the Scriptures interpret, to their own destruction.

Farewell. The 5th of the Calends of April.

THE REPORT OF PILATE THE GOVERNOR, CONCERNING OUR LORD JESUS CHRIST; WHICH WAS SENT TO AUGUSTUS CAESAR, IN ROME.

THE LOST BOOKS OF THE BIBLE

IN those days, when our Lord Jesus Christ was crucified under Pontius Pilate, the governor of Palestine and Phoenicia, the things here recorded came to pass in Jerusalem, and were done by the Jews against the Lord. Pilate therefore sent the same to Caesar in Rome, along with his private report, writing thus:

To the most potent, august, divine and awful Augustus Caesar, Pilate, the administrator of the Eastern Province:

I have received information, most excellent one, in consequence of which I am seized with fear and trembling. For in this province which I administer, one of whose cities is called Jerusalem, the whole multitude of Jews delivered unto me a certain man called Jesus, and brought many accusations against him, which they were unable to establish by consistent evidence. But they charged him with one heresy in particular, namely, That Jesus said the Sabbath was not a rest, nor to be observed by them. For he performed many cures on that day, and made the blind see, and the lame walk, raised the dead, cleansed lepers, healed the paralytic who were wholly unable to move their body or brace their nerves, but could only speak and discourse, and he gave them power to walk and run, removing their infirmity by his word alone. There is another very mighty deed which is strange to the gods we have: he raised up a man who had been four days dead, summoning him by his word alone, when the dead man had begun to decay, and his body was corrupted by the worms which had been bred, and had the stench of a dog; but, seeing him lying in the tomb he commanded him to run, nor did the dead man at all delay, but as a bridegroom out of his chamber, so did he go forth from his tomb, filled with abundant perfume. Moreover, even such as were strangers, and clearly demoniacs, who had their dwelling in deserts, and devoured their own flesh, and wandered about like cattle and creeping things, he turned into inhabiters of cities, and by a word rendered them rational, and prepared them to become wise and powerful, and illustrious, taking their food with all the enemies of the unclean spirits which were destructive in them, and which he cast into the depth of the sea.

And, again, there was another who had a withered hand, and not only the hand but rather the half of the body of the man was like a stone, and he had neither the shape of a man nor the symmetry of a body: even him He healed with a word and rendered whole. And a woman also, who had an issue of blood for a long time, and whose veins and arteries were exhausted, and who did not bear a human body, being like one dead, and daily speechless, so that all the physicians of the district were unable to cure her, for there remained unto her not a hope of life; but as Jesus passed by she mysteriously received strength by his shadow falling on her, from behind she touched the hem of his garment, and immediately, in that very hour, strength filled her exhausted limbs, and as if she had never suffered anything, she began to run along towards Capernaum, her own city, so that she reached it in a six days' journey.

And I have made known these things which I have recently been informed of, and which Jesus did on the Sabbath. And he did other miracles greater than these, so that I have observed greater works of wonder done by him than by the gods whom we worship.

THE LOST BOOKS OF THE BIBLE

But Herod and Archelaus and Philip, Annas and Caiaphas, with all the people, delivered him to me, making a great tumult against me in order that I might try him. Therefore, I commanded him to be crucified, when I had first scourged him, though I found no cause in him for evil accusations or dealings.

Now when he was crucified, there was darkness over all the world, and the sun was obscured for half a day, and the stars appeared, but no lustre was seen in them; and the moon lost its brightness, as though tinged with blood; and the world of the departed was swallowed up; so that the very sanctuary of the temple, as they call it, did not appear to the Jews themselves at their fall, but they perceived a chasm in the earth, and the rolling of successive thunders. And amid this terror the dead appeared rising again, as the Jews themselves bore witness, and said that it was Abraham, and Isaac, and Jacob, and the twelve patriarchs, and Moses, and Job, who had died before, as they say, some three thousand five hundred years. And there were very many whom I myself saw appearing in the body, and they made lamentation over the Jews, because of the transgression which was committed by them, and because of the destruction of the Jews and of their law.

And the terror of the earthquake continued from the sixth hour of the preparation until the ninth hour; and when it was evening on the first day of the week, there came a sound from heaven, and the heaven became seven times more luminous than on all other days. And at the third hour of the night the sun appeared more luminous than it had ever shone, lighting up the whole hemisphere. And as lightning-flashes suddenly come forth in a storm, so there were seen men, lofty in stature, and surpassing in glory, a countless host, crying out, and their voice was heard as that of exceedingly loud thunder, Jesus that was crucified is risen again: come up from Hades ye that were enslaved in the subterraneous recesses of Hades. And the chasm in the earth was as if it had no bottom; but it was so that the very foundations of the earth appeared, with those that shouted in heaven, and walked in the body among the dead that were raised. And He that raised up all the dead and bound Hades said, Say to my disciples He goeth before you into Galilee, there shall ye see Him.

And all that night the light ceased not shining. And many of the Jews died in the chasm of the earth, being swallowed up, so that on the morrow most of those who had been against Jesus were not to be found. Others saw the apparition of men rising again whom none of us had ever seen. One synagogue of the Jews was alone left in Jerusalem itself, for they all disappeared in that ruin.

Therefore being astounded by that terror, and being possessed with the most dreadful trembling, I have written what I saw at that time and sent it to thine excellency; and I have inserted what was done against Jesus by the Jews, and sent it to thy divinity, my lord.

THE REPORT OF PONTIUS PILATE, GOVERNOR OF JUDEA;

Which was sent to Tiberius Caesar in Rome.

To the most potent, august, dreadful, and divine Augustus, Pontius Pilate, administrator of the Eastern Province.

I HAVE undertaken to communicate to thy goodness by this my writing, though possessed with much fear and trembling, most excellent king, the present state of affairs, as the result hath shown. For as I administered this province, my lord, according to the command of thy serenity, which is one of the eastern cities called Jerusalem, wherein the temple of the nation of the Jews is erected, all the multitude of the Jews, being assembled, delivered up to me a certain man called Jesus, bringing many and endless accusations against him; but they could not convict him in anything. But they had one heresy against him, that he said the sabbath was not their proper rest.

Now that man wrought many cures and good works: he caused the blind to see, he cleansed lepers, he raised the dead, he healed paralytics, who could not move at all, but had only voice, and all their bones in their places; and he gave them strength to walk and run, enjoining it by his word alone. And he did another yet more mighty work, which had been strange even among our gods, he raised from the dead one Lazarus, who had been dead four days, commanding by a word alone that the dead man should be raised, when his body was already corrupted by worms which bred in his wounds. And he commanded the fetid body, which lay in the grave, to run, and as bridegroom from his chamber so he went forth from his grave, full of sweet perfume. And some that were grievously afflicted by demons, and had their dwellings in desert places, and devoured the flesh of their own limbs, and went up and down among creeping things and wild beasts, he caused to dwell in cities in their own houses, and by a word made them reasonable, and caused to become wise and honorable those that were vexed by unclean spirits, and the demons that were in them he sent out into a herd of swine into the sea and drowned them. Again, another who had a withered hand, and lived in suffering, and had not even the half of his body sound, he made whole by a word alone. And a woman who had an issue of blood for a long time, so that because of the discharge all the joints of her bones were seen and shone through like glass, for all the physicians had dismissed her without hope, and had not cleansed her, for there was in her no hope of health at all; but once, as Jesus was passing by she touched from behind the hem of his garments, and in that very hour the strength of her body was restored, and she was made whole, as if she had no affliction, and began to run fast towards her own city of Paneas. And these things happened thus: but the Jews reported that Jesus did these things on the sabbath. And I saw that greater marvels had been wrought by him than by the gods whom we worship. Him then Herod and Archelaus and Philip, and Annas and Caiaphas, with all the people, delivered up to me, to put him on his trial. And because many raised a tumult against me, I commanded that he should be crucified.

Now when he was crucified darkness came over all the world; the sun was altogether hidden, and the sky appeared dark while it was yet day, so that the stars were seen, though still they had their lustre obscured, wherefore, I suppose your excellency is not unaware that in all the world they lighted their lamps from the sixth hour until evening. And the moon, which was like blood, did not shine all night long, although it was at the full, and the stars and Orion made lamentation over the Jews, because of the transgression committed by them.

And on the first day of the week, about the third hour of the night, the sun appeared as it never shone before, and the whole heaven became bright. And as lightnings come in a storm, so certain men of lofty stature, in beautiful array, and of indescribable glory, appeared in the air, and a countless host of angels, crying out and saying, Glory to God in the highest, and on earth peace, good will among men: Come up from Hades, ye who are in bondage in the depths of Hades. And at their voice all the mountains and hills were moved, and the rocks were rent, and great chasms were made in the earth, so that the very places of the abyss were visible.

And amid the terror dead men were seen rising again, so that the Jews who saw it said, We beheld Abraham and Isaac, and Jacob, and the twelve patriarchs, who died some two thousand five hundred years before, and we beheld Noah clearly in the body. And all the multitude walked about and sang hymns to God with a loud voice, saying, The Lord our God, who hath risen from the dead, hath made alive all the dead, and Hades he hath spoiled and slain.

Therefore, my lord king, all that night the light ceased not. But many of the Jews died, and were sunk and swallowed up in the chasms that night, so that not even their bodies were to be seen. Now I mean, that those of the Jews suffered who spake against Jesus. And but one synagogue remained in Jerusalem, for all the synagogues which had been against Jesus were overwhelmed.

Through that terror, therefore, being amazed and being seized with great trembling, in that very hour, I ordered what had been done by them all to be written, and I have sent it to thy mightiness.

THE TRIAL AND CONDEMNATION OF PILATE.

NOW when the letters came to the city of the Romans, and were read to Caesar with no few standing there, they were all terrified, because, through the transgression of Pilate, the darkness and the earthquake had happened to all the world. And Caesar, being filled with anger, sent soldiers and commanded that Pilate should be brought as a prisoner.

And when he was brought to the city of the Romans, and Caesar heard that he was come, he sat in the temple of the gods, above all the senate, and with all the army, and with all the multitude of his power, and commanded that Pilate should stand in the entrance. And Caesar said to him, Most impious one, when thou sawest so great signs done by that man, why didst thou dare to do thus? By daring to do an evil deed thou hast ruined all the world.

And Pilate said, King and Autocrat, I am not guilty of these things, but it is the multitude of the Jews who are precipitate and guilty. And Caesar said, And who are they? Pilate saith, Herod, Archelaus, Philip, Annas and Caiaphas, and all the multitude of the Jews. Caesar saith, For what cause didst thou execute their purpose? And Pilate said, Their nation is seditious and insubordinate, and not submissive to thy power. And Caesar said, When they delivered him to thee thou oughtest to have made him secure and sent him to me, and not consented to them to crucify such a man, who was just and wrought such great and good miracles, as thou saidst in thy report. For by such miracles Jesus was manifested to be the Christ, the King of the Jews.

And when Caesar said this and himself named the name of Christ, all the multitude of the gods fell down together, and became like dust where Caesar sat with the senate. And all the people that stood near Caesar were filled with trembling because of the utterance of the word and the fall of their gods, and being seized with fear they all went away, every man to his house, wondering at what had happened. And Caesar commanded Pilate to be safely kept, that he might know the truth about Jesus.

And on the morrow when Caesar sat in the capitol with all the senate, he undertook to question Pilate again. And Caesar said, Say the truth, most impious one, for through thy impious deed which thou didst commit against Jesus, even here the doing of thy evil works were manifested, in that the gods were brought to ruin. Say then, who is he that was crucified, for his name hath destroyed all the gods? Pilate said, And verily his records are true; for even I myself was convinced by his works that he was greater than all the gods whom we venerate. And Caesar said, For what cause then didst thou perpetrate against him such daring and doing, not being ignorant of him, or assuredly designing some mischief to my government? And Pilate said, I did it because of the transgression and sedition of the lawless and ungodly Jews.

And Caesar was filled with anger, and held a council with all his senate and officers, and ordered a decree to be written against the Jews thus:—

To Licianus who holdeth the first place in the East Country. Greeting:

I have been informed of the audacity perpetrated very recently by the Jews inhabiting Jerusalem and the cities round about, and their lawless doing, how they compelled Pilate to crucify a certain god called Jesus, through which great transgression of theirs the world was darkened and drawn into ruin. Determine therefore, with a body of soldiers, to go to them there at once and proclaim their subjection to bondage by this decree. By obeying and proceeding against them, and scattering them abroad in all nations, enslave them, and by driving their nation from all Judea as soon as possible show, wherever this hath not yet appeared, that they are full of evil.

And when this decree came into the East Country, Licianus obeyed, through fear of the decree, and laid waste all the nation of the Jews, and caused those that were left in Judea, to go into slavery with them that were scattered among the Gentiles, that it might be known by Caesar that these things had been done by Licianus against the Jews in the East Country, and to please him.

And again Caesar resolved to have Pilate questioned, and commanded a captain, Albius by name, to cut off Pilate's head, saying, As he laid hands upon the just man, that is called Christ, he also shall fall in like manner, and find no deliverance.

And when Pilate came to the place he prayed in silence, saying, O Lord, destroy not me with the wicked Hebrews, for I should not have laid hands upon thee, but for the nation of lawless Jews, because they provoked sedition against me but thou knowest that I did it in ignorance. Destroy me not, therefore, for this my sin, nor be mindful of the evil that is in me, O Lord, and in thy servant Procla who standeth with me in this the hour of my death, whom thou taughtest to prophecy that thou must be nailed to the cross. Do not punish her too in my sin, but forgive us, and number us in the portion of thy just ones. And behold, when Pilate had finished his prayer, there came a voice from heaven, saying, All generations and the families of the Gentiles shall call thee blessed, because under thee were fulfilled all these things that were spoken by the prophets concerning me; and thou thyself must appear as my witness at my second coming, when I shall judge the twelve tribes of Israel, and them that have not confessed my name. And the Prefect cut off the head of Pilate, and behold an angel of the Lord received it. And when his wife Procla saw the angel coming and receiving his head, she also, being filled with joy, forthwith gave up the ghost, and was buried with her husband.

THE DEATH OF PILATE, WHO CONDEMNED JESUS.

NOW whereas Tiberius Caesar emperor of the Romans was suffering from a grievous sickness, and hearing that there was at Jerusalem a certain physician, Jesus by name, who healed all diseases by his word alone; not knowing that the Jews and Pilate had put him to death, he thus bade one of his attendants, Volusianus by name, saying, Go as quickly as thou canst across the sea, and tell Pilate, my servant and friend, to send me this physician to restore me to my original health. And Volusianus, having heard the order of the emperor, immediately departed, and came to Pilate, as it was commanded him. And he told the same Pilate what had been committed to him by Tiberius Caesar, saying, Tiberius Caesar, emperor of the Romans, thy Lord, having heard that in this city there is a physician who healeth diseases by his word alone, earnestly entreateth thee to send him to him to heal his disease. And Pilate was greatly terrified on hearing this, knowing that through envy he had caused him to be slain. Pilate answered the messenger, saying thus, This man was a malefactor, and a man who drew after himself all the people; so, after counsel taken of the wise men of the city, I caused him to be crucified. And as the messenger returned to his lodgings he met a certain woman named Veronica, who had been acquainted with Jesus, and he said, O woman, there was a certain physician in this city, who healed the sick by his word alone, why have the Jews slain him? And she began to weep, saying, Ah, me, my lord, it was my God and my Lord whom Pilate through envy delivered up, condemned, and commanded to be crucified. Then he, grieving greatly, said, I am exceedingly sorry that I cannot fulfil that for which my lord hath sent me.

Veronica said to him, When my Lord went about preaching, and I was very unwillingly deprived of his presence, I desired to have his picture painted for me, that while I was deprived of his presence, at least the figure of his likeness might give me consolation. And when I was taking the canvas to the painter to be painted, my Lord met me and asked whither I was going. And when I had made known to him the cause of my journey, He asked me for the canvas, and gave it back to me printed with the likeness of his venerable face. Therefore, if thy lord will devoutly look upon the sight of this, he will straightway enjoy the benefit of health.

Is a likeness of this kind to be procured with gold or silver? he asked. No, said she, but with a pious sentiment of devotion. Therefore, I will go with thee, and carry the likeness to Caesar to look upon, and will return.

So Volusianus came with Veronica to Rome, and said to Tiberius the emperor, Jesus, whom thou hast long desired, Pilate and the Jews have surrendered to an unjust death, and through envy fastened to the wood of the cross. Therefore, a certain matron hath come with me bringing the likeness of the same Jesus, and if thou wilt devoutly gaze upon it, thou wilt presently obtain the benefit of thy health. So Caesar caused the way to be spread with cloths of silk, and ordered the portrait to be presented to him; and as soon as he had looked upon it he regained his original health.

Then Pontius Pilate was apprehended by command of Caesar and brought to Rome. Caesar, hearing that Pilate had come to Rome, was filled with exceeding wrath against him, and caused him to be brought to him. Now Pilate brought with him the seamless coat of Jesus, and wore it when before the emperor. As soon as the emperor saw him he laid aside all his wrath, and forthwith rose to him, and was unable to speak harshly to him in anything: and he who in his absence seemed so terrible and fierce now in his presence is found comparatively gentle.

And when he had dismissed him, he soon became terribly inflamed against him, declaring himself wretched, because he had not expressed to him the anger of his bosom. And immediately he had him recalled, swearing and protesting that he was a child of death, and unfitted to live upon earth. And when he saw him he instantly greeted him, and laid aside all the fury of his mind.

All were astonished, and he was astonished himself, that he was so enraged against Pilate while absent, and could say nothing to him sharply while he was present. At length, by Divine suggestion, or perhaps by the persuasion of some Christian, he had him stripped of the coat, and soon resumed against him his original fury of mind. And when the emperor was wondering very much about this, they told him it had been the coat of the Lord Jesus. Then the emperor commanded him to be kept in prison till he should take counsel with the wise men what ought to be done with him. And after a few days sentence was given against Pilate that he should be condemned to the most ignominious death. When Pilate heard this he slew himself with his own dagger, and by such a death put an end to his life.

When Pilate's death was made known Caesar said, Truly he has died a most ignominious death, whose own hand has not spared him. He was therefore fastened to a great block of stone and sunk in the river Tiber. But wicked and unclean spirits, rejoicing in his wicked and unclean body, all moved about in the water, and caused in the air dreadful lightning and tempests, thunder and hail, so that all were seized with horrible fear. On which account the Romans dragged him out of the river Tiber, bore him away in derision to Vienne, and sunk him in the river Rhone. For Vienne means, as it were, Way of Gehenna, because it was then a place of cursing. And evil spirits were there and did the same things.

Those men, therefore, not enduring to be so harassed by demons, removed the vessel of cursing from them and sent it to be buried in the territory of Losania. But when they were troubled exceedingly by the aforesaid vexations, they put it away from them and sunk it in a certain pool surrounded by mountains, where even yet, according to the account of some, sundry diabolical contrivances are said to issue forth.

THE LOST GOSPEL ACCORDING TO PETER

[In the valley of the Upper Nile, on the right bank of the river, is the mysterious town of Akhmim. It was called Panopolis in ancient times when it was the capital of the district. The remnants of monasteries and the ruins of temples mark the intellectual life of a former day.

In 1888, the French Mission excavating in the grave of a monk, came upon a parchment codex. Six years later a translation of this was published in the Memoirs of the French Archaeological Mission at Cairo. Scholars realized for the first time that a striking discovery, possibly of overwhelming importance, had been made. A portion of The Gospel According to Peter appeared to have been restored to the Christian Community after having been lost for ages. But until now, this document has never been made available to the general public.

Centuries rolled over that remote tomb at Akhmim, while nations rose and fell, wars blasted civilization, science metamorphosed the world, Shakespeares and Miltons wrote their names and passed on, the American nation was born and grew up—all the while the ink on the parchment in that Egyptian tomb was scarcely changing—and the beautiful words of this Scripture were preserving for us this version of the most tragic and momentous event in history. That briefly is the romance of The Lost Gospel According to Peter.

Such a gospel was referred to by Serapion, Bishop of Antioch, in 190 A.D.; Origen, historian, in 253 A.D.; Eusebius, Bishop of Caesarea in 300 A.D.; Theodoret in 455 in his Religious History said that the Nazarenes used The Gospel According to Peter; and Justin Martyr includes the Memoirs of Peter in his "Apostolic Memoirs." Thus scholars have always recognized that such a document existed long ago, although its whereabouts and fate were a mystery until the discovery at Akhmim.

While in general the story of the trial and crucifixion that Is revealed here follows that of the canonical gospels, in detail it is very different. This account is freer from constraint; and with the events between the burial and resurrection of our Lord, it is much more ample and detailed than anything in the canonical tradition.

There are indeed twenty-nine variations of fact between this Lost Gospel According to Peter and the four canonical gospels. Some of the most important that the reader will note are as follows: 1. Herod was the one who gave the order for the execution. 2. Joseph was a friend of Pilate. 3. In the darkness many went about with lamps and fell down. (That is a startling glimpse of the confusion that seized the people.) 4. Our Lord's cry of "My power, my power." 5. The account of how the disciples had to hide because they were searched for as malefactors anxious to burn the temple. 6. The name of the centurion who kept watch at the tomb was Petronius.

It is also interesting to note the prominence assigned to Mary Magdalene; and how this account tends to lay more responsibility on Herod and the people, while relieving Pilate somewhat of his share in the action that was taken. Also, the Resurrection and Ascension are here recorded not as separate events but as occurring on the same day.

There will be a great divergence of opinion as to the place of this document and its relation to the canonical scriptures. Its existence is here proclaimed, and beyond that every reader may form his own estimate of its value. The Rev. D. H. Stanton, D.D., in the Journal of Theological Studies, commenting on Justin Martyr's ancient testimony, and this present document, says: "The conclusion with which we are confronted is that The Gospel of Peter once held a place of honor, comparable to that assigned to the Four Gospels, perhaps even higher than some of them . . ."]

BUT of the Jews none washed his hands, neither Herod nor any one of his judges. And when they had refused to wash them, Pilate rose up. And then Herod the king commandeth that the Lord be taken saying to them, What things soever I commanded you to do unto him, do.

And there was standing there Joseph the friend of Pilate and of the Lord; and, knowing that they were about to crucify him, he came to Pilate and asked the body of the Lord for burial. And Pilate sent to Herod and asked his body. And Herod said, Brother Pilate, even if no one has asked for him, we purposed to bury him, especially as the sabbath draweth on: for it is written in the law, that the sun set not upon one that hath been put to death.

And he delivered him to the people on the day before the unleavened bread, their feast. And they took the Lord and pushed him as they ran, and said, Let us drag away the Son of God, having obtained power over him. And they clothed him with purple, and set him on the seat of judgment, saying, Judge righteously, O king of Israel. And one of them brought a crown of thorns and put it on the head of the Lord. And others stood and spat in his eyes, and others smote his cheeks: others pricked him with a reed; and some scourged him, saying, With this honor let us honor the Son of God.

And they brought two malefactors, and they crucified the Lord between them. But he held his peace, as though having no pain. And when they had raised the cross, they wrote the title: This is the king of Israel. And having set his garments before him they parted them among them, and cast lots for them. And one of those malefactors reproached them, saying, We for the evils that we have done have suffered thus, but this man, who hath become the Saviour of men, what wrong hath he done to you? And they, being angered at him, commanded that his legs should not be broken, that he might die in torment.

And it was noon, and darkness came over all Judaea: and they were troubled and distressed, lest the sun had set, whilst he was yet alive: [for] it is written for them, that the sun set not on him that hath been put to death. And one of them said, Give him to drink gall with vinegar. And they mixed and gave him to drink, and fulfilled all things, and accomplished their sins against their own head. And many went about with lamps, supposing that it was night, and fell down. And the Lord cried out, saying, My power, my power, thou hast forsaken me. And when he had said it he was taken up. And in that hour the vail of the temple of Jerusalem was rent in twain.

THE LOST BOOKS OF THE BIBLE

And then they drew out the nails from the hands of the Lord, and laid him upon the earth, and the whole earth quaked, and great fear arose. Then the sun shone, and it was found the ninth hour: and the Jews rejoiced, and gave his body to Joseph that he might bury it, since he had seen what good things he had done. And he took the Lord, and him, and rolled him in a linen cloth, and brought him to his own tomb, which was called the Garden of Joseph.

Then the Jews and the elders and the priests, perceiving what evil they had done to themselves, began to lament and to say, Woe for our sins: the judgment hath drawn nigh, and the end of Jerusalem. And I with my companions was grieved; and being wounded in mind we hid ourselves: for we were being sought for by them as malefactors, and as wishing to set fire to the temple. And upon all these things we fasted and sat mourning and weeping night and day until the sabbath.

But the scribes and Pharisees and elders being gathered together one with another, when they heard that all the people murmured and beat their breasts saying, If by his death these most mighty signs have come to pass, see how righteous he is,—the elders were afraid and came to Pilate beseeching him and saying, Give us soldiers, that we may guard his sepulchre for three days, lest his disciples come and steal him away, and the people suppose that he is risen from the dead and do us evil. And Pilate gave them Petronius the centurion with soldiers to guard the tomb. And with them came elders and scribes to the sepulchre, and having rolled a great stone together with the centurion and the soldiers, they all together who were there set it at the door of the sepulchre; and they affixed seven seals, and they pitched a tent there and guarded it. And early in the morning as the sabbath was drawing on, there came a multitude from Jerusalem and the region round about, that they might see the sepulchre that was sealed.

And in the night in which the Lord's day was drawing on, as the soldiers kept guard two by two in a watch, there was a great voice in the heaven; and they saw the heavens opened, and two men descend from thence with great light and approach the tomb. And that stone which was put at the door rolled of itself and made way in part; and the tomb was opened, and both the young men entered in.

When therefore those soldiers saw it, they awakened the centurion and the elders; for they too were hard by keeping guard. And as they declared what things they had seen, again they see three men come forth from the tomb, and two of them supporting one, and a cross following them: and of the two the head reached unto the heaven, but the head of him who was lead by them overpassed the heavens. And they heard a voice from the heavens, saying, Thou hast preached to them that sleep. And a response was heard from the cross, Yea.

They therefore considered one with another whether to go away and shew these things to Pilate. And while they yet thought thereon, the heavens again are seen to open, and a certain man to descend and enter into the sepulchre. When the centurion and they that were with him saw these things, they hastened in the night to Pilate, leaving the tomb which they were watching, and declared all things which they had seen, being greatly distressed and saying, Truly he was the Son of God. Pilate answered and said, I am pure from the blood of the Son of God: but it was ye who determined this. Then they all drew near and besought him and entreated him to command the centurion and the soldiers to say nothing of the things which they had seen: For it is better, say they, for us to be guilty of the greatest sin before God, and not to fall into the hands of the people of the Jews and to be stoned. Pilate therefore commanded the centurion and the soldiers to say nothing.

And at dawn upon the Lord's day Mary Magdalene, a disciple of the Lord, fearing because of the Jews, since they were burning with wrath, had not done at the Lord's sepulchre the things which women are wont to do for those that die and for those that are beloved by them—she took her friends with her and came to the sepulchre where he was laid. And they feared lest the Jews should see them, and they said, Although on that day on which he was crucified we could not weep and lament, yet now let us do these things at his sepulchre. But who shall roll away for us the stone that was laid at the door of the sepulchre, that we may enter in and sit by him and do the things that are due? For the stone was great, and we fear lest some one see us. And if we cannot, yet if we but set at the door the things which we bring as a memorial of him, we will weep and lament, until we come unto our home.

And they went and found the tomb opened, and coming near they looked in there; and they see there a certain young man sitting in the midst of the tomb, beautiful and clothed in a robe exceeding bright; who said to them, Wherefore are ye come? Whom seek ye? Him that was crucified? He is risen and gone. But if ye believe not, look in and see the place where he lay, that he is not [here]; for he is risen and gone thither, whence he was sent. Then the women feared and fled.

Now it was the last day of the unleavened bread, and many were going forth, returning to their homes, as the feast was ended. But we, the twelve disciples of the Lord, wept and were grieved: and each one, being grieved for that which was come to pass, departed to his home. But I Simon Peter and Andrew my brother took our nets and went to the sea; and there was with us Levi the son of Alphaeus, whom the Lord . . .

Here ends the book.

THE LOST BOOKS OF THE BIBLE

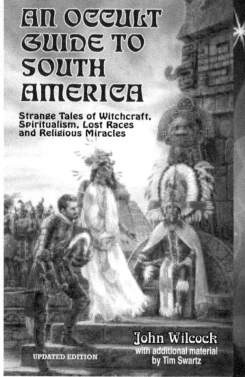

CPSIA information can be obtained
at www.ICGtesting.com
Printed in the USA
LVHW021531150519
617950LV00010B/412/P